Exploring Phys Anthropology

A LAB MANUAL AND WORKBOOK

Second Edition

Suzanne E. Walker-Pacheco

Missouri State University

Morton Publishing Company
925 W. Kenyon Avenue, Unit 12
Englewood, CO 80110

www.morton-pub.com

Book Team

Publisher	Douglas N. Morton
Project Manager	Dona Mendoza
Editorial Assistant	Desireé Coscia
Cover and Interior Design	Bob Schram, Bookends, Inc.
Copyeditor	Carolyn Acheson
Composition	Ash Street Typecrafters, Inc.

For Pearl Walker and Julián Pacheco
In memory of Warren Walker and Jesús Pacheco

Suzanne E. Walker-Pacheco, Ph.D.

Suzanne E. Walker-Pacheco, Ph.D, is Associate Professor of Anthropology in the Department of Sociology, Anthropology, and Criminology at Missouri State University in Springfield. She received the doctorate from the City University of New York and the undergraduate degree from San Diego State University. Previous to her arrival at Missouri State University in 1999, she taught in northern California. Her primary research area has been field primatology, with a focus on primates in Venezuela and Brazil. Since 1997 she has assisted coroners and medical examiners with forensics cases involving skeletal identification. Her recent research interests include medical anthropology, particularly dealing with health issues of Latino immigrants to Southwest Missouri. She currently is conducting a diabetes and obesity prevention program for Latino children in Springfield, Missouri.

Printed in the United States of America
by Morton Publishing Company
925 W. Kenyon Ave., Unit 12, Englewood, CO 80110

10   9   8   7   6   5   4   3   2   1

ISBN-10: 0-89582-811-1

ISBN-13: 978-089582-811-8

Library of Congress Control Number: 2009926158

Preface

Features new to this edition include...

- Full-color format
- 22 new lab exercises for existing chapters
- 11 sets of new self-study questions
- New exercises that provide practice in the use of basic statistical techniques
- New section with exercises to learn about relative and absolute dating techniques
- Significant changes to Chapter 13, covering early hominids
- Significant changes to Chapter 14, covering later hominids
- A discussion of tooth anatomy in Chapter 7
- The addition of information boxes for the genetics and evolutionary forces chapters (Chapters 2 through 6) to stimulate students' interest
- An index of fossil primates and of fossil hominids as appendices
- An expanded Glossary
- Expanded References (25 new reference entries added)
- An entirely new chapter, Chapter 15, covering modern human biological variation

How did humans become human? Physical anthropology delves into the historical and biological context in which we evolved as a species, using empirical evidence. This subdiscipline of anthropology places humans in perspective relative to our extinct relatives and other living creatures of today. Although the various themes within the umbrella of physical anthropology range widely, they are tied together by the thread of an underlying evolutionary framework.

This laboratory manual enables a hands-on approach to learning about the evolutionary processes that resulted in humans through the use of numerous examples and exercises. It offers solid grounding in the main areas of an introductory physical anthropology lab course: genetics, evolutionary forces, human osteology, forensic anthropology, comparative/functional skeletal anatomy, primate behavior, paleoanthropology, and now, in this new edition, modern human biological variation.

This book is intended to be used primarily as a text for an introductory laboratory course in physical anthropology but also can serve as a supplementary text or workbook for a lecture class, particularly in the absence of a laboratory offering. Because it provides numerous photos and illustrations, it can be used with a minimum of laboratory materials.

What's New in This Edition

Many new changes accompany this new edition, the most notable being an entirely *new chapter (Chapter 15) on modern human biological variation*, which includes sections on

ancestry, anthropometrics, and dermatoglyphics. Another important addition is the new *One Step Further* at the end of each chapter, containing between one and four new lab exercises that allow students to delve deeper into one or more topics or offers opportunities for additional practice with lab techniques. This section can be added to the course content or readily skipped in classes that do not allow time to cover the added material.

Most of the additions and changes to this edition are those originally suggested by instructors using the manual. Anyone with comments or suggestions about this manual is strongly encouraged to contact the author (suzannewalker@missouristate.edu) or the publisher www.morton-pub.com.

Features

A lab class typically provides appropriate specimens (skeletal material, fossil casts, and the like), but not all institutions possess a complete collection. This manual can fill in many gaps by providing a full set of graphics and photos to supplement a laboratory collection.

Additional specimens and greater detail can be obtained by also using *A Photographic Atlas for Physical Anthropology*, by Paul F. Whitehead, William K. Sacco, and Susan B. Hochgraf (Morton, 2005) and the brief edition (abbreviated br. ed.) of the atlas (Morton, 2005). Throughout this lab manual, citations for these atlases are identified as (Atlas, p. 000, Figure 000; br. ed., p. 000, Figure 000).

- Apart from skeletal and fossil specimens, few laboratory supplies are needed. Many of the experiments and exercises utilize common, everyday materials.

- The graphics provided here make it possible to use this manual as a workbook for lecture classes to reinforce the material. (Chapter 8 is the only chapter that is primarily dependent upon lab specimens to complete the exercises.)

- Throughout the book, reference is made to the discussions in earlier chapters, building on previously gained knowledge.

- A list of necessary materials now appears at the beginning of each chapter instead of being included in the online *Instructor's Manual*.

- The exercises are planned to be easily completed in the course of a 15-week semester.

- Flexibility is built in by the following:

  - Longer chapters are broken into sub-sections; instructors can choose to include or leave out portions to fit their schedule.

  - The *Self-Test* feature within each chapter may be used either in or out of class.

  - The *One Step Further* section at each chapter's end includes at least one new *Additional Exercise* to be completed if time permits.

Please note that many of the photographs in this lab manual are not taken in the Frankfurt horizontal. Instead, the various photographic views allow for observation of specific features for successful completion of lab exercises without the limitation of one particular orientation.

Organization of the Book

This book is organized into six main topical areas:

1. An introductory chapter that reviews the meaning and practice of science, introduces evolution as a scientific endeavor, and provides examples about how evolution works (Chapter 1).

2. Coverage of the genetic basis for evolution and the forces of evolution, to make the evolutionary process understandable and to trace the path from DNA to organism. Examples, empirical exercises, graphics, and self-tests are used to study genes in individuals and in populations (Chapters 2 through 6).

3. A primer in skeletal anatomy and anthropometric techniques to analyze human variation in populations. The list of skeletal features is not exhaustive; primarily demonstrated are those that allow for siding bones, sexing skeletal material, and interpreting locomotion from fossil remains (Chapters 7 and 8).

4. An explanation of functional complexes for diet and locomotion, evolutionary relationships, and comparative mammalian anatomy, with a focus on the nonhuman primates. This information, together with knowledge of skeletal anatomy, provides a basis for interpreting the fossil evidence for human evolution. Knowledge of primate behavior allows us to place humans in a behavioral as well as an evolutionary context, and to model the presumed behavior of early members of the human family. Lab exercises demonstrating primate behavior can be conducted at any zoo. Alternatively, they may be substituted by exercises presented in the *One Step Further* feature, based on videos. Some videos are recommended in the *Instructor's Manual* (Chapters 9 through 11).

5. A straightforward presentation of the nonhuman and human primate fossil record, despite the complexity of the real-life picture. The emphasis is on the basics of morphology and techniques for interpreting fossil remains rather than on evolutionary relationships (Chapters 12 through 14).

6. The book is made complete with the final, newly added, chapter on modern human biological variation, which includes an up-do-date section on ancestry, and exercises on anthropometrics and dermatoglyphics (Chapter 15).

Organization of the Chapters

Each chapter begins with one or more question that nonspecialists typically ask about each topic (for example: "If humans evolved from apes, why are there still apes?"). The chapters subsequently provide the information needed to answer these questions. Following boxed lists of materials needed and of objectives for the chapter, basic information is presented to prepare the student for the lab exercises—the crux of each chapter.

Following the lab exercises are the *Self-Tests*, which may be completed either in or out of lab and do not depend upon direct observation of specimens. The new *One Step Further* feature adds some material to the chapter and/or reinforces existing material with more exercises. These exercises enhance the flexibility of the lab manual, allowing the instructor to decide whether to cover these areas.

Ancillaries

The associated online *Instructor's Manual* (www.morton-pub.com) offers the following features:

- A set of high-quality photos that correlate with those in the lab manual, from Chapters 7 through 14. These may be printed out (preferably in color, on cardstock) and used by the instructor for practice sessions, lab exercises, or testing purposes.
- Answers to Lab Exercises and Self-Tests
- "Helpful Hints" section for the instructor, as needed for some chapters
- "Additional Resources," particularly websites, for material covered in each chapter

In sum, Physical Anthropology is a fascinating area of study that encompasses a wide range of themes. Learning this material should be as hands-on, engaging, and dynamic as possible, and that has been the aim of this book.

Skeletal specimens, fossil casts, and modern human traits were photographed by the author, using a Canon EOS Digital Rebel XT camera.

Acknowledgments

This lab manual benefited greatly from discussions with and suggestions from Susan Ford at Southern Illinois University, Marilyn Norconk of Kent State University, Lakhbir Singh at Chabot College, Elizabeth Sobel of Missouri State University, Elizabeth Strasser of California State University Sacramento, and Mary Willis at University of Nebraska Lincoln. Helpful reviews for the current edition were provided by Douglas Broadfield at Florida Atlantic University, Timothy McAndrews of University of Wisconsin LaCrosse, and Daniel Osborne at University of Nebraska Lincoln, as well as numerous instructors who filled out an online survey review.

Mary Willis of the University of Nebraska made fossil casts available for photography, and Lesa Davis of Northeastern Illinois University made casts available and also provided some new photos for this edition. Mélida Gutierrez helpfully provided her radiometric dating exercise, and Lisa Sattenspiel and Carol Ward (University of Missouri, Columbia) offered the use of exercises from their laboratory book. The working environment and moral support of colleagues and students at Missouri State University are greatly appreciated. I thank the following individuals for their permission to photograph some of their physical traits: Kristin Arnette, Thomas Dicke, Mary and Daisy Garland, Julián Pacheco, James Smith, and Elizabeth Sobel.

The book team at Morton Publishing has been wonderful to work with, from the early and willing support of Doug Morton, to Desireé Coscia for obtaining permissions for specimens to photograph, and especially editor Dona Mendoza for her wonderfully encouraging and patient manner. I also am grateful for the professional copyediting skills of Carolyn Acheson, Joanne Saliger of Ash Street Typecrafters for her typesetting, and Jessica Ridd for the illustrations. John Crawley's photographic advice early in the process has continued to be invaluable.

My parents, Pearl Walker and the late Warren Walker, and my late husband, Jesús (Quique) Pacheco provided continual encouragement for me to follow my interests. I thank my mother for her support while I worked on the new edition, and I thank my son, Julián Enrique Pacheco, for his loving patience.

Suzanne E. Walker-Pacheco, Ph.D.
Missouri State University

Contents

8 Forensic Anthropology 181

9 Comparative Osteology and Functional Complexes 217

Physical Anthropology as a Science

"Have you ever wondered . . . ?"

- If humans evolved from apes, why do apes still exist?
- Is evolution really "just" a theory?

OBJECTIVES

- Thoroughly understand the definition of science
- Become familiar with the steps in the scientific method
- Practice using the scientific method
- Understand the nature of evolution and the difference between evolution and natural selection
- Explain how evolutionary theory is scientific
- Examine biological variation with use of data collection, and learn about the importance of variation in natural selection
- Be introduced to some basic principles of descriptive statistics, particularly measures of central tendency

MATERIALS NEEDED

- Rulers and/or calipers
- Graph paper
- Measurable plant part (at least one per set of lab partners, but a total of at least 20); suggested are:
  - ◆ Snow peas
  - ◆ Leaves from the same tree species (if time, students could collect them)
  - ◆ String beans, etc.

The Scientific Method: Definition and Steps

Humans have an inquisitive nature. We like to be able to explain things that we perceive through our senses. Science—the activity of seeking out reliable explanations for natural phenomena—allows us to do that. The procedure that scientists follow is called the **scientific method**. The steps are:

1. **Observation:** Looking at some phenomenon empirically, using the five senses: sight, touch, smell, hearing, taste.

2. **Question:** Asking how the phenomenon came to be? (why, what, how, etc.)

3. **Hypothesis:** Proposing a suggested answer to a question; taking an educated guess at the answer. *A hypothesis must be testable.* It must be formulated so that if it is not true, it may be disproved through experimentation or data collection.

4. **Experimentation/data collection:** Testing the reliability of a hypothesis to corroborate or disprove it.

5. **Theory** or **law**: Based on confirmation of the hypothesis, postulating a theory or law. Both are based upon confirmed hypotheses, but they differ in some fundamental ways.

   a. A theory usually explains a phenomenon in which the explanation is supported by a body of evidence. Many theories are longstanding and well-accepted. Examples are the theory of relativity, gravitational theory, and atomic theory.

   b. A law is often a description of a phenomenon consistently observed under a specific set of conditions. Laws are more common in sciences such as physics and chemistry than the science of biology, and frequently can be described mathematically.

Science strives to explain phenomena and search continually for the most accurate explanation. Thus, theories and even laws are not absolute but, rather, are subject to being disproved in the face of new evidence.

The Process of Evolution

Evolution is best explained from the perspectives of what it is and what it isn't, as well as how it occurs.

What It Is

Evolution is *a change in gene frequency in a population from generation to generation*. If we consider any trait, in any population, and track the frequency of the genes that determine the trait, we'll find that the frequency of the gene changes over time. This occurs in nature, in a laboratory, on the farm, and in your garden. Examples of evolution are the changing nature of a virus as it is transmitted from one species to another, the bacterial strain that changes to become resistant to antibiotics, and the anatomical and behavioral changes that occur between generations as humans selectively breed for certain features in a dog breed.

What It Isn't

Evolution is *not* simply the changing over time from ape into human! Evolution can *result* in changes that accumulate over time so organisms differ from their ancestors, but that is not the *definition* of evolution.

Within a population (a group of potentially interbreeding organisms), a certain number of individuals will have, for example, type A blood, type B blood, type O blood, and type AB blood. Also, certain numbers of individuals will have blue eyes, green eyes, or brown eyes.

For any given **trait** (such as blood type or eye color), if you count the number of people with each **form of a trait** (how many with type A blood, green eyes, etc.), your total count is a **frequency** of individuals with each form of a trait. Frequencies are expressed in percentages. For example, in

a population of 1,000 people, the frequency of individuals with various eye colors may be: 650 with brown eyes, 250 with blue eyes, 100 with green eyes, and 50 with hazel eyes. In this population the percentages are 65% with brown eyes, 25% with blue eyes, 10% with green eyes, and 5% with hazel eyes.

Many physical traits (as well as some behavioral traits) have a strong genetic, rather than environmental, influence. You have blood type A or B because of the **genes** you've inherited from your parents. You have green or brown or blue eyes for the same reason. Genes are functional segments of our **deoxyribonucleic acid**, or **DNA**. DNA is the genetic material and, together with certain proteins, makes up the chromosomes in the nucleus of cells. The set of genes on the chromosomes that we inherited from our parents provides the "blueprint" to produce each one of us, and a copy of this blueprint resides in each of our cells.

In any population we can figure out the frequencies for the number of *individuals* with blood type A, B, O, or AB. We also can determine the number of actual *genes* for a given trait. The number of genes in a population that exists for each form of a trait (for example, blood type A, or brown eyes) is called the **gene frequency**. Again, evolution is defined most accurately as *the change in gene frequency within a population from generation to generation.*

How Evolution Occurs

To illustrate evolution in action, imagine a hypothetical experiment: You will stand at the entrance to your student union for one week, blood-typing kit in hand. You'll take a blood sample from all who pass by (with their permission, of course) to figure out how many of them have the blood types A, B, O, and AB. From the frequency of blood types, you can calculate the gene frequency for the A, B, and O genes (**alleles**, actually) in this sample.

With the results from the current generation of university "inhabitants," you'll wait 20 years for the second part of the experiment. Returning 20 years later to the steps of the student union, you will repeat the experiment, typing the blood of the next generation. The *gene frequency will have changed*. It may be just a little different from the previous generation, but it *will* be different, because the factors that cause evolution are constantly in action. In this case, **migration** has occurred as new people moved in to replace those who left and, because of chance, they won't have genes in the *exact* same frequencies as those who left.

A second cause of differences in gene frequency between generations is that only a *sample* of the sperm and egg cells produced in a given generation will combine to form new individuals in the next generation. Thus, it is highly improbable that the next generation will have exactly the same frequencies of blood types as the last generation. This illustrates one form of **genetic drift**.

Migration and genetic drift are two types of **evolutionary forces**. A third is **mutation,** and the fourth is **natural selection**. Individuals with features best suited to their specific environment are more likely to pass on their genes in greater numbers. Evolution thus results from this change in gene frequency.

Although discussions regarding evolutionary change had been taking place for many years, not until the mid-1800s was a feasible mechanism for evolution proposed. At that time, Charles Darwin and Alfred Russell Wallace independently established this series of steps by which evolution could work. It is called natural selection.

Steps in Theory of Evolution by Natural Selection

The steps in natural selection are:

1. Within each species, more individuals are produced than can possibly survive.

2. Variation exists within each species, making some individuals better adapted than others to their environment.

3. Members of a population compete for limited resources. (Other factors that limit population growth are also at play here—disease, predation, etc.)

4. Individuals with inherited traits that allow them to be better adapted to their environment will be more likely to survive and reproduce than will those with traits that make them less well-adapted.

5. Individuals with the well-adapted traits are likely to reproduce more, passing on their genes to the next generation in higher numbers than those with the less favorable traits, thereby causing a change in gene frequency.

6. If a certain form of a trait continues to have a **selective advantage** in a given environment, it is likely to become more and more common in the population. Accumulated changes in a number of traits over many generations eventually can result in descendants that are sufficiently different from their ancestors to be considered a new species.

These steps are illustrated in the example in Figure 1.1, showing the process of natural selection for short, broad wings over a few generations. In this example, selection favors the shape of bird wing that is most efficient for fast take-offs—short and broad. Observe how the variation in wing shape already is present in the population (as a result of inherited features), but because those with the shortest, broadest wings are the most successful at surviving and reproducing, they pass on more of their genes, increasing the frequency of the genes that determine the short, broad wing shape in the next generation. The four evolutionary forces will be discussed further in Chapter 6.

All populations evolve from one generation to the next. Gene frequencies change as a result of individuals moving between populations, random sampling of parental genes that produce a different combination of individuals making up the next generation, mutations in the genetic material, and natural selection.

Evolutionary Theory as Science

In writing about evolutionary theory, Darwin was aware of two separate tasks:

1. establishing the fact of evolution; and

2. proposing a theory to explain the mechanism by which evolution worked ("theory of evolution *by natural selection*").

FIGURE 1.1 *Process of natural selection for short, broad wings*

No set of ideas has been proposed that provides a scientific alternative to evolutionary theory. That is, no alternatives to evolution have been proposed in the form of *testable hypotheses* that explain the genetic and anatomical similarities in groups of organisms, the origin of new species, and the changes occurring within a lineage through time. Although numerous arguments have been advanced to detract from theories of evolution, the arguments against evolutionary ideas are based on a lack of understanding of what evolution is and how the scientific method works. Without going into great detail, two main arguments of detractors of evolution are the following:

1. Evolution is *just* a theory, not a "proven" fact. This statement is unfounded and rests on the confusion of the terms *hypothesis* (an untested idea) and *theory* (an idea that has a basis in a corroborated hypothesis; theories are structures of ideas that explain and interpret facts). The two terms often are mistakenly used interchangeably, which is wrong.

2. Evolutionists themselves disagree as to how evolution works.

In science, it is often said that hypotheses are never *proved*, just *disproved*. We attempt to explain phenomena based on the most reasonable explanations, but theories are always subject to change.

Evolution is a fact. It occurs. Gene frequencies change in each population, even from one generation to the next. That is established, and we can see it all around us. The *theoretical* part is *how* it occurs. For example, natural selection is a *mechanism* for evolution. Scientists may argue about whether natural selection or mutation is what plays the larger role in producing evolutionary change, but this is *not* an argument over whether evolution does or does not occur.

Gravitational theory describes how gravity is thought to work, but people don't clamor to claim that gravity doesn't exist because it is "just a theory." Keep in mind the key difference between hypotheses and theories: Theories already have been tested and have been stated based upon confirmed/corroborated hypotheses; hypotheses have not yet undergone testing.

Decades (in fact, centuries) of scientific discoveries in the areas of geology, biology, anthropology, paleontology, physics, and chemistry have brought us to the level of knowledge at which we find ourselves now. Questioning, probing, critiquing—these are qualities in the nature of scientists, and we continue to engage in them to better provide explanations for natural phenomena. But *if it's not testable, it's not science!*

Measuring Evolutionary Success

We have established that because gene frequencies change in all populations from one generation to the next, evolution occurs continually in all populations. Evolution is nonprogressive, which means that a species doesn't strive to achieve some specific form by evolving consciously in a particular way. Rather, random factors (such as mutation) and nonrandom factors (such as natural selection) combine to change gene frequencies in a population.

If a species is well-adapted to its environment and the environment remains the same, the species may undergo little or no obvious change. Two excellent examples are sharks (see Figure 1.2), which first evolved over 400 million years

FIGURE 1.2 *Sharks—little change through time*

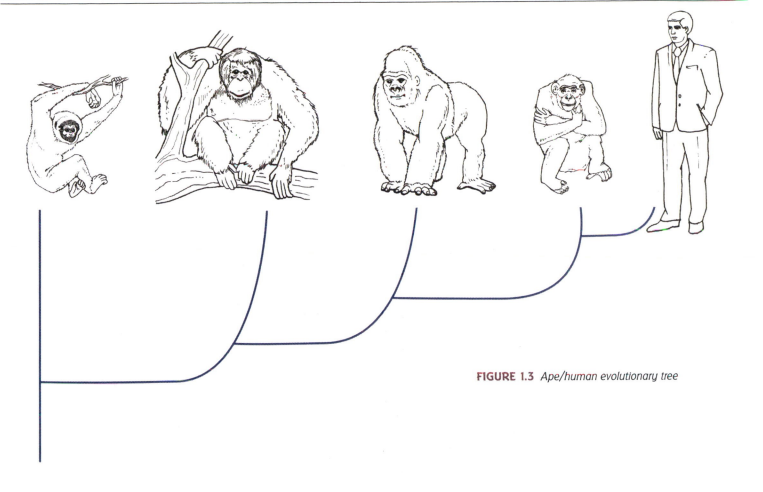

FIGURE 1.3 *Ape/human evolutionary tree*

ago in the Devonian period of the Paleozoic Era, and cockroaches, which first evolved about 305 million years ago in the Carboniferous period (also in the Paleozoic Era).

A long period of existence is one way to measure evolutionary success. Another is the diversity of species within a taxonomic group. Examples within the Class Mammalia are the more than 2,000 species in the Order Rodentia (rodents) and the approximately 1,100 species in the Order Chiroptera (bats). By contrast, the aardvark order (Order Tubulidentata) has only one species!

Evolution and Human Ancestry

The fossil record and genetic data agree in telling us that the modern African apes (chimpanzee and gorilla) and humans shared a common ancestor between 7 and 8 million years ago (see Figure 1.3). This common ancestor would have been quite ape-like, and the earliest members of the human family indeed do have many ape-like features (such as a small brain and a forward-jutting jaw).

Keep in mind that evolution continues to occur, depending on environmental conditions and random changes (mutations) in the DNA. Thus, while both modern apes and humans have evolved since our shared ancestor several million years ago, we have diverged from that ancestor to a much different extent. The apes have undergone little *obvious* change since that common ancestor, and humans have changed a great deal in our appearance and behavior. While the apes have their own unique evolutionary history, their environment and lifestyle have changed less than ours—resulting in less selection pressure to cause species change.

LAB EXERCISE 1.1

NAME _____

SECTION _____ DATE _____

Working together in pairs or groups of three:

1. Make up a simple experiment to investigate one of the following phenomena, using all the steps of the scientific method:

    a. Your neighbor's rooster crows every morning at daylight.

    b. Your cookie dough disappears from the refrigerator every night.

    c. Make up your own phenomenon.

2. Using rulers, calipers, your imagination, or any other tool, document variation in the class population. List three traits that differ among students (physical or behavioral). How might each of these traits have been selected for in certain (hypothetical) environments? Write a couple of paragraphs to illustrate how that variation might be acted upon by natural selection to change gene frequency in this population. In your answer, clearly incorporate all of the steps of evolution by natural selection.

3. As accurately as possible, draw (don't trace) the dog illustrated below. Compare your drawings to those of your classmates. Notice that all drawings look somewhat different from the original. This is analogous to the intraspecific (within-species) variation that all individuals acquire from their parents and contribute to a population. Without variation, natural selection cannot occur!

LAB EXERCISE 1.2

NAME _____

SECTION _____ DATE _____

As stated earlier in this chapter, **biological variation** within populations of a species is necessary for the action of natural selection. When environmental change occurs, variation allows for individuals with characteristics that are most beneficial to survive and reproduce at higher rates than those that are less well adapted.

The purpose of this exercise is to draw attention to the range of variation inherent within each population of living organisms, and to take steps toward describing characteristics that relate to that variation.

Your instructor has brought to class a measurable plant part, such as snow peas. (Leaves or other plant parts may be substituted, as determined by the instructor.)

1. Using a ruler or calipers, with your lab partner measure the maximum length from tip to tip in millimeters (refer to illustration below). Then measure up to 20 additional snow peas (yours and those of other students). Record the measurements in the chart below.

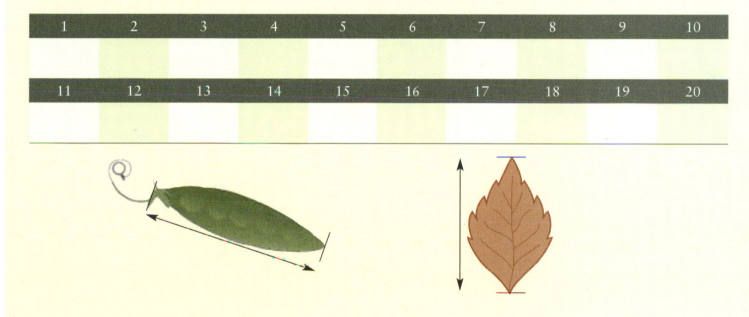

1	2	3	4	5	6	7	8	9	10

11	12	13	14	15	16	17	18	19	20

Your results will probably exhibit a cluster around the middle size value, and few very long and very short values.

2. You now will examine the variation in your group, or **sample**, of snow peas and the manner in which your measurements are dispersed around the average size. You will figure out the following:

   a. What is the **range** of measurements in your sample?

   _____ mm to _____ mm
         shortest   longest

   b. What is the **mean** of your sample? Add up your individual measurements and divide by the number of snow peas. This will give you the average size of the snow peas in your sample.

c. What is the **median**? List your measurements from shortest to longest, then note the length of the snow pea in the middle of the list (if there are two in the middle, take the mean of the two).

d. What is the **mode**? Record the number of snow peas of each length in your sample. If your sample is small (and 20 is generally a small sample), you may not have a mode: that is, all of the snow peas may have different lengths.

If you had a larger sample size, and were to draw the results on a graph, the result probably would be a **normal curve**. A normal, or **bell-shaped curve**, is typical of measurements that represent a range of variation. Most *measurable* characteristics of living organisms can be represented in this way, and exhibit a continuous range of variation, or **continuous variation**.

Answer the following in terms of your results.

3. How does the *median* compare to the *mean*? What is the effect of one very long snow pea in your sample on the median? On the mean?

4. In your sample, is there much variation in snow pea size? Are most snow peas close to the mean in size or do they vary widely from the mean?

To understand variation within species, we must think in terms of **adaptive significance**, or the advantage of certain forms in the process of natural selection. The size of wild pods in legumes similar to snow peas may be associated with plant success. A larger pod with more and/or larger seeds may have increased competitive ability because of the larger seeds' greater probability of seedling establishment, ability to withstand environmental hazards, and production of larger, hardier seedlings. Advantages, however, of larger seeds are most significant in deep shade, while in more exposed conditions, smaller seeds may mature faster.

Thus, current conditions determine which forms are best adapted within the environment, and the range of variation within each species provides the basis for selection. Keep in mind that the larger pods/seeds in your sample (if they belonged to a wild species) may be better adapted under one set of environmental conditions and less so under other conditions.

SELF-TEST
1.1

NAME _____

SECTION _____ DATE _____

By now you should have enough knowledge and information to answer the "Have you ever wondered…?" questions at the beginning of the lab—along with a few additional questions.

1. If humans evolved from apes, why are there still apes?

2. What is the difference between a hypothesis and a theory?

3. What is an example of a "good" (useful or testable) hypothesis?

4. What is an example of a useless (untestable) hypothesis?

5. What is the definition of evolution?

6. What is gene frequency?

7. How do we know that evolution occurs and is not "just a theory?"

8. What are the four main evolutionary forces?

9. Why is variation within each species so important for evolution?

ONE STEP FURTHER

NAME _____

SECTION _____ DATE _____

Additional Lab Exercise 1.1

1. With your lab partner(s), come up with two natural phenomena about which you are curious, and list them below.

   Phenomenon A:

   Phenomenon B:

2. For each of the phenomena, formulate a *testable hypothesis*.

   Phenomenon A:

   Phenomenon B:

3. What is an example of an *untestable* hypothesis for each?

   Phenomenon A:

   Phenomenon B:

4. Outline an experiment or set of observations that would allow you to test your testable hypothesis for each phenomenon.

   Phenomenon A:

   Phenomenon B:

ONE STEP FURTHER

NAME _____

SECTION _____ DATE _____

Additional Self-Test Questions

1. What is the difference between a hypothesis and a theory?

2. Put the steps of the scientific method in order, and fill in the blanks.

   _____ Question(s) (why, what, how, etc.)

   _____ Experiment or data collection

   _____ Propose a _____, which may be more generally applicable

   _____ Observe some phenomenon

   _____ Propose a _____, which must be _____

3. Describe the steps of natural selection clearly, in the context of a hypothetical example of its occurrence.

The Organism and the Cell

2

> ## "Have you ever wondered . . . ?"
>
> - What are cells made of?
> - How can you tell if a cell is from a male or a female?
>
> ### OBJECTIVES
>
> - Understand the levels of organization of the body
> - Understand cell structure
> - Become familiar with chromosomes, what they're made of, and their structure
> - Learn to compose a layout (karyotype) of the human genome
>
> ### MATERIALS NEEDED
>
> - Scissors
> - Glue or tape
>
> *(One Step Further will require additional materials; see Additional Lab Exercise 2.1.)*

Because all living organisms share a common ancestry from more than 3.6 billion years ago, we also share the same code for our genetic material, deoxyribonucleic acid. All of our cells contain DNA, and in most living organisms it is contained within the nucleus.

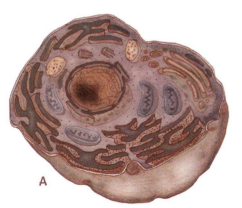

A

Organisms in which the DNA is within the nucleus are **eukaryotes** (G *eus*: true, *karyon*: nut, kernel) (Figure 2.1A) and include members of the kingdoms Protista, Fungi, Plantae, and Animalia. The more primitive kingdom Monera (sometimes divided into two kingdoms) are **prokaryotes** (G *pro*: before, *karyon*: nut, kernel). Prokaryotes (Figure 2.1B) lack a nucleus to enclose the DNA, which floats freely throughout the cell.

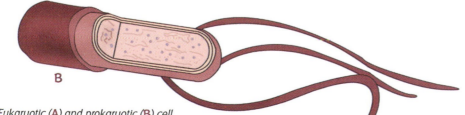

B

FIGURE 2.1 *Eukaryotic (A) and prokaryotic (B) cell*

The Basic Body Plan

In comparing the human body plan with those of other organisms, we have greater similarity to those with whom we share a more recent ancestry. All living vertebrates shared a common ancestor more than 500 million years ago. The genetic material (DNA) passed down from that common ancestor dictates the development of the same features in various groups. We have a femur, a humerus, and a mandible, as do salamanders, crocodiles, birds, and horses, because our shared common ancestor also had those bones. Features that we have in common because of our shared ancestry are called **homologous features** (Figure 2.2).

The human body plan thus shares some basic similarities with other animals, particularly the vertebrates. We are composed of **cells**, the fundamental units of life. Cells are organized into **tissues**, which form **organs** (for example, heart and lungs). Organs function together as part of various **organ systems** (for example, cardiovascular system and muscular system), and all of the organ systems are "packaged" into an **organism**. In Figure 2.3 observe the relationship of these various levels of organization from the organs to the cells making up the organ tissues.

Over the next few chapters, we'll be "zooming in and out" from looking at entire organisms to the component parts and their functions, then back to the whole organism. In this way we'll get a look at the whole picture.

Now that you are familiar with the basic body plan, you will learn about its genetic basis. First we will discuss the cell, the fundamental unit of living things. Then we will cover the structures that are made up of the genetic material—the **chromosomes**—and conclude the chapter with how they all fit together.

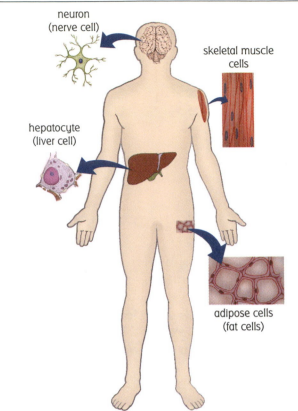

FIGURE 2.3 *Human body plan: Organs made of cells*

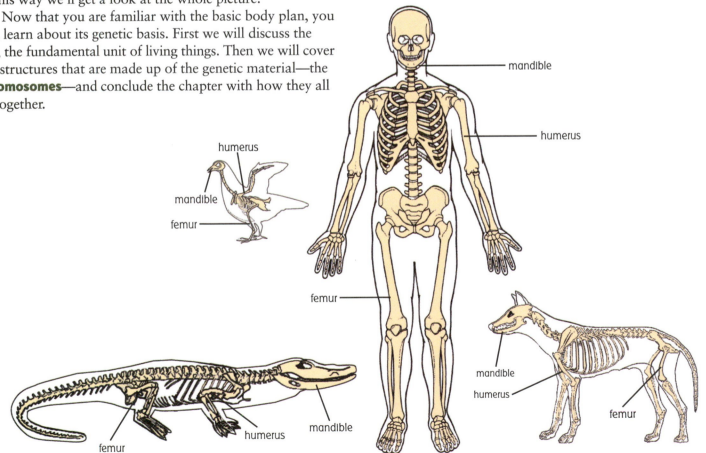

FIGURE 2.2 *Various vertebrates demonstrating homologous features*

Cells

Cells are responsible for arranging molecules into living matter. Most plants and animals have millions—or even billions or trillions—of cells, with various types specialized for specific roles in the body. The human body is estimated to have anywhere from 10 trillion to 100 trillion cells; the number differs from individual to individual and throughout our lifetime. Each cell has a full set of genetic information that directs life and its processes: growth, development, and metabolism. This genetic information is passed from parent to offspring.

Cell Structure

A typical cell is composed of water, salt, proteins, lipids, carbohydrates, and nucleic acids, all held within a permeable membrane. In eukaryotes a nucleus separates the genetic material from the **cytoplasm.** In the cytoplasm the various **organelles** each have a function. You should be familiar with the structure and function of the following cell components (see Figure 2.4):

- **plasma membrane** A double-layered membrane, composed of phospholipids and protein molecules, that gives form to the cell and controls passage of material into and out of the cell.

- **nucleus** Contains the genetic material (DNA), separated from the rest of the cell by a **nuclear membrane**.

- **nucleolus** Seen as a dark mass in the nucleus, made up of proteins and ribosomal RNA, and the site of ribosome production.

- **cytoplasm** Fluid, jelly-like substance, between the cell membrane and the nucleus, in which organelles are suspended.

- **mitochondria** Oblong organelle where adenosine triphosphate (ATP) production occurs; ATP is the carrier of chemical energy in the cell.

- **ribosomes** Small structures made of proteins and RNA that "read" the RNA strand during protein synthesis; occur free and on endoplasmic reticulum.

- **endoplasmic reticulum (e.r.)** Membranous network of channels in cytoplasm, continuous with nuclear membrane, that forms a pathway for transporting substances within the cell and stores synthesized molecules (intracellular circulatory system).

- **centriole** Pairs of organelles composed of microtubules; organizes the cytoskeleton for cell division.

- **lysosome** Sac-like attachment to cell membrane that digests unneeded molecules; formed from vesicles of Golgi body.

- **Golgi body and vesicles** Delivery system of cell, which collects, modifies, packages, and distributes **vesicles**, molecules that are synthesized at one location and used at another.

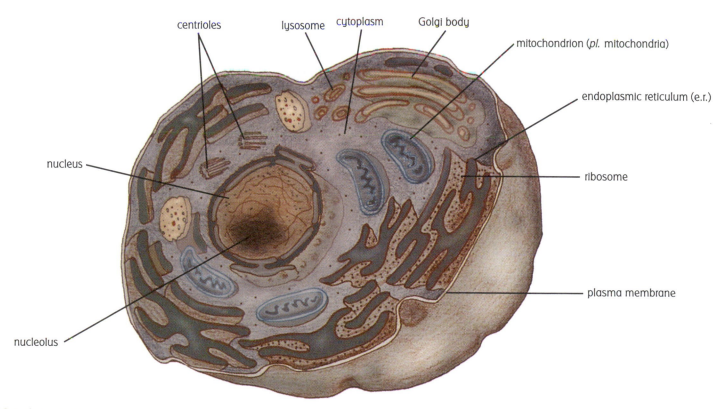

FIGURE 2.4 *Generalized eukaryotic cell*

In addition, you should be familiar with the following terms:

- **cytoskeleton** Network of microtubules and microfilaments; dispersed in cytoplasm to provide a structural framework for cell division; composed of the proteins tubulin, actin, and myosin.

- **chromosomes** Structures in the nucleus; composed of genetic material (DNA) wound around proteins.

Classes of Cells

The body has two classes of cells (see Figure 2.5):

1. **Somatic cells**, the thousands of types of cells making up our body structure, and

2. **Gametes**, or **sex cells—egg** or **sperm** cells.

Take a look at two types of somatic cells by following these instructions:

1. Pull out a hair. The expanded base of your hair is embedded in a **hair follicle**, which is like a little sac housed in your skin. The portion of a hair you can see sticking out of your scalp is the hair shaft, which consists of dead cells and proteins. The part of your hair that is buried beneath the surface of your skin is made up of living cells. You can see evidence of this if, when you pluck out a hair, you can see a white covering at the end. This is the hair bulb, which is made up of living cells.

2. Now scratch your elbow or knee, where skin is often relatively dry. The white flakes you may see are dead skin cells (Figure 2.6). They were produced about a week ago, through cell division in the deeper skin layers, then migrated to the surface. The basal cell layer of your epidermis is constantly producing new skin cells.

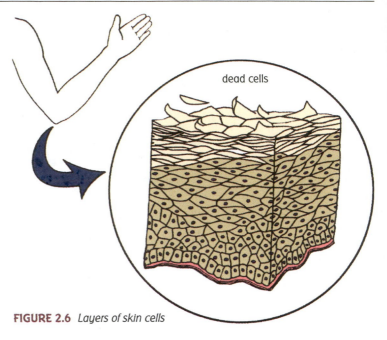

FIGURE 2.6 *Layers of skin cells*

Development

All of the cells in an individual are derived from the fertilized egg, the **zygote**. In this single original cell the hereditary information (DNA) is stored in the nucleus. One-half of this hereditary information (23 chromosomes) has come from the mother's egg, and one-half (23 chromosomes) from the father's sperm. Immediately after fertilization the zygote first replicates its hereditary material (DNA), then divides into two cells, apportioning one-half of its DNA into each of the two newly formed cells. Each new cell divides in the same way.

This cell division continues until a mass of cells with the appearance of a mulberry is formed. These cells, which up to this point had been identical to one another, begin the process of **differentiation** from one another. That is, after cell division, they suddenly begin to grow in different ways from each other. This results in three embryonic layers:

1. endoderm,

2. mesoderm, and

3. ectoderm.

These layers eventually develop into the inner primitive gut and other internal organs, the musculoskeletal system and the kidney, and the outside covering of the body together with the nervous system and the eye (see Figure 2.7).

Continued cell division and differentiation result in hundreds of types of cells, each with a different function. These cells eventually develop into the various tissues and organs of the body. A complete set of hereditary information remains stored, intact, in each of the body's somatic cells.

The process of cell division in which somatic cells divide to produce more somatic cells is called **mitosis**. Cell division will be discussed in detail in Chapter 4. Keep in mind that,

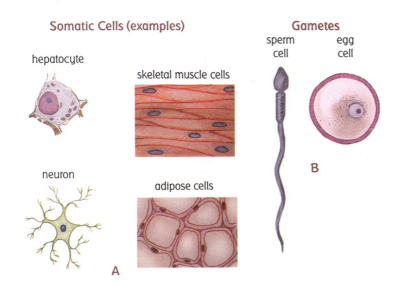

FIGURE 2.5 **A** *Examples of somatic cells and* **B** *gametes*

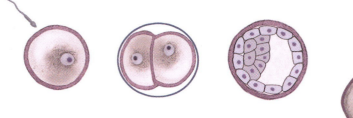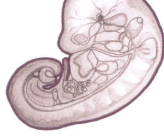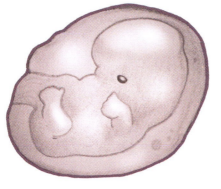

FIGURE 2.7 *Overview of embryological development*

although individuals each have many types of somatic cells, they produce only one type of gamete—eggs or sperm. Sperm originate in the testes of males, and eggs in the ovaries of females. Both types of gamete arise by **meiosis**. In the process of gamete formation, an individual's genetic information is "reshuffled" to produce the variation that prepares for passing genetic information to the offspring. Each sperm and egg cell that an individual produces is unique in terms of its combination of genetic information.

Chromosomes

We soon will be delving into the molecular world of the actual genetic material, but first we will discuss how it is packaged. Most of the genetic material, deoxyribonucleic acid (DNA), is found in the nucleus of cells. This nuclear DNA, together with the proteins that it is coiled around, is packaged into **chromosomes** (G *chrome*: color; *soma*: body). Chromosomes are visible in the form shown in Figure 2.8 only during cell division, when the genetic material condenses and contracts. Note the **arms**, the **centromere** (L *centro*: central; *mere*: part), and the **sister chromatids**. When the cell is not in the process of cell division, the chromosomes remain uncoiled and diffuse into a form called **chromatin**.

The chromosome is shown in Figure 2.8 in its doubled state, the way it appears early in the process of cell division. This is a result of DNA replication, which always occurs prior to cell division. The two sister chromatids are identical.

The number of chromosomes, and thus the amount of genetic material, is the same for all members of a species. For example, a goldfish has 92 chromosomes in each of its somatic cells; a chicken and a dog each have 78; a rat has 42; and a fruit fly has 4 chromosomes. A baboon has 42 chromosomes, a chimpanzee 48, and a human 46. The number of chromosomes does not correlate with "complexity" or place within the biological classification system, as chromosomes of different species are of varying sizes, with different proportions of active regions.

Chromosomes in Humans

In humans, the chromosome number of 46 refers to the number in *somatic cells*. Remember that all of these cells

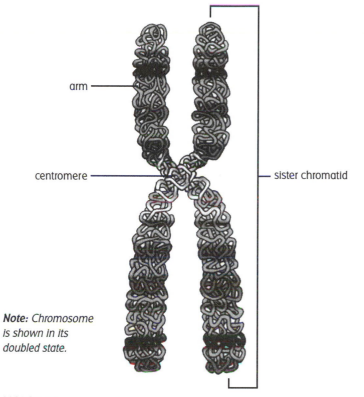

arm

centromere ———   ——— sister chromatid

Note: Chromosome is shown in its doubled state.

FIGURE 2.8 *Chromosome structure*

originally were derived, via continual mitosis, from the zygote, which consisted of one set of 23 chromosomes from the mother's egg and 23 from the father's sperm. These two sets of 23 chromosomes make up the full complement of 46 chromosomes, referred to as the **diploid** number. The single set of 23 chromosomes contained within each *gamete* (egg or sperm cell) is referred to as the **haploid** number. When a haploid sperm and egg combine, the zygote they form will have the full (diploid) complement of 46 chromosomes.

Humans have 23 different chromosomes, which can be identified based on their *size, centromere location,* and *banding pattern* (the bands show up after chemical staining). With one exception, resulting from mistakes before microscopes were as powerful as they are today, the chromosomes are numbered according to their size, with number 1 being the largest. Chromosome 21 is actually smaller than 22. The 23rd chromosome is a sex chromosome, X or Y.

Because each person inherits 23 chromosomes from the mother and 23 from the father, each cell has two sets of chromosomes. All of the 23 members of a set can be arranged into pairs so we have two chromosome 1s, two 2s, and so on. The pairs are referred to as **homologous**. Figure 2.9 demonstrates a **karyotype**, the chromosomal complement of an individual. Is the individual in Figure 2.9 a male or a female?

Karyotypes

A set of chromosomes can be organized into such a karyotype by first isolating some cells during cell division when the chromosomes are condensed and in visible form. For example, if you scrape the inner surface of your cheek with a toothpick, you almost certainly will obtain some dividing cells. After staining, you would put these on a slide to be viewed under a microscope and photograph the image. From the resulting photograph, you would arrange the chromosomes into matching (homologous) pairs based on the criteria listed.

This completes your karyotype. The 23 chromosomes fall into several groups, based on their size and centromere location. Keep in mind that these same 46 chromosomes are found in the nucleus of *each* somatic cell and are identical copies of those in the nucleus of *you* back when you were just a zygote (Figure 2.10).

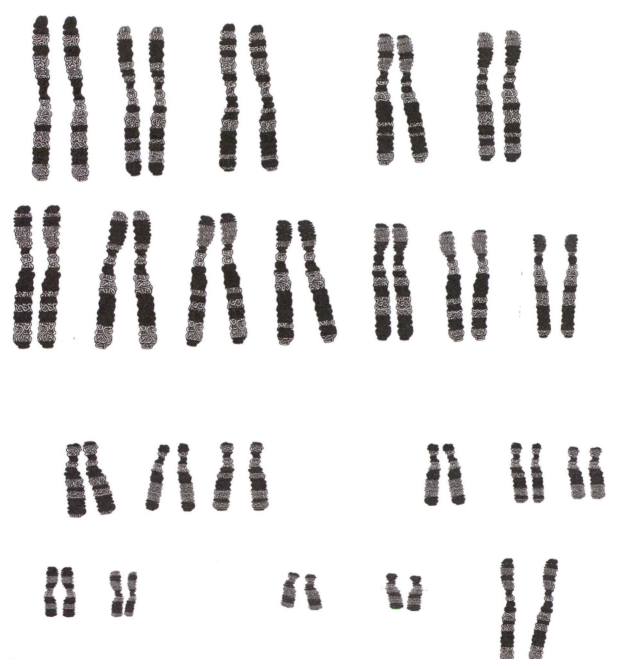

FIGURE 2.9 *Sample karyotype*

Recent Advances: Epigenetics

A new, fascinating area of research called epigenetics (G *epi*: on top of) deals with the question of why some regions of DNA (genes) are expressed and others are not. A set of chemical reactions switch parts of the genome off and on at various times and in various cells. Factors that influence the epigenome include diet, stress, and culture. These factors play an important role in the development (or lack of development) of certain diseases, including cancer. **Epigenetics** is the study of how these environmental factors influence the genes we have.

One use of a karyotype is to evaluate the health of a developing fetus by examining its chromosomes. During pregnancy, a karyotype is made with cells taken from the amniotic fluid surrounding the fetus. Chromosomal anomalies, or abnormalities, usually are fatal (discussed further in Chapter 4).

Chromosome pairs numbered 1 through 22 are called **autosomes**, and pair number 23 consists of the **sex chromosomes**, **X** and **Y**. Chromosomes X and Y determine an individual's sex. Each female has two X chromosomes along with the 22 pairs of autosomes in each somatic cell. Each male has one X and one Y chromosome. The much larger X chromosome has more than 1,100 genes, and the Y chromosome has only about 250 genes.

Homologous Chromosomes

What makes a chromosome pair homologous? Although the size, shape, and banding pattern can help identify the members of a pair, what makes a pair homologous is *what is on the chromosomes*. A **gene** is a segment of DNA that codes for a specific polypeptide or protein (which eventually determines one's traits). The position a gene occupies on a chromosome is called a **locus** (*pl.* loci). A locus is analogous to a street address, with many loci on each chromosome. Larger chromosomes have more loci and more genes than do smaller chromosomes.

Two chromosomes are **homologous** when the genes at a given locus code for the same trait on both chromosomes. Figure 2.11 gives examples of genes on chromosomes. We'll learn more about genes in Chapter 3.

Because the karyotype represented within each somatic cell of an individual consists of two sets of chromosomes (one set originally from the mother's egg and another set from the father's sperm), different "versions" of a gene may

appear on each member of a pair of homologous chromosomes. For example, at the locus for ABO blood type, the mother's egg may have carried a gene coding for type B blood (see Figure 2.12). The corresponding locus on the chromosome contributed from the father's sperm may have a

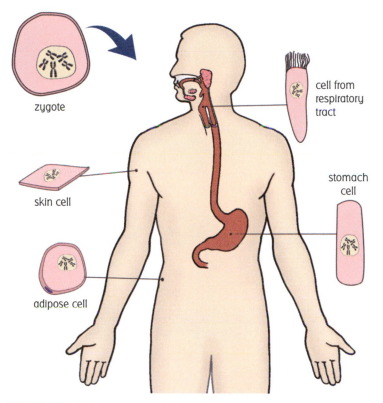

FIGURE 2.10 *Body's somatic cells, all derived from zygote*

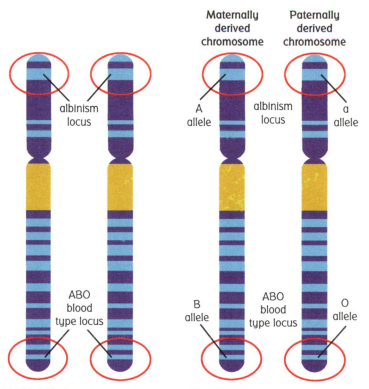

FIGURE 2.11 *Sample gene loci on chromosome 9*

FIGURE 2.12 *Sample alleles for genes on chromosome 9*

gene coding for type O blood. These alternative versions of a gene are called **alleles** (in the example, B allele, O allele).

Organisms, Cells, and Chromosomes

Chromosomes are made up of our genetic material, DNA. DNA controls all cell processes, and thus dictates the development, metabolism, and repair of the body in case of illness or injury. Chromosomes are replicated to allow for the production of new cells for two purposes:

1. to make new somatic cells that maintain the body

2. to make gametes that combine in a new individual and carry our genetic information to the next generation.

The reshuffling of genetic material during the process of gamete formation, together with the combining of parental genes in sexually reproducing species, leads to incredible variation within each species. This variation among individual organisms is what provides the raw material upon which natural selection can act.

LAB EXERCISE
2.1

NAME _____

SECTION _____ DATE _____

Pretend that you've just scraped the inside of a classmate's cheek with a toothpick to get a cell sample. You put this cellular "extract" on a microscope slide, observe it under magnification, then take a black-and-white photo of the magnified slide. The result will appear similar to the set of chromosomes below.

  Compare this set of chromosomes to that of Figure 2.9. The set on this page is in the doubled, or replicated, state, because that is how they will appear in a microscope.

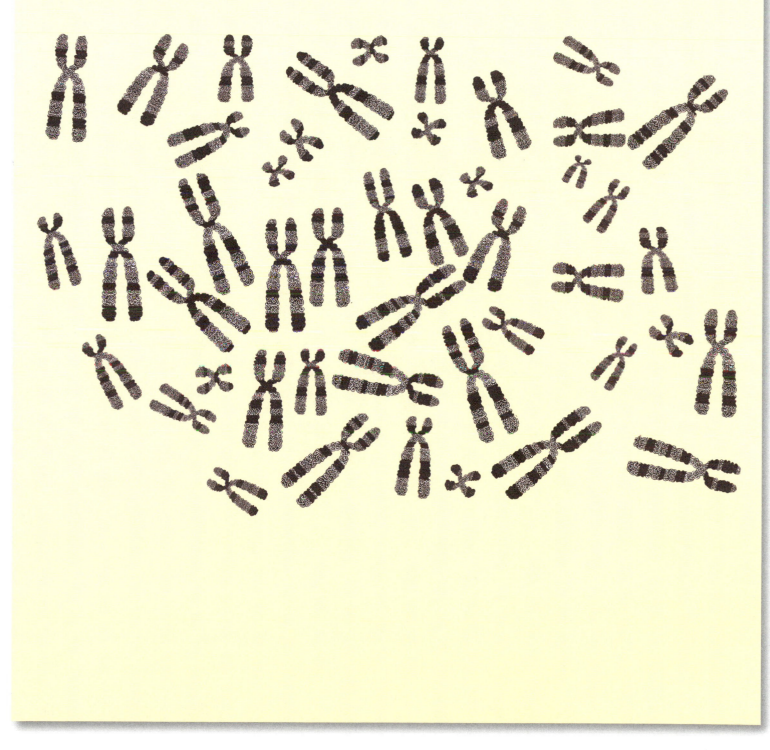

LAB EXERCISE 2.1 (CONT.)

NAME _____

SECTION _____ DATE _____

1. Cut out the chromosomes on page 25.

2. Match the homologous pairs, and put them in the proper order according to size and banding pattern, gluing or taping them below. Remember that Chromosome 21 is smaller than Chromosome 22 (the only exception to the size-numbering rule). Use the karyotype form below to categorize them into the seven groups (plus the sex chromosomes) listed. You will place two chromosomes in each blank (a homologous pair).

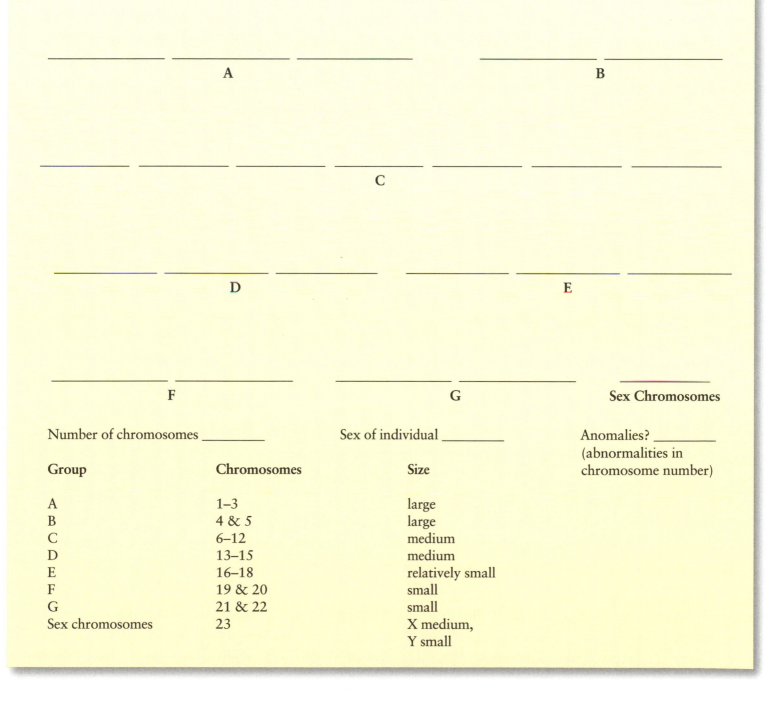

_____ _____ _____   _____ _____

A   **B**

_____ _____ _____ _____ _____ _____ _____

C

_____ _____ _____   _____ _____ _____

D   **E**

_____ _____   _____ _____   _____

F   **G**   **Sex Chromosomes**

Number of chromosomes _____   Sex of individual _____   Anomalies? _____
                                                                                    (abnormalities in
                                                                                    chromosome number)

Group	Chromosomes	Size
A	1–3	large
B	4 & 5	large
C	6–12	medium
D	13–15	medium
E	16–18	relatively small
F	19 & 20	small
G	21 & 22	small
Sex chromosomes	23	X medium, Y small

SELF-TEST

2.1

NAME _____

SECTION _____ DATE _____

1. What are cells made of?

2. How can you tell if a somatic cell is from a male or a female?

3. Fill in the blanks to label the structures in the cell, and briefly note the basic function of each structure.

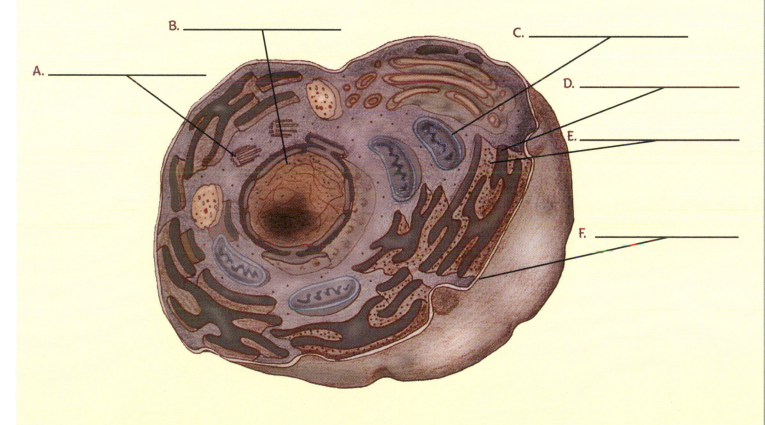

B. _____   C. _____

A. _____   D. _____

E. _____

F. _____

4. The full complement of chromosomes (found in a somatic cell) is called the _____ number.

5. Regarding the previous question, what is this number for humans? _____

6. Pretend that you are observing a skin cell from a chicken under a microscope.

   a. What is the *class* of cell you're looking at? _____

   b. If the nucleus of this cell has 78 chromosomes, how many chromosomes would the chicken's sperm cell have?

   _____

7. What are gametes, and how many chromosomes do they each contain in humans?

8. What is a zygote?

9. How many chromosomes does a human zygote have, and where did these chromosomes come from originally?

10. What is a gene?

11. What makes homologous chromosomes homologous?

12. What are alleles? What are examples of two alleles for a given gene?

13. a. Draw a chromosome in its
doubled (replicated) state, and
label the parts: arms, centromere,
and sister chromatids.

    b. Draw three different chromosomes,
and show how they can differ in
terms of size, centromere location,
and banding pattern.

    c. Draw a pair of chromosomes, and
demonstrate one hypothetical locus
for a gene on each. Choose (or make
up) a trait and two possible alleles.
Label these similar to Figure 2.12.

14. What are autosomes? What is a chromosome if it is not an autosome?

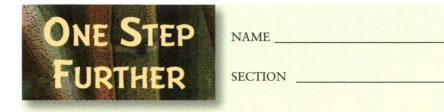

ONE STEP FURTHER

NAME _____

SECTION _____ DATE _____

Additional Lab Exercise **2.1**

ADDITIONAL MATERIALS NEEDED:

- Various examples of karyotypes: The instructor should print out and bring to class, or show in class without their labels. Some karyotypes are available at:
  - ◆ www.biology.iupui.edu/biocourses/N100/2K2humancsomaldisorders.html
  - ◆ http://www.biology.arizona.edu/human_bio/activities/karyotyping/karyotyping2.html
  - ◆ http://www.emc.maricopa.edu/faculty/farabee/BIOBK/BioBookhumgen.html#Human%20chromosomal%20abnormalities
  - ◆ http://www.bioedonline.org/slides/slide01.cfm?q=genetic+abnormalities
- Microscopes
- Microscope slides of various cell(s), preferably with visible organelles, or at least to show cell variety. Some examples:
  - ◆ skeletal muscle cell   ◆ bone cell (osteocyte)   ◆ adipocyte (fat cell)
  - ◆ cartilage (fibrocartilage, elastic cartilage, hyaline cartilage)

1. Observe four different karyotypes provided by your instructor. Determine the following for each:

	Sex	Any genetic anomalies? (or are all chromosomes present and whole?)
Karyotype 1	_____	_____
Karyotype 2	_____	_____
Karyotype 3	_____	_____
Karyotype 4	_____	_____

2. Examine various cell slides under a microscope, one at a time.

   a. List the cells you observed.

   b. Could you distinguish the nucleus in any of the cells? If so, which ones? Do any have more than one nucleus?

   c. What are two things you might expect to be visible in the nucleus?

3. For each of the cells you observed, list any of the identifiable organelles in the cytoplasm.

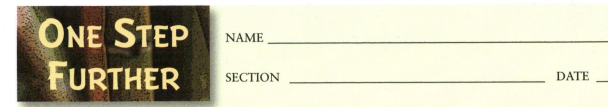

ONE STEP FURTHER

NAME _____

SECTION _____ DATE _____

Additional Self-Test Questions

1. A homologous pair of chromosomes is homologous because:
   a. the chromosomes come from the same parent
   b. both have loci that contain alleles for the same traits
   c. they are found only in somatic cells
   d. the alleles on both chromosomes are identical

2. Alternative forms of a gene are called:
   a. alleles
   b. centromeres
   c. homologs
   d. loci

3. Draw a cell with the following components: centrioles, mitochondria, endoplasmic reticulum, nucleus, chromatin, ribosomes.

4. What does a karyotype represent?

5. What are the two classes of cells in the body? How do they differ in terms of: number of chromosomes, type of cell division that produces them, and where in the body they are found?

The Double Helix

3

"Have you ever wondered . . . ?"

- I've heard of DNA, but *how* is DNA our genetic material?
- What exactly *are* genes anyway?
- How do you get from DNA to a person? Or an eel? Or a nectarine tree?
- How is cloning possible?

OBJECTIVES

- Understand the genetic material, its structure and function
- Understand processes dictated by DNA—DNA replication and protein synthesis
- Know how DNA replication allows for cell division
- Know how DNA sequence determines protein production
- Extract and observe the DNA from an organism (a banana)

MATERIALS NEEDED

- Blender—one (two if possible) for the entire class
- Bananas—one banana per pair of lab partners
- 1 teaspoon per lab pair
- One small clear glass per lab pair
- Coffee filters (thin ones recommended) or strainer—one or two per lab pair
- Sharp knife and cutting surface—per lab pair
- Toothpicks—enough for one per student
- Liquid dish detergent
- Meat tenderizer
- Isopropyl (91% alcohol recommended) or regular rubbing alcohol
- Paper towels

(One Step Further will require additional materials; see Additional Lab Exercises 3.1 and 3.2.)

The processes that occur in our cells are amazing in precision and scope. The cellular process, and thus the functioning of our entire body, is controlled by our genetic material, DNA. This chapter covers the structure and function of DNA.

The Genetic Material

Although the component parts of **deoxyribonucleic acid,** or **DNA,** had been identified, its structure was unknown until 1953. Several scientists were engaged in a race to discover DNA's structure. The race was won by James Watson and Francis Crick, who published their results in a 1953 issue of *Nature* and shared the Nobel Prize in 1962 with Maurice Wilkins. Rosalind Franklin, who worked in Wilkins' lab and whose X-ray diffraction photo provided the final piece to the puzzle, died before the prize was awarded.

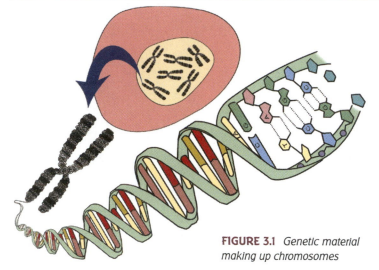

FIGURE 3.1 *Genetic material making up chromosomes*

DNA is a large molecule in the nucleus of all eukaryotic cells and, together with several types of proteins, is "packaged" into chromosomes that are contained in the nucleus of every cell in the body (see Figure 3.1). DNA is an extremely long molecule, but very thin—approximately 6 feet of DNA are coiled and crowded into *each cell!* DNA is responsible for two vital processes:

1. **replication** (making a copy of itself), and
2. **protein synthesis** (the manufacture of proteins).

The structure enables DNA to carry out these processes, which allow for growth and development, and for genetic information to be passed from generation to generation.

Why should we care about a *molecule*? What is its relevance or interest to us? Knowledge of the structure and function of DNA, and how DNA sequences are inherited, allows us to:

- be aware of the risks of transmitting genetic diseases to our children, based upon the genetic makeup of both biological parents.
- identify perpetrators of various crimes.
- identify biological relationships among individuals and among species.
- track historical events in our species, as the story of our ancestry lies in our DNA sequence.

Nucleic Acids

Within the nucleus of all eukaryotic cells are two types of **nucleic acids**. They are referred to as "nucleic" because they are found in the nucleus, and acidic because they release H+ ions when they disassociate in water. Molecules that release OH− or accept H+ are basic. The two variants of nucleic acids are DNA (deoxyribonucleic acid) and **RNA (ribonucleic acid)**. DNA is the actual genetic material, and RNA is a

Recent Advances: DNA Fingerprinting

DNA is used in identifying individuals, establishing relationships, and diagnosing genetic disease. **DNA fingerprinting** (or genetic fingerprinting, or DNA typing) is based on the fact that although humans are genetically similar to one another, the portions that do vary are highly useful for differentiating us from each other. While the usable portions of DNA (coding regions) are more similar between individuals, the unused portions (noncoding regions, or "junk" DNA) mutate more frequently because these portions are not subjected to selection pressure.

Some of these portions consist of repeating sequences of bases, and these typically are similar in related individuals and dissimilar in unrelated individuals. Thus, DNA fingerprinting is used to establish paternity or maternity. But DNA fingerprinting is best known for its forensic uses: Any DNA left at a crime scene can be reliably matched to a suspect's DNA, and it also can be used to identify otherwise unidentifiable victims of crimes or accidents.

similar substance that can be thought of as a vital "helper" for some DNA functions.

The "building blocks" of the nucleic acids are called **nucleotides** (see Figure 3.2). A nucleotide is the most basic unit of both DNA and RNA. Each nucleotide has three components:

1. a **sugar molecule**. DNA has a type of sugar called **deoxyribose**, and RNA has a sugar called **ribose**. These sugars differ from one another only slightly in chemical structure, with deoxyribose having one fewer oxygen atom than ribose.
2. a **phosphate molecule**, and
3. a **base**.

Bases are one of four chemical substances, each of which is made of simple atoms of hydrogen, carbon, oxygen, and nitrogen. Three of the four bases of DNA and RNA are the same: **adenine (A)**, **guanine (G)**, and **cytosine (C)**. The fourth base differs, with **thymine (T)** found only in DNA and the chemically similar **uracil (U)** found only in RNA.

Because nucleotides are composed of simple atoms such as carbon, hydrogen, oxygen, and nitrogen, the nucleus of cells has a constant supply of free DNA and RNA nucleotides. These are used in DNA replication and protein synthesis.

DNA nucleotides

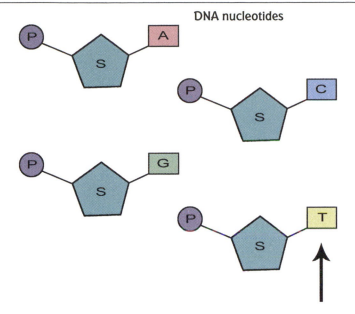

RNA nucleotides

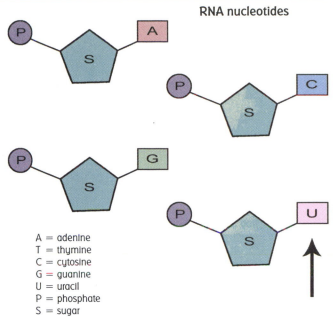

A = adenine
T = thymine
C = cytosine
G = guanine
U = uracil
P = phosphate
S = sugar

FIGURE 3.2 *Nucleotides of DNA and RNA*

The Structure of DNA

A number of nucleotides strung together are referred to as a **polynucleotide** (*poly:* many) **chain**. DNA consists of two polynucleotide chains, or strands. The DNA molecule is called the **double helix** because of its helical (twisted) structure and because it has two strands. Its overall appearance is that of a twisted ladder. The "backbone" of DNA, or sides of the ladder, is composed of alternating molecules of phosphates and sugars. The pairs of bases, or **base pairs**, make up the "rungs" of the ladder (see Figure 3.3). The human genome has nearly 3 billion base pairs, and the rat has about 2.75 billion (Rat Genome Sequencing Project Consortium, 2004). By comparison, a fruit fly has 1.2 billion base pairs and an *Escherichia coli* bacterium has 4.6 million (Blattner et al., 1997; Adams et al., 2000).

On each strand, the phosphates and sugars of adjacent nucleotides and those between sugars and the bases are held together by strong chemical bonds. The bonds holding the base pairs together, however, are weak bonds, called **hydrogen bonds**, which can be easily broken by enzymes.

The pairing of bases in DNA has specific "rules," based upon the size of the four different bases and their available sites for bonding with one another. Adenine and thymine consistently bond together, as do cytosine with guanine (see Figure 3.3).

Important to understanding DNA structure is that the two strands (polynucleotide chains) are *complementary*, not identical, to one another. Thus, by knowing the sequence of one strand, you can easily infer the sequence of the other strand. This complementarity in its structure allows for the two vital processes of replication and protein synthesis that are directed by the DNA.

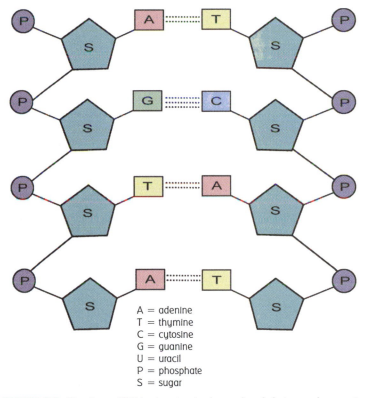

A = adenine
T = thymine
C = cytosine
G = guanine
U = uracil
P = phosphate
S = sugar

FIGURE 3.3 *Structure of DNA, showing hydrogen bonds between base pairs*

Summary of Genetic Material

To summarize—DNA is a nucleic acid whose double helix (twisted ladder) structure is based upon sugar and phosphate molecules comprising the "backbone," and paired combinations of the four types of bases (A,C,T,G) making up the "rungs" of the ladder. The smallest unit of DNA, a nucleotide, consists of one sugar molecule, one phosphate, and one base. The two polynucleotide chains in DNA are linked by weak hydrogen bonds between the bases.

In Watson and Crick's famous 1953 publication announcing the discovery of the structure of DNA, the ending reads, "It has not escaped notice that the specific pairing we have postulated immediately suggests a possible copying mechanism for the genetic material" (p. 738). We will deal with these functions next, but before you go on—and preferably without looking at the previous discussion—answer the questions in Self-Test 3.1.

SELF-TEST
3.1

NAME _____

SECTION _____ DATE _____

1. How many nucleotides are represented below?

2. The "backbone" of DNA is made up of _____ and _____ molecules.

3. The four bases in DNA are:

_____   _____

_____   _____

4. In the DNA molecule, the base adenine always forms a complementary pair with _____.

5. Which of the following is *not* a base found in DNA?
   a. uracil
   b. guanine
   c. thymine
   d. adenine

   Where *is* it found? _____

6. What would the complementary strand of the DNA section A G T G A T T C C be?
   a. A G T G A T T C C
   b. A G U G A U U C C
   c. T C A C T A A G G
   d. T C A C T A A C C

7. The DNA molecule can be described as a:

   a. single-stranded chain

   b. double helix

   c. rung of a ladder

   d. sphere

8. A DNA nucleotide:

   a. is composed of a base, a sugar, and a phosphate molecule.

   b. is the same thing as an RNA molecule.

   c. codes for the production of an amino acid.

   d. can include the base uracil.

9. DNA is found in the _____ of all cells.

10. The two processes for which DNA is responsible are _____ and _____.

11. How many polynucleotide chains are in each DNA molecule? _____

12. Fill in the blanks in the illustration below.

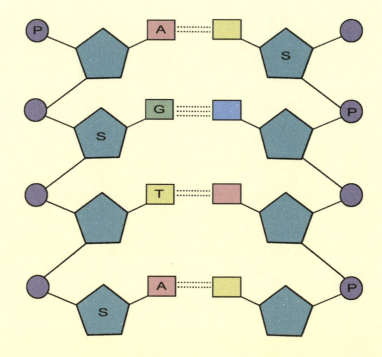

DNA Function: Replication

DNA replication is a vital process that *always* occurs just before cell division, so that a full set of genetic information is passed on to the daughter cells. Thus, *the DNA making up the chromosomes is identical in the nucleus of all somatic cells within an individual's body*. DNA replication enables cell division to occur successfully and allows for hereditary information to be passed from parent to offspring. The fact that the same copy of DNA is in all of our body cells is the basis for **cloning**.

The replication process is controlled by **enzymes**, a class of proteins in the body that carry out metabolic activity in cells. For DNA replication, two important enzymes are DNA polymerase and DNA ligase. The steps by which the DNA in each cell replicates itself before it divides are listed below (see Figure 3.4).

1. Enzymes cause the double helix to unwind by breaking the hydrogen bonds between the bases.

2. The two DNA strands separate from each other as they are unwinding, leaving the bases exposed on each strand.

3. These exposed bases attract free DNA nucleotides that are in the cell's nucleus, and these free nucleotides bond to the appropriate (A with T, and C with G) exposed bases on both of the original (and now separated) DNA strands.

4. The DNA nucleotides that have just arrived to bond with the exposed bases on each of the original DNA strands now bond together by their phosphates and sugars, forming a new strand (polynucleotide chain) on each side.

5. This process has resulted in two double-stranded DNA molecules (each is one sister chromatid, connected via the centromere), which are identical to each other and consist of one original strand and one new strand. These newly forming molecules begin to wind up into double helices, even as the original strands are still unwinding and separating along their length (see Figure 3.5).

6. Remember the idea of complementarity? This allows each original strand to serve as a "template" for the production of a new strand.

7. The newly replicated DNA molecule coils and condenses into the recognizable form of the chromosome prior to cell division in its doubled (replicated) state (see Figure 3.6).

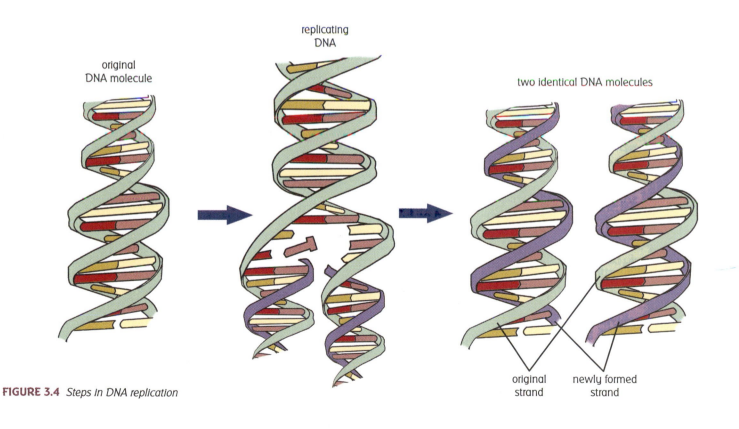

replicating
DNA

original
DNA molecule

two identical DNA molecules

original   newly formed
strand   strand

FIGURE 3.4 *Steps in DNA replication*

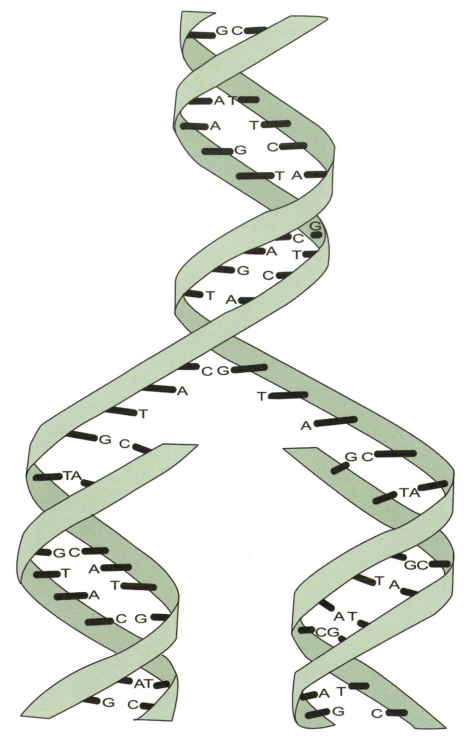

FIGURE 3.5 *Summary of DNA replication*

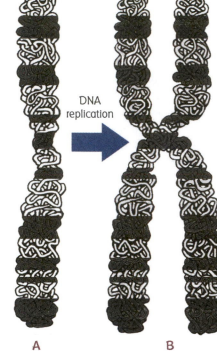

FIGURE 3.6 *Chromosome form in single (**A**) and doubled (**B**), or replicated, state*

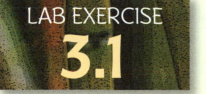

LAB EXERCISE 3.1

NAME _____

SECTION _____ DATE _____

The goal of today's exercise is to isolate the nucleic acids in a banana and see firsthand what DNA looks like. You will break open the cells of a banana, letting the cells' molecules spill into a solution. This solution at first will contain proteins, lipids, and carbohydrates in addition to the DNA and RNA, but you'll bind up the proteins with detergent to separate the DNA. See the first page of this chapter (p. 35) for materials needed.

Method

Step 1. Peel and slice banana into thin disks.

Step 2. Place sliced banana into blender, and add a little water to dampen the banana.

Step 3. Blend until a semi-thick paste forms in the blender (about 10 seconds blend time). Blending will break up the banana tissue; the goal is a solution of proteins and DNA.

Step 4. Add two dashes of meat tenderizer on top of the banana slices. The meat tenderizer contains papain, which is a mixture of enzymes that cleave proteins, serving to help isolate the DNA and catalyze (speed up) chemical reactions in the cell. Papain is derived from unripe papaya juice.

Step 5. Place coffee filters around the rim of the glasses. If you dampen the coffee filters, they will grip the glasses around the edges so you won't have to hold them on by hand.

Step 6. Pour contents of blender proportionally into the coffee filter-topped glasses.

Step 7. Filter to separate the DNA and proteins from the other cell components. If filtering occurs too slowly, gently use a toothpick to poke small holes into the coffee filters to quicken the drainage time. Avoid making large tears in the filters. (Filtration time usually is 5–10 minutes). After fluid drainage begins to slow, hasten the filtering process by gently lifting up the coffee filter (being careful not to spill the contents) over the glass, and then gently squeeze the filter by hand. (This can be messy, so have towels handy to wipe off your hands.) If a few banana chunks accumulate in the glass in this way, it shouldn't harm the outcome.

Step 8. Add small amounts of detergent into opposite sides of the glasses in three or four spots. This serves to dissolve the lipids and proteins of the cell by disrupting the bonds that hold the cell membrane together. Breaking open the plasma and nuclear membranes releases DNA into the solution. The detergent then binds to the lipid–protein layers, forming complexes with them so they can be separated from the DNA.

Step 9. Gently mix the contents of the glass with a toothpick, and continue stirring for a few minutes. Do not stir too roughly, as this can break up the DNA into fragments (this is bad). A gentle diagonal pattern of stirring usually yields the best results.

Step 10. Place a teaspoon gently on top of the banana–detergent mixture (as if you were about to eat it). Be careful not to dip the spoon into the banana mixture itself.

Step 11. Carefully pour the isopropyl alcohol so it runs down the spoon into the banana–detergent mixture (rather than dumping the alcohol directly in the banana mixture). The alcohol will form a layer on top of the banana mixture because it is less dense than the solution under it. *Note*: Fill the glass with alcohol proportional to the amount of banana fluid in the glass (should be 50/50). Alcohol serves as a gradient for the DNA to precipitate up through.

Step 12. In a successful experiment, the DNA should rise to the surface of the mixture in only a few seconds; it will appear as a cotton-like material forming where the banana mixture meets the alcohol layer.

Step 13. You now should be able to spool the DNA up, using a toothpick. The clumped DNA is a whitish substance with a mucous-like consistency. Although this method extracts RNA as well as DNA, much of the RNA is cut by ribonucleases (a type of enzyme) that are released when the cells are broken open. Thus, most of what you spool up will be DNA. Keep in mind that your DNA is the same "stuff" as the banana's DNA, as well as that of all organisms.

SELF-TEST 3.2

NAME _____

SECTION _____ DATE _____

1. The steps of DNA replication are as follows:
   Choose from the following to fill in the blanks:

identical	new	sugar	unzip
original	free nucleotides	phosphate	hydrogen

   The _____ bonds between the bases break, and the two DNA strands unwind and

   _____. _____ _____ are brought in, and they attach to

   _____. Bonds form between the _____ and _____ molecules of the

   free DNA nucleotides, forming a new strand. DNA replication results in two DNA double helices, each composed of

   one _____ and one _____ strand. The new DNA is _____

   to each other and to the original DNA.

2. Why is DNA replication so important?

3. Fill in the blanks in the illustration.

4. Draw and label the components of a segment of DNA (include all four bases, phosphates, and sugars). Be sure to bond the correct molecules together. Make your segment at least eight base pairs long.

5. Draw this same segment undergoing the process of DNA replication. Show the original strands separating and the new strands forming. Label all parts.

Protein Synthesis: How Genes are Expressed

Before describing the process of protein synthesis, we'll briefly discuss what a protein is, and why proteins are so vitally important in the body. Keep in mind that the sequence of bases in our DNA is what ultimately determines the proteins we produce.

Proteins

Proteins make up about 50% of the weight of each cell, after the water is squeezed out. The human body has approximately 250 kinds of proteins, with up to 10,000 proteins in a single human cell! Many proteins are structural proteins, which make up body structures such as tendons and ligaments, cores of bones and teeth, hair filaments, and nails. Functions of other proteins include facilitating the transport of molecules into and out of cells, regulating metabolism, performing mechanical work such as that involved in muscle contraction, or participating in the immune system.

If proteins are heated, or are degraded by stomach acids, they break down into their subunits, which are **amino acids**. Strings of amino acids, called polypeptides, combine to form the various proteins. Most proteins have 20 common types of amino acids. About half of the amino acids are produced by the body, and the others, called **essential amino acids**, must be taken in as food.

Thus, when you take in proteins from foods, they are broken down by digestive enzymes and the amino acids are released into your bloodstream. The amino acids then circulate, ready and available to be taken up by any cell in your body that needs them for manufacturing a specific kind of protein.

Amino acids are joined end to end by **peptide bonds**; hence the name **polypeptide**, or **polypeptide chain** (see Figure 3.7). Polypeptides vary in length (they average approximately 100 amino acids) and their amino acid sequence. After a polypeptide chain has been formed, it often joins with another such chain to form a protein.

Keep in mind that the protein, not the polypeptide, *is the functional unit*. One or more polypeptides together make up a protein. The complex shape of a protein determines its function in the body, and its shape is determined by the amino acid sequence and by the number and kinds of polypeptides comprising it. Proteins have "nooks and crannies" to fit specific molecules whose chemical reactions they are controlling.

An example of a protein that is familiar to all of us is **hemoglobin**. It is the molecule in our red blood cells that carries oxygen to our tissues, and it also removes carbon dioxide from tissues to be carried back to the lungs and exhaled. The iron-containing portion gives the molecule its red color. Hemoglobin is made of four polypeptide chains—two "alpha" chains and two "beta" chains. The alpha chains each are made of 141 amino acids, and the beta chains are 146 amino acids long. We'll now see how proteins such as hemoglobin are manufactured in the process dictated by the sequence of bases in the DNA.

Although *all* of our cells contain the "blueprint" to synthesize *all* of the proteins that the body produces, each type of protein is produced in cells of only specific parts of the body (see Figure 3.8).

An overview of protein **synthesis** demonstrates how we get from a gene (a segment of DNA on a chromosome) to a protein. The general flow of genetic information from the DNA to a protein is:

DNA → mRNA → amino acid → polypeptide → protein
sequence sequence   sequence

The blueprint used to make an individual's proteins (and thus comprise their physical traits) remains in the DNA in the nucleus of cells. Proteins, however, actually are constructed outside the nucleus—in the cytoplasm of cells, where the "workbench" for protein synthesis is found. To form a protein, information contained in the nuclear DNA somehow must be taken out to the cytoplasm, where proteins are put together. This process is analogous to the information you may need from a book in the Reserve Book Room of your library (the nucleus). You can't check out and remove the book (the DNA) from the library, but you can make a copy (transcription into mRNA) so the information can leave the library with you (go out into the cytoplasm).

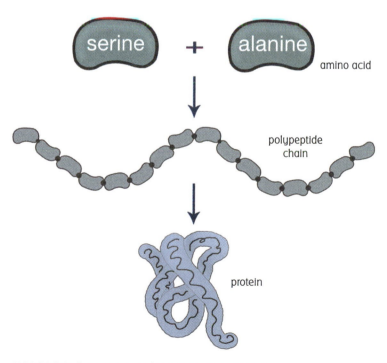

FIGURE 3.7 *From amino acids to polypeptide to protein*

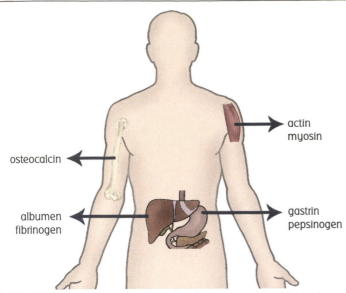

osteocalcin

actin
myosin

albumen
fibrinogen

gastrin
pepsinogen

FIGURE 3.8 *Examples of proteins produced in various parts of the body*

Cell Components Involved in Protein Synthesis

In protein synthesis, the component parts of a protein are put together, based upon the sequence ("code") that ultimately is dictated by the DNA. The components of the cells that are involved in synthesizing proteins are primarily the following:

- ribosomes,
- the three kinds of RNA,
- DNA,
- amino acids,
- various enzymes, and
- an energy source (ATP).

Again, the two types of nucleic acids are RNA and DNA. The actual genetic material is DNA, and RNA is a vital "assistant" in protein synthesis. The basic differences in structure between RNA and DNA are shown in Figure 3.9.

There are three types of RNA—mRNA, tRNA, and rRNA—which differ from one another in structure and in their function during protein synthesis (see Figure 3.10) despite the fact that all have, as their most basic unit, the RNA nucleotide. All are essential in the manufacture of protein.

Steps in Protein Synthesis

The complex process of protein synthesis has two main steps.

1. The first step occurs in the cell nucleus where the DNA resides and results in the formation of a strand of mRNA.

2. The second step carries the message of the DNA sequence to the cell's cytoplasm and "translates" it into a specific order of amino acids that will form a polypeptide.

First Step: Transcription Picture a DNA double helix and zoom in on it in your mind. "Highlight" a portion of the DNA on just one side, or strand. This portion represents a **gene**. The human genome, as discovered recently, is made up of about 25,000 genes. A gene is a functional unit, not a structural one. A gene begins and ends at the nucleotides that comprise the beginning and end of a sequence that will "code for" a specific polypeptide. The gene coding for hemoglobin's alpha chain is on chromosome 16, and a gene on

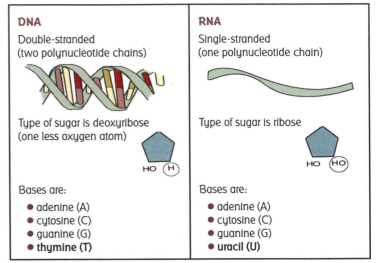

DNA
Double-stranded
(two polynucleotide chains)

Type of sugar is deoxyribose
(one less oxygen atom)

Bases are:
- adenine (A)
- cytosine (C)
- guanine (G)
- **thymine (T)**

RNA
Single-stranded
(one polynucleotide chain)

Type of sugar is ribose

Bases are:
- adenine (A)
- cytosine (C)
- guanine (G)
- **uracil (U)**

FIGURE 3.9 *Differences between DNA and RNA*

	Messenger RNA (mRNA)	Transfer RNA (tRNA)	Ribosomal RNA (rRNA)
Idealized drawing		2 — amino acid binding site / 1 — anticodon	Shown: ribosome
Function	Carries the message of the sequence of DNA bases for a gene	Brings amino acids to appropriate place along the mRNA strand in the formation of a polypeptide chain	Together with proteins, rRNA makes up the *ribosomes,* where the mRNA strand is read and decoded
Form	A simple single strand	Single stranded; folds back on itself so parts are double-stranded. Important functional parts: (1) the three exposed bases at one end—the **anticodon**; (2) amino acid binding site	Ribosomes are the site at which amino acids are bonded together to form polypeptides; comprised of a large and small subunit that together clamp onto the mRNA strand for decoding
Length	Between 300 and 10,000 nucleotides	Between 75 and 90 nucleotides	Between 120 and 4800 nucleotides

FIGURE 3.10 *Differences among the three types of RNA*

chromosome 11 codes for the beta chain. Hemoglobin synthesis occurs in the stem cells that divide to develop into red blood cells, so the hemoglobin is produced as the cells that house them are developing.

Remember that the first step of protein synthesis results in the *formation of a strand of mRNA*. This part of the process is called **transcription** (see Figure 3.11):

1. The process begins in a manner similar to that of DNA replication. The two DNA strands begin to separate and unwind, the result of enzyme action. But in protein synthesis the strands separate along only a small portion—along the gene. Bases now are exposed on both DNA strands. Remember that a gene is a segment of DNA along only one side (one strand).

2. This is where RNA comes into the picture. Numerous free RNA nucleotides are present in the nucleus. The exposed bases along the DNA gene will attract these free RNA nucleotides. As the RNA nucleotides line up along the DNA gene, they bond together to form a strand. They line up with the DNA bases following the same base-pairing rules as for DNA, but with one exception: There is no thymine (T) in RNA; instead, uracil (U) of RNA acts as a substitute for T and bonds with A (Figure 3.11a). Thus, the portion of the DNA gene that reads:

CACGTGGACT

would attract the following RNA nucleotides:

GUGCACCUG

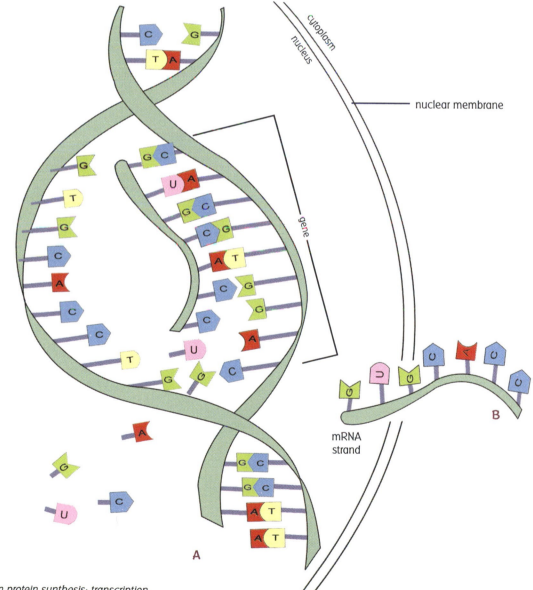

FIGURE 3.11 *First step in protein synthesis: transcription*

Again, this occurs only along the *gene side* (the exposed bases along the corresponding segment on the other DNA strand merely wait patiently for transcription to be done). The RNA nucleotides will continue to line up and bond with the appropriate DNA base and with each other, forming an RNA strand, until no more exposed DNA bases remain with which to bond. This will correspond to the end of the DNA gene.

3. The RNA strand forms quickly (30–50 nucleotides are added per second!), then breaks away immediately from the DNA. Now it has what it needs: It has formed itself on the basis of the DNA sequence of a specific gene, so in its very form carries the message of the code for the production of a particular protein. (Before continuing on to the next step of protein synthesis, the RNA strand goes through "processing," in which parts of the strand are removed while still in the nucleus.) The strand now is referred to as mRNA. The mRNA leaves the nucleus, passing through the nuclear membrane into the cytoplasm, for the process of translation (Figure 3.11B).

4. The final product of transcription is

   - a single-stranded RNA molecule, complementary to the sequence of bases of the original DNA gene (DNA was used as a blueprint) an average of 5,000 nucleotides long

   - called mRNA (messenger RNA), because it now is carrying the message of the sequence of the DNA bases.

Second Step: Translation In the second step of protein synthesis, the message of the DNA sequence will be "translated" into a specific order of amino acids, which will be joined end-to-end to form a polypeptide (remember, a chain of amino acids). A protein is made of one or more polypeptides. The specific protein that is formed depends upon the order of the amino acids that comprise it. Thus, the DNA sequence of a gene determines the amino acid sequence, which in turn determines the protein that will be produced.

   Translation involves the newly formed *mRNA, tRNA, ribosomes, amino acids,* and more *enzymes*.

1. After passing through the nuclear membrane into the cytoplasm, the mRNA goes to a ribosome and is clasped between its two subunits (Figure 3.12A). The ribosome, in effect, "reads" the mRNA strand three bases at a time. These "words" made of triplets of mRNA bases are called **codons**. Each codon corresponds to a specific amino acid.

2. Next, the corresponding amino acids are brought into place along the mRNA strand. This is accomplished by the tRNA. As each codon is "read" by the ribosome, a tRNA is "called over," carrying with it the correct amino

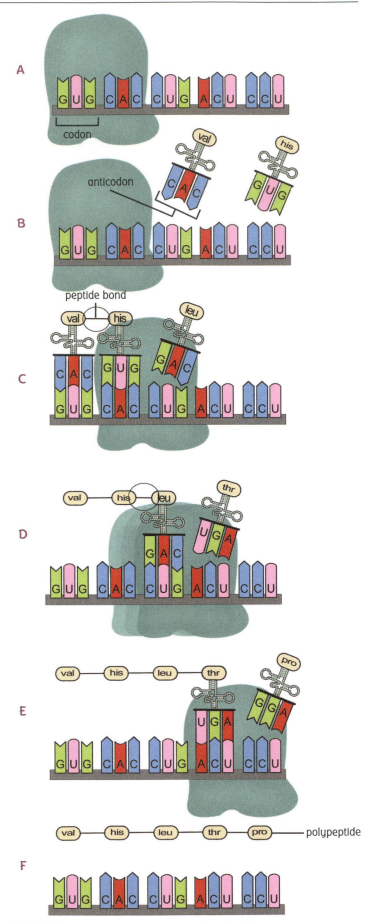

FIGURE 3.12 *Second step in protein synthesis: translation*

acid for each codon (Figure 3.12B). The tRNA must have some way to briefly "dock" onto the mRNA to transfer its cargo. This is accomplished by chemical bonds that are formed briefly between the bases making up a codon and the three exposed bases at the end of the tRNA. These three bases comprise the **anticodon**. Each anticodon of tRNA is complementary to the codon's bases. Thus, each codon of mRNA (for example, AAU) has a counterpart of tRNA (UUA).

3. As each amino acid is brought into place by its tRNA, it immediately forms a chemical bond (a peptide bond) with the previously transferred amino acid (Figure 3.12C, D, E). The chain of amino acids grows as the ribosomes read the mRNA strand. As in the building of the mRNA strand in transcription, the amino acid chain grows quickly, with the growing polypeptide chain adding about 10 to 15 amino acids per second. A beta chain of hemoglobin takes only about 10 seconds for its 146 amino acids to be brought together into a polypeptide.

4. Eventually a ribosome reads a **mRNA codon** for which there is no tRNA anticodon. This will be the **stop codon**, or **terminating triplet** (not shown in Figure 3.12). The codons UAA, UAG, and UGA are all stop codons. At that point the ribosome dissociates, its parts separate, and the newly formed polypeptide (chain of amino acids) floats free (Figure 3.12F).

5. When a polypeptide chain has been formed, it may join with another such chain to form a protein, and protein synthesis is complete. For example, remember that a gene on chromosome 16 and a gene on chromosome 11 determine the four polypeptide chains (alpha and beta) contributing to the protein hemoglobin. The *protein* (not the polypeptide) is the actual functional unit, and its complex shape determines its function in the body.

The Genetic Code

The 20 amino acids each correspond to a specific sequence of three bases (a codon) on the mRNA strand, consistent in all species. There are 64 combinations of the three bases (64 different codons) but only about 20 amino acids, so some amino acids have more than one codon coding for them (some have up to 6). For example, the codons that code for phenylalanine are UUU or UUC. This is what is referred to as the **genetic code** (see Table 3.1).

TABLE 3.1: The Genetic Code (mRNA codons corresponding to amino acids)

		U		C		A		G
U	UUU UUC	phenalalynine	UCU UCC UCA UCG	serine	UAU UAC	tyrosine	UGU UGC	cysteine
	UUA UUG	leucine			UAA UAG	Stop codon Stop codon	UGA	Stop codon
							UGG	tryptophan
C	CUU CUC CUA CUG	leucine	CCU CCC CCA CCG	proline	CAU CAC	histidine	CGU CGC CGA CGG	arginine
					CAA CAG	glutamine		
A	AUU AUC AUA	isoleucine	ACU ACC ACA ACG	threonine	AAU AAC	asparagine	AGU AGC	serine
	AUG	methionine Start codon			AAA AAG	lysine	AGA AGG	arginine
G	GUU GUC GUA GUG	valine	GCU CCC GCA GCG	alanine	GAU GAC	aspartic acid	GGU GGC GGA GGG	glycine
					GAA GAG	glutamic acid		

Summary of Protein Synthesis

1. *Transcription:* Occurs in the nucleus; a complementary copy (blueprint) of DNA is made and transcribed onto an mRNA strand, which leaves the nucleus to the cytoplasm.

2. *Translation:* The mRNA carries its message of the sequence of DNA bases out to the cytoplasm. With the aid of ribosomes "reading" the mRNA bases three at a time (codon by codon), tRNA brings the appropriate amino acids into place along the mRNA strand to form a polypeptide.

3. Thus, the DNA has been transcribed into RNA, then translated into amino acids, then synthesized (put together) into a polypeptide, one or more of which comprise a protein.

Note: Because in prokaryotes (like bacteria) the nucleus is not separated from the cytoplasm, transcription and translation can occur at the same time!

Mutations

As you are well aware, genetics processes sometimes go awry, or the genetic material can be affected by an external source (for example, radiation). An inherited change in the DNA is called a **mutation**. Mutations can occur at various levels, from an extra or missing set of chromosomes, an extra or missing single chromosome or piece of one, to an extra or missing base or bases.

We will discuss mutations at the level of the chromosome, or chunks of chromosome, in Chapter 4. A mutation involving only a single nucleotide out of place can have devastating effects on an individual's development and survivability. Such a mutation can be inherited from a parent's DNA, or it may occur in an individual during early DNA replication or protein synthesis. Three main types of such mutations are **single-base substitution (point mutation), insertion**, and **deletion**.

In a single-base substitution mutation, one nucleotide is replaced mistakenly by another. For example, a C may be inserted in DNA where a T should be. If the same amino acid is coded for after the mutation, it is known as a **silent mutation** and results in successful production of the correct protein.

For example, look at the genetic code chart (Table 3.1), at the mRNA codon CCU. It codes for the amino acid proline. A substitution that results in another C instead of the U also would code for proline, thereby producing the same protein as if no mutation had occurred. If the second C were replaced by a U, however, this new codon CUU would code for leucine.

This is a **missense mutation**, with the mutated codon coding for a different amino acid. If the mutation causes a change in the codon such that it becomes a stop codon, it is known as a **nonsense mutation**. This causes premature halting of translation, and thus a truncated polypeptide length and almost certainly a malformed protein.

Insertions add one or more nucleotides to the DNA, while deletions remove them. Because codons are composed of groups of three bases, inserting or deleting a base from a codon changes the reading of all of the rest of the codons on the mRNA strand. This difference in the way the ribosome now will read the mRNA strand is referred to as a **frameshift mutation**, and this affects the final production of the protein.

As mentioned in Chapter 1, mutation is one of the four evolutionary forces. It is the only evolutionary force to produce *new* variation to introduce into a population, which is vital for the action of natural selection. The evolutionary forces will be covered more extensively in Chapter 6.

LAB EXERCISE
3.2

NAME _____

SECTION _____ DATE _____

1. The illustration below represents a portion of the DNA strand for production of hemoglobin's beta chain. The strands are in the process of separating for transcription. Transcribe and translate the entire shaded portion into an mRNA strand, and using the genetic code chart (Table 3.1), translate it into a part of the hemoglobin protein.

DNA strand __ __ __ __ __ __ __ __ __ __ __ __ __ __ __ __ __ __ __

mRNA strand __ __ __ __ __ __ __ __ __ __ __ __ __ __ __ __ __ __ __

amino acids _____ _____ _____ _____ _____

2. Numerous known mutations of the genes dictate hemoglobin production. In this exercise you will trace the route from DNA to a faulty type of hemoglobin.

   a. Draw a double helix.

   b. Highlight (or circle) a portion that will represent a segment of DNA on one strand (your gene).

   c. Now re-draw this segment of DNA, making it large enough to see the DNA bases. Use the DNA sequence from question 1 for your gene, but change the 17th base from T to A.

   d. You have just caused a mutation. Transcribe and translate your strand as you did in question #1. Is your amino acid sequence the same or different?

   DNA strand   ___ ___ ___   ___ ___ ___   ___ ___ ___   ___ ___ ___   ___ ___ ___   ___ ___ ___

   mRNA strand   ___ ___ ___   ___ ___ ___   ___ ___ ___   ___ ___ ___   ___ ___ ___   ___ ___ ___

   amino acids   _____   _____   _____   _____   _____   _____

   e. This mutation results in abnormal hemoglobin production, and if an individual receives this mutated gene from both parents, he or she will have sickle-cell anemia.

3. Diagram the steps of protein synthesis, labeling these parts: *nucleus, DNA, RNA, ribosomes, mRNA, tRNA,* and *amino acids.*

SELF-TEST 3.3

NAME _____

SECTION _____ DATE _____

1. Proteins are made of _____.

2. DNA and RNA are both _____, found in the _____ of cells.

3. Which is the actual genetic material, DNA or RNA? _____

4. What are three structural differences between DNA and RNA?

   a. _____

   b. _____

   c. _____

5. Answer the following questions about the molecule illustrated at right.

   a. What is this molecule (the entire thing)? _____

   b. What is its function? _____

   c. Identify A _____

   d. Identify B _____

6. Hereditary information (in the form of the sequence of DNA bases) is taken from the nucleus to the cytoplasm by:

   a. the nucleotides

   b. mRNA

   c. ribosomes

   d. tRNA

7. A segment of DNA that codes for the synthesis of a particular protein (or polypeptide) is a _____.

8. In protein synthesis, the process called *translation* is the:

   a. manufacture of transfer RNA

   b. assembly of polypeptide chains

   c. manufacture of messenger RNA

   d. production of amino acids

9. Which of the following sequences is correct?

    a. DNA → mRNA → tRNA → protein

    b. mRNA → DNA → tRNA → protein

    c. DNA → tRNA → mRNA → protein

    d. tRNA → DNA → mRNA → protein

10. Proteins are manufactured within the cell at structures called:

    a. mitochondria

    b. nuclei

    c. nucleoli

    d. ribosomes

11. What is a mutation?

    Why is it so important for evolution?

12. The amino acids used by the cell to manufacture proteins are:

    a. manufactured by the body

    b. derived from ingested protein food

    c. both a and b

    d. found on the DNA molecule

13. Describe the basic structure and main functions of mRNA.

14. What is a polypeptide?

15. What is the name for a triplet of mRNA bases? _____

    Of tRNA bases? _____

16. Where does transcription occur?

    Translation?

SELF-TEST
3.3 (CONT.)

NAME _____

SECTION _____ DATE _____

17. What process, and what portion of
this process, is represented here?

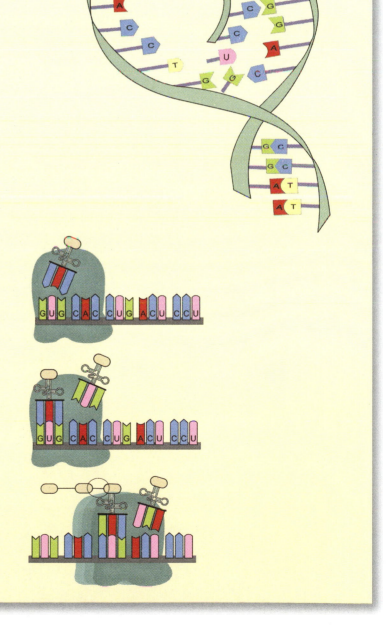

18. What process, and what portion of this
process, is represented in the illustration?

19. What is an important difference in the potential outcome of a *single base substitution mutation* and the other two types of point mutations—*insertions* and *deletions*?

20. Why is *all* of your DNA in *each* of your somatic cells?

ONE STEP FURTHER

NAME _____

SECTION _____ DATE _____

Additional Lab Exercise 3.1

ADDITIONAL MATERIALS NEEDED:

For each set of lab partners:
- 12" pipe cleaners (or string cut into 12" lengths) of two different colors, two of each
- 36 beads of a single color to fit snugly on pipe cleaners; 9 beads will be placed along each pipe cleaner (see below for alternative to beads)
- Scissors (one for every set of lab partners probably is not necessary; several circulating scissors can be shared throughout the class)
- Cut-outs of bases from Appendix A

In this exercise, the pipe cleaners will represent DNA strands—one color representing the strands of the original DNA molecule and the other for the two strands that form during the process of DNA replication. The beads will represent sugar molecules along the DNA strand.

To prepare, you will set up your double-stranded DNA molecule as shown in the photo.

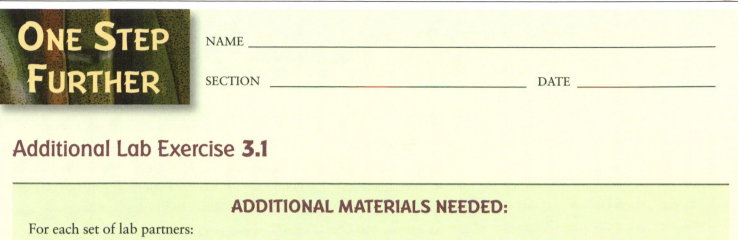

1. On two of the pipe cleaners of the same color, slide 9 beads on each, placed approximately 1" apart. (Alternatively, a permanent marker could be used to demonstrate the position of sugar molecules along the strand.)

2. Cut out the DNA bases from Appendix A in your lab manual. Note that the four bases fall into two different size classes, one larger and one smaller.

You are now ready to re-create the process of DNA replication.

3. Construct a DNA molecule on the table, laying out the paper cut-out bases next to the 9 sugar molecules of both pipe cleaners. You choose the order to lay the bases out, but be sure to follow the correct base pairing rules. You will have one extra pair of bases.

Record the DNA sequence below for your DNA segment.

Strand 1   __ __ __ __ __ __ __ __ __

Strand 2   __ __ __ __ __ __ __ __ __

Using the paper cut-outs, you will replicate your DNA.

4. Pull apart your two DNA strands until they are separated from each other by a few inches.

5. Prepare two pipe cleaners of the *second color* with nine beads to represent sugar molecules, as for the original DNA strands.

6. Cut out the free DNA bases from Appendix A and place each one next to the appropriate base along your newly separated DNA strands, following the base pairing rules.

7. Once all of your new DNA bases are lined up next to the ones from the original strands, place the prepared pipe cleaners of the second color alongside for the phosphate/sugar "backbone" of the DNA strand. (Of course, a real DNA base will be part of a nucleotide, and will include its own sugar and phosphate molecule.)

You now can easily see the end result of DNA replication, in which each DNA molecule consists of an original and a newly formed strand.

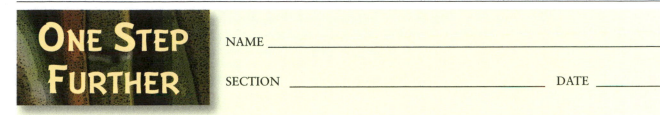

NAME _____

SECTION _____   DATE _____

Additional Lab Exercise 3.2

ADDITIONAL MATERIALS NEEDED:

- In addition to those for Lab Exercise 3.1:
  - One 12" pipe cleaner of a *third color*, to represent a mRNA strand, with beads placed 1" apart to represent sugar molecules
- Cut-outs from lab manual in Appendix A:
  - RNA bases
  - tRNA molecules
  - Amino acids
  - Ribosome

In this section, you will re-create the process of protein synthesis.

Transcribing a mRNA strand

1. Choose one of your double-stranded DNA molecules, removing the other molecule completely (you won't need it again). Because any particular gene is located on only one side of the DNA, choose *one* of the DNA strands to be the "gene side"—the one that will be expressed, or used, in your protein synthesis process. Remove the other strand with its bases, leaving your chosen DNA strand (with its bases) on the table in front of you.

   Record the sequence of bases in your gene.

   DNA gene __ __ __ __ __ __ __ __ __

   Remember that the first step in protein synthesis is *transcription*, the forming of an RNA strand.

2. Cut out your free RNA bases.

3. To begin your mRNA strand, bring in and match up the correct RNA bases with the bases on your DNA strand (following the base pairing rules: RNA has no thymine (T), but instead contains the chemically similar uracil (U), which will pair with adenine (A).

4. Once all exposed DNA bases have "bonded" with an RNA base, use a pipe cleaner of the third color to serve as the phosphate/sugar "backbone" for the mRNA strand (normally, the RNA bases will be part of an entire nucleotide, complete with phosphate and sugar molecule.)

5. Pull the newly formed mRNA strand and its bases away from the DNA, mimicking the end of transcription, where the mRNA separates from the DNA and leaves the nucleus. (Keep in mind also that at the end of the process, your DNA sense strand will rejoin and rewind with the other DNA strand.) Orient the strand so it is horizontal on the table.

   Record the sequence of bases in your mRNA strand.

   mRNA strand   __ __ __ __ __ __ __ __

Translating mRNA codons into an amino acid sequence

The next step of protein synthesis, **translation**, occurs in the cell's cytoplasm.

1. Cut out the rest of the components involved from your cut-out page: the ribosome, the tRNA molecules, and the amino acids.

2. Normally, the ribosome clasps the mRNA strand between its large and small subunits to "read" and "translate" the mRNA strand, three bases (a codon) at a time. In this exercise, you will simply place the ribosome below the mRNA strand, underneath the first codon.

3. Take one of the tRNA molecules and place it so the three blanks underneath (representing the anticodon) line up with the first mRNA codon. Label the tRNA anticodon so it is complementary to the codon of the mRNA strand.

4. The tRNA will have carried with it a particular amino acid. Place an amino acid cut-out above the tRNA molecule.

5. To find out which amino acid the tRNA will have brought into place, use the genetic code chart, Table 3.1. On this chart, look up the appropriate amino acid by using the sequence of bases in your **mRNA codon** (the first one on your mRNA strand). Fill in the name on the amino acid cut-out.

6. Move the ribosome along the strand to the next mRNA codon, and repeat the process with the tRNA and the amino acid, filling in the anticodon and the amino acid name according to the genetic code chart. Draw a connection between the two amino acids to represent the peptide bond that forms.

7. Do the same with the last mRNA codon. You can remove the tRNA molecules, and your amino acid chain, or polypeptide, will float free. Remember that real polypeptides are an average of 100 amino acids long (rather than only three as in this exercise).

Record the following:

mRNA strand (again)   __ __ __ __ __ __ __ __ __

tRNA anticodons   __ __ __ __ __ __ __ __ __

amino acids   _____ _____ _____

                    (see genetic code chart for mRNA codons, Table 3.1)

A polypeptide likely will join with another such amino acid chain to form a protein; most proteins consist of more than one polypeptide.

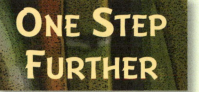

NAME _____

SECTION _____ DATE _____

Additional Self-Test Questions

1. Enzymes are composed of:

   a. nucleic acids
   b. phosphates
   c. amino acids
   d. proteins

2. In protein synthesis, the process called *transcription* is the:

   a. manufacture of transfer RNA
   b. assembly of polypeptide chains from amino acids
   c. manufacture of messenger RNA strand
   d. production of amino acids
   e. manufacture of ribosomal RNA

3. The bases of RNA are:

   a. uracil, guanine, thymine, adenine
   b. thymine, guanine, adenine, cytosine
   c. guanine, adenine, cytosine, uracil
   d. adenine, uracil, guanine, ribose

4. The genetic information is contained in the DNA molecule in the sequence of codons. Each codon is made up of three:

   a. nucleic acids
   b. amino acids
   c. proteins
   d. nucleotides

5. Use the genetic code chart (Table 3.1) to fill in the blanks below. What are the corresponding mRNA codons for the DNA triplets? What are the anticodons of the tRNA that will have brought the appropriate amino acids into place? What are the associated amino acids for each mRNA codon?

DNA	mRNA codon	tRNA anticodon	amino acid
TAA	_____	_____	_____
GGG	_____	_____	_____
ATA	_____	_____	_____
GTC	_____	_____	_____
ACT	_____	_____	_____
CCA	_____	_____	_____
TAC	_____	_____	_____

6. What is a gene?

7. Below are two sets of normal DNA segments, with a mutated segment below each. Describe, in as much detail as possible, what kinds of mutations are involved (there may be more than one in each strand). Use the genetic code chart (Table 3.1). (*Don't forget that you will need to first transcribe your DNA into an mRNA strand to use the genetic code chart of amino acids!*)

  a. Normal DNA AAAGTCCTGACTGTTAAAAAAGGG

    Mutated DNA AAAGTCCTGACTGTTTAAAAAGGG

  b. Normal DNA TACAAATCACGCGTATTTGTCACT

    Mutated DNA TACAAATCACGCGTATTCGTACT

How Cells Are Made

4

"Have you ever wondered . . . ?"

- How did the genetic material from my parents combine to form me?
- How long does it take a cell to divide?
- How many times can a cell divide?

OBJECTIVES

- Know the two main classes of cells and their main characteristics
- Understand the process of somatic cell production (mitosis)
- Understand the process of gamete production (meiosis) and how variability is introduced into the gene pool
- Be familiar with somatic cell function
- Be familiar with gamete function
- Understand how mistakes (mutations) in cell division can occur, and how these mutations affect further development
- Recognize some of the common syndromes (chromosomal anomalies) that result from mutations arising during cell division
- Understand the differences between mutations in autosomes and sex chromosomes

MATERIALS NEEDED

- Scissors to cut out chromosomes (one pair per two or three pairs of lab partners)
- Tape or glue (tape is recommended)

(One Step Further will require additional materials; see Additional Lab Exercise 4.1.)

Cell Division

We start our lives as a fertilized egg cell, a zygote. From this cell we derive all the cells of our body. The vast majority and most diversity of our cells consist of somatic cells. Each human somatic cell normally has 46 chromosomes (the diploid number) in its nucleus, derived from the two sets of 23 chromosomes contributed by our parents' egg and sperm. The cell division that produces somatic cells is called mitosis and occurs throughout our life for growth, body maintenance, and healing. Gametes are produced by a more complex type of cell division called meiosis, which produces egg and sperm cells with 23 chromosomes each (the haploid number). Remember that *gametes do not divide*; *only somatic cells divide*, whether by mitosis to produce more somatic cells, or by meiosis to produce gametes.

When cell division begins, the DNA in the nucleus has just replicated itself, so when the chromosomes condense and become visible, they already are in their doubled state (made up of two sister chromatids).

Mitosis

Mitosis begins early—immediately after fertilization. The zygote divides to produce two embryonic cells, each of which divides in turn. The developing embryo continues to divide many times into many identical cells until cells begin to undergo differential development and become specialized for different functions. Each of these more specialized cells then divides into two identical daughter cells.

All of your somatic cells are produced in this way. Mitosis occurs often throughout life, during growth and for healing. Many types of cells, such as skin cells, are replaced almost constantly by new ones. Others, such as nerve cells and liver cells, are rarely, if ever, replaced once cells are mature. In mammals the entire cell cycle (cell growth, DNA replication, chromosome division, and cytoplasm division) takes 18 to 24 hours. The actual mitosis portion, however, usually lasts only an hour at most.

Mitosis begins with a somatic cell whose nucleus contains 46 chromosomes (in humans). *The end result is two identical daughter cells, each also with 46 chromosomes.* Keep in mind that each somatic cell maintains a *complete DNA blueprint* of an individual: All of the DNA that makes up the chromosomes is present in each cell.

When cells divide, we can observe a series of phases as these phases are visible under a microscope. Figure 4.1 illustrates the phases of mitosis and what happens to the chromosomes in each phase. It is less important to memorize these phases in detail than to understand the overall process, how chromosomes come to be distributed equally in the daughter cells, and the end result of cell division. The portion of the cell cycle in which cell division is *not* occurring is called the **interphase**. At this time the cell is anything but inactive. For example, replication of DNA is in progress, and organelles are replicating themselves.

Follow along with Figure 4.1 as the process of mitosis is demonstrated for a cell with only four chromosomes (the diploid number for fruit flies, for example). Remember that if this somatic cell were from a human, it would have 46 chromosomes.

Meiosis

The term *meiosis* derives from the Greek *diminution*, meaning to make smaller, or reduce, which roughly translates to "reduction division." Meiosis is the production of gametes (sperm in males and eggs in females). Meiosis is a more complex process than mitosis and produces cells with a different function. The end result of meiosis is the production of haploid gametes that carry genetic information and introduce genetic variability among the daughter cells. This ensures that each individual is different from any other individual, thereby causing variability in populations.

The meiotic process begins with a somatic cell specialized to divide and produce another kind of cell. The specific

Interphase

- DNA is replicating.
- DNA is in the form of chromatin, so the chromosomes are not visible.
- Mitochondrial DNA is replicating.
- Organelles are replicating, preparing to be split into two different cells when the original cell divides.

Prophase

- Nuclear membrane of phospholipids is breaking down into small vesicles, or sacs.
- Chromatin has condensed and contracted into visible chromosomes, which are in their doubled state after DNA replication.
- The cytoskeleton is organizing into a spindle apparatus, making a framework for chromosome movement in the cell.
- The cell's two centrosomes (each composed of a pair of centrioles) are separating and moving to opposite poles of the cell.
- Spindle fibers coming from centrioles at opposite poles of the cell are attaching to the protein complexes on *both sides* of the chromosomes' centromeres.

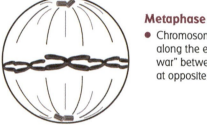

Metaphase

- Chromosomes are being pulled into place along the equator of the cell by a "tug-of-war" between spindle fibers from centrioles at opposite poles of the cell.

Anaphase

- Continued tugging by the spindle fibers is resulting in the chromosomes being pulled apart at the centromeres, resulting in the separation of the sister chromatids of each chromosome—known as disjunction.
- These are now referred to as chromosomes; temporarily, the cell has eight chromosomes.
- The two groups of chromosomes are gathering at opposite poles of the cell.

Telophase

- Nuclear membrane is re-forming around the chromosomes grouped at each pole.
- The cell wall is pinching in, eventually causing the original cell to separate into two daughter cells; this process is called **cytokinesis**.

FIGURE 4.1 *Phases of mitosis: Somatic cell production*

type of cell to undergo meiosis and produce egg cells is the **primary oocyte**, and **primary spermatocytes** divide to produce sperm. Primary oocytes are found in the ovaries of females, and primary spermatocytes in the testes of males. Because *these are somatic cells*, each has 46 chromosomes. After the process of meiosis is complete and gametes have been produced, no more cell division occurs in the resulting cells. Again, the *gametes themselves do not undergo cell division*!

In males, the production of sperm cells begins at puberty. Sperm are produced regularly and stored in the epididymis for 10 to 20 days, with the off-chance that during that time one of these sperm will enter the female reproductive tract and fertilize an egg. In females, the process of meiosis begins in the ovaries before birth (beginning at about the 12th week), and the precursor egg cells are held in "suspended animation" until puberty. At that time they begin to mature and are released from the ovary, one per month, until menopause.

Until recently, each female was thought to be born with the full complement of precursor egg cells that she will produce in her lifetime, while males continue to produce sperm throughout their lifetime (see Figure 4.2). More recent work on mice and humans, however, suggests that egg production continues into adulthood (Bukovsky et al., 2005; Johnson et al., 2006). The differences between meiosis in males and females are summarized in Table 4.1.

The stages are named the same as in mitosis, but to accomplish the goals of producing four haploid cells that differ in their genetic makeup, there are two meiotic divisions, **Meiosis I** and **Meiosis II**. The first of these reduces the number of chromosomes from 46 in the parent cell to 23 in the

daughter cells, and the second division cleaves the sister chromatids apart so the chromosomes in the final daughter cells are in their single state.

The most important thing to remember is the end result of each part of the process, as well as the phenomenon that enables genetic variability. As you will see from the process outlined in Figure 4.3, homologous pairs of chromosomes will exchange pieces of one another to "reshuffle" genes, and the distribution of chromosomes into the daughter cells is a random process. These factors increase the potential genetic combinations that can result in the gametes.

Follow along with Figure 4.3 as it illustrates the process of meiosis for gamete production in a species (again, such as the fruit fly) with only four chromosomes in its somatic cells (the diploid number is four). If this were a human, the cell we would start with would have 46 chromosomes, and each of the four daughter cells would have 23 chromosomes.

TABLE 4.1: Differences in Meiosis Between Males and Females		
DIFFERENCE	**MALES**	**FEMALES**
Meiosis begins	At puberty	Before birth (~12 weeks)
Meiosis ends	At death	At menopause
Location of gamete production	Testes	Ovaries
Number of functional gametes produced	Four sperm	One egg

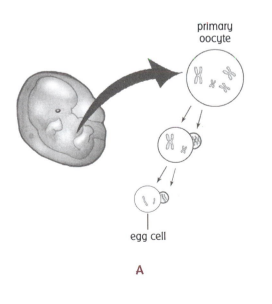

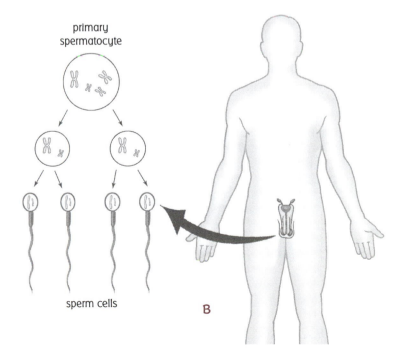

FIGURE 4.2 *Meiosis in females (A) versus males (B)*

What's Happening?

Meiosis 1

Interphase

- DNA replication is occurring.
- DNA is in the form of chromatin, so the chromosomes are not visible.
- Mitochondrial DNA is replicating.
- Organelles are replicating, preparing to be split into two different cells when the original cell divides.

Prophase 1

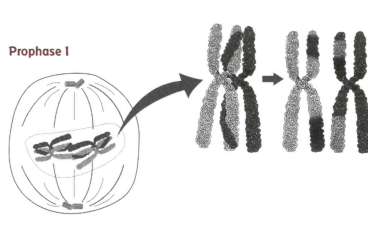

As in mitosis, the following events occur:

- Nuclear membrane of phospholipids breaks down into small vesicles, or sacs.
- Chromatin has condensed and contracted into visible chromosomes, now in their doubled state after DNA replication.
- Cytoskeleton organizes into a spindle apparatus, making a framework for chromosome movement in the cell. (This is the longest stage and contributes to meiosis taking days to complete!)
- Centrioles separate and move to opposite poles of the cell.

A vital event unique to meiosis is as follows:

- The homologous pairs of chromosomes join together, lining up next to each other with point-by-point precision.
- Because the chromosomes occur in pairs, and are each in their doubled state (with sister chromatids), each pair is referred to as a **tetrad**.
- The members of the homologous pairs *exchange portions of each other* where they touch along their length so that pieces of the maternally derived chromosome are exchanged with exact precision with pieces of the paternally derived chromosome in each pair! This is called **crossing over,** or recombination of genes.
- Spindle fibers from opposite poles of the cell attach to the protein complex on the centromere of each of the chromosomes of the homologous pair, so when the fibers pull, the pairs will be pulled apart.

Metaphase 1

- Chromosome pairs are pulled into place along the equator of the cell by the spindle fibers, like couples lined up opposite their partners at a barn dance.
- The sister chromatids of each chromosome are no longer identical because crossing over has occurred.
- Within each tetrad is a random assignment of sides (so either maternally or paternally derived chromosome could end up on either side; this is called **independent assortment** of chromosomes).

Anaphase 1

- Continued tugging by the spindle fibers results in pulling apart of the homologous pairs so the *maternally and paternally derived chromosomes are separated –* disjunction.
- These two groups of 23 chromosomes, each still consisting of two sister chromatids, collect at opposite poles of the cell.

Telophase 1

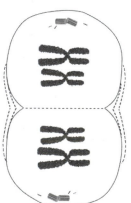

- As the chromosomes are grouped at each pole of the cell, the cell wall constricts (cytokinesis), which causes separation of the original cell into two daughter cells.

The end result of Meiosis 1 is:

1. two haploid daughter cells (23 chromosomes each), chromosomes still in doubled state.
2. homologous pairs have been separated (so the chromosome number drops from 46 to 23).
3. daughter cells now are different from each other in their chromosomal makeup, because pieces of the maternally and paternally derived chromosomes have been interchanged (crossing over), with a random distribution of maternally and paternally derived chromosomes in the daughter cells during cell division (independent assortment).

   In a male, the two daughter cells resulting from Meiosis 1 are the same size. In a female, one of the two daughter cells keeps most of the cytoplasm so it is much larger than the other (see Figure 4.2). The smaller cell is called a polar body, which is left with its 23 chromosomes, but little else. This polar body may or may not divide again, but it will never develop into a functional egg, and is reabsorbed by the body.

FIGURE 4.3 *Phases of meiosis: Gamete production*

Continued

Meiosis II

Prophase II

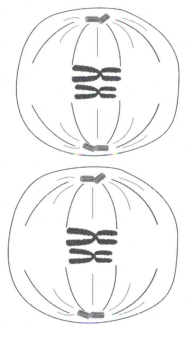

- Begins with the end products of Meiosis I: two daughter cells whose homologous pairs have been separated, so now each cell has only one set of the 23 chromosomes in each cell; chromosomes are still in their doubled state.
- Spindle apparatus begins to form in each of the two new cells.
- Spindle fibers coming from centrioles at opposite poles of the cell attach to the protein complexes on both sides of each chromosome's centromeres.

Metaphase II

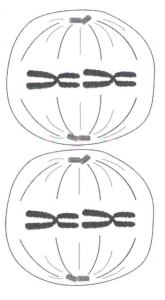

- As in mitosis, all of the chromosomes in each cell are pulled by the spindle fibers into lining up on the equator of the cell.

Anaphase II

- Continued tugging by the spindle fibers results in the pulling apart, or disjunction, of the chromosomes at the centromeres, so the *sister chromatids of each chromosome are separated*.
- The two groups of 23 chromosomes, now in their single state, gather at opposite poles of the two cells.

Telophase II

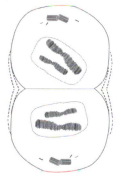
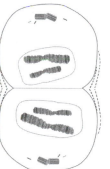

- Nuclear membrane re-forms around the 23 chromosomes grouped at each pole.
- The chromosomes are uncoiling and taking the form of chromatin.
- Cytokinesis occurs, eventually causing separation of each of the two original cells into two daughter cells, for a total of four haploid cells.

The end result of Meiosis II is:
Four haploid cells (each with 23 chromosomes), now in their single state because the sister chromatids of each chromosome have been separated. In a male, a total of four sperm eventually develop.

    In a female, the second division also results in one big cell with most of the cytoplasm from the parent cell, and one polar body. Only the larger daughter cell continues to develop into an egg cell (see Figure 4.2).

The key to learning the process of meiosis to be aware of:

1. *where the chromosomes originally came from.* The 46 chromosomes in the specialized somatic cell that is about to divide (a cell in the ovary or testis) were originally derived from the zygote, which formed from the 23 chromosomes of the mother's egg cell and the 23 chromosomes of the father's sperm. Remember that each somatic cell now in your body contains an exact replica of those original chromosomes, 23 maternally and 23 paternally derived.

2. *what happens to those maternally and paternally derived chromosomes during this process.* Their "behavior" is what makes meiosis such a unique and important process and introduces the genetic variability that typifies sexual reproduction.

3. *how many chromosomes are present* in the parent and daughter cells before and after each of the two meiotic divisions, and whether they are in their single or doubled state.

In addition to females' beginning to produce egg cells while still in the womb, the chromosomes actually begin crossing over. In this state, the precursor eggs are held in "limbo" until puberty, when the meiotic process continues at the rate of only one cell per month.

Summary of Meiosis

Meiosis I Homologous pairs are separated into different daughter cells, immediately reducing the number of chromosomes from 46 in the parent cell to 23 in daughter cells (crossing over has occurred, so the pairs are no longer identical).

Meiosis II Sister chromatids of each chromosome are separated from each other.

Variation Each gamete is now unique as a result of crossing over, and the independent assortment that occurs during meiosis. These events are vital in producing variation, and ensuring that gametes are produced that are different from one another!

Mitosis Versus Meiosis

The differences between somatic cell production (mitosis) and gamete production (meiosis) are summarized in Table 4.2. Again, keep in mind that mitosis is the division of an existing somatic cell into two daughter somatic cells, whereas meiosis is the division of a specialized kind of somatic cell into first two, then four cells, which mature into gametes and never will undergo cell division.

TABLE 4.2: Differences Between Mitosis and Meiosis

DIFFERENCE	MITOSIS	MEIOSIS
End result of process	Division of somatic cell to produce more somatic cells for growth and tissue repair	Division of specialized somatic cell to produce haploid gametes that can combine with another gamete to form a new individual
Number of divisions	One	Two
Chromosome number in daughter cells	Chromosome number of 46 is maintained from parent cell to daughter cells	Chromosome number is *reduced* from 46 in the parent cell to 23 in each of the resulting daughter cells (gametes)
Similarity of DNA of daughter cells to that in parent cells	Identical	Each gamete unique in its genetic makeup
Location in body	Throughout body	Ovaries or testes only

Chromosomal Aberrations

Fortunately, cell division proceeds smoothly most often, but mistakes do happen. Mistakes that result in an extra or missing piece of chromosome, an entire chromosome, or even a set of chromosomes are called **chromosomal mutations**. Having too many or too few chromosomes is a **chromosomal anomaly** or **chromosomal aberration** and can cause an early miscarriage in pregnancy (often before a woman even knows she is pregnant) or can lead to serious or fatal conditions.

Chromosomal mutations can occur in various ways. A common cause is failure of chromosomes to separate properly from one another during cell division. The separation of chromosomes to move toward opposite poles of the cell during anaphase is called **disjunction**; failure to separate is **nondisjunction** (see Figure 4.4).

If nondisjunction occurs during mitosis of the embryo in very early development, all subsequent cells deriving from that cell will have the wrong number of chromosomes. If nondisjunction occurs during meiosis, gametes with the improper number of chromosomes will be produced. A zygote (or later, an embryo) without some of the genes necessary for development, or a zygote that possesses too many genes, will develop either improperly or not at all. Nondisjunction during Meiosis I results in all daughter cells having the wrong number of chromosomes, and in Meiosis II one-half of the daughter cells will be normal and one-half will have chromosomal anomalies (see Figure 4.5).

In addition to nondisjunction, mutations can result in the wrong number of chromosomes, called **aneuploidy**; diploid rather than haploid gametes; or fertilization of an egg with more than one sperm. The correct number of chromosomes is referred to as **euploidy** (G *eu*: good, *ploid*: set).

Normally, the set of chromosomes in a human zygote includes 23 homologous pairs, consisting of two chromosomes of each "type" (two chromosome number 1s, two number 2s, two sex chromosomes, etc.). This normal condition is called **disomy** (referring to the two chromosomes that make up each pair). When one of a pair is missing, it is called a **monosomy**, and when there is an extra chromosome, it is a **trisomy**.

For most chromosomes, missing one of a pair or having an extra chromosome is a fatal condition. One important exception is **Trisomy 21**, which produces the condition known as **Down syndrome**. Because chromosome 21 is the smallest chromosome, less damage occurs by having three copies of its genes than with trisomy of larger chromosomes.

Anomalies in number of sex chromosomes are less damaging. Because survivability is not affected, sex chromosomal aberrations are observed more commonly in living individuals. An individual may have an extra of one of the sex chromosomes, or have only one, but at least one X chromosome must be present because survival without any X chromosome is incompatible with life. The conditions caused by this type of mutation are outlined in Table 4.3.

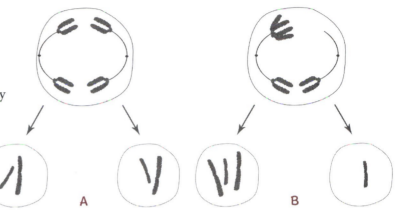

FIGURE 4.4 *Anaphase of normal mitosis* (**A**) *and nondisjunction of chromosomes during anaphase* (**B**)

Recent Advances: Cloning

Cloning refers to the process of producing a genetically identical individual (or individuals). The various types of cloning techniques are: **recombinant DNA technology** (or DNA cloning), **reproductive cloning**, and **therapeutic cloning**.

1. In DNA cloning only small pieces of DNA are copied (cloned) to produce many copies that will produce some desired protein (for example, insulin).

2. In reproductive cloning an entire organism is produced from a cell (at least the nucleus with the genetic material) of an existing organism. The most famous example is Dolly the sheep, as she represented the first successful mammalian cloning from an adult cell. This technique could contribute to saving endangered species.

3. Therapeutic cloning is the production of human embryos with the goal of harvesting stem cells that can be "trained" to become any type of cell needed for medical purposes.

Keep in mind that even the growing of a plant from a cutting is a type of cloning, and identical twins are an example of cloning in nature.

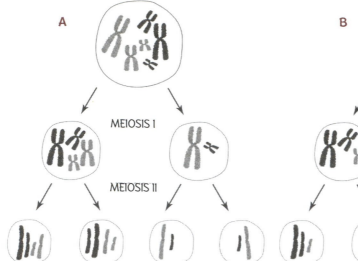

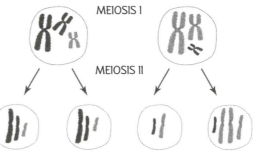

Note: The results of crossing over are not shown here.

If male, all four will develop into sperm, all with the wrong number of chromosomes. If female, only one egg matures, with the wrong chromosome number.

One-half of gametes produced will have the wrong number of chromosomes, and one-half will have the correct number.

FIGURE 4.5 *Nondisjunction during gamete formation: In Meiosis I (A) and in Meiosis II (B)*

TABLE 4.3: Examples of Sex Chromosomal Anomalies			
SEX CHROMOSOMES	**NAME OF CONDITION**	**SYMPTOMS**	**INCIDENCE**
XO	Turner syndrome	Underdeveloped breasts, infertile, rudimentary ovaries, lack of menstruation, short stature, neck webbing, heart problems, skeletal abnormalities[1]	1 in 2,000 female births[2]
XXY	Klinefelter syndrome	Malformed and/or small testes, lack of sperm development, some with breast development, low fertility, some with mild retardation[1]	1 in 500 to 1,000 male births[2]
XYY	XYY syndrome	Poorly known	1 in 1,000 male births[1]
XXX	XXX syndrome	Tall, thin, some with menstrual difficulties and mental retardation[1]	1 in 1,000 to 1 in 2,000 female births[1]

[1]Mange and Mange, 1990.
[2]National Institute of Child Health and Human Development, 2004.

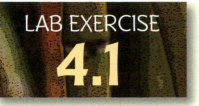

LAB EXERCISE

4.1

NAME _____

SECTION _____ DATE _____

1. Before completing this question, review the process of mitosis so you can fill out the diagrams and answer the questions without looking at the preceding information.

MITOSIS

Interphase:

a. In the cell provided, draw the form the DNA takes in the nucleus at this stage.

b. What is the "main event" occurring in the nucleus *before* cell division?

Prophase:

a. Draw four chromosomes in the blank cell. Think about the state in which they will appear (single or doubled).

b. If this were a human, how many chromosomes would appear?

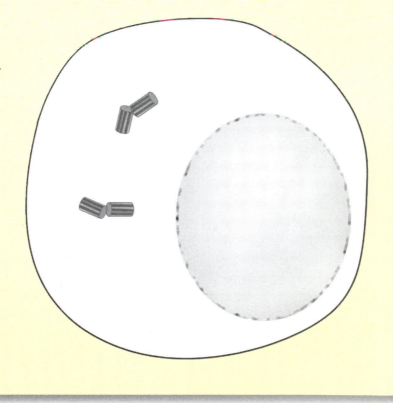

Metaphase:

a. Draw the chromosomes along the equator of the cell.

b. Draw the pairs of centrioles at opposite poles of the cell, and add spindle fibers connecting them to the centromeres of the chromosomes.

Anaphase:

a. Draw the chromosomes. In what form are they now?

b. What exactly is happening to the chromosomes?

LAB EXERCISE 4.1 (CONT.)

NAME _____

SECTION _____ DATE _____

Telophase:

a. Draw the chromosomes at each pole, surrounded by their newly formed nuclear membranes.

b. In this example, how many chromosomes are in each nucleus?

c. If this were a human, how many chromosomes would be in each nucleus?

d. Note the cell walls at the sides of the cell pinching in. This is accomplished by a ring of elastic proteins around the cell, constricting much the way a rubber band tightening around a balloon would appear. What is the term for this process of separating the one cell into two?

2. You will re-create the process of meiosis in an individual whose diploid chromosome number is six. From the sample of chromosomes given in Appendix B, choose and cut out the appropriate ones to fill in the stages of meiosis. Tape or glue them inside the blank cells. All of the sample chromosomes should be used; none should be left over.

a. Look at the chromosomes in Appendix B. What do the two different colors of chromosome represent?

MEIOSIS I

b. Would this example be more representative of the meiotic process in males or in females? Why?

MEIOSIS II

3. In Figure 4.1 you saw a diagram of normal anaphase of mitosis occurring, and nondisjunction in Figure 4.4. Take another look at these figures. In the illustration, anaphase is in progress. Draw the remaining four chromosomes (in the right half of the cell) as though nondisjunction were occurring for the chromosome indicated by the arrow (and anaphase proceeding normally for the other three chromosomes). Then draw the outcome in the daughter cells.

4. Determine from the karyotype below whether the individual represented is chromosomally normal or abnormal. If abnormal, which syndrome do you see, from the information you were given in this chapter? What is the sex of this individual?

SELF-TEST

4.1

NAME _____

SECTION _____ DATE _____

1. a. What process is represented here?

   b. How do you know?

   c. What kind of cell is being produced?

   d. If you find out that the diploid number of chromosomes for this species is eight, will that change your answers to 1.a and 1.c?

2. a. What process is represented here?

   b. How do you know? (Give two reasons.)

   c. The original cell that is dividing is what kind?

   d. What is the end result of this process?

   e. How similar or different are the daughter cells?

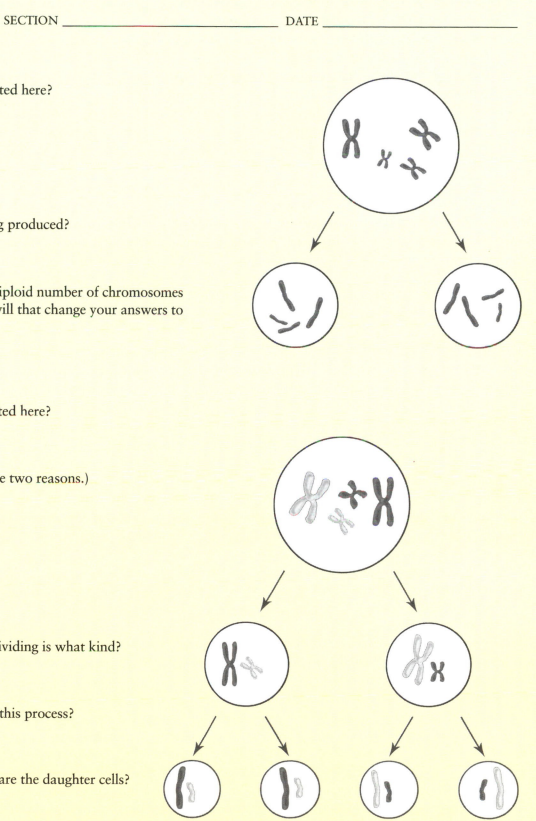

3. a. What kind of cells have the haploid number of chromosomes?

   b. Why do these cells have the haploid number?

   c. What is the haploid chromosome number for humans?

4. a. What kind of cells have the diploid number of chromosomes?

   b. What is the diploid chromosome number for humans?

5. a. What process occurs in the cell nucleus *before* cell division begins?

   b. Why is this process necessary?

6. What are chromosomes made of?

7. Explain how the genetic material from your parents combined to form you as a zygote.

8. Why doesn't the DNA get reduced by half every time cell division occurs?

ONE STEP FURTHER

NAME _____

SECTION _____ DATE _____

Additional Lab Exercise **4.1**

ADDITIONAL MATERIALS NEEDED:

- Microscope(s)
- Microscope slides of cell(s) at various stages of cell division

1. Examine at least three slides of cells in the microscope. For each, answer the following questions:

   a. Can you distinguish the nucleus?

   b. Can you see that the chromosomes are in their doubled (replicated) state?

   c. Can you identify the stage of cell division?

   d. Are any other organelles visible? If so, list them.

NAME _____

SECTION _____ DATE _____

Additional Self-Test Questions

1. Which is the "best" kind of chromosomal anomaly (abnormality) to have, in terms of survivability? That is, which type of chromosome is the least damaging if there is an extra or missing one?

2. True or False? Which of the following statements about meiosis is correct?

   _____ Meiosis takes place only in the testes of the male and the ovaries of the female

   _____ During the process of meiosis, the chromosome number is doubled between the parent cell and the daughter cells.

   _____ Two cycles of division are involved in meiosis.

3. The process of meiosis begins with a _____ cell specialized for the production of gametes.
   a. somatic
   b. sperm
   c. sex
   d. both a and b

4. What is a zygote?

5. _____ is the type of cell division that results in four new cells, each different from the other.

6. What is the term for the exchange of genetic material between members of a homologous pair of chromosomes during the prophase of meiosis?

7. Why is this (see #6) so important?

8. Name at least two ways by which meiosis differs between males and females.

9. What is the difference between somatic and sex cells (gametes) in terms of:

	somatic	sex
a. number of chromosomes in nucleus	_____	_____
b. location in the body	_____	_____
c. type of cell division by which they are produced	_____	_____

10. Each of the somatic cells in chickens has 78 chromosomes.

Thus, the _____ number for chickens is 78.

The haploid number is _____.

What type of chicken cell would have this number? _____

11. If nondisjunction occurs during Meiosis I (in a male), the result would be:
    a. two normal sperm (one of each kind of chromosome) and two with one extra chromsome
    b. two sperm with one extra chromosome and two sperm missing that chromosome
    c. two sperm with two extra chromosomes and two sperm with the normal number
    d. two normal sperm, one sperm with an extra chromosome and one sperm missing that chromosome

12. If nondisjunction occurs during meiosis II (in a male), the result would be:
    a. two normal sperm and two with an extra chromosome
    b. two sperm with one extra chromosome and two sperm missing that chromosome
    c. two normal sperm and two missing a chromosome
    d. two normal sperm, one sperm with an extra chromosome, and one sperm missing that chromosome

13. Which of the following chromosomal aberrations are incompatible with life (fatal)?
    a. Trisomy 21
    b. XXXY
    c. Trisomy 2
    d. all of the above

14. Describe the results of the first division of meiosis.

15. What is the difference *in function* between mitosis and meiosis? (What is the purpose of mitosis, and what is the purpose of meiosis?)

Inheritance

5

"Have you ever wondered . . . ?"

- Why do I look so much more like my father than my mother, if each contributed 50% of my genes?
- How can a set of parents with brown eyes produce a child with blue eyes?

OBJECTIVES

- Understand the relationship between Mendel's laws, molecular genetics, and gamete production
- Be introduced to the concept of probability and its role in transmission of genetic traits
- Learn the modes of transmitting genetic traits determined by genes on autosomes and sex chromosomes
- Understand the difference between simple and complex inheritance
- Learn to predict outcomes from parental crosses in offspring
- Learn steps of segregation analysis in determining the mode of inheritance demonstrated in a pedigree
- Understand the difference between continuous and discrete traits
- Become familiar with the process of identifying blood type

MATERIALS NEEDED

- PTC (phenylthiocarbimide) taste papers
- Food coloring bottles (preferably blue and/or green)
- Coins for coin-tossing (presumably, the students will supply their own coins)

(One Step Further will require additional materials; see Additional Lab Exercise 5.1.)

Gregor Mendel

In Darwin's time genetics were unknown. He knew the importance of variation within species for the action of natural selection, but didn't know how this variation occurred. During Darwin's lifetime a monk in what is now Czechoslovakia solved the mystery, although the importance of his discoveries wouldn't be discovered until after his (and Darwin's) death. Johann (later changed to Gregor) Mendel conducted breeding experiments with pea plants, leading to his discovery of the laws of inheritance. His results predicted the then-unknown behavior of chromosomes during meiosis.

Mendel was successful partly through luck but mainly because of carefully planned experiments, a large sample size (about 28,000 individual plants!), use of a statistical approach (probability), and his fortuitous choice of genetically **simple traits** (those controlled by only one gene). These traits now are called **Mendelian traits**.

Mendel's experiments included observing the transmission of a single trait at a time and also observing two traits at a time. From these experiments he concluded these two "laws" of inheritance:

1. For any given trait, members of a pair of "characters" separate (segregate) from each other during the formation of gametes, so only one copy (one gene) is passed on from each parent. This is his **principle of segregation**. We now know that this explains the separation of members of a gene pair from each other during the formation of gametes (when homologous pairs separate).

2. Genes on one set of homologous chromosomes don't influence the distribution of gene pairs on other chromosomes (for example, the chance for a pea seed to be round or wrinkled is independent of its chance of being yellow or green). This is because genes from homologous chromosomes separate independently from each other during meiosis and are assorted randomly in the gametes. This is the **principle of independent assortment**.

Recall from Chapter 2 that a **gene** is a segment of a chromosome's DNA coding for a specific protein, and an **allele** (G *allelo*: one another, parallel) is an alternative form of a gene. For any trait, an individual inherits one allele from each parent so each individual always has two alleles for each trait. The two alleles at a given locus make up an individual's **genotype**. The alleles are represented by letters (see Figure 5.1). As first shown in Chapter 2, chromosome 9 has genes for melanin production and for blood type for the ABO blood group. These are only a handful of the thousands of genes on this chromosome.

If an individual inherits two alleles coding for the same form of the trait, they are said to be **homozygous** for that trait. If the alleles code for different forms of the trait, the genotype is **heterozygous**. Thus, for example, if someone inherits one allele that does not result in normal melanin production and the other allele that does code for melanin production, what determines which form the trait will take? Will the person produce melanin or not?

Many traits have a consistent pattern of expression such that one allele may be expressed whenever it is present and the other allele is expressed only if it has been passed on by both parents. If an allele is always expressed when present, this allele codes for the dominant form of the trait. The **recessive** form of a trait is expressed only when both recessive alleles are present and no allele for the **dominant** form of the trait is present. Genotypes can be **homozygous dominant**, **heterozygous**, or **homozygous recessive**.

The physical expression of a trait is the **phenotype** (G *pheno*: show, seem, appear). Thus, the *genotype* consists of the genes (alleles) present at a specific locus on a homologous pair of chromosomes, and the *phenotype* is the resulting observable form of the trait.

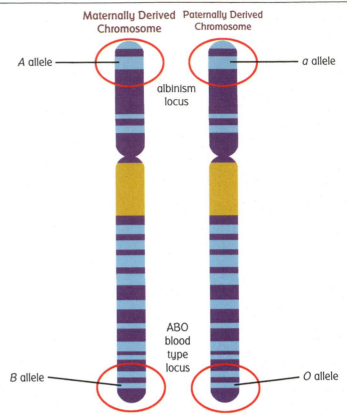

FIGURE 5.1 *Chromosome 9 for a hypothetical individual, showing samples of loci for two traits*

If a specific trait is coded for by a gene on a chromosome numbered 1–22 (the autosomes), it is an **autosomal trait**. A trait coded for by a gene on the 23rd pair (the sex chromosomes) is a **sex-linked trait**.

Autosomal Traits

"Simple" Genetic Traits

Many traits traditionally thought to be simple, or Mendelian, traits actually are controlled by genes at more than one locus and also may have some environmental component (e.g., Martin, 1975, for tongue-rolling). At least some of these traits, however, appear to be controlled primarily by one gene and usually follow a straightforward pattern of inheritance; thus, they serve as useful learning tools. Several examples of such traits are found in Table 5.1 (and Photos 5.1 to 5.5). The traits used in Lab Exercise 5.1 may be recorded simply upon observation; thus, the technique used to study them is called **anthroposcopy** (G *anthropos*: man, *scopy*: observation). We will use these traits in a later chapter as well.

The type of traits we deal with in this section are **discrete traits**; that is, there are only a few clear *categories* of phenotypes rather than an infinite number of possibilities of phenotypes. Discrete traits are not measurable, unlike **continuous traits** (e.g., height), which are measurable and

TABLE 5.1: Traits for Use in Exercises

TRAIT	DESCRIPTION	DOMINANT FORM OF TRAIT	LETTERS REPRESENTING DOM. AND REC. ALLELES
Albinism	Lack of production of pigment melanin	Production of melanin	A, a
Tongue-rolling*	Muscular capacity to curl the out edges of the tongue upward	Ability to tongue-roll	R, r
Earlobe attachment*	Earlobes may be either free-hanging (unattached), or the front lower portion of the earlobe may be attached to the skin around the location of the jaw joint	Unattached earlobes	E, e
Cleft chin*	Dimple in center of chin	Possession of cleft chin	C, c
Hand clasping*	With hands clasped and fingers interlocked, it feels more natural to have either left or right thumb on top	Left thumb on top feels more natural	L, l
Earwax form	Sticky yellow/brown vs. dry grayish earwax	Sticky earwax	G (dominant) A (recessive)
PTC tasting	Ability to taste bitterness of chemical phenylthiocarbamide	Ability to taste	T, t
ACHOO syndrome (Autosomal Dominant Compelling Helio-Ophthalmic Outburst)	Overstimulation of the optic nerve may affect the trigeminal nerve, inducing sneezing multiple times	Sneezing upon exposure to bright light	S, s (to be used here; no standard found)
ABO blood type	Antigens on blood cell surface determine blood type for ABO blood group	Alleles coding for A and B antigens are codominant (O is recessive)	A, B, O
Rh blood type	Antigens on blood cell surface determine blood type for Rh blood group	Rh^+	D, d

*See Photos 5.1 through 5.5.

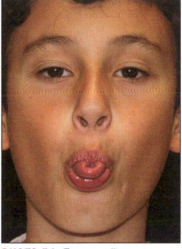

PHOTO 5.1 *Tongue-rolling*

PHOTO 5.2 *Cleft chin*

can have any number of possibilities for their measurement. Examples of continuous traits are the snow peas or leaves you measured in Chapter 1; they have a continuous distribution, which you also learned about previously.

The following two sections describe how to predict possible outcomes of various genetic crosses, considering first one trait at a time, then two at a time.

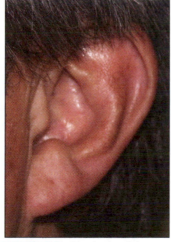

PHOTO 5.3 *Attached earlobe*

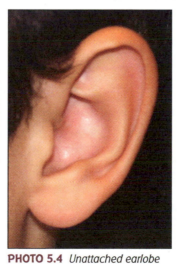

PHOTO 5.4 *Unattached earlobe*

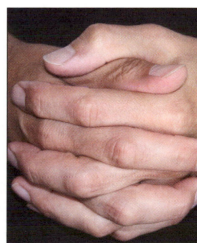

PHOTO 5.5 *Hand clasping*

Transmission of Traits: One at a Time

The transmission of *one* autosomal trait from parents to off-spring is straightforward. We'll use albinism as an example (see Table 5.1).

Albinism is coded for by a recessive autosomal gene with two alternative alleles: *A* (the dominant allele) and *a* (the recessive allele). Therefore, the genotypes *AA* and *Aa* (homozygous dominant and heterozygous, respectively) would result in normal melanin production and, therefore, in phenotypes with normally pigmented coloration. The genotype *aa* would result in the recessive form and, thus, an albino phenotype.

To predict the probability of offspring from a cross between an *albino woman* and a *man heterozygous for albinism*:

1. List the genotype of the mother as *aa* and the father as *Aa*.

2. Figure out what alleles for this trait will be carried by the gametes in the mother and the father. Remember that during meiosis the homologous chromosome pairs are separated from each other during the first division (see Chapter 4 and Figure 5.2). Although an individual has two alleles for each trait in each somatic cell (one maternally and one paternally derived), each gamete produced

will have only *one* allele representing each trait (to potentially combine with an allele from an individual of the opposite sex).

In our example, the mother has only *a* alleles, so all of her eggs will carry an *a* (see Figure 5.2A). The father is heterozygous, so approximately half of his sperm will carry an *A*, and half an *a* (see Figure 5.2B).

3. Set up a **Punnett square**. This is a simple tool, developed in the early 1900s by geneticist Reginald Punnett, to predict offspring outcomes depending upon the parental genotypes.

   List the alleles possessed by one parent along the top of the square and those of the other parent along the left side of the square (our example shows the mother's alleles along the top). Thus, these will represent the kinds of alleles present in the eggs of the mother and the sperm cells of the father (Figure 5.3). Keep in mind that we are focusing only on *one* trait—actually, in each gamete alleles will be present for *all* traits.

4. Fill in your Punnett square. The results represent possible outcomes of allele combinations (genotypes) in the zygote (Figure 5.4).

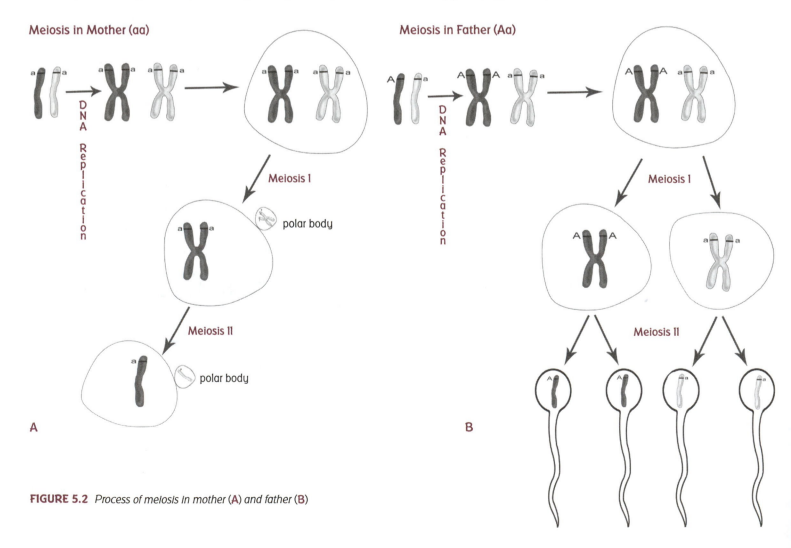

FIGURE 5.2 *Process of meiosis in mother (A) and father (B)*

FIGURE 5.3 *Punnett square, showing alleles in gametes to be passed on*

FIGURE 5.4 *Completed Punnett square*

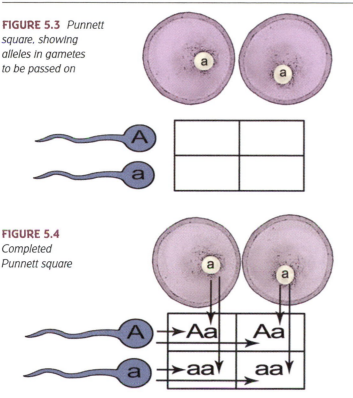

5. From your completed Punnett square, list the possible genotypes and phenotypes of the offspring, and the probability of each type.

genotypes	phenotypes	probability
Aa	nonalbino	1/2 (50%)
aa	albino	1/2 (50%)

6. List the ratio of the phenotypes and the genotypes, in terms of probabilities:

   a. **genotypic ratio**—number of homozygous dominant to heterozygous to homozygous recessive: 0:2:2

   b. **phenotypic ratio**—number expressing the dominant form of the trait to number expressing the recessive form: 1:1

Transmission of Traits: Two at a Time

If we consider *two* traits at once, Mendel's principle of segregation becomes important in demonstrating that the chance of inheriting one trait has no effect on the chance of inheriting the other. That is because, during gamete formation, the alleles (on their respective chromosomes) segregate/assort independently from one another and are assorted randomly in the gametes. Thus, the chances for someone's blood type to be A or B is independent of his or her chances of being an albino or not.

The Punnett square also can be used to determine the probabilities of outcomes of more than one trait considered together. We'll use the traits of tongue-rolling and albinism in this example. Remember that albinism is inherited recessively

Recent Advances: Genetic Counseling and Prenatal Detection of Genetic Disease

To minimize the chances that their child will be born with a serious genetic disorder, parents can enlist (1) genetic counseling prior to pregnancy, and (2) prenatal testing during pregnancy. As a result of the Human Genome Project, we know more than ever about people's medical future and about the health of offspring they potentially may produce. In addition, this and other studies of population genetics have provided invaluable information about the likelihood of specific diseases in specific populations, assisting genetic counselors in their advising of patients. Thus, studies of family histories together with ancestry information are used to advise couples about the risk of producing an infant with an inherited disorder.

Parents also are advised about the disorder itself and dealing with a child with that disorder in case of that eventuality. These days we also have the option of undergoing genetic testing, which can identify the likelihood of passing on certain genetic diseases to your children. Some of the common genetic disorders tested for are: Down syndrome, cystic fibrosis, sickle cell disease, Tay-Sachs, and spina bifida.

by a gene on one of the autosomes. Tongue-rolling is inherited as an autosomal dominant trait (Table 5.1), so someone who is heterozygous (*Rr*) for the trait can roll the tongue, and someone who is homozygous recessive (*rr*) does not have the musculature to tongue-roll.

Work through this example of a woman who cannot roll her tongue and is homozygous dominant for albinism, who marries a man who is heterozygous for tongue-rolling and is an albino.

1. List the genotypes of the parents for both traits:
   Mother: *rrAA*   Father: *Rraa*

2. Figure out what alleles are present in the gametes of the mother and father. *This is a crucial step! Do it carefully, and ask your instructor if you do not understand!* See Figure 5.5. The process of meiosis will result in the following:

   a. In the mother's eggs, the tongue-rolling trait will be represented only by the *r* allele (the mother's genotype is *rr*), and the albinism trait will be represented only by the *A* allele (the mother's genotype is *AA*). Thus, all eggs she produces will have an *r* and an *A* to represent those two traits. This can be written as *rA* (Figure 5.5A).

   b. The father's sperm will have two possible combinations of alleles. Because he is heterozygous for tongue-rolling, half of his sperm will have the *R* allele and half will have the *r* allele. All of his sperm will be produced carrying the *a* allele for albinism. Thus, half his sperm will have *Ra* and half will have *ra* (Figure 5.5B).

3. Set up your Punnett square. The number of columns and rows will depend on the number of possible combinations in the parents' gametes. Because there is only one possible type of egg, the mother will produce (*rA*) and the father will have two types of sperm (*Ra* and *ra*). The Punnett "square" can be as small as a 1 × 2 table (Figure 5.6).

4. Fill in the Punnett square with the expected types of offspring (Figure 5.7).

5. List the possible genotypes and phenotypes of the offspring, as well as the probability of each type.

genotype	phenotype	probability
RrAa	tongue-roller, non-albino	½ (50%)
rrAa	non tongue-roller, non-albino	½ (50%)

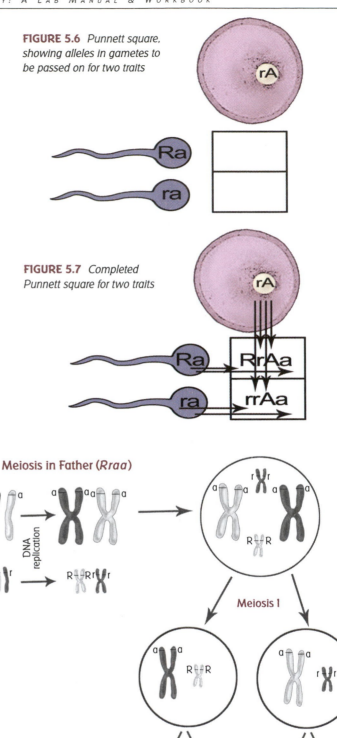

FIGURE 5.6 *Punnett square, showing alleles in gametes to be passed on for two traits*

FIGURE 5.7 *Completed Punnett square for two traits*

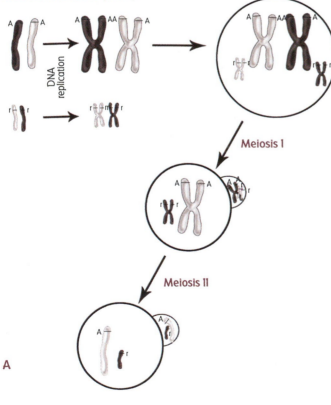

Meiosis in Mother (*rrAA*)

Meiosis in Father (*Rraa*)

A

B

FIGURE 5.5 *Process of meiosis in female (A) and Male (B), considering two traits*

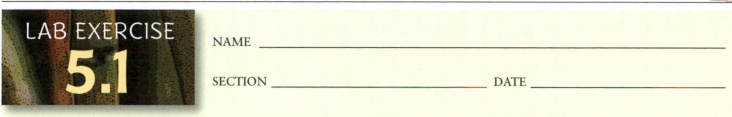

LAB EXERCISE

5.1

NAME _____

SECTION _____ DATE _____

1. Fill out the chart below for the form of each of these traits (phenotype) you possess, your possible genotype(s), and the types of alleles present in the gamete you produce. Refer to Table 5.1.

    An extra row is provided at the bottom for your instructor to record an additional trait, if desired

	PHENOTYPE	POSSIBLE GENOTYPE(S)	WHICH ALLELES PRESENT IN YOUR GAMETES?
Tongue-rolling			
Earlobe attachment			
Cleft chin			
Hand-clasping			

    a. How similar or different are your phenotypes, genotypes, and alleles from those of your lab partner?

    b. Do you have any trait(s) for which you know the genotype for certain? If so, which one(s), and how do you know?

    c. Choose *two* of the traits for which you know the phenotype in your family members (such as earlobe attachment and cleft chin). By knowing phenotypes for siblings and/or parents, does that help narrow the possibilities for your genotypes for these traits?

2. Make a Punnett square for the following exercise to answer these questions.

    a. If you can roll your tongue, let's (for the purposes of this exercise) assume that you're heterozygous. If you produce offspring with another heterozygote, what are the possible genotypes of these offspring? Their phenotypes? (Remember, use the letter *R* and *r* to represent the dominant and recessive alleles.)

b. If you cannot roll your tongue and you produce offspring with someone who is heterozygous for tongue-rolling, what are the possible genotypes of these offspring? Their phenotypes?

3. Represented in the illustration below is a hypothetical chromosome 11, taken from the karotypes of three individuals—1, 2, and 3 (keep in mind that the actual genes present on chromosome 11 are different from these).

Using the information in Table 5.1, you will create genotypes for each chromosome pair for three traits: cleft chin, earwax form, and PTC tasting.

a. Fill in the alleles on the chromosomes illustrated below, using whatever combination of dominant and recessive alleles you wish. (The tongue-rolling example is filled in for you.)

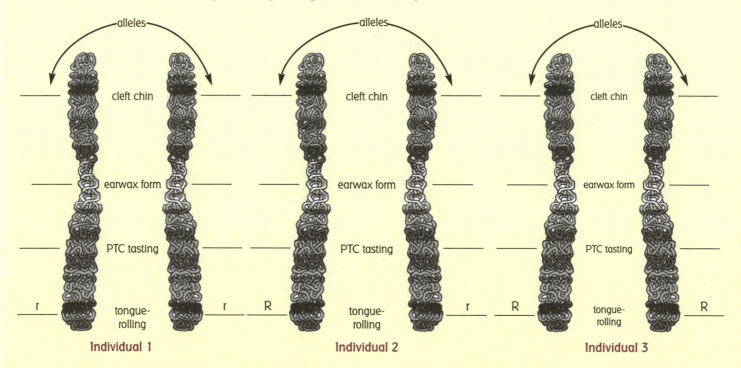

b. Fill in the chart below, making the genotype for each trait different for individuals 1, 2, and 3.

	INDIVIDUAL 1		INDIVIDUAL 2		INDIVIDUAL 3	
	GENOTYPE	PHENOTYPE	GENOTYPE	PHENOTYPE	GENOTYPE	PHENOTYPE
Cleft chin						
Earwax form						
PTC tasting						
Tongue-rolling	rr	inability to tongue-roll	Rr	ability to tongue-roll	RR	ability to tongue-roll

NAME _____

SECTION _____ DATE _____

c. Compare the genotypes and phenotypes for your three individuals with a classmate's results. Are your results the same?

This demonstrates the variation that can result from the different combinations of alleles produced by the parents and randomly passed on to the next generation (Mendel's principles). There are several hundred thousand possible combinations of genotypes for these four traits for any group of three individuals randomly chosen from the population. Imagine the possible allelic combinations if we consider all approximately 25,000 traits represented by the genes on all 23 chromosomes!

4. At DuPont Company in 1931, a chemist instigated an accident in which some synthesized compound phenylthiocarbamide (PTC) exploded into the air (Gadsby, 2000). Some of the workers actually could taste bitterness in the air and others couldn't. This led to the "taste test" for PTC. When the compound was handed out as crystals at the 1932 American Academy for the Advancement of Sciences (AAAS) conference, about a quarter of the people could not taste it ("non-tasters"), and the others ("tasters") said it was incredibly bitter.

It was quickly noted that the ability to taste was determined genetically, and it was transmitted in a simple Mendelian fashion. Phenotypes were divided into non-tasters and tasters. The ability to taste is dominant to the inability to taste, so a non-taster would be homozygous recessive.

a. Taste the PTC paper, and note your:

phenotype   **genotype (or at least any known alleles—use the letters *T,t*)**

More recently, human taste specialist Linda Bartoshuk (1994), found a third level of tasters, and thus divided people into supertasters, tasters, and non-tasters. These may correlate with homozygous dominant, heterozygous, and homozygous recessive genotypes.

The tongue has four types of **papillae**. The papillae house the receptor cells (taste buds). Molecules with sweet, salty, sour, or bitter tastes stimulate the receptors, which stimulate nerve endings inside the tongue, and the message of the type of taste is carried along the nerve cells to the brain. The number of taste buds embedded in the tips of the tongue are controlled by our genes. The types of papillae are **circumvallate**, **filiform**, **foliate**, and **fungiform** (the mushroom-shaped bumps concentrated more at the tongue's tip), as illustrated.

b. Drip a small drop of food coloring (green or blue works best) onto a thin strip of paper, then use it to paint the tip of your tongue (Scientific American Frontiers Archives, 1999).

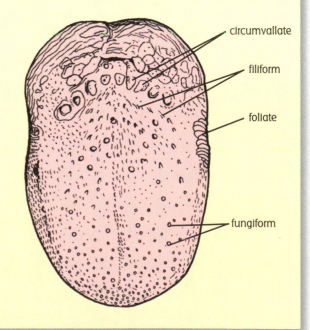

circumvallate

filiform

foliate

fungiform

c. Punch a hole in an index card and place the hole over the tip of your tongue. This small area of your tongue will serve as your sample of taste buds (Shahbake et al., 2005). The edge of the hole should be on the tip of the tongue, in the center.

d. Have someone else count (using a magnifying glass, if available) the fungiform papillae (these should appear pale against the food-colored tongue background). *Super-tasters* may have up to 50 fungiform papillae. *Tasters* usually have 15 to 30, and *non-tasters* may have as few as 10 (Bartoshuk et al., 1994, 1998; Gadsby, 2000).

e. Are you a PTC taster? According to fungiform-counting, what is your tasting level? Do your taste preferences match the results of PTC-tasting and fungiform papillae-counting? Super-tasters often avoid black coffee, grapefruit, and very sweet desserts. (More females than males tend to be super-tasters.)

f. Take a count of the phenotypes of all of your classmates so you have a total number of supertasters, tasters and non-tasters.

Super-tasters: _____   Tasters: _____   Non-tasters: _____

Blood Typing

Although we usually hear about types A, B, O, and AB, as well as positive and negative blood, we each actually have not two but about 24 blood types! Each different blood type is coded for by genes at different loci on our chromosomes. A blood type is determined by the kind of antigen on the surface of our red blood cells. Blood types are useful for tracking genetic traits within and between populations, investigating their biomedical effects and learning about inheritance. Punnett squares are useful for predicting offspring outcomes for blood type as well.

ABO Blood Group

In the blood serum, each person has **antibodies** against foreign blood antigens. By determining the type of antibodies in the blood, you can determine the individual's blood type. The simplest way to test for the type of antibody present is to add **antigens**. If the antibodies attack the antigens, the result is a clumping affect, called **agglutination**. The surface of the red blood cells has antigens with the same common name as the person's type of blood (A or B).

The **ABO blood group** is coded for at a locus on chromosome 9; alleles called I^A, I^B, and I^O (hereafter referred to simply as A, B, and O alleles) determine enzymes that are responsible for the type of antigens that are produced and reside on the surface of red blood cells. These antigens are composed of a chain of simple sugar molecules and differ just slightly from each other depending upon the alleles present. The difference between A and B antigens (determined by A or B alleles) is that each has an extra sugar molecule (different from each other) on the end of the chain, which is lacking in the chain produced by someone with only O alleles.

The various genotypes for this trait are: AA, AO, AB, BO, OO, and BB. A and B alleles are both dominant over O but are **codominant** with regard to each other (Table 5.1). Thus, if both an A and a B allele are present, both A-type and B-type antigens are produced (and the genotype is type AB). O alleles are expressed only if they occur without an A or a B allele to "mask" their appearance in the phenotype: An OO genotype (type O blood) is the only one to produce a sugar chain with no end sugar as in blood types A, B, and AB. Table 5.2 lists the genotypes, phenotypes (blood types), antigens, and antibodies for each blood type in the ABO group.

Blood types for the ABO blood group must match if blood from one person (a donor) is to be used for another (a recipient), as a result of the reaction of anti-A and anti-B antibodies against the A and B antigens, respectively, on the surface of the red blood cells. Because type O blood has neither A nor B antigens on its cell surface, it has both anti-A and anti-B antibodies in its serum. For that very reason (lack of A or B antigens), however, type O blood does not provoke a reaction (**agglutinate**) with type A, B, or AB blood. Therefore, individuals with type O blood are known as **universal donors**. Type AB blood has neither anti-A nor anti-B antibodies with which to attack incoming blood cells, so it can receive any blood—type A, type B, type AB, or type O. Thus, type AB individuals are referred to as **universal recipients.**

Rh Blood Group

The blood types associated with the **Rh blood group** are Rh^+ and Rh^- (A^+, B^-, etc. really represent blood types from two different blood groups, ABO and Rh). Actually, several alleles code for Rh blood types, determined by simple dominant/recessive inheritance. If an individual is homozygous dominant or heterozygous (DD or Dd), he or she is Rh^+; the individual is Rh^- if homozygous recessive (dd). (See Table 5.1.) A person who is Rh^+ has antigens (called D antigens) on the surface of the red blood cells that can provoke the production of antibodies in the serum of someone without those antigens (an Rh^- person).

The Rh blood group has great significance medically because of potential problems with **Rh incompatibility** between a mother and her developing fetus. If the antibodies are produced by a (Rh^-) mother's immune system in response to antigens on her (Rh^+) fetus' red blood cells, the mother's antibodies can attack the fetal cells and break them open, releasing the hemoglobin within and resulting in severe **anemia** in the infant around the time of its birth. If the mother receives prenatal care, medical advances have virtually eliminated the problem in our society today.

TABLE 5.2: Characteristics of ABO Blood Group			
GENOTYPE	PHENOTYPE (BLOOD TYPE)	TYPE OF ANTIGENS ON RED BLOOD CELL SURFACE	TYPE OF ANTIBODIES IN SERUM
AA or AO	Type A blood	A antigens	Anti-B
BB or BO	Type B blood	B antigens	Anti-A
OO	Type O blood	None	Anti-A and anti-B
AB	Type AB blood	A and B antigens	None

SELF-TEST
5.1

NAME _____

SECTION _____ DATE _____

1. Two normally pigmented parents have an albino child. What are the parents' genotypes? The child grows up and marries another albino. What is the probability of their having an albino child?

2. A zebra population has a mutant allele for spots. The spot trait (*S*) is dominant to the striped allele (*s*).

   a. A spotted male mates with a striped female. Assuming that he is homozygous, what is the probability that they will have striped offspring?

   b. If one of their daughters mates with a spotted (heterozygous) male, what is the probability that the offspring will be striped?

3. If a male who is Rh⁻ mates with a female who is Rh⁺ (heterozygous), what are the possible genotypes and phenotypes of their offspring? (Use the letters *D* and *d* to represent the dominant and recessive alleles, respectively; use a Punnett square.)

4. A normally pigmented woman and an albino man have nine normally pigmented children and one albino child. What is the woman's genotype?

5. The ability to taste the chemical PTC is transmitted as a dominant allele, represented by *T*; the recessive allele is *t*. Two normally pigmented taster parents have an albino son and a non-taster daughter with normal pigmentation.

   a. What are the genotypes of the parents?

   b. What is the chance that the albino son is a taster?

   c. What is the chance that the non-taster daughter is heterozygous for the gene controlling albinism?

   d. The non-taster, non-albino daughter marries a taster man with normal pigmentation; his mother was a non-taster albino. What is his genotype?

   e. What is the chance that a child of theirs will be a taster albino if the wife is heterozygous for albinism?

6. A case of disputed paternity involves a woman (W) and her children (i, ii, iii, iv) and two men (Y and Z). The analysis is limited to the ABO and MN blood group systems. The phenotypes are as follows:

		father:
W: A, MN	i: A, MN	_____
Y: B, MN	ii: A, M	_____
Z: AB, N	iii. AB, M	_____
	iv. O, N	_____

    Assuming that only Y or Z could be the father of these children, assign the children to their appropriate father. In the ABO blood group system, A and B are codominant, and both are dominant over the recessive O allele. In the MN blood group system, M and N are codominant. You can solve this problem either with Punnett squares for both possible parental crosses (W with Y; W with Z) or without a Punnett square, working with a process of eliminating possibilities.

7. You are typing your blood. What is your blood type if:

   a. there is no agglutination?
   b. there is agglutination with anti-A but not anti-B?
   c. there is agglutination with both anti-A and anti-B?

   Which blood type is known as a universal donor? _____

   Why?

   d. Which blood type is known as a universal receiver? _____

   Why?

8. A female who is a PTC taster and a tongue-roller mates with a male who is also a PTC taster but is not a tongue-roller. Use the letters *T,t* (for PTC tasting) and *R,r* (for tongue-rolling). The ability to taste is dominant, and the ability to tongue-roll is dominant.

   a. What do we know of their genotypes? Female _____ Male _____
      (Fill in only the alleles you know at this point, without looking ahead.)

   b. They have three kids with the following phenotypes:

      Kid 1: PTC taster and tongue-roller
      Kid 2: PTC taster and non-tongue-roller
      Kid 3: PTC non-taster and tongue-roller

   c. With the knowledge of the next generation's phenotypes, now what do we know of the parents' genotypes?

   Female _____   Male _____

9. In a case of disputed paternity, a woman has a daughter with type A, Rh$^+$ blood. The woman's blood type is A, Rh$^-$. What blood types could a possible father have?

10. How could a set of parents with brown eyes produce a child with blue eyes?

Sex-Linked Traits

Sex-linked traits can be coded for by genes on either the X or the Y chromosome. Traits coded for by genes on the X chromosome are X-linked, and those on the Y chromosome are Y-linked. Most traits that are sex-linked are X-linked because X is a much larger chromosome, possessing many more genes than the Y chromosome. Genes on the Y chromosome relate to male sexual development. Most genes on the X chromosome have nothing to do with female sexual development but are vital for individuals of both sexes.

An example of an X-linked trait is red/green colorblindness. On the X chromosome is a gene coding for **opsin** proteins (proteins in cone cells of the retina that enable us to perceive color); these opsins bind to visual pigments in the red-sensitive cones, green-sensitive cones, or blue-sensitive cones, making the visual pigment/opsin complex sensitive to light of a particular wavelength. If the opsin protein (a product of a gene, via protein synthesis) is absent or defective, the color vision is affected.

The vast majority (93%) of people who are colorblind are males, because this trait is transmitted by a recessive gene on the X chromosome. When denoting the genotype for a sex-linked trait, *always include the sex chromosomes*, X and Y, as shown below. This is significant because the pattern of transmission of a sex-linked trait differs for males versus females. Below, C denotes the normal, dominant allele, and *c* the recessive, faulty allele. The genotypes for males and for females are as follows:

Genotypes for Males	Phenotypes
$X^C Y$	Male with normal color vision
$X^c Y$	Colorblind male

Genotypes for Females	Phenotypes
$X^C X^C$	Female with normal color vision (non-carrier)
$X^C X^c$	**Carrier** for colorblindness (but normal color vision)
$X^c X^c$	Colorblind female

Note that females can be homozygous dominant, heterozygous, or homozygous recessive. Because males have only one X chromosome, and thus one allele for each trait coded for by this chromosome, they cannot be referred to as any of these! They are **hemizygous.** Recessive alleles on the X chromosome are always expressed in males because there is no dominant allele to "compensate."

The steps for predicting outcomes for a sex-linked trait are demonstrated by this example. A man with normal color vision and a woman who is a carrier for colorblindness are expecting a child. What are the possible genotypes for the child?

1. List the genotypes of each parent. Man: $X^C Y$

   Woman: $X^C X^c$

2. Set up your Punnett square, remembering to include the sex chromosomes with the allele that is on it, as shown in Figure 5.8.

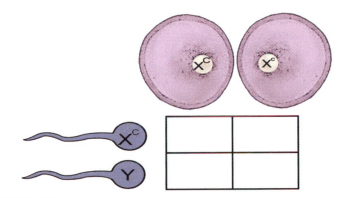

FIGURE 5.8 *Punnett square for X-linked trait, colorblindness*

3. Fill in the Punnett square with the expected types of offspring, as shown in Figure 5.9.

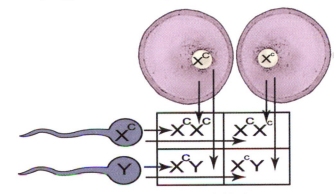

FIGURE 5.9 *Completed Punnett square for colorblindness*

4. List the possible genotypes and phenotypes of each, and their associated probabilities of occurrence.

Genotypes	Phenotypes	Probability
$X^C X^C$	normal female	1/4 (25%)
$X^C X^c$	carrier female	1/4 (25%)
$X^C Y$	normal male	1/4 (25%)
$X^c Y$	colorblind male	1/4 (25%)

Pedigrees

Important in the study of inheritance is the search for patterns of transmission of traits from one generation to the next. Does a specific trait follow a definite and predictable pattern of transmission? Knowledge of the mode of inheritance has important implications for biomedical research, genetics studies, and genetic counseling.

We can visualize patterns of inheritance by constructing a **pedigree**, which is a diagram that delineates the genetic relationships of family members over two or more generations. **Segregation analysis** is used to determine which of several modes of inheritance is responsible for producing specific patterns in a familial line. This involves proposing a genetic hypothesis (a possible mode of transmission), testing it, and continuing the process until a hypothesis is proposed that accounts for the observed patterns of inheritance with high accuracy and cannot be rejected.

The five modes of inheritance (which follow a Mendelian pattern) discussed here are: autosomal recessive, autosomal dominant, sex-linked recessive, sex-linked dominant, and Y-linked. Each has a set of characteristics that can be used to identify it from a pedigree, listed in the accompanying box.

The way to "test" a hypothesis is to provisionally assume a particular mode of inheritance and try out associated genotypes to see which fits for parents and offspring. Below are examples of abbreviated pedigrees for autosomal and sex-linked traits, with sample genotypes and explanations. Keep in mind that to determine a pattern of inheritance, one normally would observe several generations of a family or extended family rather than only a set of parents and their offspring. Read over the boxed information, then try these. The actual mode of inheritance for each is listed at the end of this section.

Characteristics of Modes of Mendelian Inheritance

Autosomal Recessive
- Most affected individuals are children of unaffected parents
- All children of two affected parents (homozygous recessive) are affected
- It is expressed in males and females to (approximately) same degree
- May skip generations

Autosomal Dominant
- Each affected individual has at least one affected parent
- Number of affected males and females is roughly equal
- Two affected individuals may have an unaffected child (because affected individuals can be heterozygotes)

Sex-linked

X-linked Dominant
- Affected males produce all affected daughters and no affected sons
- A heterozygous-affected female will transmit the trait to half of her children, with males and females affected equally.
- Twice as many females as males are affected.

X-linked Recessive
- Hemizygous males and homozygous females are affected
- Males express the trait when it is present (because hemizygous)
- It is more common in males than in females
- Affected males get mutant allele from the mother
- Males transmit the allele to all daughters (via X chromosome), but not to sons (pass only Y to sons)
- It may skip generations

Y-linked
- This mode appears only in males
- Affected males pass trait to sons but not to daughters
- Every Y-linked trait should be expressed

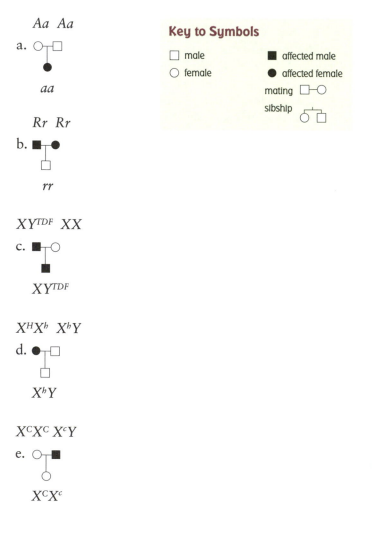

Key to Symbols

- □ male
- ○ female
- ■ affected male
- ● affected female
- mating □—○
- sibship

a. *Autosomal recessive:* If two unaffected parents have an affected offspring, the trait must be "hidden" in the parents' genotypes, and thus be recessive. If the trait were dominant, at least one parent would be affected.

b. *Autosomal dominant:* If two affected parents have an unaffected offspring, the trait must be dominant. Two affected parents with a recessive disorder would have all affected children.

c. *Y-linked:* Father-to-son transmission rules out X-linked inheritance. All sons of affected fathers are affected; no females are affected.

d. *X-linked dominant:* An affected woman with an unaffected son rules out X-linked recessive, because both of her chromosomes would have the recessive allele—so the son would be affected, but he is not.

e. *X-linked recessive:* An unaffected daughter from an affected father can't be X-linked dominant because the father has only one type of X (with affected allele) to give a daughter, so she also would be affected.

Genetics Recap

By this point you have gone through the major genetics processes. Try to keep the big picture in mind, from the DNA comprising the chromosomes in all of our cells, to the expression of our physical characteristics via protein synthesis, and their probability of occurrence from generation to generation. Remember also how we got our own set of genes in the first place—from the meeting of the nucleus of our mother's egg cell and that of our father's sperm cell. The contents of the nucleus of all of our somatic cells are basically photocopies of that original cell, the zygote.

As for the genetic material we contribute to the next generation, in the process of producing our sperm or egg cells, we shuffle up the DNA sequences we received from our father and mother before passing it on to our children. Individuals together comprise populations, and the sum total of our genetic contributions to the next generation results in the gene pool. The difference in the gene frequency between the gene pools of succeeding generations is a function of evolution.

LAB EXERCISE

5.2

NAME _____

SECTION _____ DATE _____

1. Using the color-blindness chart below, check your color vision. If you can see the green number against the reddish background, you have normal color vision. If you cannot distinguish the number, you are (red/green) colorblind.

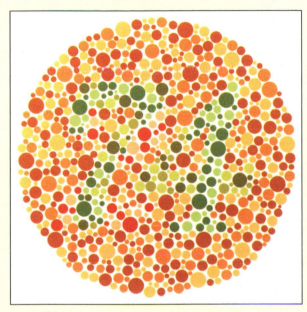 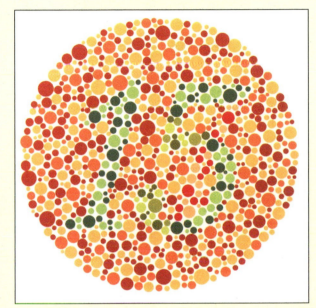

a. Do you have normal color vision?

b. What is your genotype, or your possible genotypes, for the colorblindness trait?

   (Remember, because it's a sex-linked trait, you will include the sex chromosomes in your genotype.)

2. With a lab partner, you will use coin-tossing to simulate the random nature of allele combinations in offspring, and "create" a family for which you will construct a pedigree. Use the boxed information and the sample short pedigrees on page 98 for directions on the symbols to use. Although a Punnett square gives you all of the *possible* outcomes of various crosses and their probabilities of occurrence, this method will mimic the passing on of alleles for the *particular outcome* determined by your coin tosses.

   Begin with a woman and a man with the following genotypes for the colorblindness trait:

$$\text{Woman: } X^C X^c \qquad \text{Man: } X^C Y$$

a. Start your pedigree by putting the symbols for this couple at the top (center) of a blank piece of paper. Fill in the blanks below, and record the genotypes next to the male/female symbols on the pedigree itself. Throughout the pedigree, remember to darken the symbol if an individual is affected by colorblindness.

b. This couple will produce gametes with what kind of alleles?

   Woman: _____   Man: _____

c. This couple has three children whose sex and color-vision acuity are determined by your coin tosses.
   • The *first coin toss* will be to determine which chromosome (X or Y) the father contributes. Use heads for the X chromosome and tails for the Y chromosome.

- The *second coin toss* will be to determine which of the two X chromosomes the offspring receives from the mother. Use heads for an X chromosome with a dominant allele and tails for an X chromosome with a recessive allele.

  Offspring 1

  Chromosome contributed by the father? _____ (determines sex of offspring)

  Chromosome contributed by the mother? _____

  Genotype of offspring? _____

  Offspring 2

  Chromosome contributed by the father? _____ (determines sex of offspring)

  Chromosome contributed by the mother? _____

  Genotype of offspring? _____

  Offspring 3

  Chromosome contributed by the father? _____ (determines sex of offspring)

  Chromosome contributed by the mother? _____

  Genotype of offspring? _____

d. Add these three offspring to your pedigree, and write the genotypes next to the symbols for each.

e. "Create" mates for each of these offspring—you will know the sex of the mate because it will be opposite from the offspring. Flip a coin to determine whether a male mate carries a *C* or a *c* on his X chromosomes, and to determine whether a female carries a *C* or a *c* on each of her X chromosomes. Draw these mates on your pedigree.

f. Produce one offspring for each of these second-generation couples by coin-tossing for sex and to determine which alleles are passed on for the color vision trait. Depending upon the parents' genotypes, you may have to toss either more or fewer coins.

  Record the genotypes for your third generation.

Offspring Couple 1	*Offspring Couple 2*	*Offspring Couple 3*
_____	_____	_____

g. Add them to your pedigree.

h. Compare your three generations to those of at least three lab partner pairs, and briefly comment on those comparisons below.

SELF-TEST
5.2

NAME _____

SECTION _____ DATE _____

1. Hemophilia is a rare, sex-linked recessive trait. Making a Punnett square may help you answer some of the following questions. Use the letter *H, h* to represent the dominant and recessive allele.

   a. What is the genotype of a male with hemophilia?

   b. What is the genotype of a female who is a carrier?

   c. If a female who is a carrier mates with a normal male, what are the chances that they will have an offspring with hemophilia?

   d. Will this offspring (with hemophilia) be a male or a female?

   e. What are the chances of their having a carrier daughter?

2. What is the probability that a colorblind male and a colorblind female will have an offspring with normal vision?

3. A cross between a colorblind man and a woman who is a carrier will result in what kinds of offspring, and in what proportions?

For the remaining questions, refer to the box on p. 98 entitled "Characteristics of Modes of Mendelian Inheritance."

 4. What is the most likely mode of inheritance for this pedigree? Briefly explain your answer.

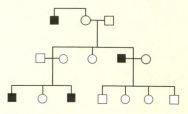

5. What is the most likely mode of inheritance for this pedigree? Briefly explain your answer.

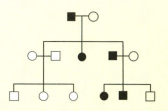

True-False

1. _____ X-linked recessive traits are expressed more frequently in females than in males.

2. _____ People with type A blood have anti-A antibodies in their blood plasma.

3. _____ Autosomal recessive traits often demonstrate affected individuals only every other generation.

4. _____ Segregation analysis is the process of proposing, testing, and rejecting (or supporting) genetic hypotheses to explain patterns observed in pedigrees.

5. _____ ■ in a pedigree would represent an affected female.

6. _____ For traits inherited as autosomal recessives, all of the children of two affected parents are affected.

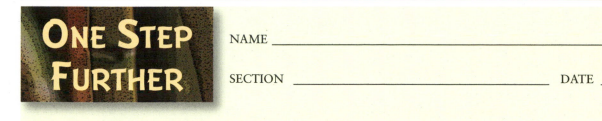

NAME _____

SECTION _____ DATE _____

Additional Lab Exercise **5.1**

Because of the potential health risks involved in experiments with real blood, synthetic blood will be used to learn the technique of blood typing. This lab is designed to be carried out using Carolina Biological Supply Company's 70-0101 blood typing kit. Any blood type kit, however, may be substituted (preferably with four different types); most come with their own instructions.

Blood Typing To Solve a Crime

You will solve a hypothetical criminal case based on an apparent violent homicide. The crime scene presents evidence of considerable blood spatter, in which most of the blood is that of the unfortunate victim, who was stabbed to death. The victim's blood type is A, Rh$^+$. Also present at the scene is a small amount of blood of another type: AB, Rh$^-$. The second blood sample is thought to have come from the perpetrator, possibly from wounds inflicted by the victim in self-defense before his death. Although new, more sophisticated techniques of analysis often are used for genetic identification, blood typing still proves to be a simple and cost-effective way of narrowing the possibilities, as you will see.

Four suspects (numbered Suspect 1, 2, 3, and 4) are in custody. Blood samples that have been drawn from them are in the four vials that you will analyze. These vials are labeled Sample 1, Sample 2, Sample 3, and Sample 4, corresponding to their respective suspect number.

At this point it would be helpful to review the section on blood types, paying special attention to Table 5.1 and Table 5.2. You will be applying drops of synthetic blood serum with antibodies specific to the antigens A and B for the ABO blood group, and the antibody for the D antigen (which determines Rh$^+$ blood type) for the Rh group. The response you will look for is **agglutination**, or clumping of antibodies with red blood cells. This response will produce a spotted appearance.

You will use the blood test cards on pages 107–108 to analyze each subject's blood. (Alternatively, at your instructor's discretion, you may use whatever card or slide came with your blood type kit.)

1. Label each of the cards with the Suspect/Sample number, 1 through 4.

2. Carefully drop a drop of synthetic blood from Sample 1 on Suspect 1's card, into the lefthand circles of each of the three sections (where it reads "Blood").

3. Have a mixing stick (colored toothpick) ready for *each* of the three antibody sera. The Carolina Biological kit has antibody sera colors that match the toothpick colors (e.g., blue Anti-A and blue toothpick, etc.). You will use each toothpick for mixing only one drop of blood with one type of antibody serum so no contamination will occur.

4. Still on the Suspect 1 card, place a drop of Anti-A in the proper circle, and do the same for Anti-B and Anti-D. Recap all vials.

5. Using the blue toothpick, stir the blood together gently with the Anti-A serum in the adjoining circle. Continue to mix for 30 seconds, then discard the toothpick. Mix the blood drops as well with the respective Anti-B and Anti-D drops, each with its own toothpick.

6. When you mixed the antibodies with the blood, did the blood "puddle" remain shiny and clear, or does one or more have a spotty appearance from an agglutination response? Look closely—the response may be weak! See the chart below to interpret your results, and fill in the blood type at the bottom of the card, for both ABO and Rh blood groups.

BLOOD MIXED WITH:	IF RESPONSE IS . . .	THEN . . .
Anti-A	agglutination	it is type A blood.
	no agglutination	check for agglutination with Anti-B.
		If none, it is type O.
Anti-B	agglutination	it is type B blood.
	no agglutination	check for agglutination with Anti-A.
		If none, it is type O.
Anti-D	agglutination	it is type Rh$^+$ blood.
	no agglutination	it is type Rh$^-$ blood.

7. Follow the same procedure for the other three suspects on their respective cards, filling in the blood type for each.

Answer the following questions about Additional Lab Exercise 5.1.

1. What blood type is represented by agglutination with both Anti-A and Anti-B?

2. Do any of the subjects provide a match for the crime scene blood? If so, which one?

3. If Suspect 2 is released and he is hit by a truck at the street corner and requires a transfusion, can Suspect 4 provide the blood for him? Why or why not?

4. What type of antibodies are present in the blood serum of Suspect 1? Of Suspect 3?

5. For each of the suspects, list the possible genotypes for each blood type (for both ABO and Rh blood groups.)

	ABO BLOOD TYPE	ABO GENOTYPES POSSIBLE	RH BLOOD TYPE	RH GENOTYPES POSSIBLE
Suspect 1				
Suspect 2				
Suspect 3				
Suspect 4				

Blood Test Cards

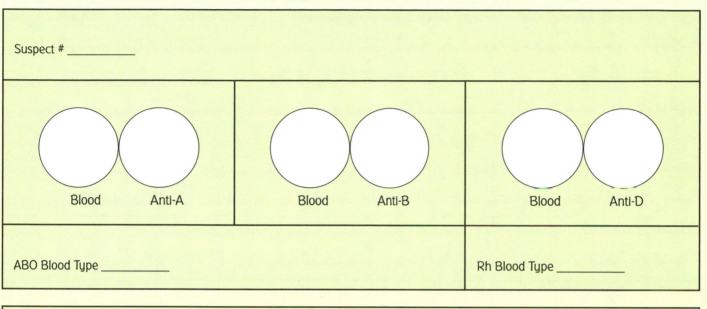

Suspect # _____

Blood   Anti-A   Blood   Anti-B   Blood   Anti-D

ABO Blood Type _____   Rh Blood Type _____

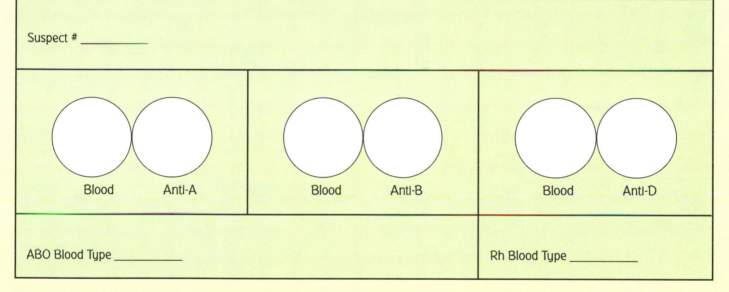

Suspect # _____

Blood   Anti-A   Blood   Anti-B   Blood   Anti-D

ABO Blood Type _____   Rh Blood Type _____

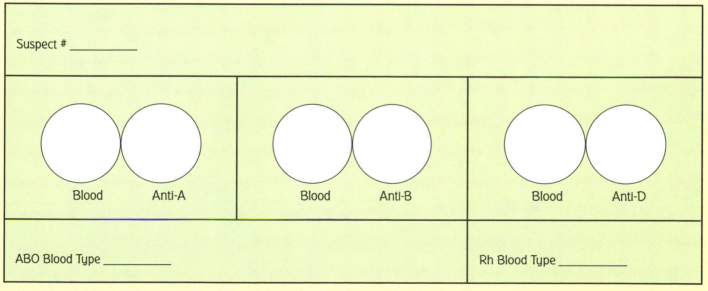

Suspect # _____

Blood   Anti-A   Blood   Anti-B   Blood   Anti-D

ABO Blood Type _____   Rh Blood Type _____

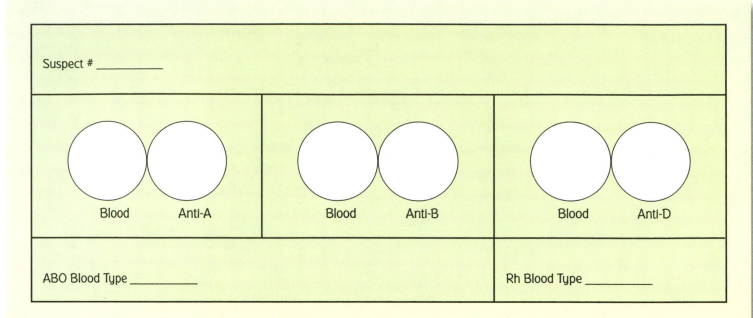

Suspect # _____

Blood   Anti-A   Blood   Anti-B   Blood   Anti-D

ABO Blood Type _____   Rh Blood Type _____

NAME _____

SECTION _____ DATE _____

Additional Lab Exercise 5.2

You probably will have to consult family members for this exercise; alternatively, you could "invent" the phenotypes for everyone. (You could even invent family members for a larger family.)

1. Construct a pedigree for your family, using one or more of the following traits:

   • Blood type for the ABO group
   • Blood type for the Rh group
   • Earlobe form
   • Tongue-rolling
   • ACHOO (Autosomal Dominant Compelling Helio-Ophthalmic Outburst) syndrome (sneezing after looking at a bright light)

2. Label the phenotype for each individual, as well as the genotype or possible genotypes. Include a total of three generations. Refer to Table 5.1 for information on the traits.

NAME _____

SECTION _____ DATE _____

Additional Self-Test Questions

1. In a population of 500 people, 160 are homozygous dominant for tongue-rolling. If 90 people cannot roll their tongue, how many dominant alleles for tongue-rolling are in the gene pool? (Remember—each person has two alleles for each trait!)

2. If a person with A type blood mates with a person with AB type blood, which type of blood will *not* appear among their children?

3. If a couple, neither of whom can roll the tongue, produce offspring:
   a. all of these offspring will be tongue-rollers
   b. some of the offspring will be tongue-rollers and some won't be able to roll their tongue
   c. their offsprings' phenotypes will depend on the actual genotypes of the couple
   d. none of these offspring will be tongue-rollers

4. If you have the genotype AB for the ABO blood group, what is your *blood type*? _____

   If you have the phenotype O, what is your *genotype*? _____

5. In this hypothetical paternity case, a blood group, the tongue-rolling trait, and earlobe attachment were examined. The mother is type A for the ABO blood group, is a tongue-roller, and has attached earlobes. The man she assumes to be the father is type B, is a tongue-roller, and has free-hanging earlobes. Her child has the following phenotype: type O, not a tongue-roller, and free-hanging earlobes. (Tongue-rolling is dominant to the inability to tongue-roll, and free-hanging earlobes are dominant to attached earlobes.)
   On the basis of this information, can the man be the father of the child? Briefly explain your answer.

6. ABO, MN, and Rh are examples of:
   a. genotypes
   b. blood types
   c. blood groups
   d. phenotypes

7. Only _____ traits are expressed in the heterozygous condition.
   a. recessive
   b. autosomal
   c. dominant
   d. Y-linked

8. In a case of disputed paternity, a child has type A, Rh$^+$ blood. The mother's blood type is A, Rh$^-$. What are the possible blood types of the father, for both ABO and Rh blood groups?

The Major Forces of Evolution

"Have you ever wondered . . . ?"

- What causes evolution to occur?
- What does "survival of the fittest" actually mean?

OBJECTIVES

- Learn about each of the four evolutionary forces and how they cause changes in gene frequency between generations (evolution)
- Understand the role of probability in the change in gene frequency between generations in a population
- Reenact the "mechanics" of each evolutionary force and follow-through with the results of their actions on changes in gene frequency in populations
- Learn to "translate" allele and genotype frequencies into a mathematical formula (Hardy-Weinberg formula)
- Use the Hardy-Weinberg formula to determine change in gene frequency in populations and determine allele frequency from genotype frequency, and vice versa
- Understand the influence of population size on gene frequency size, especially with regard to small populations
- Use the Hardy-Weinberg formula to examine allele frequency and genotype frequency in the class "population" from collection of data in Chapter 5

MATERIALS NEEDED

- 3 lengths of string (approx. ½ meter each) for each lab pair
- Have students bring calculators
- Toothpicks—approx. 250 per lab pair (flat or square toothpicks are recommended so they won't roll off the table)
- Red markers (preferably 1 per lab pair)

Evolution is a change in gene frequency in a population over time. What can cause this change from one generation to the next? Four main factors, called **evolutionary forces**, are involved. You were briefly introduced to these in Chapter 1:

1. **natural selection,**
2. **migration (gene flow),**
3. **genetic drift,** and
4. **mutation.**

The first three forces result in changes in the frequency of various genes in a population by "redistributing" the existing alleles; the fourth, mutation, is the only one to introduce *new variation* into the gene pool. Some scientists would add a fifth separate force, that of **nonrandom mating**.

Natural Selection

Two important scientists—Charles Darwin (1809–1882) and Alfred Russell Wallace (1823–1913)—were independently involved in formulating a unified theory of evolution. Both realized that several factors were involved: the struggle for existence, extinction of species, variation, and adaptation. But how did these fit together? Darwin knew about **artificial selection** but knew of no mechanism for selection in nature, or **natural selection**. A key question for each dealt with population growth. If human (and therefore animal) population growth could increase at high rates, why weren't species overrunning the earth?

Both Darwin and Wallace had read an essay by the economist Thomas Robert Malthus (1826), which stated that "animal population growth was checked [stopped] in the struggle for existence," but humans had to restrain population growth artificially. The earth's resources are limited while potential population growth is unlimited.

Darwin realized that not all individuals could survive, so "favorable variations would tend to be preserved, and unfavorable ones destroyed," and that this would result in change within a species. He realized that *selection acts upon the individual*. Wallace, while suffering from a bout of malaria in Indonesia, also solved his problem of why species don't overrun the earth, and why some species become extinct and others continue to live: "The less well adapted don't survive, and the best-adapted survive." Social scientist Herbert Spencer coined the now-familiar phrase "survival of the fittest" to describe this concept, although he used it in relation to human societies rather than in nature.

The steps in natural selection are:

1. Within all populations of a species, more individuals are produced than can survive.

2. Each population exhibits a great deal of variation and, as a result of this variation, some individuals are better adapted to their environment than others (see Figure 6.1).

3. Members of a population compete for limited resources. (Other factors that limit survival and reproduction include death from disease, predation, and so on.)

4. Those best adapted to their environment, because of their inherited traits, will be more likely to survive to reproductive age—and to reproduce—than those that are less well-adapted. Therefore, the genes coding for the well-adapted traits will be passed onto the next generation in higher numbers than the genes for the less well-adapted traits. *At this point, a change in gene frequency, and thus evolution, has occurred.*

5. If populations of a species become reproductively isolated from each other, many generations of accumulated genetic change between the populations eventually may result in sufficient differences between their genetic makeup to prevent interbreeding. At this point, speciation, or the production of new species, has occurred.

For natural selection to occur, traits must be

- *variable:* Variation must be present in the population for natural selection to act upon; individuals must differ from each other in the expression of traits. For example, they may have individual differences in thickness of the enamel covering the teeth, length of limbs, thickness of fur, attractiveness to members of the opposite sex, or susceptibility to disease. Darwin and Wallace knew the importance of variation but did not know from where it arose. The field of genetics has provided us with that information.

- *heritable:* The trait(s) must be inherited through the genes passed by the parents rather than acquired in an individual's lifetime or influenced by the environment.

FIGURE 6.1 *Natural selection occurring in a population, resulting in more thick-furred individuals*

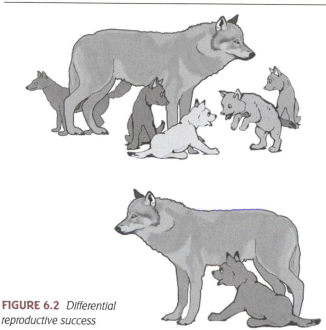

FIGURE 6.2 *Differential reproductive success*

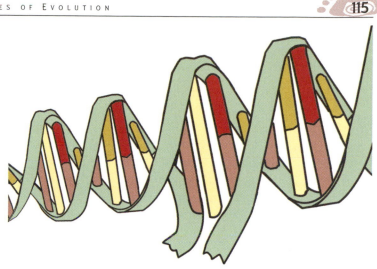

FIGURE 6.3 *Mutation*

Natural selection acts on *individuals*, not species. Each individual either reproduces a lot, or only a little (Figure 6.2), or not at all. The additive effects of this **differential reproductive success** result in a change in gene frequency in a population. Individuals with inherited traits that are better adapted to their environment will leave more descendants than others. Perhaps some are better able to crack harder nuts because of their thicker tooth enamel, or more efficient at escaping from predators because of their longer limbs, or better able to deal with extreme temperatures because of their thicker fur, or more successful at attracting more (or better quality) mates. The **fitness** (reproductive success) of any variation will change as the environment changes. A result of natural selection is **adaptation**.

Mutation

A heritable change in the genetic material (DNA) is a **mutation** (see Figure 6.3), a vital source of new variation in a population. Overall, mutation rates tend to be low, so mutations rarely have a great effect on gene frequency change by themselves. But the action of natural selection together with mutation, particularly in small populations, can change gene frequency more rapidly.

As you learned in Chapter 3, mutations can occur at various levels of the genome, from a "mistake" of a single base to entire sets of chromosomes. A mutation can occur during various genetic processes—mitosis, meiosis, DNA replication, or protein synthesis. Mutations are random; they do not occur because of an organism's "need," although they occasionally can provide a benefit in a specific environment. Some specific parts of certain chromosomes are more susceptible to mutation, and environmental **mutagens** such as some chemicals or radiation also can cause mutation.

Migration (Gene Flow)

Migration occurs constantly among populations within a species. When individuals move from one population to another, they obviously take their genes with them! Thus, an individual who has type AB blood takes his or her *A* allele and *B* allele along, thereby taking away an *A* allele and a *B* allele from the old population and contributing these to the new population. This change—obviously minor in the case of one individual—changes the gene frequency for ABO bloodtype in the population that was left behind, as well as the population the individual moves into.

If we think of a population as being made up of genes rather than individuals, we are referring to the **gene pool**. A gene pool comprises all the genes in a population. As individuals of each species move among populations, **gene flow** causes gene frequencies to fluctuate, resulting in evolutionary change.

Figure 6.4 depicts three gene pools experiencing losses and gains in various genes as individuals move among them. The light blue and dark blue dots represent different alleles for a given trait.

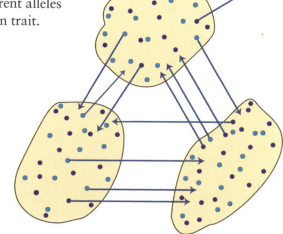

FIGURE 6.4 *Migration/gene flow of alleles among gene pools*

Recent Advances: Can a Single Mutation Cause Speciation?

A clear understanding of how new species arise would contribute a great deal to our knowledge of evolution, so examples of real cases that may represent speciation (development of new species) in action are exciting to biologists. In various snail species a single gene mutation in a female can cause her offspring to develop coils in a direction opposite from the majority of the population. Most snails are dextral (right-coiling); the mutation results in sinistral (left-coiling) snails.

In many species mating is difficult between dextral and sinistral snails. If mating is difficult enough to cause a consistent reproductive barrier, dextral and sinistral snails may, over time, develop into separate species (or coiling may at least contribute to speciation). Research is ongoing, but investigations in the combined areas of snail genetics, ecology, and behavior eventually, we hope, will provide us with an answer.

Random Genetic Drift

The gene frequency of populations fluctuates over time. From one generation to the next, random events cause changes in the gene pool. One generation's gene frequencies may not accurately represent the frequency of its previous generation's genes. Two frequent causes of these fluctuations are the **founder effect** and the **population bottleneck**.

Genetic drift is similar to a *sampling error* in that the smaller the sample, the less likely that the sample will be representative of the population at large. A common analogy is coin-tossing. If you toss a coin four times, the probability that it will come up heads and tails an equal number of times is relatively low. You're quite likely to toss three heads or all four rather than the number expected relative to the possibilities—two heads and two tails. If you toss a coin 100 times, you're more likely to come up with a "representative sample" of tosses—approximately 50 heads and 50 tails.

Or, say you have a huge vat of marbles, half red and half blue, well-mixed. You reach in and grab eight marbles (see Figure 6.5). Because of this small sample, you might just as readily draw three blue marbles and five red marbles as four and four, or even seven blue marbles and one red marble. If you scoop 200 marbles out of a pitcher full of marbles, this larger sample is more likely to accurately reflect the color proportion of the entire marble "pool," and to be made up of half red marbles and half blue marbles.

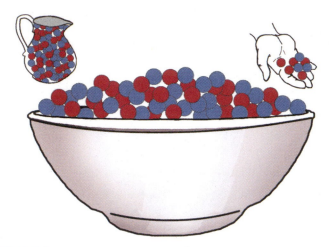

FIGURE 6.5 *Genetic drift similar to sampling error*

Genes in a gene pool can be envisioned in a way similar to the marble example. A small sub-population that separates itself from the rest of the population to "found" a new population will not represent accurately the frequency of the genes in the population at large, called the parent population. The parental gene frequency will exhibit fewer differences in a larger population than in a smaller population. This is the *founder effect* (see Figure 6.6). Results of such small populations include:

- a higher proportion of recessive genes, which can be "lost" more easily in a large population
- a greater chance of two recessive alleles coming together in zygote formation
- more recessively expressed traits, sometimes including genetic diseases
- loss of genetic diversity overall, because fewer individuals contribute their genes to the gene pool.

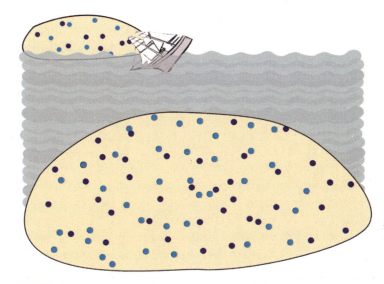

FIGURE 6.6 *Founder effect: Founding a new population*

A similar effect is achieved by a drastic reduction in the number of individuals in a population. This is called a *population bottleneck* (see Figure 6.7). Highly endangered species, such as the cheetah, have suffered from such a phenomenon. Their reduced genetic diversity and some recessive traits relating to fertility hinder their chances for future survival as a species.

By summing up the reproductive success of all the individuals in a population resulting from selective processes in nature and adding the influence of mutation, migration/gene flow, and genetic drift, the gene frequency of an entire population will be affected. These are evolutionary changes. Therefore, *the "unit" of evolution is the population*.

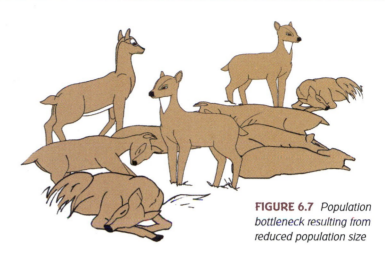

FIGURE 6.7 *Population bottleneck resulting from reduced population size*

LAB EXERCISE 6.1

NAME _____

SECTION _____ DATE _____

In this lab we will be tracking, and actually *causing* the changes in, allele frequency of an imaginary population and documenting the effects of all four evolutionary forces. We will simulate the action of the four evolutionary forces over a few generations. You will be working in pairs.

Our study animal is a species of a small African mammal similar to a raccoon, as illustrated. These animals are omnivorous and spend most of their time on the ground. Although they sometimes search for food in trees, their climbing abilities are limited so they often must wait for fruit to fall to the ground. Their environment is woodland, consisting of small patches of forest with interspersed savannah; it is more wooded along the Pengbai River, which runs through their habitat.

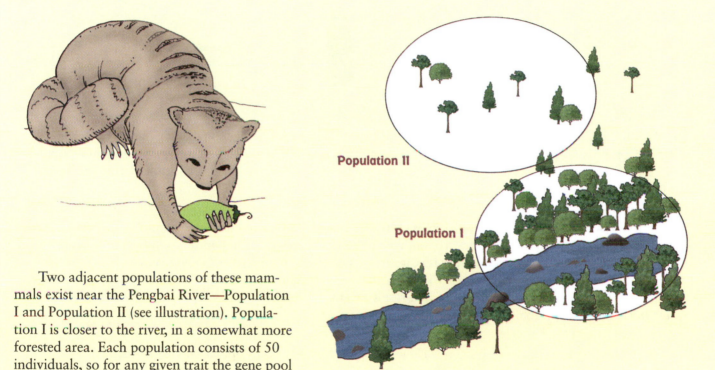

Population II

Population I

Two adjacent populations of these mammals exist near the Pengbai River—Population I and Population II (see illustration). Population I is closer to the river, in a somewhat more forested area. Each population consists of 50 individuals, so for any given trait the gene pool has 100 alleles. We'll use toothpicks to represent alleles and a pair of toothpicks to represent the genotype of an individual. Set up Population I and Population II by placing 100 "alleles" (toothpicks) within the boundaries of each of two pieces of string.

Mutation

Let's cause a mutation. This mutation occurs on chromosome 16, on the short (p) arm. At a specific locus on this portion of the chromosome is a gene that dictates muscle development, and particularly affects a muscle that inserts on the big toe. The DNA sequence for a portion of this gene normally reads: TAC GGG TGA CGC ACT. After the mutation, it reads: T A C   G G G   *G* G A   C G C   A C T.

mRNA   ___ ___ ___   ___ ___ ___   ___ ___ ___   ___ ___ ___   ___ ___ ___

tRNA   ___ ___ ___   ___ ___ ___   ___ ___ ___   ___ ___ ___   ___ ___ ___

amino acid _____   _____   _____   _____   _____

1. Fill in the blanks for the mRNA codons on the strand, and the anticodons on the tRNA.

2. Still regarding Question 1, what amino acids will the tRNAs carry to the mRNA strand?

Use the genetic code chart in Chapter 3 (Table 3.1) to see which amino acids will be coded-for during protein synthesis. Fill in the blanks.

3. What amino acid normally is coded-for by the third codon on the mRNA strand (in the *non-mutated* sequence)?

_____

In our hypothetical mammal species, the resulting phenotypic difference from this mutation is increased development in the abductor hallucis muscle, which increases grasping strength for the big toe, and therefore greatly enhances climbing ability. The illustration of chromosome 16 shows the region of the mutated gene causing excessive toe muscle development.

4. In Population I, use a red marker to "mutate" 20 toothpicks (alleles) by coloring complete bands around their middles. This trait is now **polymorphic**; it has more than one form. (In reality, 20 mutations occurring in a population of 50 individuals would be exceedingly high, but it will serve our purpose for this lab, considering the limited time to carry out this exercise.)

5. In Population II, also consisting of 50 individuals (100 alleles in the gene pool), the same mutation also occurs, but at a lower rate. Use a marker to "mutate" 10 toothpicks (alleles) by coloring red bands around them.

This mutation is inherited recessively; that is, it is expressed in the phenotype of an individual only if the alleles inherited from both parents are recessive. We'll use H and h to represent the dominant and recessive alleles, respectively, for this trait. The recessive form of the trait results in enhanced muscular development; only homozygous recessive (hh) individuals exhibit the trait.

6. Record the allele frequency for your baseline below. The allele frequency for Population I is provided below. Remember that individuals have two alleles for each trait. Thus, this population of 50 individuals has 100 total alleles—20 recessive and 80 dominant.

> Population I:
>
> > h allele = 20/100, so 20%
> >
> > H allele = 80/100, so 80%
>
> Population II:
>
> > h allele = _____
> >
> > H allele = _____

Natural Selection

In the current woodland environment, there is little recognizable difference in the activities or fitness of individuals on the basis of their genes for the abductor hallucis muscle, and the animals continue to feed on insects, roots, and fallen fruits. Let's focus on Population I to emulate the selection process.

LAB EXERCISE 6.1 (CONT.)

NAME _____

SECTION _____ DATE _____

First, although we know how many *H* and *h* alleles are in the gene pool, we don't know how many individuals are homozygous dominant, heterozygous, or homozygous recessive. Actually, we can use a simple formula, the **Hardy-Weinberg formula,** to figure it out. Wilhelm Weinberg (1908) and Godfrey H. Hardy (1908) independently stated that in a large, randomly mating population, there is a mathematical relationship between allele frequency and genotype frequency such that the frequencies of specific genotypes can be predicted from allele frequencies.

The **Hardy-Weinberg law** also states that allele and genotype frequencies will remain constant from one generation to the next (in equilibrium) if the following conditions are met:

- random mating,
- no selection or genetic drift, and
- neither migration nor mutation.

This equilibrium has not been observed to be maintained in natural populations, but it is basically a "null hypothesis" and can be used as a model against which we can measure genetic change.

The Hardy-Weinberg formula is:

$$p^2 + 2pq + q^2 = 1$$

where *p* represents the dominant allele and *q* the recessive allele, and
the number 1 represents the entire population (100%).

We will use this formula to estimate the actual *genotypes* from the number of *H* and *h* alleles in the population. In our Population I:

p is 80%, and *q* is 20%.
Adding these two, we get 100%, or 1.
because $p + q = 1$, $p = .8$ and $q = .2$.

Look at the formula above.

- p^2 represents the number of homozygous dominants
- $2pq$ represents the number of heterozygotes
- q^2 represents the number of homozygous recessives.

Simply plug our numbers into the above formula. Remember: $p = .8$ and $q = .2$.

$p^2 = .8^2 = .64$ (64%)
$2pq$ (this translates to $2 \times p \times q$) $= 2 \times .8 \times .2 = .32$ (32%)
$q^2 = .2^2 = .04$ (4%)

We now know how many of each genotype is expected to exist in our population. In reality, the numbers *may* differ somewhat from these *expected numbers* of individuals with the three genotypes, as you'll see.

$$
\begin{array}{lll}
HH & = 64\% & = 32 \\
Hh & = 32\% & = 16 \\
hh & = \underline{4\%} & = \underline{2} \\
   & 100\% & 50 \text{ individuals}
\end{array}
$$

The results indicate that we would expect 64% homozygous dominant, 32% heterozygous, and 4% homozygous recessive individuals. Only the latter, *hh*, would have the enhanced toe muscle development. In our population of 50 individuals, the expected numbers would be 32 *HH*, 16 *Hh*, and 2 *hh*. Always keep in mind that each individual possesses *two alleles* for each trait.

1. How do these expected numbers compare to *your Population I*? Mix up the toothpicks thoroughly, then close your eyes and put all of them into pairs to emulate the gametes that joined to form the individuals in your population. Each pair of alleles represents the genotype of an individual.

_____ individuals, or _____% *HH*

_____ individuals, or _____% *Hh*

_____ individuals, or _____% *hh*

_50_ individuals   100 %

Your random combinations of alleles are probably similar to the expected numbers. However, any change from expected indicates that one or more of the evolutionary forces are acting on the population.

2. Now let's produce another generation to see what happens to our gene pool. Taking our allele pairs as representatives of one of our individual mammals, we will pair individuals into "couples." We'll assume that each individual reproduces with one other individual. Close your eyes, or by using some other random process, pair your individuals (toothpick/allele pairs) into couples. (Continue to maintain the integrity of the individuals throughout the exercise, until directed otherwise.) When this pairing process is done, you will have 25 groups of four toothpicks.

3. Fill in the Outcomes Chart #1. First list all 25 of the parental crosses, then fill in probabilities for each kind of genotype. (You did this in Chapter 5 using Punnett squares.) For example:

PAIR #1	CROSS	HOMOZYGOUS DOMINANT	HETEROZYGOUS	HOMOZYGOUS RECESSIVE
1	*HH* × *Hh*	2	2	0

Outcomes Chart #1: Second Generation of Population I

PAIR #___	PARENTAL CROSS	HOMOZYGOUS DOMINANT	HETEROZYGOUS	HOMOZYGOUS RECESSIVE
1				
2				
3				
4				
5				
6				
7				
8				
9				
10				
11				
12				
13				
14				
15				
16				
17				
18				
19				
20				
21				
22				
23				
24				
25				
Totals				100%

NAME _____

SECTION _____ DATE _____

Second generation outcomes totals (Population I):   HH   Hh   hh

_____% + _____% + _____ = 100%

We'll assume the population size of the second generation hasn't changed, so:

HH   Hh   hh

_____% + _____% + _____ = 50 individuals

4. How do the genotype frequencies of the parental generation of Population I (p. 123, #1) compare with those of their offspring (second generation outcomes totals above)?

5. Compare your results to those of at least one other set of lab partners, and note your comparisons here.

Selective Pressure

We now know how many individuals of the various genotypes are in Population I. Suddenly the climate changes, becoming cool and dry. The fruiting seasons are shorter. Fallen fruit now is increasingly scarce, and the climatic change affects the entire food web, influencing the availability of foods for our little mammal. Younger trees become less likely to survive because of the lack of moisture, causing some shrinking of forests in areas farther from the Pengbai River. Along the river the forests continue to be lush and green.

Individuals who are homozygous recessive (*hh*) for the abductor hallucis trait can move around more efficiently in the trees and thus exploit a wider part of their habitat. They no longer have to wait for fruit to fall to the ground but can get to the increasingly hard-to-obtain fruit by seeking it out where it grows. In doing so, they also have learned about a new source of food: birds' eggs. These individuals fulfill their dietary requirements more easily and have more energy available to seek mates and reproduce successfully.

Previously, the likelihood of reproduction was equal for all individuals. Now we have a **selective pressure** that acts to enhance the fitness for some and lower the fitness for others. Individuals with the *hh* genotype are highly likely to reach reproductive age and reproduce successfully. Those with either *Hh* or *HH* are only half as likely to survive to reach reproductive age and reproduce.

Now we will see how selection acts to change gene frequencies in the next generation, and how selection is a non-random process, acting on existing variation in the gene pool.

1. Modify your Population I individuals (your toothpicks) so the number of *HH*, *Hh*, and *hh* offspring represent your second generation's genotypes (second generation outcome totals). For example, if you had 30 *HH* individuals from Outcomes Chart #1, set aside 30 pairs of unmarked toothpicks. Do the same for *Hh* (pairs consisting of one marked and one unmarked toothpick) and *hh* (two marked toothpicks). Your frequencies may not have been all whole numbers; if there are numbers beyond the decimal point, you will have to round up or down slightly. Also, depending upon your second generation outcomes totals, you may have to get (or create) more marked or unmarked toothpicks.

2. Now you are going to apply your selective pressure, with the climatic change selecting for the *hh* individuals. Because *HH* and *Hh* are only half as likely to reach reproductive age, choose half of the *HH* and *Hh* individuals and "select them out" of the gene pool, leaving an even number of individuals (even if you have to leave in an extra pair of toothpicks). Remember—the individuals represented here are not necessarily dying off but simply are not reproducing.

3. For the remaining toothpicks, close your eyes (or use some other random process) and pair them up into "couples."

4. For each couple, produce offspring by closing your eyes (or otherwise randomly choosing) and picking one allele to be passed on from each member of the pair. Obviously, if an individual is homozygous (either *HH* or *hh*), it has only one possible allele to pass on. Use new (marked and unmarked) toothpicks to "create" an offspring for each couple according to the allele combination you have randomly selected from the parents.

5. Place each offspring directly below the parents so you can record the frequencies of their genotypes in Outcomes Chart #2.

Outcomes Chart #2

HOMOZYGOUS DOMINANT	HETEROZYGOUS	HOMOZYGOUS RECESSIVE	TOTAL # OFFSPRING
			N =
			100%

Now you have genotype frequencies for Population I from before and after the action of natural selection. Describe this change between the two generations.

The size of Population I appears smaller because you have removed the nonreproducing individuals (one-half of the *HH* and *Hh*), and the couples have produced only one offspring each thus far. But before the next breeding season . . .

Genetic Drift

Population I is located closer to the Pengbai River and its associated forested area than is Population II. The river is quite low in the dry season, at which time animals cross back and forth over it on the exposed large rocks in a shallow portion. During the wet season, however, our mammal species typically stays within its more familiar range on the side of the river within the boundaries of Population I (or II).

In one year during the dry season, 10 members of Population I are foraging on the other side of the river, when a deluge quickly fills the river and covers the usually exposed rocks. These terrified little mammals are very wet and, further, are trapped. While they are isolated on the far side of the river, the water level doesn't decrease enough during the dry season for them to

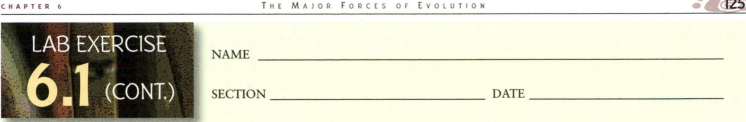

NAME _____

SECTION _____ DATE _____

return. They go on about their daily lives, which end up being spent on the far side of the river because a geographical barrier has now formed. They will produce offspring, thereby founding a new population, Population III. As mentioned previously, the type of genetic drift that changes gene frequency by forming a population from a small splinter subgroup is called the founder effect.

1. Close your eyes, choose 10 individuals (toothpick pairs) from Population I (these may be parents or offspring), and set them apart from the others with a string around them. You have just formed Population III.

2. a. What is the allele frequency of this new population?

    H _____ + h _____ = 20

    H _____% + h _____% = 100%

   b. What is the genotype frequency? Use the Hardy-Weinberg formula: $p^2 + 2pq + q^2 = 1$

    (p = % of H alleles; q = % of h alleles)

    HH Hh hh

    _____% + _____% + _____% = 100%

3. Compare the allele and genotype frequencies to Population I from the beginning of the lab exercise (p. 122, #1). How different are these proportions?

4. This small population will serve as the *founder* of subsequent generations. The *next generation's* genes will represent the actual evolutionary change that has occurred. What effect will continued selective pressure have on this small population?

5. What might have happened if the climatic change had occurred but the mutation on chromosome 16 had not?

Migration (Gene Flow)

Let's go back briefly to our Population I, to the members that did not become stranded on the opposite side of the river. We'll look at the action of the final evolutionary force by causing the migration of individuals between Populations I and II.

1. From Population I, close your eyes and choose 10 individuals. Likewise, from Population II, randomly select 10 pairs of alleles (toothpicks) to represent 10 individuals. Switch them between populations.

2. What is the allele frequency now for each population? Compare this to before migration occurred.

Population I

H _____ + h _____ = _____ alleles

H _____% + h _____% = 100%

Population II

H _____ + h _____ = _____ alleles

H _____% + h _____% = 100%

You now have reenacted all four evolutionary forces and seen firsthand how gene frequencies fluctuate within populations based upon both random and nonrandom factors.

SELF TEST
6.1

NAME _____

SECTION _____ DATE _____

1. Using the example of our hypothetical mammal populations, briefly explain how each of the four evolutionary forces causes evolution.

2. Which evolutionary force would seem to change gene frequency the fastest? Why?

3. Which evolutionary forces seem to work together to cause evolution?

4. To which evolutionary force does the saying "survival of the fittest" apply?

5. In which evolutionary force does competition play the biggest role?

6. What evolutionary force is represented by founder effect and population bottleneck? How are these similar to a "sampling error?"

7. As mentioned, some scientists consider non-random mating to be a separate evolutionary force. In our hypothetical mammal example, if the individuals with the big toe mutation suddenly were to mate only with other individuals with the mutation, what would be the result?

8. In a population of 200, an allele Z has a frequency of 80%. What is the frequency of allele Z? Using the Hardy-Weinberg equation, estimate the numbers of homozygous dominant, heterozygous, and homozygous recessive genotypes. (Remember that the formula is $p^2 + 2pq + q^2 = 1$, where p represents the dominant allele and q the recessive allele. The number 1 represents the entire population, or 100%.)

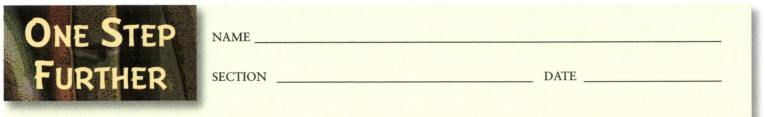

NAME _____

SECTION _____   DATE _____

Additional Lab Exercise 6.1

In Chapter 5 you collected data on a few discrete traits that follow largely a Mendelian (simple) pattern of inheritance. Now that you have been introduced to some principles of population genetics, you will apply that knowledge to data from your class. In this exercise your class is the population.

Your instructor will guide you in terms of how many of the traits you will use from the chart below, and whether students will collect data individually for the entire class, or whether the data are compiled as a group (perhaps with the instructor or one student filling out a chart on the board as they ask how many students exhibit each form of the traits).

1. For your trait (or traits), fill out the chart below, noting down how many individuals in your class have the dominant form of each trait and how many have the recessive form.

2. Fill out the column for the total number of alleles in your classroom population. This will be twice the number of students in class because (as you remember) each trait has two alleles, one from each of our parents.

TRAIT	# DOMINANT PHENOTYPE	# RECESSIVE PHENOTYPE	TOTAL NUMBER OF ALLELES IN "POPULATION"
Tongue-rolling (Tongue-roll ability dominant)			
Earlobe form (Unattached dominant)			
Cleft chin (Cleft dominant)			
PTC tasting (Tasting dominant)			

You now have the phenotypic frequency of your class "population." With this information you can estimate the allele frequency and then the genotype frequencies using the Hardy-Weinberg formula. This estimate is based on an assumption of how a particular frequency of dominant alleles (p) and recessive alleles (q) will combine in the population to form genotype frequencies. This also assumes that the population is in equilibrium (not subject to evolutionary forces), which is unrealistic for most real populations.

Before you calculate estimated genotype frequencies for your class population, an example will be presented here, using the trait of tongue-rolling (remember, this trait is not actually controlled by only one gene, but the influence of additional genes seems to be minimal).

We will assume a population of 50, with 40 able to roll the tongue and 10 not able to tongue-roll. Remember that each person has two alleles, so the population for this trait has 100 alleles.

The question we'll answer is: How many of the 40 tongue-rollers are homozygous dominant (RR), and how many are heterozygous (Rr)?

• Your first goal is to find the allele frequencies, p and q. Always *begin with the known quantity*, which is the *homozygous recessive genotype*. In this case there are 10 rr individuals; therefore, 20 r alleles of the total 100 alleles.

(Remember that q^2 represents the number of homozygous recessives.)

$q^2 = 20/100 = .2$

thus, $q = .45$ (we round off the remaining decimal points)

Since $p + q = 1$ (representing the entire population):

$p = .55$

thus, $p^2 = .3$

- We now can reconstruct the estimated frequencies of the other genotypes, *RR* and *Rr*, by plugging the known quantities for p and q into the Hardy-Weinberg equation:

$p^2 + 2pq + q^2 = 1$, which translates to: $.30 + .50 + .20 = 1$

$(RR) + (Rr) + (rr)$

so there are 30 *RR*, 50 *Rr*, and 20 *rr*

Your turn. Choose a trait, and use the information from your filled-out chart above.

1. Figure out the allele frequency (p and q) for the trait. Remember to use the known quantity to begin: homozygous recessive genotypes.

2. Calculate the estimated genotype frequency ($p^2 + 2pq + q^2$) for the three genotypes (you already knew q^2 for the homozygous recessive genotype).

   # of individuals with the following genotypes:

   Homozygous dominant _____

   Heterozygous _____

   Homozygous recessive _____

3. How many dominant alleles does your population have?

If we know all of the genotypes of a trait in a population, we can take Hardy-Weinberg a step farther and see how much the genotype frequencies in an actual population differ from what we would expect if the alleles were combined in a completely random manner (that is, if no evolutionary forces were acting, and if mating were random).

The following example uses the MN blood group, whose alleles, M and N, are codominant. Thus, we know the genotypes automatically from the phenotypes (blood types).

Blood type	Genotype	Number of Individuals
Type M	MM	40
Type MN	MN	20
Type N	NN	40

NAME _____

SECTION _____   DATE _____

Additional Lab Exercise **6.1** (cont.)

Obtain the actual number of alleles present in the population to obtain allele frequency (for p and q). This population of 100 individuals has 200 alleles.

Number of M alleles: MM individuals have 80 (2 M alleles each)
                          MN individuals have 20 (1 M allele each)
                              Total of M alleles: 100

Number of N alleles: NN individuals have 80 (two N alleles each)
                          MN individuals have 20 (one N allele each)
                              Total of N alleles: 100

Frequency of M allele (p) = 100/200 = .5

Frequency of N allele (q) = 100/200 = .5

Now that we know the allele frequencies from the genotypes, we'll plug them into the Hardy-Weinberg formula to see whether the actual genotype frequencies above conform to expectations if the population were in equilibrium (not evolving, and experiencing random mating).

$$p^2 + 2pq + q^2 = 1 \qquad .5^2 + 2(.5)(.5) + .5^2 = .25 + .50 + .25 = 1$$

Thus, the genotype frequencies expected if the alleles were to combine in a completely random manner would be:

Blood Type	Percent	Number of Individuals
MM	.25	25
MN	.50	50
NN	.25	25

(Remember this population has 100 individuals)

Compare these expected numbers to those observed in our actual population (40 MM, 20 MN, 40 NN). They are very different from one another. We would assume either that mating is nonrandom in this population or that evolutionary forces are in action, or both.

From the information given below:

- Figure out the allele frequencies, and
- Calculate the genotype frequencies, then
- Compare the calculated (expected) frequencies to those presented as the actual observed genotype frequencies.

Genotype	Number of Individuals
RR	25
Rr	40
rr	35
	100

1. Number of *R* alleles _____   Number of *r* alleles _____
   (Remember the total number of alleles in the population)

   Frequency of *R* allele (*p*) _____   Frequency of *r* allele (*q*) _____

2. Plug *p* and *q* into the Hardy-Weinberg equation:

3. Frequency of expected genotypes: *RR* _____   *Rr* _____   *rr* _____

4. Number of individuals with expected genotypes: *RR* _____   *Rr* _____   *rr* _____

5. Do the expected numbers differ much from the actual population genotype frequencies? Does the population appear to be in equilibrium, or are either evolutionary forces or nonrandom mating occurring?

NAME _____

SECTION _____   DATE _____

Additional Self-Test Questions

1. Genetic drift is said to occur if:
   a. genes move from one population to another
   b. the genes of siblings are different from each other
   c. the gene frequency of a population does not accurately represent that of its parental population
   d. there is too much genetic variation

2. What is a population?

3. What is a gene pool?

4. In one particular population, 4% of the individuals cannot roll their tongues.
   a. What is the frequency of the *r* allele? _____
   b. What is the frequency of the *R* allele? _____
   c. What proportion of the population is heterozygous for tongue-rolling? _____

5. For the previous question, if the population is composed of 1,500 individuals, how many *r* alleles are present?

The Bones Within Us

The human skeleton is composed of bones and cartilage, assembled into a rigid framework that has a variety of functions during life and offers a wealth of information after death. This lab focuses on the structure and function of bone and the terminology used to describe the position of various bones in the body.

Although we may not think about it much, we see a part of our own skeleton every day—our teeth. We also don't tend to think about our bones as being alive until we break a bone or need a root canal. Then the nerves and blood vessels that course through our skeleton make their presence known.

Bones are actually organs, but they are solid because of the deposition of mineral salts around protein fibers. Bone is a living, dynamic tissue that changes during life in response to forces placed upon it, as well as to disease and injury. Bones are part of the phenotype, and, therefore, are the products of both the genotype and the environment. Bones have a great deal of individual variation because of differences in age, sex, geographic origin, activity during life, and diseases or injuries.

Functions of the Skeleton

The skeleton has various functions, summarized as follows.

1. *support:* structural support, framework for attachment of soft tissues, holds organs
2. *protection:* protects vital organs (for example, the cranium protects the brain, the rib cage protects the heart and lungs, the vertebral column protects the spinal cord)
3. *movement/leverage:* framework for muscle attachment; allows movement at the joints

4. *mineral and lipid (fat) storage:* stores calcium and phosphate, which can be released as needed to maintain normal concentration of these ions in body fluids (calcium is the most abundant mineral in the body; each individual has 1–2 kilograms; energy reserves are stored as lipids in yellow bone marrow)

5. *blood cell formation* (hemopoiesis) and *storage:* blood cells are produced in red bone marrow; in children this occurs in long bones, in adults in the ribs, spleen, and **diploë** (porous portion of flat bones of skull)

What Can We Tell From Bone?

The types of information that can be obtained from bone include age, sex, race, and physical activities that were important in an individual's life. Upon closer analysis, especially with a narrow range of possible identities, unknown skeletons can be identified on the basis of X-rays—for example, comparing teeth to dental records, or skeletal elements with healed fractures to medical records. We often can diagnose disease from bone, even from prehistoric populations. By observing the form of bones and the joint surfaces of human or nonhuman remains, we can make inferences about how they moved around, whether bipedal, quadrupedal, climbing, or leaping.

Classification, Development, and Anatomy of Bone

Bones can be divided into four main categories, or classes (see Figure 7.1).

1. *long bones:* the limb bones as well as finger and toe bones

2. *short bones:* the blocky, often cube-shaped bones of the wrist and ankle, as well as **sesamoid** bones (these form within a tendon, such as the patella)

3. *flat bones:* those of the cranium, shoulder, pelvis, and rib cage

4. *irregular bones:* the vertebrae, facial bones, and some bones of the wrist and ankle

The skeleton of the fetus serves as a cartilaginous model upon which the adult bony skeleton is based. The skeleton can be separated into two main portions, according to its developmental sequence before birth (Figure 7.2).

The **axial skeleton** develops first and consists of the midline structures, such as the skull, vertebral column, rib cage, sternum, and hyoid. The **appendicular skeleton**, which develops later, consists of the limb bones and their connections to the axial skeleton (pelvic and pectoral girdles).

A typical long bone, such as the humerus (upper arm bone) or femur (thigh bone) consists of the following portions (see Figure 7.3 and *Atlas* pp. 186–187):

1. *diaphysis:* the shaft, or main portion of the bone

2. *epiphyses:* portions at the extremities, or ends of the bone

3. *articular cartilage:* a cartilaginous layer covering the epiphyseal ends

4. *metaphysis:* the region in a mature bone where the diaphysis meets the epiphysis; in growing bone, it is where calcified cartilage is replaced by bone

5. *epiphyseal line:* the remnant of epiphyseal plate, which consisted of hyaline cartilage before being replaced by bone; same area as the metaphysis

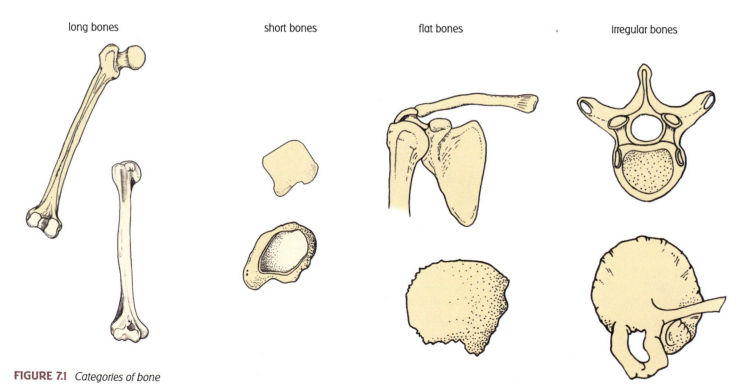

long bones   short bones   flat bones   irregular bones

FIGURE 7.1 *Categories of bone*

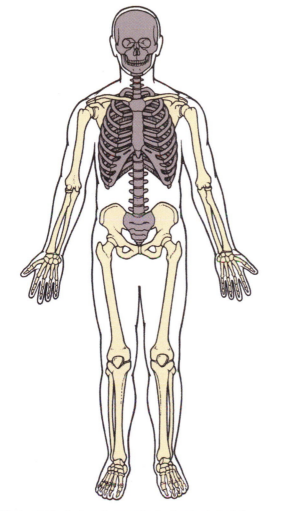

FIGURE 7.2 *Axial (shaded) and appendicular (unshaded) skeleton*

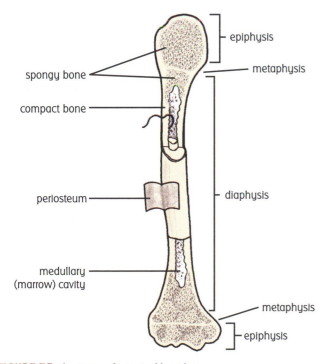

FIGURE 7.3 *Anatomy of a typical long bone*

6. *periosteum:* the connective tissue covering bone in places where there is no articular cartilage; consists of an outer fibrous layer of connective tissue with blood vessels, lymph vessels, and nerves that pass into bone, and an inner layer that is involved with the production of new bone for growth and repair

7. *medullary (marrow) cavity:* the space along the inside of the diaphysis that contains yellow marrow (in adults), consisting mostly of fat cells and some scattered blood cells

Throughout the skeleton are two distinct types of bone based upon differences in the cellular (histological) makeup.

1. **Compact bone**, or **dense bone**, usually is in the more external portions of bone. It is deposited in a layer over the other bone type, the spongy bone, and is thickest in the diaphysis of long bones. Compact bone provides protection and support and resists stress.

2. **Spongy bone**, or **cancellous bone**, usually is found more internally within bone. This is the type of bone that surrounds the marrow cavity and is found within the ends of long bones. Spongy bone contains many large spaces, which are filled with mostly red marrow.

Anatomical Terminology

Osteologists and anatomists often describe bones, or parts of bones, in what is called **anatomical terminology.** They use terms that describe the relationship of the bone to a body in **anatomical position**. Anatomical position for **orthograde** (bipedal) animals such as humans is a standing position with the arms down at the sides and the palms of the hands facing forward with the thumbs out to the sides. When using anatomical terms, we assume the body to be in anatomical position.

Like any three-dimensional object, the body can be divided by three basic imaginary planes (see Figure 7.4):

1. *midsagittal,* or *median plane:* divides the body into equal left and right halves (see *Atlas* p. 23; br. ed. p. 23)

2. *coronal,* or *frontal plane:* divides the body into front and back portions

3. *transverse,* or *horizontal plane:* divides the body into upper and lower parts.

Many anatomical terms describe the position of structures based on their relationship to these three planes, when the body is in anatomical position (Figure 7.5). These terms are often used to describe the position of one structure relative to another. The major terms are follows:

medial:	closer to the midline, or the median plane
lateral:	farther from the midline, or the median plane

anterior: toward the front
posterior: toward the back

superior: above
inferior: below

superficial: near the body's surface
deep: away from the body's surface; internal

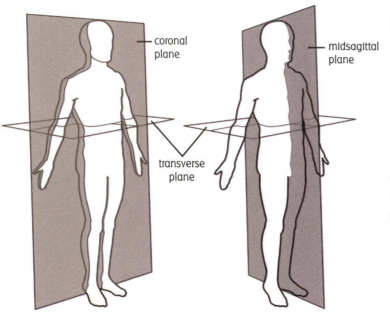

FIGURE 7.4 *Planes of the body*

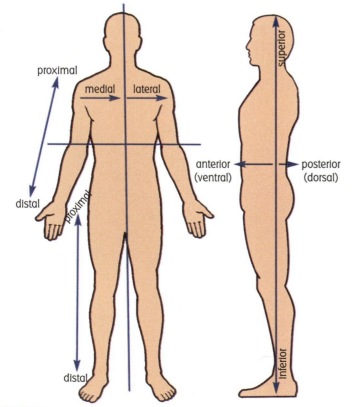

FIGURE 7.5 *Anatomical position: Directional terms*

A specific set of terms refers to how far up or down a limb a particular point is. These terms are:

proximal: closer to the attachment of the limb to trunk of body (nearer the hip or shoulder)

distal: farther from the attachment of the limb to trunk of body (away from the hip or shoulder)

Some examples of how these terms are used are the following.

● The ears are *lateral* to the nose.
● The wrist is *distal* to the elbow.
● The head is *superior* to the feet.
● The thumb is *lateral* to the fourth digit (in anatomical position).

Keep in mind that some of these terms do not apply as well to **pronograde** (quadrupedal) animals, in which the backbone is parallel to the ground. Terms that help to avoid confusion are:

ventral: closer to the belly

dorsal: closer to the back

cranial: closer to the head

caudal: closer to the tip of the tail

Features of Bone

The human body typically has 206 complete bones, each of which is influenced during life by the soft tissues that surround it. Raised areas or lumps on bone appear where the tendons of muscles attach. The bones may have grooves where blood vessels lie over the surface. Vessels and nerves enter bones by holes called *foramina* (singular: *foramen*). These bumps, grooves, and so on, referred to collectively as **features,** present us with important information. Features on bone can indicate the level of activity to which a limb was subjected during life, and they allow us to distinguish bones that came from the right versus the left side of the body.

In the following discussion we will cover the bones of the skull. Then we will review a sample of the features found on each bone.

Axial Skeleton Part 1: The Skull

The 22 skull bones are separated from one another by sutures, which allow them to grow independently of one another. Sutures are highly visible in a young individual's skull and become obliterated with advancing age. Some of the skull bones are paired, with a left and a right. The bones in the midline are single.

Bones of the Skull

Using the description of each of the skull bones listed below, identify each bone on a real skull (if available). As you identify each bone, pay attention also to the surrounding bones. With which bones do they articulate (are they adjacent to)? Often, the nature of the articulation of two bones determines their shape at the joint ends, depending upon the type of joint that occurs between them. If no skull is available, you may use Photos 7.1 through 7.3 (see also *Atlas* p. 78) instead. This list refers to Photo 7.1, unless otherwise noted.

1. *frontal:* The "forehead bone" is a single bone whose lower margins are occupied largely by the *orbits,* or eye sockets.

2. *parietals:* These paired bones articulate with the frontal bone; they make up the "walls" of the skull, meeting at the suture that runs in the midsagittal plane on top of the head.

3. *temporals:* This pair of bones on the sides of the head houses "ear holes" and provides articulation for the mandible (lower jaw).

4. *occipital:* The midline bone at the back of the skull houses the large hole (foramen magnum) at the base of the skull for passage of the spinal cord.

5. *maxilla:* These paired bones make up much of the face between the orbits and the mouth.

6. *zygomatics:* These are the paired "cheekbones."

7. *nasals:* These small, paired bones lie just superior to the nasal opening, between the orbits.

8. *ethmoid:* This single bone entirely within the skull can be seen from the frontal view (at the back of the orbit, medial side) or the lateral view (just posterior to lacrimals in orbits) or the superior view with the top of skull removed.

9. *sphenoid:* The large, butterfly-shaped single bone is mostly within skull, but portions are visible laterally (anterior to the temporals), inferiorly (much of underside of the skull posterior to the maxillae, anterior to the occipital), anteriorly (back of orbits lateral to the ethmoid), and superiorly with the top of the skull removed.

10. *lacrimals:* The small, delicate, paired bones just inside the rim of the orbits house the canal for tear ducts (lacrimal ducts)

11. *mandible:* This is the lower jaw (single bone after about one year of age)

12. *inferior nasal conchae:* These are small, curved bones, one on each side within nasal opening (Photo 7.2)

13. *palatine:* These small, paired bones lie just posterior to the bony palate (of the maxillae) (Photo 7.3)

14. *vomer:* This is a single midline bone visible just posterior to palatine (Photo 7.3)

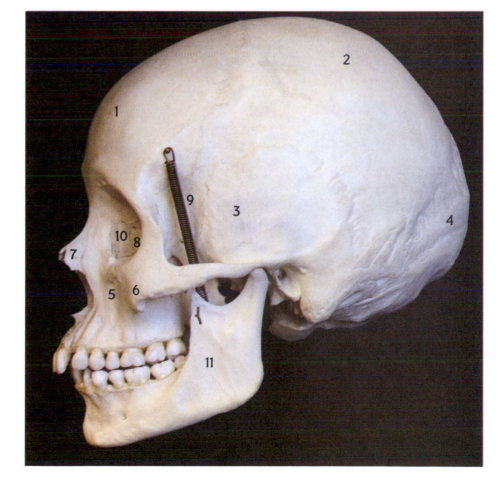

PHOTO 7.1

Lateral view of skull

1. frontal
2. parietal
3. temporal
4. occipital
5. maxilla
6. zygomatic
7. nasal
8. ethmoid
9. sphenoid
10. lacrimal
11. mandible

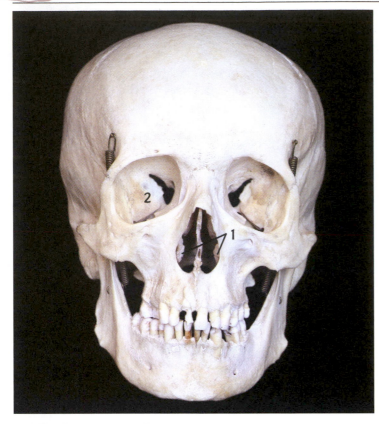

PHOTO 7.2 *Anterior view of skull*

1. inferior nasal conchae   2. sphenoid

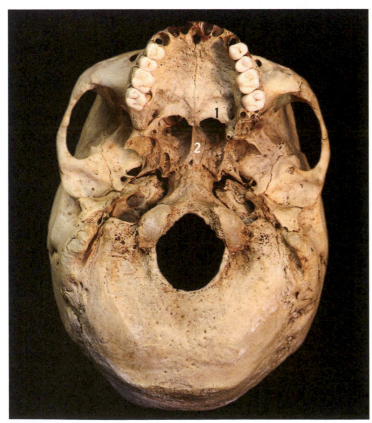

PHOTO 7.3 *Inferior view of skull*

1. palatine   2. vomer

Skull Sutures

The skull has many sutures, usually named for the two bones they separate (Photos 7.4–7.6 and *Atlas* pp. 83, 85, 88, 89). The primary five sutures, though, have their own names. Identify each of the following major sutures on a skull:

1. *sagittal:* separates the two parietal bones; along the midsagittal plane.

2. *coronal:* separates the frontal from the two parietal bones.

3. *squamosal:* separates the parietal from the temporal bone.

4. *lambdoidal:* separates the parietal bones from the occipital bone.

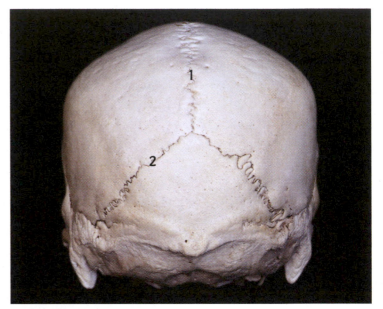

PHOTO 7.4 *Sutures, posterior view*

1. sagittal suture   2. lambdoidal suture

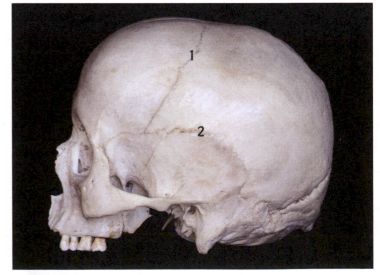

PHOTO 7.5 *Sutures, lateral view*

1. coronal suture   2. squamosal suture

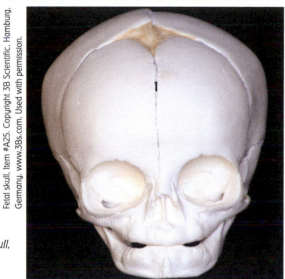

Fetal skull. Item #A25. Copyright 3B Scientific. Hamburg, Germany. www.3Bs.com. Used with permission.

PHOTO 7.6
Sutures: Fetal skull, anterior view
1. metopic suture

5. *metopic:* separates the two halves of the frontal bone until approximately 2 years of age in humans; in most mammals and in some primates it is retained throughout life.

Middle Ear Bones

The mammalian ear is a complex organ, originally derived from ancestral reptilian bones that made up the articulation of the mandible with the cranium. The *ear canal* is the portion (in humans, taking the form of a bony tube) that leads to the *tympanic membrane*, or eardrum. This is the point of entrance to the *middle ear,* a space that houses the three small ear bones, or *ossicles*: the *malleus, incus,* and *stapes* (see Figure 7.6).

Incoming sound waves vibrate the tympanic membrane, which in turn vibrates the three ossicles. The last of these,

the stapes, vibrates against the membrane leading to the *inner ear,* which contains the cochlea and the semicircular canals. Nerve receptors inside the cochlea transmit impulses via the acoustic nerve, to be perceived by the brain. The middle ear is housed inside of a highly mineralized part of the temporal bone, the *petrous portion* (G *petr:* rock).

The Teeth

As mammals, we have a heterodont (G *hetero:* different; *dont:* tooth) dentition, with teeth specialized for different functions. Our four different types of teeth—*incisors, canines, premolars,* and *molars*—allow us to process various foods efficiently. As adults, we typically have 32 teeth (assuming that none have been removed). The deciduous dentition, or set of baby teeth (G *decid:* falling off) is composed of 20 teeth.

Look at the teeth of a skull, and identify the four types of teeth. The incisors and canines are blade-like and chiseled. The premolars (often called bicuspids; L *bi:* two) have two cusps, and the molars (L *mola:* grind) have four or five cusps.

In one quadrant of the jaw, a human with a full complement of teeth has two incisors, one canine, two premolars, and three molars. This is known as **the dental formula**. Because it is the same for the top and the bottom in humans, the dental formula is $\frac{2}{2} \frac{1}{1} \frac{2}{2} \frac{3}{3}$. Children's teeth are all deciduous until about age 6, when these begin to be replaced by permanent teeth. Thus, they have the dental formula $\frac{2}{2} \frac{1}{1} \frac{0}{0} \frac{2}{2}$. The mouth has its own set of directional terms, as shown in Figure 7.7 and *Atlas* p. 22; br. ed. p. 22.

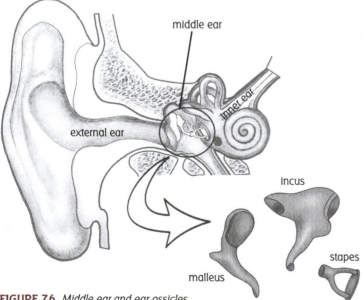

FIGURE 7.6 *Middle ear and ear ossicles*

FIGURE 7.7 *Directional terms for tooth row; functional tooth types*

The anatomy of a tooth is depicted in Figure 7.8.

- *alveolus*: tooth socket consisting of spongy bone surrounding each tooth in the maxilla and mandible
- *apical foramen*: opening at the tip of the tooth's root through which pass nerves and vessels
- *cementum*: hard substance adhered to directly outside of tooth root
- *crown*: portion of the tooth above the gumline; enamel-covered
- *dentin*: organic substance, softer than enamel, that makes up most of the tooth's area throughout its length
- *enamel*: hard inorganic mineralized substance; covers the crown of the tooth
- *neck*: constricted area at the junction of the tooth root and the crown
- *pulp cavity*: open space along the inner tooth, filled with blood
  vessels, nerves, and soft
  connective tissue
- *periodontal ligament*: fibrous connective tissue "fastening" the tooth in the alveolus
- *root*: portion of the tooth below the gumline; portion in alveolus

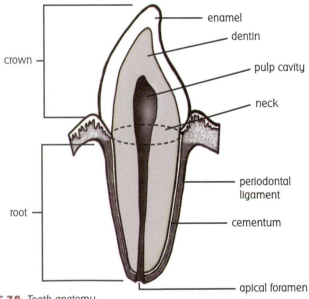

enamel

dentin

crown

pulp cavity

neck

periodontal ligament

root

cementum

apical foramen

FIGURE 7.8 *Tooth anatomy*

Features on Skull Bones

Now that you have identified the skull bones, you are prepared to learn the names of the *features* on these bones. (Again, features are the bumps, crests, and grooves that result from the influence of soft tissue during development. These features allow us to distinguish female from male skulls and help us identify activities during life (for example, the size of a bump indicates the size of a muscle).

Some of the terminology used for features throughout the skeleton is defined next. Many specific features include one of these words as a part of their name. You are *not* expected to memorize this list.

Terms that describe *raised areas on bone* are:

process: general term for an area that protrudes on bone

Articular surface found at a movable joint:

condyle: large rounded articular projection or surface

head: dome-shaped articular projection

Areas of muscle attachment:

tubercle: small rounded process

tuberosity: large rounded, rough process

trochanter: large blunt process (only on femur)

ridge: raised elongated area of bone

torus: thickened ridge

crest: relatively sharp narrow ridge

linea or *line*: raised elongated area that is not as marked as a ridge or a crest

spine: sharp slender projection

epicondyle: prominence above a condyle

Terms that refer to concave areas on bone:

fissure: narrow crack-like opening

foramen: holes for blood vessels and nerves to pass through (*plural:* foramina)

meatus: short canal

sulcus: furrow-like depression

fossa: dug-out area, depression

notch: indentation

An additional term is:

facet: a smooth flat surface for articulation; typically where little movement occurs

Selected Skull Features Below are some examples of prominent features found on some of the skull bones. Keep in mind that there are a multitude of such features. Your instructor may want to add more features to this list. Refer to a skull and to Photos 7.7–7.10 (and *Atlas* pp. 78, 83, 86, 87) to identify these features.

Skull bones:

> **Temporal** (Photos 7.7, 7.8):
> *external auditory meatus*
> *mastoid process*
> *styloid process*
> *mandibular fossa*
> *zygomatic process of zygomatic arch (together with zygomatic bone)*

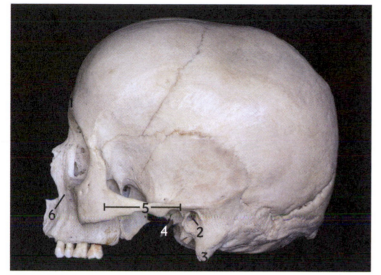

PHOTO 7.7 *Skull: Lateral view*

1. supraorbital ridge
2. external auditory meatus
3. mastoid process
4. styloid process
5. zygomatic arch
6. infraorbital foramen

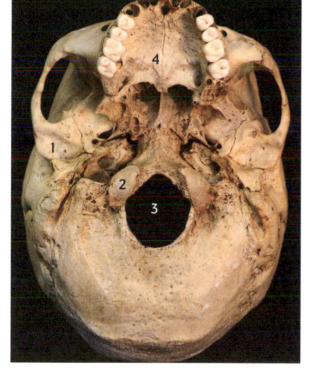

PHOTO 7.8
*Skull:
Inferior view*

1. mandibular
   fossa
2. occipital
   condyle
3. foramen
   magnum
4. hard palate
   (palatine
   process)

Zygomatic (Photo 7.7):
zygomatic arch (together with the temporal bone)

Ethmoid (Photo 7.9):
crista galli
cribriform plate (where olfactory bulbs sit)

Sphenoid (Photo 7.9):
sella turcica (the "compartment" for the pituitary
   gland; the gland "sits" in a depression called the
   hypophyseal fossa)

Mandible (Photo 7.10):
mental foramen
mandibular condyles (condyloid process)
body
ramus

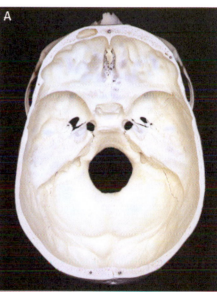

PHOTO 7.9 *Skull,
superior view*

1. crista galli
2. cribriform plate
3. sella turcica
4. hypophyseal fossa
5. frontal sinus

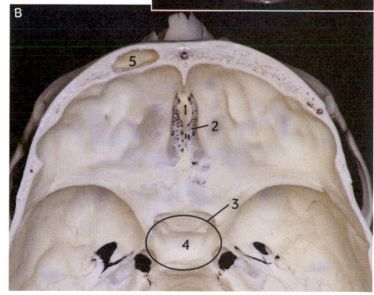

Occipital (Photo 7.8):
occipital condyles
foramen magnum

Maxilla (photos 7.7, 7.8):
infraorbital foramen
hard palate (palatine process)

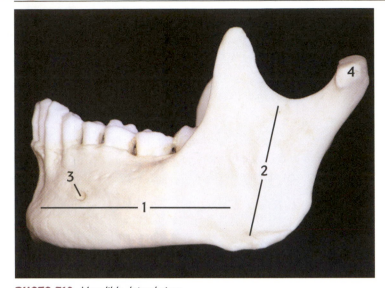

PHOTO 7.10 *Mandible, lateral view*

1. body
2. ramus
3. mental foramen
4. mandibular condyle (condyloid process)

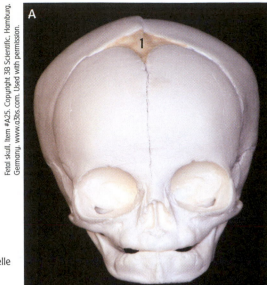

Fetal skull. Item #A25. Copyright 3B Scientific. Hamburg, Germany. www.a3bs.com. Used with permission.

PHOTO 7.11
Fetal skull

1. anterior fontanelle
2. sphenoidal fontanelle
3. mastoid fontanelle

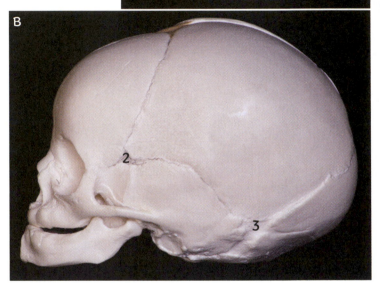

Fetal Skull A fetal or an infant skull exhibits some important differences from an adult skull. Take a look at a fetal skull and/or at Photo 7.11 and *Atlas* pp. 95–97. Notice the open sutures, allowing room for growth, and the large spaces between some of the bones. These spaces, termed **fontanels**, are the so-called "soft spots" on a baby's skull. Review the **metopic suture** in Photo 7.6. In an infant, the frontal bone and the mandible are composed of two bones. As the metopic suture and the mandibular symphysis *fuse, or* **ossify**, by 1 or 2 years of age, these bones combine into one.

Hyoid Bone

The bony support for your larynx, or voice box, is the hyoid bone. It connects via muscles and ligaments to the larynx and the temporal bones (see Figure 7.9). It is the only bone in the body without any direct bony articulations.

Etymology

In learning the names of bones and their features, it is helpful to know something about their Greek or Latin roots (etymology), because they typically are descriptive terms. Some of these roots are listed in the text when new bones or features are introduced. Others are given in Appendix C. The roots can be useful in memorizing the names.

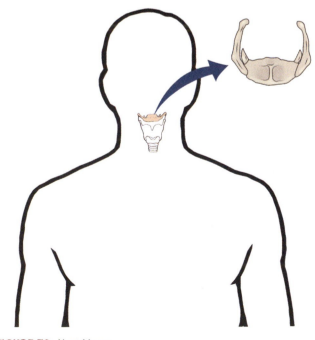

FIGURE 7.9 *Hyoid bone*

LAB EXERCISE
7.1

NAME _____

SECTION _____ DATE _____

1. Label the parts of a typical long bone.

a. _____

b. _____

c. _____

d. _____

e. _____

f. _____

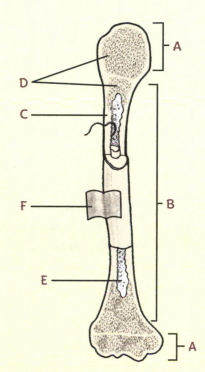

2. Label the planes of the body on the diagram at right.

a. _____

b. _____

c. _____

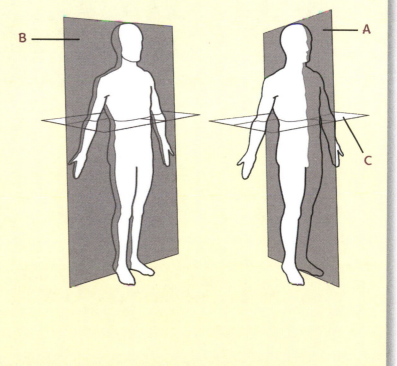

For the following, fill in the correct anatomical term:

3. Your knee is _____ relative to your navel.

4. Your navel is _____ relative to your right side.

5. Your nose is _____ relative to your ears.

6. Your ankle is _____ relative to your hip.

7. Provide labels for all of the bones learned so far.

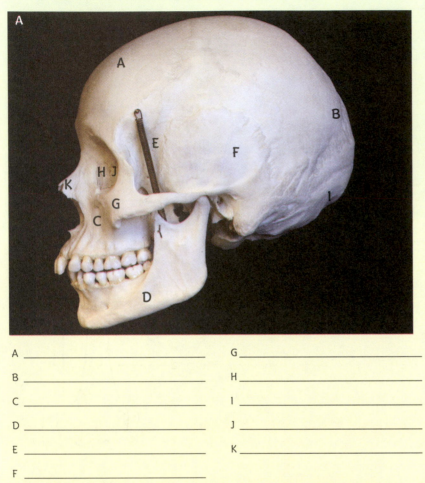

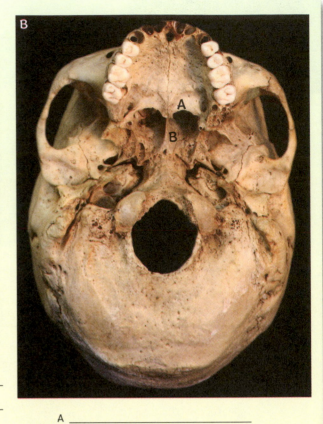

A _____   G _____

B _____   H _____

C _____   I _____

D _____   J _____

E _____   K _____

F _____

A _____

B _____

8. Label the four main sutures on the adult skull and the one learned for the fetal skull.

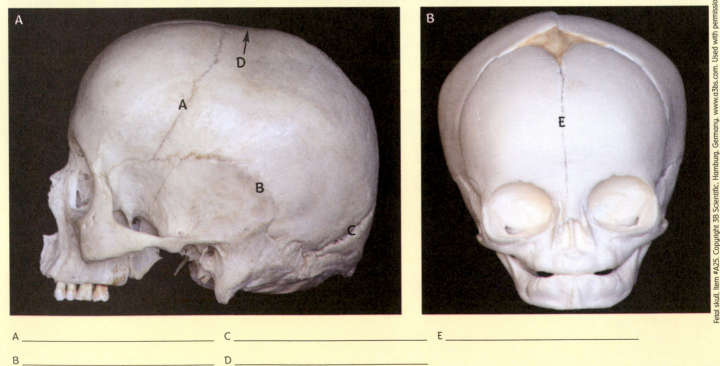

A _____   C _____   E _____

B _____   D _____

LAB EXERCISE
7.1 (CONT.)

NAME _____

SECTION _____ DATE _____

9. Which is which? Label each of the middle ear ossicles.

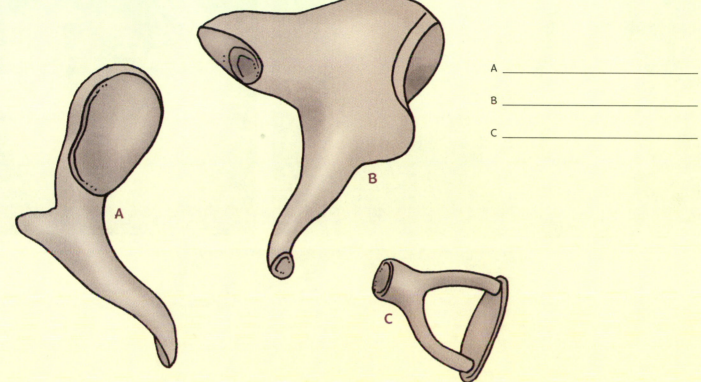

A _____

B _____

C _____

10. How many teeth, and of which type, do you have in your own mouth? Which have been pulled or otherwise lost?

11. Your canine is _____ relative to your first molar. (Use the directional terms for the tooth row, shown in Figure 7.7.)

12. Provide labels for all of the features learned so far.

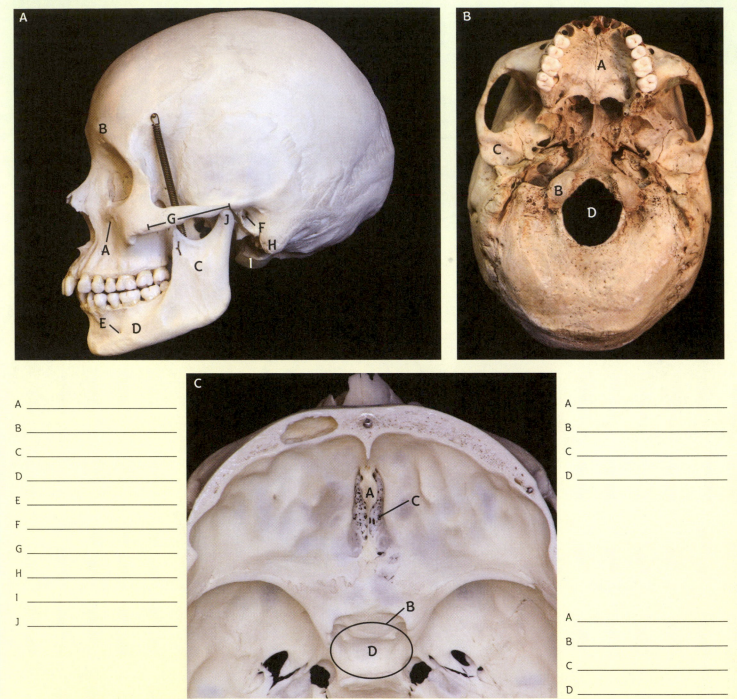

A _____

B _____

C _____

D _____

E _____

F _____

G _____

H _____

I _____

J _____

A _____

B _____

C _____

D _____

A _____

B _____

C _____

D _____

13. Take a look at the frontal bone. With which other bones does it articulate?

14. The bump on your skull just posterior to your ear is the _____.

15. Which bone is visible from anterior, lateral, and inferior views, and articulates anteriorly with the temporal bone?

| SELF-TEST | NAME _____ |
| **7.1** | SECTION _____ DATE _____ |

1. What are the five main functions of the skeleton? Briefly explain each.

2. What are some kinds of information that can be obtained from a skeleton?

3. What is an example of a long bone?

4. What are the two "portions" of the skeleton?

   a.

   b.

   Which appears first developmentally?

5. What are the two types of bone?

6. What set of terms is used specifically to refer to a position up or down the limbs?

7. What plane divides the body into left and right halves?

   Into front and back portions?

8. The name for the structures separating skull bones is _____.

9. In directional terms, where is:

   a. your thumb relative to your palm?

   b. a dog's tail relative to its lumbar vertebrae?

   c. your shin relative to your calf?

   d. a horse's belly relative to its back?

   e. your pinkie relative to your elbow?

10. The ear ossicles are found in the _____. Name these three bones.

    a. _____

    b. _____

    c. _____

11. What is the dental formula for humans (adults)?

12. If a mammal's entire top row of teeth consists of four incisors, two canines, two premolars, and four molars, and its lower tooth row consists of four incisors, two canines, two premolars, and two molars, what is its dental formula? (Remember: Dental formulae refer to one *quadrant* of a jaw!)

13. Where is the ethmoid bone relative to the lacrimal bone?

14. The name for a hole through bone is _____.

15. The real name for a "soft spot" on an infant's skull is _____.

16. The only bone in the body that does not articulate with any other bone is the _____.

Axial Skeleton Part II: Vertebral Column

The vertebral column is made up of five main regions, each of which has vertebrae with distinguishing characteristics based upon their function and their position in the column. Look at Figure 7.10 and *Atlas* p. 158. As you follow the vertebrae inferiorly, you'll see how they become larger and larger as they provide support for more and more body weight. Also notice the various regions of the spine and the characteristic curves, which together serve to bring the weight-bearing axis directly under the body.

All four types of vertebrae share several features. Photo 7.12 uses a thoracic vertebra as an example. The features found on most vertebrae include:

- *spinous process*
- *transverse processes*
- *superior and inferior articular surfaces.*
- *body*
- *vertebral foramen*
- *arch*

You should be able to identify each of these listed features on a vertebra (preferably a thoracic or lumbar), using Photo 7.12 as a guide.

Next we will learn the characteristics of individual types of vertebrae.

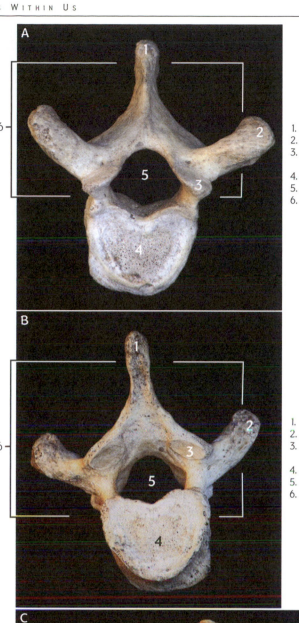

1. spinous process
2. transverse process
3. superior articular surface
4. body
5. vertebral foramen
6. arch

1. spinous process
2. transverse process
3. inferior articular surface
4. body
5. vertebral foramen
6. arch

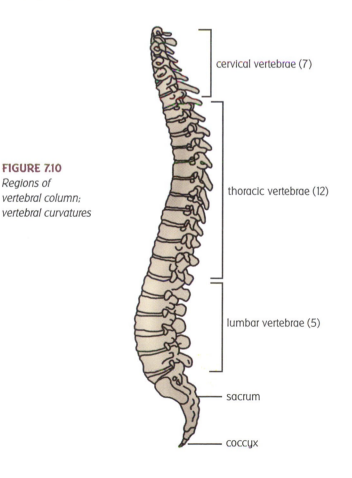

FIGURE 7.10
Regions of vertebral column; vertebral curvatures

cervical vertebrae (7)

thoracic vertebrae (12)

lumbar vertebrae (5)

sacrum

coccyx

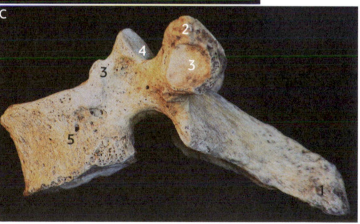

1. spinous process
2. transverse process
3. rib facets (only on thoracic)
4. superior articular surface
5. body

PHOTO 7.12 *Features of a typical vertebra (shown is a thoracic):* (**A**) *superior view,* (**B**) *inferior view,* (**C**) *lateral view*

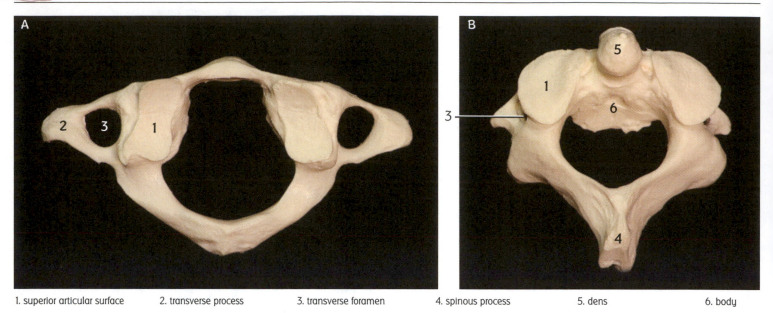

| 1. superior articular surface | 2. transverse process | 3. transverse foramen | 4. spinous process | 5. dens | 6. body |

PHOTO 7.13 *Features of an atlas (A) and an axis (B), superior view*

Cervical Vertebrae

The neck vertebrae are called *cervical vertebrae* (L *cervi:* neck). The homologous condition of the number of cervical vertebrae—seven—is common to all mammals and presumably is inherited from the mammalian common ancestor.

The two most superior vertebrae have some distinguishing features because of their unique role relative to the other vertebrae. The *atlas (CI)* supports the skull and has large articular facets for a wide range of movement (Photo 7.13A). The *axis (C2),* just inferior to the atlas, has a superior projection, the *dens,* which serves as an axis for the atlas to move about (Photo 7.13B). The other cervical vertebrae (C3 through C7) are more similar to one another (see Photo 7.14).

All seven cervical vertebrae have *transverse foramina* for passage of the transverse artery, vein, and nerve. Features of the cervical vertebrae are as follows (see also *Atlas* pp. 159, 160).

atlas (C1):
- no body
- large superior articulating facets
- barely discernable spinous process

axis (C2):
- dens (odontoid process)
- larger body than atlas

C3–C7:
- larger body than atlas or axis
- more prominent spinous process
- spinous process often bifid (forked)

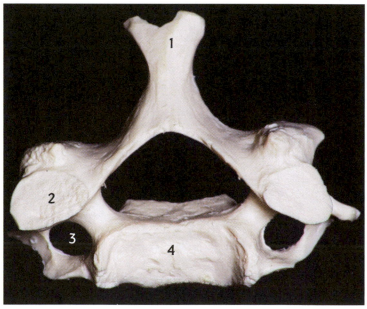

| 1. spinous process | 3. transverse foramen |
| 2. superior articular surface | 4. body |

PHOTO 7.14 *Cervical vertebrae C3–C7, superior view*

Thoracic Vertebrae

The *thoracic vertebrae* all articulate with ribs; hence, there are 12 of them. (Refer again to Photo 7.12, and *Atlas* pp. 161, 162). Features are:

- long, skinny, spinous process (except for the most inferior thoracic vertebrae)
- transverse process, thick compared to those of lumbar vertebrae

3B Classic Skeleton Skin, Item #A10. Copyright 3B Scientific, Hamburg, Germany, www.a3Bs.com. Used with permission.

PHOTO 7.15 *Articulation of thoracic vertebra with rib*
1. spinous process   2. transverse process   3. rib   4. articular facet on rib

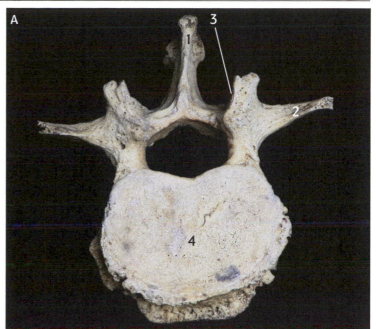

1. spinous process   2. transverse process   3. superior articular surface   4. body

- superior and inferior articular surfaces oriented laterally (side to side)
- rib facets on body of vertebra and on transverse process.

Looking at an articulated skeleton (or, in its absence, Photo 7.15), observe the articulations of the ribs with the thoracic vertebrae. Most of the ribs articulate with the thoracic vertebrae in two places, on the flattened **facets** located laterally on the body and on the transverse processes.

Lumbar Vertebrae

The five *lumbar vertebrae* bear the most weight and thus are the largest vertebrae (*see* Photo 7.16 and *Atlas* pp. 163, 164)

- spinous processes short and squared-off
- is superior and inferior articular surfaces oriented antero-posteriorly (front to back)
- has no rib facets.

The adjacent 12th thoracic vertebra and first lumbar vertebra are similar in size and overall shape. Photo 7.17 highlights the differences so you can learn to distinguish them from each other (see also *Atlas* p. 162, Figure 5.13).

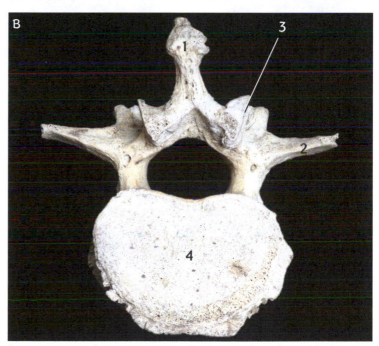

1. spinous process   2. transverse process   3. inferior articular surface   4. body

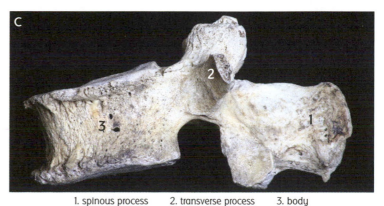

1. spinous process   2. transverse process   3. body

PHOTO 7.16 *Lumbar vertebrae, (A) superior view, (B) inferior view, (C) lateral view*

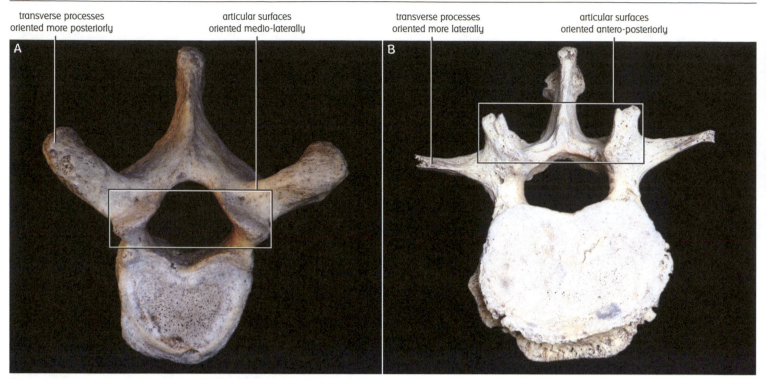

transverse processes oriented more posteriorly | articular surfaces oriented medio-laterally | transverse processes oriented more laterally | articular surfaces oriented antero-posteriorly

PHOTO 7.17 *Comparison of thoracic and lumbar vertebrae, superior view*

Sacrum

The *sacrum* is made up of five fused vertebrae (see Figure 7.11 and *Atlas* p.165). Together, the sacrum and the two pelvic (*innominate*) bones articulate at the sacroiliac joint to form the pelvic girdle.

Coccyx

The *coccyx* is the small remnant of the caudal vertebrae that make up the tail in most vertebrates—hence the nickname "tailbone." It is made up of about four fused vertebrae (see Photo 7.18 and *Atlas* p. 165), and sometimes is fused to the sacrum.

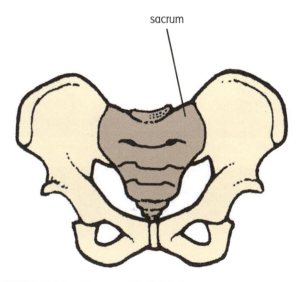

sacrum

FIGURE 7.11 *Pelvis with sacrum highlighted*

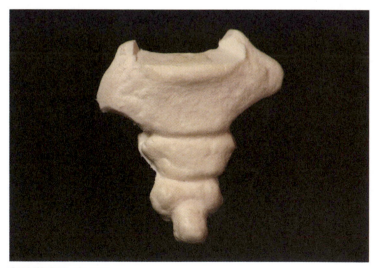

PHOTO 7.18 *Coccyx*

Axial Skeleton Part III: Thorax

The bony thorax provides protection for the heart and lungs. It consists of

- the *sternum* (breastbone)
- the *ribs*
- the *costal cartilage*

Referring to Photo 7.19, the uppermost seven ribs (the "true" ribs) articulate with the thoracic vertebrae posteriorly, then come around anteriorly to articulate with the sternum. The 8th through the 10th ribs (called "false" ribs) have no direct connection. Here, a cartilaginous structure, the costal cartilage (L *cost*: rib), stretches between the anterior margin of the ribs and the sternum. Particularly note the 11th and 12th ribs in the photo. These, the smallest and most inferior ribs, articulate posteriorly with the 11th and 12th thoracic vertebrae. Because they have no anterior connection, they are called "floating" ribs. There are no differences between the sexes in numbers of ribs—both males and females have 12!

Sternum

The three main parts of the sternum are (see Photo 7.20 and *Atlas* p. 166)

- *manubrium*
- *body*
- *xiphoid process*.

Obvious features include the *clavicular notches* and the *jugular notch* (both on the manubrium, but not shown here), and the *costal notches* for the attachment of the ribs (or the costal cartilage) on the body of the sternum.

PHOTO 7.20 *Features of the sternum*

1. manubrium
2. body
3. xiphoid process
4. costal notches

Ribs

Most ribs have the following features (see Photo 7.21 and *Atlas* pp. 166, 167):

- *head*: articulates with the rib facet on the transverse process of a thoracic vertebra
- *tubercle*: a process near the head for articulation with the rib facet on the body of a thoracic vertebra
- sharpened *inferior border*, useful for siding the ribs

To distinguish the left from the right ribs, find the sharpened lower (inferior) border of the rib, then orient it so the head of the rib is on the posterior aspect.

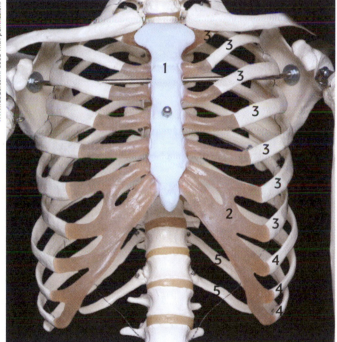

PHOTO 7.19 *Thorax, showing ribs, sternum, and costal cartilage*

1. sternum
2. costal cartilage
3. true ribs
4. false ribs
5. floating ribs

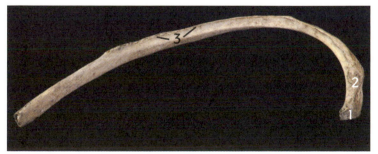

PHOTO 7.21 *Features of a typical "true" rib, inferior view*

1. head   2. tubercle   3. inferior border

LAB EXERCISE
7.2

NAME _____

SECTION _____ DATE _____

1. In your lab, find and identify the following vertebrae, then note, below, the features you used for your identifications. If no skeletal material is available, use Photos A–E (not all vertebrae are represented by photos here):

atlas:

axis:

representative of C3–C7:

thoracic vertebra:

lumbar vertebra:

sacrum:

coccyx:

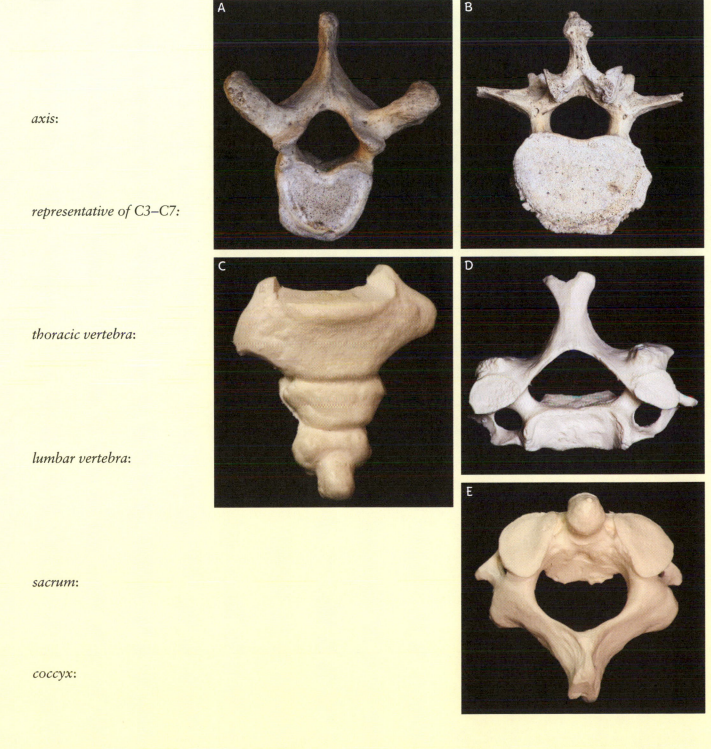

2. Observe a sternum (or a photo). Identify and list the three main portions.

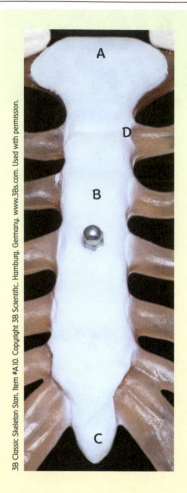

3. In your lab collection, side three ribs (the top ones are more difficult, so you may want to choose other, more "typical" ribs). How did you go about determining which side of the body they were from?

4. Look at a rib and a thoracic vertebra. Identify the head and the tubercle of a rib. Point out the corresponding points of articulation on a thoracic vertebra, and fit them (at least approximately) together.

SELF-TEST
7.2

NAME _____

SECTION _____ DATE _____

1. What are the components of the axial skeleton?

2. What are the five kinds of vertebrae?

3. Name a feature that differentiates all seven cervical vertebrae from the other vertebrae.

4. Name two features that are used to distinguish each of these vertebral types from one another.

   cervical:

   thoracic:

   lumbar:

5. Why does the human vertebral column have curves?

6. What are the three components of the thorax?

7. What is the difference between a true rib, a false rib, and a floating rib?

8. Point to the approximate location of the xiphoid process on yourself.

Appendicular Skeleton

The human body is unique. We exhibit features in the *post-cranial* skeleton (the skeleton from the neck down) that reflect our bipedal ancestry. We evolved from arboreal hominoids with a highly mobile upper limb, which we still possess. Our lower limb obviously is adapted for **bipedalism**, for which we use only two limbs to support all of our body weight. Therefore, we have a robust and relatively long lower limb.

We will explore the relationship between body form and function further in Chapter 9. For the remainder of this chapter, we will learn the bones, some relevant features, and function of the appendicular skeleton.

You will work your way through the appendicular skeleton, identifying the bones and their features using the figures in this chapter and any laboratory material available to you. In learning the features, pay attention to their location on the bone (using anatomical terminology). Knowledge of the position of features on paired bones will allow you to successfully distinguish whether a specific bone is from the right or the left side of the body. To "side" a bone, it is helpful to hold it close to your body as if it were your own bone.

Muscle Attachments

Muscles insert onto bone via tendons. Most muscles cross one joint, *originating* on one bone and *inserting* on another. When a muscle contracts, it shortens and reduces the angle between the two bones. A muscle **origin** is the site from which a muscle arises. A muscle pulls toward its origin, which usually is fixed and more proximal. A muscle **insertion** is the site where a muscle grabs hold of the second bone. This site is usually on the mobile bone and is more distal.

By contracting, muscles are responsible for performing various actions. The location of the origin and insertion (how near to or far from a joint) and the size of the muscle determine the magnitude of its strength and its speed. Many *muscle actions* are paired and opposites; one set of muscles produces a certain action at a joint, and another produces the opposite action. Many of the following muscle actions will be familiar to you already.

flexion:　　　acts to bend or reduce the angle between two bones

extension:　　acts to increase the angle between two bones

abduction:　　movement of a body part away from the longitudinal axis of the body (or, in the hand, from a specified digit)

adduction:　　movement of a body part toward the longitudinal body axis (or toward a specified digit)

rotation:　　the act of a bone turning around its axis; for example, rotation of the radius around the ulna produces the specific actions:

pronation:　　palm of the hand turning toward the posterior aspect

supination:　　palm of the hand turning toward the anterior aspect

inversion:　　turns the sole of the foot inward

eversion:　　turns the sole of the foot outward

protraction:　　a bone is drawn forward

retraction:　　a bone is drawn backward

circumduction:　　a circular movement at a joint, produced by numerous individual muscle actions (for example, making a cone shape with the arm, a movement produced at the shoulder joint)

Pectoral (Shoulder) Girdle

Typically, a "girdle" is a stable feature that encircles (more like the pelvic girdle). Earlier vertebrate ancestors had a more stable, encircling pectoral girdle, whereas ours is adapted to mobility. The pectoral girdle consists of two bones:

- *clavicle*
- *scapula.*

Both of these names probably are familiar to you, but they are known more commonly as the collarbone and the shoulder blade, respectively. The articulation between these two bones is only superficial and occurs at the lateral end of the clavicle (see Photo 7.22 and *Atlas* p. 168).

Feel along your clavicle out toward the lateral end. When you get to a bump, you've probably found the articulation between the lateral (acromial) end of the clavicle and the *acromion* process of the scapula.

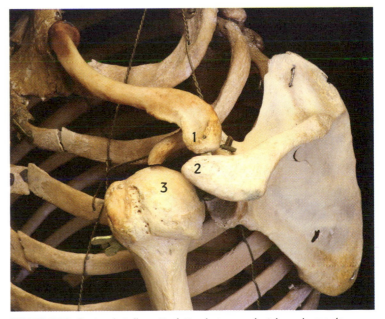

PHOTO 7.22 *Pectoral girdle; articulation between clavicle and scapula*
1. acromial end of clavicle　　2. acromion process of scapula　　3. head of humerus

Clavicle The clavicle acts as a "strut" to keep the upper limb away from the body, providing greater leverage for muscle actions taking place at the shoulder joint. Its "S" shape resists fracture more efficiently than would a straight bone. The *inferior surface* tends to be more *rugose*, or rough, than the *superior surface*, because more muscle insertions occur on the underside of the clavicle (see Photo 7.23 and *Atlas* p. 170). The *sternal end* is "fatter" and rounder than is the *acromial end*. (Remember that the sternal end is medial and the acromial end is lateral.)

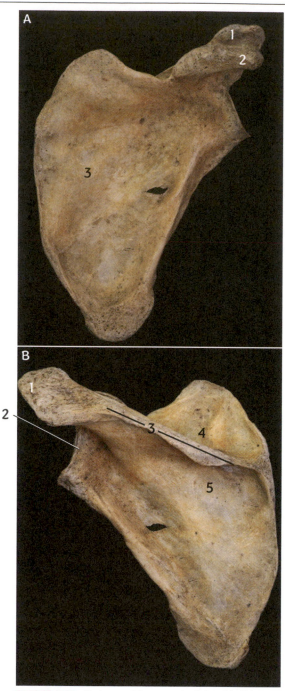

1. acromion process
2. coracoid process
3. subscapular fossa

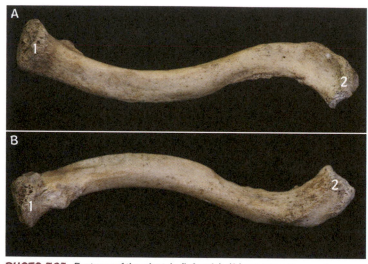

PHOTO 7.23 *Features of the clavicle (left side):* **(A)** *superior view and* **(B)** *inferior view*

1. sternal end   2. acromial end

Scapula Each scapula slides around on your back as you shrug your shoulders or move your shoulder forward or backward. It has muscular attachments to the vertebral column and to the humerus. The anterior, or ventral, side of the scapula has a somewhat "scooped out" appearance; this depression is the *subscapular fossa* (see Photo 7.24 and *Atlas* p. 168. The posterior, or dorsal, aspect has more features.

The *scapular spine* is one of the attachment sites for an important muscle that lifts the arm, the deltoid. The scapular spine divides the scapula into upper and lower sections, the *supraspinous fossa* and the *infraspinous fossa*. The articulation of the head of the humerus with the scapula occurs at the pear-shaped depression, the *glenoid fossa*. Two other important features are the *acromion process,* to which you were introduced as the articulation with the lateral end of the clavicle, and the beak-like *coracoid process* (G *cora*: crow, raven).

Study a clavicle and scapula to identify the features labeled in Photos 7.23 and 7.24, and *Atlas* p. 168–170.

1. acromion process
2. glenoid fossa
3. scapular spine
4. supraspinous fossa
5. infraspinous fossa

PHOTO 7.24 *Features of the scapula (left side):* **(A)** *anterior view and* **(B)** *posterior view*

Upper Limb

The upper limb articulates with the body axis at the *shoulder joint,* which is the connection between the scapula and the humerus. This type of articulation is referred to as a *ball-and-socket joint* and allows for a wide range of motion, particularly because there are few bony constraints surrounding the joint.

Humerus The upper arm has a single bone, the *humerus*. Locate the features listed below on Photo 7.25 (and *Atlas* p. 171) and on an actual bone. The main features located at the proximal humerus are:

head: articulates with glenoid fossa of scapula

greater tubercle: point of origin for rotator cuff muscles; anteriorly located

lesser tubercle: smaller process, antero-medially located

bicipital groove (intertubercular sulcus): tendon for a portion of the biceps muscle runs through this groove; anterior

About halfway down the *shaft* of the humerus lies the *deltoid tuberosity*: place of insertion for deltoid muscle

At the distal humerus, the main features are:

olecranon fossa: depression for articulation with the olecranon process of the proximal ulna; on posterior side

trochlea: spool-shaped feature that articulates with ulna

capitulum: rounded feature for articulation with depression at head of radius

lateral epicondyle: protrusion superior to capitulum; on lateral side

medial epicondyle: protrusion superior to trochlea; on medial side

For siding purposes, remember that the humeral head faces medially (toward the glenoid of the scapula) and the olecranon fossa is posterior.

Radius The *radius* and the *ulna* together make up the bones of the forearm. You can palpate (feel) them in your own arm, especially near your wrist. Both bones articulate with the humerus at their proximal end. The radius is located on the lateral side of the ulna. Remember to picture the body in the *anatomical position*, with palms facing forward and thumbs out to the sides. When you *pronate* your hand at the wrist, you cause the distal end of the radius to cross over the ulna.

At the proximal end of the radius, the primary features (Photo 7.26 and *Atlas* p. 174) are the

head: shaped like a horse's hoof, the very end is depressed for articulation with the rounded capitulum of the humerus

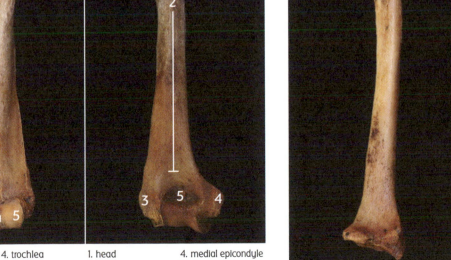

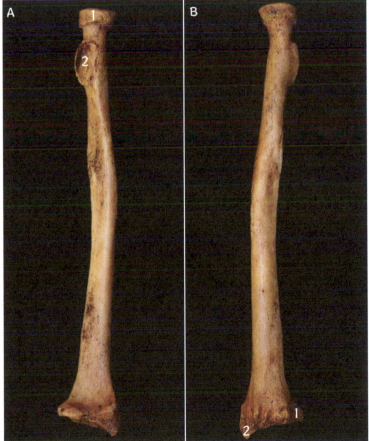

1. greater tubercle	4. trochlea
2. lesser tubercle	5. capitulum
3. deltoid tuberosity	6. bicipital groove

1. head	4. medial epicondyle
2. shaft	5. olecranon fossa
3. lateral epicondyle	

PHOTO 7.25 *Features of the humerus (left side):* **(A)** *anterior view and* **(B)** *posterior view*

| 1. head | 2. radial tuberosity |

| 1. ulnar notch | 2. styloid process |

PHOTO 7.26 *Features of the radius (left side):* **(A)** *anterior view and* **(B)** *posterior view*

| radial tuberosity: | bump near radial head; muscle attachment site |
| ulnar notch: | semilunar-shaped depression found on the medial aspect for articulation with the ulna |

The main feature at the distal end is the

| styloid process: | distal extended tip of radius |

Ulna At the proximal end are the two primary features (Photo 7.27 and *Atlas* pp. 175 and 176):

| olecranon process: | uppermost posterior portion of the ulna; in humans and apes, it is not prominent, but in quadrupeds it is large and prevents full extension of the arm at the elbow |
| radial notch: | a depression for articulation of the rounded portion of the radial head |

At the distal end of the ulna is the

| styloid process: | sharper than the like-named feature on the radius; it is a pointy extension |

PHOTO 7.27
Features of the ulna (left side)

1. olecranon process
2. trochlear notch
3. radial notch
4. styloid process

The Hand and Wrist

Carpal Bones The bones of the wrist are referred to as *carpal bones* (G *carp*: wrist). The anatomical term for the wrist is the *carpus*. Humans have eight carpal bones; apes have nine. The bones of the wrist can be roughly divided into a proximal row and a distal row (Photo 7.28 and *Atlas* p. 178). The proximal row, from the medial to the lateral side, consists of the *pisiform, triquetrum (triquetral), lunate,* and *scaphoid (navicular)*. The distal row contains the *hamate, capitate, trapezoid,* and *trapezium.*

Hand Bones The row of bones immediately distal to the carpals consists of the *metacarpals* (see Photo 7.28 and *Atlas* p. 178). These can be easily palpated between your palm and the back of your hand. The bones making up your fingers and thumb are *phalanges* (singular: *phalanx*). The first row, articulating with the metacarpals, consists of the *proximal phalanges*. You can see these as the first section of each finger and of your thumb. The next row consists of the *middle phalanges* and is found only in your fingers. Note that your thumb consists of only two sections (and thus two bones). Your finger and thumb tips are on your *distal phalanges*. The fingers are numbered one through five, with Digit I referring to the thumb, and Digit V the pinkie.

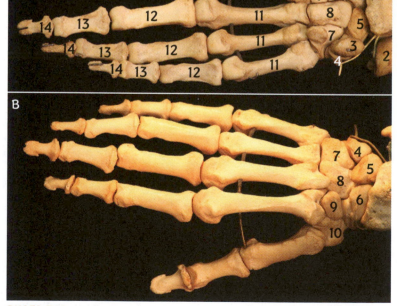

PHOTO 7.28 *Hand and carpal bones (right side):* **(A)** *palmar view and* **(B)** *dorsal view*

1. distal radius	5. lunate	9. trapezoid	13. middle phalanges
2. distal ulna	6. scaphoid	10. trapezium	
3. pisiform	7. hamate	11. metacarpals	14. distal phalanges
4. triquetrum	8. capitate	12. proximal phalanges	

LAB EXERCISE
7.3

NAME _____

SECTION _____ DATE _____

1. Review and perform the following muscle actions with your lab partner:

   a. pronation of hand
   b. flexion of arm at elbow
   c. extension of leg at knee
   d. eversion of foot
   e. flexion of leg at hip
   f. abduction of arm
   g. adduction of arm

2. Side a clavicle.

3. Side a scapula.

4. Find a clavicle and a scapula from the same side, then articulate them properly, using an articulated skeleton or Photo 7.22 as a guide.

5. Find a humerus, or use the photo of the humerus (at right).

   a. Side the humerus.

   b. List the features you used to orient the bone and determine the side.

   c. Locate and list one feature at the anterior end of the humerus, and one at the distal end.

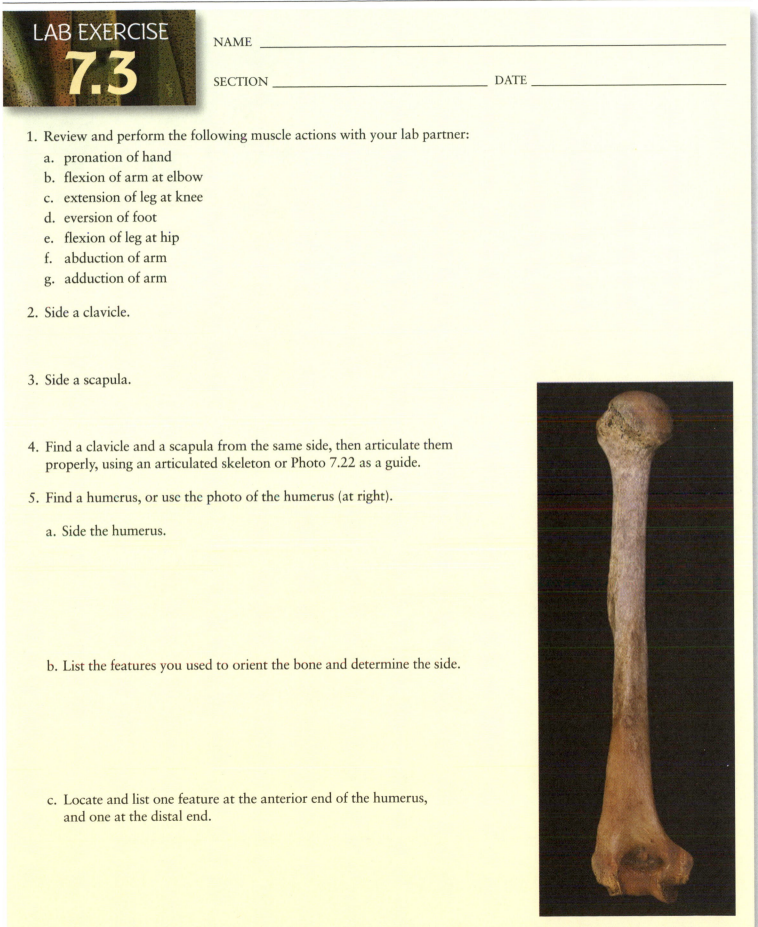

6. Find a radius and an ulna from the same side, then articulate them properly, using an articulated skeleton or the photo as a guide.

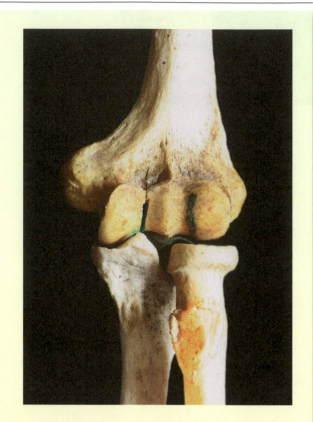

7. Two relatively easily identifiable carpal bones are the pisiform (G *pis*: pea; this is a hint!) and the hamate. The pisiform is the medial-most bone, and the hamate has an appropriately named feature called a *hook* on the anterior (palmar) side. Identify these bones on either a disarticulated or an articulated hand (or use the photo below).

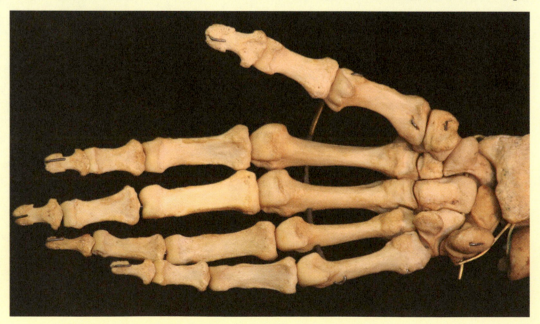

8. Observe the very tip of the distal phalanx of the thumb. You will notice a slightly rounded, expanded, roughened area. What do you think this feature relates to, and why might it be much smaller in our close relatives, the apes?

NAME _____

SECTION _____ DATE _____

1. What is the difference between the appendicular skeleton and the postcranial skeleton?

2. Briefly explain the basic way in which muscles function.

3. What is the difference between the pectoral girdle and the shoulder joint?

4. What are the points of articulation between the humerus and the scapula?

5. What are the features that serve as the articulating points between the humerus and the ulna?

Between the humerus and the radius?

6. What is the anatomical name for the wrist bones?

7. The first row of bones immediately distal to the wrist bones consists of _____.

8. The name of the bone underneath the fingertip of your index finger is the _____ _____

of digit _____.

Pelvic Girdle

Numerous features apparent in the bones of the pelvic girdle relate to bipedalism and differ from the form of these bones in the apes. Again, the pelvic girdle is composed of the two pelvic (*innominate*) bones and the sacrum (Photo 7.29A and *Atlas* p. 181).

Innominate Bones   The two innominate bones are each made up of three bones that fuse during the early teen years—the *ilium*, the *ischium*, and the *pubis* (Photo 7.29A and *Atlas* p. 182). The pelvis is extremely useful for distinguishing the sex of skeletons. As you orient the pelvis, note that the ischium is wider than the pubis. The two innominate bones articulate with each other at the pubis, where a pad of fibrocartilage makes up the *pubic symphysis*.

The pelvic features labeled in Photo 7.29 (see also *Atlas* p. 182) will be used later to side the bones, to determine sex, and to make comparisons with other species. These include the:

iliac crest:	ridge of bone along the superior margin of the ilium
iliac fossa:	internal portion of the ilium, a large scooped-out area
anterior inferior iliac spine:	large process on anterior aspect of ilium; origin for *rectus femoris* muscle, a key muscle for propulsion in bipedal locomotion
greater sciatic notch:	large notch on posterior aspect of ilium; helpful in making determination of sex
acetabulum:	large fossa for articulation with femoral head; hip socket
obturator foramen:	large foramen on anterior aspect of pelvis
ischial tuberosity:	roughened areas on the inferior-most portion of the ischium; the area we sit on
pubic symphysis:	the joining of the pubic regions of two innominates

1. Put your hands on your hips. You're putting your hands on the iliac crest (with a few layers of tissue between your hands and the actual pelvis, of course).

2. Sit down hard on a hard surface (but don't break your coccyx!). Those are your ischial tuberosities that you can feel in contact with the substrate.

3. Pick up an innominate bone. Hold it in front of your own hips, and orient it the way it would be placed if it were in your body. Remember—the pubis is anterior and must point (orient) medially if it is to meet up with the pubis from the other innominate bone.

4. Side the bone, using what you know about the position of the pubis and the ischium, and/or using an articulated skeleton or referring to Photo 7.29 of the innominate.

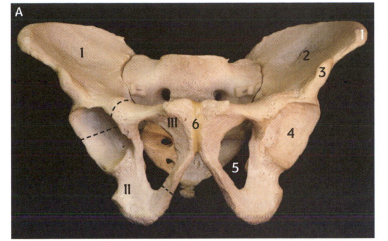

I ilium	1. iliac crest	4. acetabulum
II ischium	2. iliac fossa	5. obturator foramen
III pubis	3. anterior inferior iliac spine	6. pubic symphysis

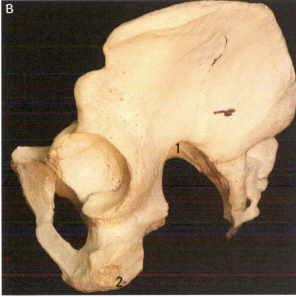

1. greater sciatic notch
2. ischial tuberosity

PHOTO 7.29 *Features of the innominate: (A) anterior, and (B) and lateral*

Lower Limb

The lower limb articulates with the body axis at the *hip joint*, which is the connection between the pelvis and the femur. Like the shoulder, the hip is a ball-and-socket joint, although the range of motion is less because of more bony constraints. The acetabulum of the pelvis is much more stable and protective than is the glenoid fossa of the scapula. This is necessary because the hip is a weight-bearing joint. Numerous changes in the lower limb occurred during the evolution of our quadrupedal ancestors to efficient bipeds.

Femur   The femur is relatively large and robust and angles inward from hip to knee, which brings the weight-bearing load more in line with our center of gravity. The features highlighted in the photo are important either for siding the bone or making comparisons of the adaptations of our extant and extinct relatives (Photo 7.30 and *Atlas* pp. 186–187).

At the proximal end, the key features are the

head: large and robust in humans; set off from the shaft of the femur by a *neck*; faces medially for articulation with acetabulum of pelvic bones

greater trochanter: large superior projection; attachment point for hip muscles

lesser trochanter: smaller process on posterior aspect

On the posterior aspect, running down much of the femoral shaft, is the

linea aspera (L *lin*: line; *asper*: rough):   insertion of the adductor muscles, which bring the leg around to the center with each step, an important aspect of human bipedalism

The primary features at the distal end are the

medial condyle: rounded articulation area for the medial condyle of the tibia

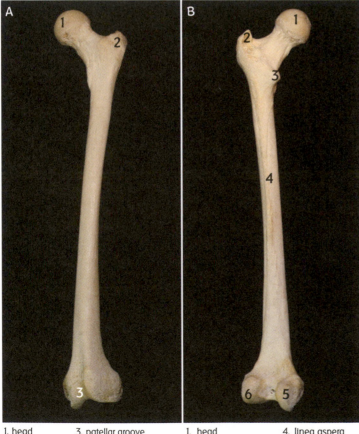

1. head   3. patellar groove
2. greater trochanter

1. head   4. linea aspera
2. greater trochanter   5. medial condyle
3. lesser trochanter   6. lateral condyle

PHOTO 7.30 *Features of the femur (left side):* (**A**) *anterior view and* (**B**) *posterior view*

lateral condyle: rounded articulation area for the lateral condyle of the tibia

patellar groove: anterior depression, the sides of which are formed by the medial and lateral condyles; the patella rests in this groove

Patella   The patella is a *sesamoid* (G *sesam*: sesame) bone. Sesamoid bones form within the tendons of some joints, acting rather like a pulley to move a muscle away from a joint and provide enhanced leverage for the muscle's action. The patella is the largest sesamoid in the body; most of the others are so small that they rarely are found with a skeleton.

Besides being able to tell anterior from posterior (the posterior side is smooth from articulation with the femur), the important distinctions to make are between these two features:

apex: pointed end; distal-most part of the patella

base: gently rounded end; proximal portion of the patella

The facet for the lateral condyle of the femur is larger than for the medial side, and the entire lateral side of the patella is somewhat larger and heavier (Photo 7.31 and *Atlas* p. 191). This makes siding the patella very simple.

To side a patella:

1. Identify the apex and the posterior (dorsal) surface of the patella.

2. Point the apex away from you and put the patella down on its posterior surface, balancing it momentarily on the ridge between the facets for the medial and lateral femoral condyles.

3. Let go. The patella will tip toward the lateral side. Thus, if it falls to the right, it is a right patella.

Tibia   The tibia articulates distally with the femur. Together, the tibia and the fibula comprise the lower leg bones (Photo 7.32 and *Atlas* p. 189). The tibia is commonly referred to as the shin bone.

medial condyle: articulates proximally with the medial condyle of the femur

lateral condyle: articulates proximally with the lateral condyle of the femur

anterior tibial tuberosity: roughened area on anterior aspect; insertion of *rectus femoris* muscle; can be palpated as a bump just distal to the patella

medial malleolus: distally located process on tibia; useful for siding the bone; located on medial side

PHOTO 7.31 *Patella (left side; note the arthritic growth):* **(A)** *anterior view and* **(B)** *posterior view*

1. base   2. apex

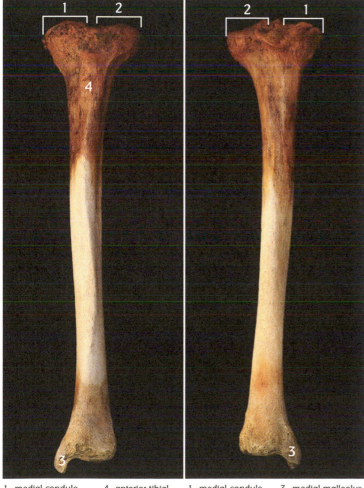

1. medial condyle   4. anterior tibial   1. medial condyle   3. medial malleolus
2. lateral condyle   tuberosity   2. lateral condyle
3. medial malleolus

PHOTO 7.32 *Features of the tibia (left side):* **(A)** *anterior view and* **(B)** *posterior view*

Fibula The fibula is a long, skinny bone that articulates laterally with the tibia (Photo 7.33 and *Atlas* p. 191). The proximal and distal ends initially can be difficult to distinguish from one another.

head: proximally located feature, which is "blockier" and more compressed than the distal end

lateral malleolus: distal end of tibia; longer and more drawn-out than the head, almost arrowhead-shaped

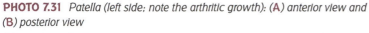

PHOTO 7.33 *Features of the fibula (left side)*
1. head   2. lateral malleolus

The medial malleolus of the tibia and the lateral malleolus of the fibula together enclose the most proximal of the ankle bones, the *talus.* Both of these processes can be felt as bumps on the medial and lateral sides of the ankle.

The Foot and Ankle

Tarsal Bones The bones of the ankle are referred to as *tarsal bones* (G *tars:* ankle), and the term for the ankle is the *tarsus*. Humans have seven tarsal bones. The two largest bones are also the most proximally located: the *calcaneus* (heel bone) and the *talus* (astragalus). The talus articulates distally with the *navicular,* and the rest of the tarsal bones—*cuboid, lateral cuneiform, intermediate cuneiform,* and *medial cuneiform*—form a row that articulates with the foot bones (*see* Photo 7.34 and *Atlas* p. 192).

Foot Bones The row of bones immediately distal to the tarsals consists of the *metatarsals* (Photo 7.34 and *Atlas* p. 192). These can be easily palpated between the sole and the back of your foot. As in the fingers, the bones making up the toes are the *phalanges* (singular: *phalanx*). The first row, articulating with the metatarsals, consists of the *proximal phalanges*. The next row contains *middle phalanges* (except in the big toe, which, like the thumb, has only two bones). The tips of the toes are the *distal phalanges*. As in the hand, the toes are numbered one through five, with Digit I referring to the big toe and Digit V, the little toe.

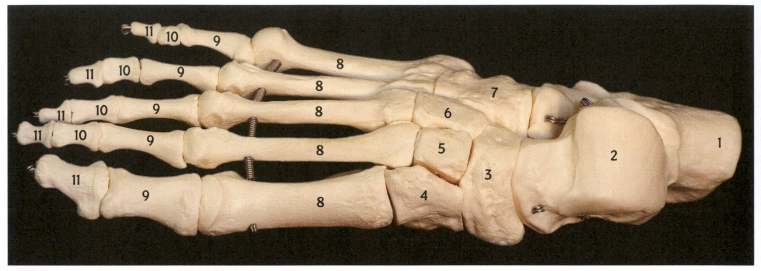

PHOTO 7.34 *Tarsal and foot bones (right side), dorsal view*

1. calcaneus	4. medial cuneiform	7. cuboid	10. middle phalanges
2. talus	5. intermediate cuneiform	8. metatarsals	11. distal phalanges
3. navicular	6. lateral cuneiform	9. proximal phalanges	

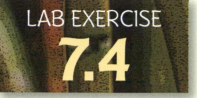

LAB EXERCISE
7.4

NAME _____

SECTION _____ DATE _____

1. Identify the following features on an innominate bone (or use the photo for identification):

   anterior inferior iliac spine   sciatic notch   pubis   ischium   obturator foramen

   Side the bone (or a specimen in your lab).

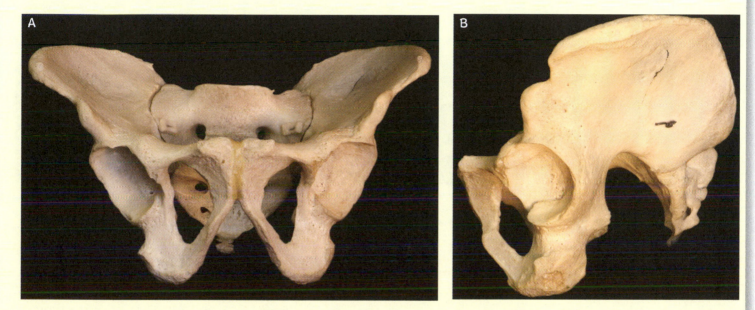

2. Side a femur. What features did you use to determine the side? (Use the photo for reference.)

3. Identify the *linea aspera* on a femur (or on the photo). What directional term best describes the location of this feature on the femur?

4. Find a tibia that comes from the same side as the femur, and articulate the two bones. What features did you use to determine the side of the tibia?

5. For a fibula, determine which is the proximal end and which is the distal end. What are the names of the features at each end?

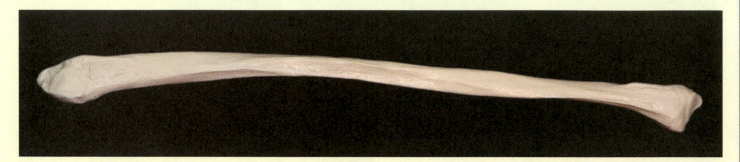

6. Identify the calcaneus and the talus on an articulated foot, disarticulated bones, or on the photo. Also identify the proximal phalanx of Digit V.

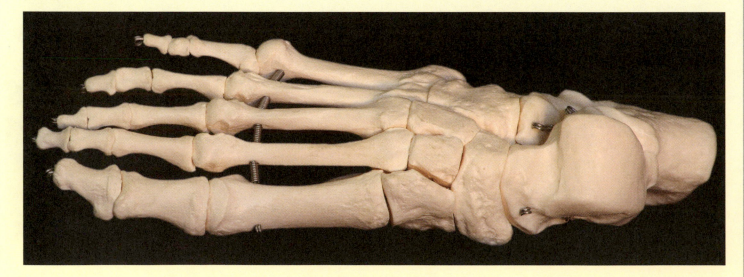

SELF-TEST 7.4

NAME _____

SECTION _____ DATE _____

1. How can you tell the difference between a humerus and a femur?

2. What bones make up the pelvic girdle?

3. What is the name for the heel bone?

4. Which is the lateral of the two lower leg bones?

5. The first row of bones distal to the ankle bones (tarsals) are the _____.

6. What are the names for the features of the femur and the innominate that articulate at the hip joint?

7. The talus is enclosed by the _____ _____ of the tibia and the _____ _____ of the fibula.

ONE STEP FURTHER

NAME _____

SECTION _____ DATE _____

Additional Lab Exercise 7.1

Work with your partner, but each use your own body to identify these parts of your skeleton.

1. Name the bone and the feature for each:
   a. the bump on the back of your wrist (posterior, medial)

   b. the bump on your inner ankle

   c. the bump on your outer ankle

   d. your knuckles

   e. your elbow

   f. your knee

   g. your chin

2. Follow your scapular spine laterally. What feature is at its end?

3. What is the bony bump behind your ear?

4. Run your fingers along your lower jaw toward the back (posteriorly). What feature is at the very back (corner of your jaw), and what is the entire bone called?

5. The tip of your nose is made of cartilage. Follow your nose up toward your forehead, until you reach bone. What bone is it (are they)?

6. Your eyebrows lie on what bone, and on what feature? (This feature usually is more pronounced on males.)

7. Put your hands on your hips. What bone, and what part of the bone, are your hands on?

8. Follow one of your cheekbones posteriorly toward your ear. What feature runs along that path, and on what two bones?

9. What features make up the bumps that you can feel along the midline of your back?

10. From a sitting position, put your hand on your kneecap (patella). Move your hand distally just an inch or so. What is the next bump that you can feel? What feature, and on what bone?

ONE STEP FURTHER

NAME _____

SECTION _____ DATE _____

Additional Self-Test Questions

Learning which bones connect with which other bones, and how to articulate them properly, is important.

1. Which two bones articulate distally with the humerus?

2. The clavicle and the costal cartilage of the ribs articulate with what bone on the ventral aspect of the body?

3. With which two other bones does the innonimate articulate?

4. What bones are proximal to the foot and distal to the femur?

5. What is the name for the bones at the tip of the second through fifth toes?

6. What bones articulate with the parietals?

7. What is a sesamoid bone? Give an example.

Forensic Anthropology

"Have you ever wondered . . . ?"

- How you can tell a male skeleton from a female skeleton?

OBJECTIVES

- Become aware of the range of information that can be obtained from a skeleton
- Understand the sources of biological variation of the skeleton
- Learn to use anthropometric tools
- Learn anthropometric techniques and gain experience in data collection
- Learn examples of qualitative and quantitative skeletal traits to estimate/determine age, sex, ancestry, and stature

MATERIALS NEEDED

- Sliding caliper
- Spreading caliper
- Calculator
- At least three human skulls
- At least three human innominate bones (from three individuals) or complete pelves
- One human femur

(One Step Further will require additional materials; see Additional Lab Exercises 8.1 and 8.2.)

Note to Instructor: In the place of, or in addition to, Chapter 8 Lab Exercises, questions associated with three forensic anthropology movies are available as links from the on-line Instructor's Manual. Complete references for these easily available movies are given as well. The Instructor's Manual is found at: www.morton-pub.com

When someone finds a skeleton, or even one bone, the police typically are called to investigate. Eventually, a forensic anthropologist likely will be asked for assistance in identifying the remains. Knowledge of how humans vary osteologically (skeletally) from each other, in terms of age, sex, ancestry, health, and activities during life, together provide information that can lead to identification of skeletal material. Forensic dentists and other medical professionals often collaborate with forensic anthropologists in consulting dental records or using imaging techniques.

Measuring Human Biological Variation

To measure variation in human biology, two tools are anthropometry and osteometry. **Anthropometry** refers to the measurement of humans, often of living individuals.

Osteometry is a subcategory of anthropometry that deals strictly with measurement of the skeleton. In this lab we'll use both skeletal material and your fellow students as experimental subjects. Osteometric techniques, together with qualitative assessment of skeletal material, provide the basis for conducting forensic anthropology analyses.

Standard methods of measuring the human body are in place for both living and skeletal specimens. The first step is to identify a few of the many sites on the skull that serve as **landmarks** (Photo 8.1) for measurement and allow us to take the same measurement consistently on a number of individuals.

Examples of some skull landmarks are:

- *euryon:* most lateral point on each side of the skull (on parietals)
- *glabella:* the most prominent point on the midline of the supraorbital ridge
- *nasion:* the most superior point of articulation of the two nasal bones, where both articulate with the frontal bone
- *nasospinale:* the midline point of the inferior margin of the nasal aperture (opening)
- *alare:* the most lateral point of each side of the nasal aperture
- *opisthocranion:* not a fixed point, but the point on the occipital bone that occurs the greatest distance from the glabella (in the mid-sagittal plane)
- *bregma:* the junction of the sagittal and coronal sutures
- *basion:* the medial, anterior-most rim of the foramen magnum

A more complete listing of landmarks can be found in the *Atlas*, pp. 206–210.

Anthropometric Techniques

The main tools for collecting data on skeletal material, particularly on skulls, are *spreading calipers* (see Figures 8.1 and 8.2) and *sliding calipers* (see Figures 8.3 and 8.4). Your instructor will review proper use of the calipers. Practice with them a few times, and compare results with your lab partner. Take each measurement two times to ensure accuracy. If they are different, measure a third time, which probably will match one of your prior measurements. If not, take an average of the two closer measurements. Record all measurements using the metric system (in cm), which is the international system for scientific measurements.

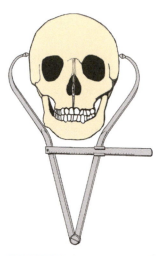

FIGURE 8.1 *Measuring cranial breadth*

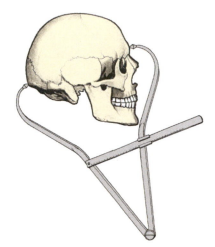

FIGURE 8.2 *Measuring cranial length*

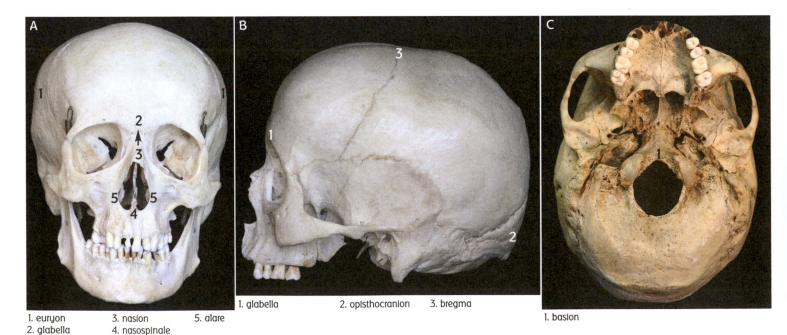

1. glabella   2. opisthocranion   3. bregma

1. euryon   3. nasion   5. alare
2. glabella   4. nasospinale

1. basion

PHOTO 8.1 *Landmarks of the skull: (A) anterior, (B) lateral, and (C) inferior views*

Head Shape

A common set of measurements used for anthropometry is related to shape of the head. Head shape is one of the many features considered in determining an individual's ancestry. The two measurements and the formula presented below can be applied to skulls as well as the heads of living humans. For **cranial** measurements, use the spreading calipers.

- *cranial breadth:* This is the maximum transverse diameter of the skull (the maximum width). Take the measurement by moving the points of the spreading caliper along the parietal bones until the maximum diameter is found, at *euryon* (Figure 8.1) on both sides of the skull.

- *cranial length:* This measurement quantifies the anterior–posterior maximum length of the skull, measured from *glabella* to *opisthocranion*. Fix one end of the spreading caliper on glabella and hold it with one hand. With the other hand move the other end of the caliper around until you find the maximum reading (Figure 8.2).

With the measurements you have obtained, you now can draw some useful information about the overall appearance of these skulls. To gauge how round-headed versus how long-headed an individual is, you would use the cranial, or **cephalic**, index:

$$\text{Cranial index} = \frac{\text{Cranial breadth} \times 100}{\text{Cranial length}}$$

The following categories have been created for results of the cranial index (*e.g.*, Bass, 1995):

	Index
Narrow or long-headed (*dolichocephalic*)	up to 74.9
Average (*mesocephalic*)	75.0–79.9
Round-headed (*brachycephalic*)	80.0–84.9
Very round-headed (*hyperbrachycephalic*)	more than 85.0

Nasal Region

Also commonly measured is the **nasal** region, which can be useful for helping to determine ancestry. The following measurements relate to the overall width of the nose. For the nasal measurements, use the sliding calipers (careful—they're sharp, and the nasal region is fragile!).

- *nasal breadth:* Measure the widest portion of the nasal aperture, between the two *alare* landmarks (Figure 8.3).

- *nasal height:* Measure from *nasion* to *nasospinale*; remember—you are measuring not only the nasal opening but actually from the inferior margin of the nasal opening to the superior margin of the nasal bones (see Figure 8.4).

You then will apply the *nasal index* to your results.

$$\text{Nasal index} = \frac{\text{Nasal breadth} \times 100}{\text{Nasal height}}$$

	Index
Wide-nosed (*platyrrhiny*)	53 and up
Medium-nosed (*mesorrhiny*)	48–52.9
Narrow-nosed (*leptorrhiny*)	up to 47.9

(*e.g.*, Bass, 1995)

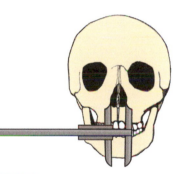

FIGURE 8.3 *Measuring nasal breadth*

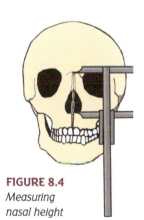

FIGURE 8.4 *Measuring nasal height*

LAB EXERCISE
8.1

NAME _____

SECTION _____   DATE _____

Using your fellow students as laboratory subjects, conduct the following measurements to determine their head shape, referring to Figures 8.1 and 8.2. Use the spreading calipers (and take care to not poke out anyone's eye) to measure, then calculate, the cranial index.

	INDIVIDUAL #1	INDIVIDUAL #2
Cranial breadth		
Cranial length		
Cranial index		

Next you will collect some osteometric data, taking these same measurements on three skulls.

	SKULL 1	SKULL 2	SKULL 3
Cranial breadth			
Cranial length			
Cranial index			

Practice using the sliding calipers for some nasal measurements, and fill out the chart below. Referring to Figures 8.3 and 8.4 again, use the sharper, pointed part of the calipers. Be gentle in taking these measurements, especially for nasal breadth, as the nasal region is fragile. Calculate the nasal index for each skull.

	SKULL 1	SKULL 2	SKULL 3
Nasal breadth			
Nasal length			
Nasal index			

SELF-TEST

8.1

NAME _____

SECTION _____   DATE _____

1. Which measurements can be taken with sliding calipers?

2. Which measurements can be taken with spreading calipers?

3. What does the cranial index tell you?

4. What does the nasal index tell you?

Male or Female?

To determine the sex of an individual, skeletal evidence usually is taken from the skull and the pelvis. It is difficult to establish sex from the skeleton prior to adulthood, although methods are being developed.

Evidence from the Skull

Sexual dimorphism refers to differences in shape or size between the sexes of a species. Living human males and females exhibit obvious differences, and skeletal correlates exist for some of these soft anatomical differences. These features relate mainly to differences in muscle development and to the widened birth canal in females.

Rugose (rough) areas or raised processes often appear where the tendons of muscles attach to bone. In general, male skeletons have more rugose muscle attachment sites than female skeletons because of their greater muscle mass (*e.g.*, France, 1986). Females usually are smaller, with shorter, more slender bones. The most distinctive differences occur on the skull and in the pelvis (Giles and Elliot, 1963; Phenice, 1969).

In this lab you will determine the sex of some individuals by examining several features of the cranial and post-cranial skeleton. Table 8.1 (and *Atlas* p. 94) lists several of the many features that differ on the skulls of males and females. Most of these are observable in Photo 8.2.

Keep in mind that because skeletons vary greatly, most skulls have at least a few characteristics that appear to belong to the opposite sex. Therefore, a suite of several features must be taken together to determine sex reliably.

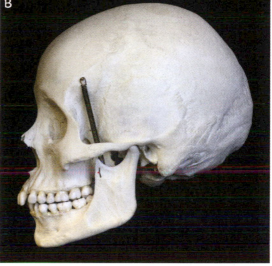

PHOTO 8.2
(A) *Male skull and* **(B)** *female skull*

Evidence from the Pelvis

Take a look at Photos 8.3 and 8.4 and Figure 8.5 (and *Atlas* p. 183) for some of the many features that can indicate an individual's sex. These are described in Table 8.2. As with the skull, there is overlap between the sexes, and a pelvis may exhibit a mix of "male" and "female" features.

TABLE 8.1: Selected Traits for Determining Sex from Skull

SKULL FEATURES	FORM IN MALE	FORM IN FEMALE
Overall skull size	Larger, more robust	Smaller, more gracile
Shape of forehead	Sloping	More vertical, rounded
Supraorbital ridge	More prominent, thicker	Less prominent, smaller
Mastoid process	Larger	Smaller
Orbital shape	Squared, low, broad	Rounded, set higher
Nuchal area and occipital protuberance	More pronounced	Less pronounced
Chin shape	More squared, broader	More rounded, narower

TABLE 8.2: Selected Traits for Determining Sex from Pelvis

FEATURES OF INNOMINATE	FORM IN MALE	FORM IN FEMALE
Sub-pubic arch size	Narrower, more V-shaped	Wider, more rounded
Pubic symphysis (height versus width)	Longer, narrower	Shorter, wider
Ventral arc	Absent	Present
Pelvic inlet	Narrower, heart-shaped	Broader, more oval
Greater sciatic notch	Narrower, deeper	Wider, shallower
Preauricular sulcus	Usually absent	Usually present

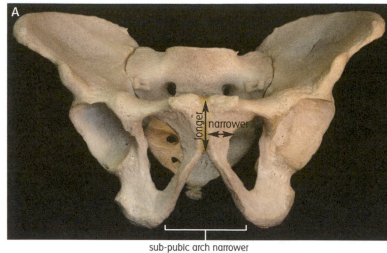

longer | narrower

sub-pubic arch narrower

PHOTO 8.3 (A) Male pelvis and (B) female pelvis

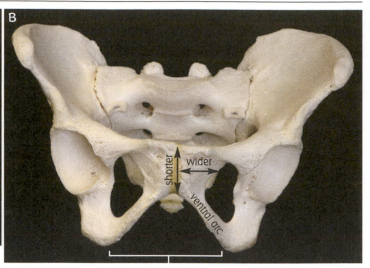

shorter | wider

ventral arc

sub-pubic arch wider

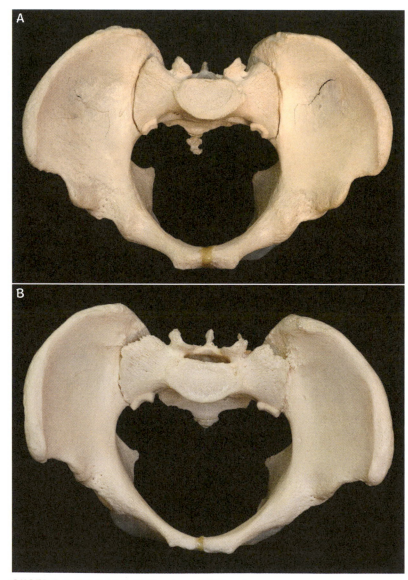

PHOTO 8.4 Pelvic inlet of (A) male and (B) female

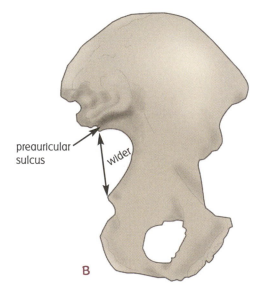

lack of preauricular sulcus | narrower

A

preauricular sulcus | wider

B

FIGURE 8.5 Sciatic notch form and preauricular sulcus in (A) male and (B) female

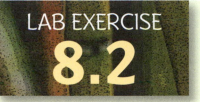

LAB EXERCISE
8.2

NAME _____

SECTION _____ DATE _____

1. "Sex" three skulls by filling out the chart below. For each feature, enter an M or an F, indicating whether each feature appears to be more masculine or more feminine, or a U to designate "uncertain." For each feature, compare all of the skulls before deciding on a sex. (In the absence of comparative skulls in your lab, use the photos here).

FEATURE	SKULL 1	SKULL 2	SKULL 3
Overall skull size			
Forehead shape			
Supraorbital ridge size			
Mastoid process			
Nuchal area, occipital protuberance			
Chin shape			
Total number of Ms			
Total number of Fs			
Sex designation			

Skull 1

Skull 2

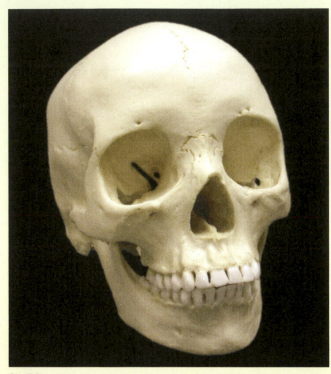

Skull 3

2. Sex three pelves (either entire pelves or casts of parts of the pelvis). Fill in the chart, again using the letters M, F, or U. (In the absence of comparative pelves in your lab, use the photos here. Some of the features listed below may not be observable from the photos.)

Feature (Use M or F)	Pelvis 1	Pelvis 2	Pelvis 3
Sub-pubic arch			
Pubic symphysis			
Ventral arc			
Greater sciatic notch			
Pelvic inlet (for entire pelvis)			
Total number of Ms			
Total number of Fs			
Sex designation			

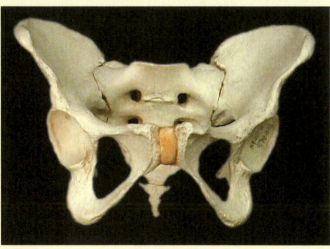

Pelvis 1

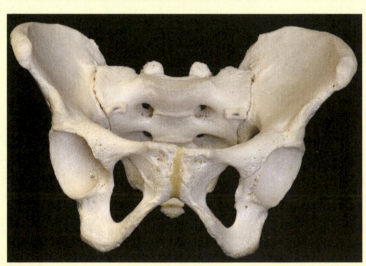

Pelvis 2

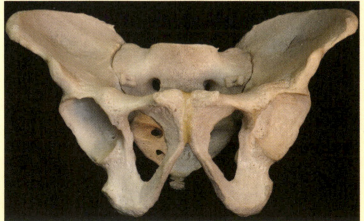

Pelvis 3

SELF-TEST
8.2

NAME _____

SECTION _____ DATE _____

1. a. What are three ways to tell male from female skulls?

   b. What are these differences related to?

2. a. What are three ways to tell male from female pelves?

   b. What are these differences related to?

3. What is the term for differences in size or shape between males and females within a species?

How Old Were They?

Numerous methods can be used to estimate the age of an individual at death. These methods depend upon knowledge of the **formative changes** that occur as we grow, and the **degenerative changes** that occur as we senesce (grow old). Methods for determining the age of skeletal material include observations of the dentition, skull suture closure, and growth areas of the long bones. We will look at a few examples.

Formative Changes

Developmental features can be a useful means to determine age until growth stops, because the developmental sequence is predetermined and known. Individuals' rate of development varies, however, so results are presented in terms of age *ranges*.

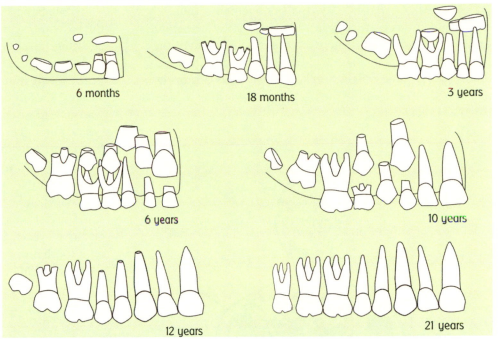

FIGURE 8.6 *Dental eruption chart*   Sources: *Digging Up Bones*, 3d ed., by D. R. Brothwell (New York: Cornell University Press, 1981), p. 64; *Human Skeletal Remains: Excavation, Analysis, Interpretation*, by D. H. Ubelaker (Chicago: Aldine, 1978); *A Photographic Atlas for Physical Anthropology* by P. F. Whitehead, W. K. Sacco, and S. G. Hochgraf (Englewood, CO: Morton, 2005), p. 73.

Age Determination Using the Teeth Several methods involving the dentition are useful. We will deal only with the third method listed here.

1. Examination of *growth ridges of tooth enamel*, which grows at a regular, measurable rate; growth lines form a new ridge each week and can be detected with scanning electron microscopy.

2. Patterns of *tooth root growth patterns*: Even after a tooth is fully erupted, its root grows for as long as 20 years. The root tips remain sharp until about 25 years of age, then they become blunt as cementum is deposited around them. They can be observed by X-ray while in the alveoli (tooth sockets).

3. *Dental eruption* pattern is the most commonly used method. The sequence of appearance of deciduous (baby) and permanent dentition provides a useful tool for determining age (*e.g.,* Ubelaker, 1978). It is most useful through about age 15. Again, in adults, the dental formula is $\frac{2}{2}\frac{1}{1}\frac{2}{2}\frac{3}{3}$. On average, females mature 1 to 2 years before males (for example, 14–17 if male, 13–16 if female). The dental formula for deciduous teeth is $\frac{2}{2}\frac{1}{1}\frac{0}{0}\frac{2}{2}$, after which the dentition will consist of a mix of permanent and deciduous teeth for a number of years.

In this lab you will look at some skulls to determine their age using an illustration of the eruption times of various teeth provided in Figure 8.6.

Epiphyseal Closure After birth, bone growth occurs in cartilaginous "plates," in which cartilage cells divide by mitosis

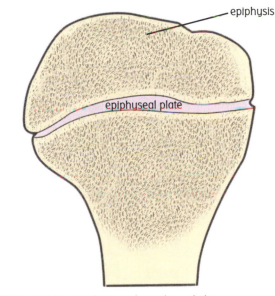

FIGURE 8.7 *Long-bone epiphysis with epiphyseal plate*

for growth. Bone cells then enter via the bloodstream and are "injected" into the cartilage. Later, minerals are deposited and the bone **ossifies**. Cartilaginous growth plates are evident while bone tissue is being deposited (see Figure 8.7). In the long bones these cartilaginous plates are located between the epiphyses and the diaphysis. When the cartilage is replaced by bone, bone growth ends.

Different bones ossify, or "fuse," at different times, generally between the early teens and the mid-20s. Because males and females mature at different rates, a different scale is used for each sex. On average, females mature 1 to 2 years before males (for example, 14–17 if male, 13–16 if female).

At death, cartilage decays but bone remains; thus, when the cartilaginous plate decays and disintegrates, the epiphyseal bone ends can separate from the main portion of the bone (see Figure 8.7). You will be using Figure 8.8, which demonstrates time ranges for the fusion of the various bones in the body to determine the age range of various skeletons (or skeletal elements).

If the bone end (the epiphysis) is fused to the diaphysis, the individual can't be younger than the minimum age of the age range given. For example, if the age range for occurrence of fusion for the femoral head is between age 14 and 20 years of age, it means that the head can be fused as young as age 14, or as old as 20 (but no older). If you find a femur whose head is fused, that individual is at least 14 years old (you cannot give a maximum value). If the epiphysis is not fused, the individual can't be any older than the maximum age of the age range given. So if the femoral head has not fused, it may be as old as 20, but not older. Use of another epiphyseal end often helps narrow the age range.

The last bone to fuse is the clavicle, which can occur as late as 28 years. Epiphyseal growth often is used together with tooth eruption information, but much of the significant tooth eruption begins much earlier than most epiphyseal growth.

Degenerative Changes

Upon reaching adulthood, wear on the skeleton becomes increasingly observable. Hints of increasing age can be seen throughout the skeleton.

Cranial Sutures As the cranium grows, the spaces making up the sutures close, and eventually they may become obliterated. Although individuals vary greatly in the timing of suture closure, the method is at least useful to distinguish younger adults from older adults (Photo 8.5).

Pubic Symphysis Surface The symphyseal "face" of the pubis changes with age, as the distinctive ridges wear down to less evenly placed bumps (Todd, 1920; Todd, 1921; Katz and Suchey, 1986). In females, bony projections at the margins of the pubic symphysis form at the birth of each child in response to stresses on that area during childbirth. Figure 8.9 demonstrates a male pubic symphysis and the changes occurring from young adult to older adult.

Dental Attrition After the teeth erupt through the gums, they are in continual use. The points of contact between the upper and lower teeth are part of the **occlusal** surface of our teeth, and this is the area we look for in determining the extent of tooth wear (**attrition**). Because the molars are the teeth that crush and grind food, they receive the most wear, and eventually degrade the tooth's enamel down to the next deeper layer, the dentin (see Figure 7.8 for tooth anatomy and *Atlas* pp. 241 and 242 for attrition).

It is important to note that comparisons between species also emphasize the molars, as they are the most intimately associated with the food and thus are the best indicators of dietary type. When studying tooth wear, we must realize that the amount of wear is *highly dependent upon diet*. More abrasive foods wear faster through the enamel, so the teeth will appear to belong to an older individual. Therefore,

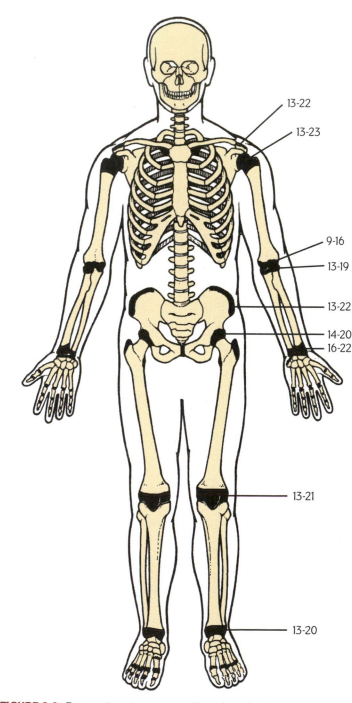

FIGURE 8.8 *Timing of epiphyseal union throughout the skeleton*

Sources: *Skeletal Age Changes in Young American Males*, by T. W. McKern and T. D. Stewart, *U.S. Army Quartermaster* (Technical Report EP-45, 1957); *Standards for Data Collection from Human Skeletal Remains*, by J. E. Buikstra, and D. H. Ubelaker (Fayetteville: Arkansas Archeological Survey), p. 43; *A Photographic Atlas for Physical Anthropology* by P. F. Whitehead, W. K. Sacco, and S. B. Hochgraf (Englewood, CO: Morton, 2005), p. 157.

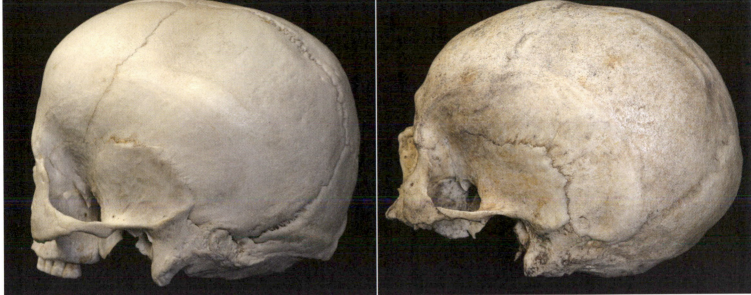

PHOTO 8.5 *Cranial suture closure in (A) younger and (B) older adults*

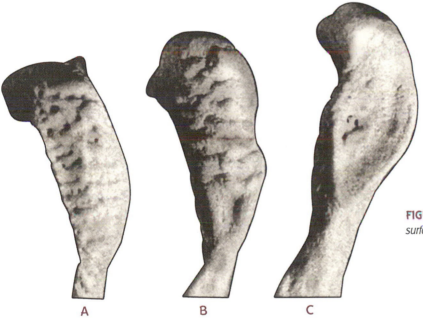

FIGURE 8.9 *Appearance of male pubic symphysis surface at (A) younger, (B) middle, and (C) older age*

A   B   C

such comparisons are best made within a population whose individuals subsist or subsisted on a similar diet. Tooth-grinding may also cause tooth wear.

The primary source for estimating age by dental attrition is based on data of an Iron Age British population (Brothwell, 1981), which would have had a much different diet from modern populations. More current studies of tooth wear in various modern populations would be highly useful for forensic anthropologists in their attempt to determine the age of skeletons. (Keep this in mind if you are searching for a master's thesis or doctoral dissertation topic some day!)

Additional changes include the following:

1. Bone microstructure changes, which can be studied by observing a thin section of long bone under a microscope.

2. Changes throughout life occurs in the ratio of two types of aspartic acid (an amino acid). Measuring their ratio can yield an estimate of age.

3. Bone density decreases with increasing age. Common sites of bone loss (reabsorption) are the clavicle and the femur. This series of transformations can be used as an aging technique.

LAB EXERCISE 8.3

NAME _____

SECTION _____ DATE _____

1. Use the dental eruption chart (Figure 8.6) to gauge the age of these two individuals or skulls in your lab. How old do you think these are?

Dentition A _____   Dentition B _____

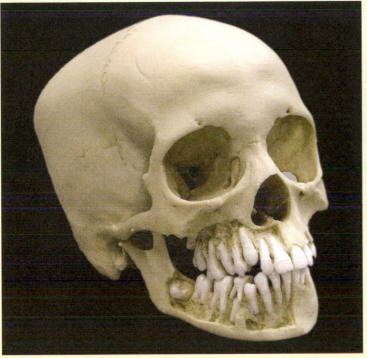

Dentition A

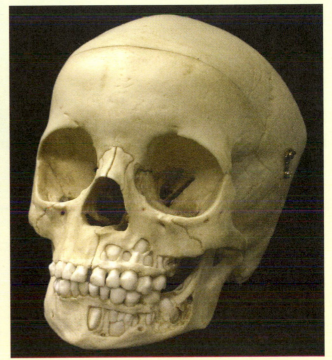

Dentition B

2. To determine the age range for specimens A, B, and C, refer to specimens in your lab or to the illustrations below. Refer to Figure 8.8 for epiphyseal fusion times.

INDIVIDUAL	EPIPHYSEAL END	AGE RANGE
A	Crest of ilium	
B	Humeral head	
C	Distal femur	

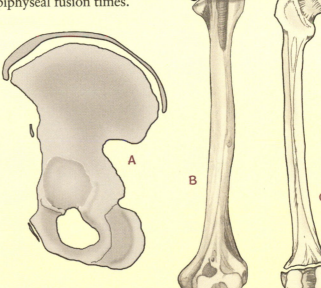

What if A and C are from the same individual?

Would that narrow the age range?

If so, how?

3. Compare the sutures on skulls A and B in the photos or in two skulls from your lab. Look at points 1, 2, and 3 on each, and, using the chart below, score them from 0 to 3 according to the closure categories (from Buikstra and Ubelaker, 1994). Normally, one would use 17 such skull points rather than only three, to gauge suture closure.

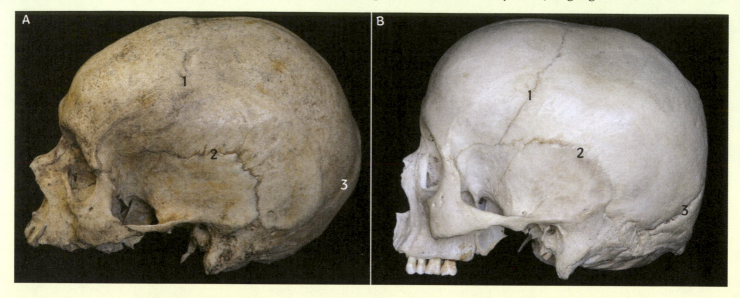

SKULL SUTURE AREA	SKULL A	SKULL B
1		
2		
3		
Average		

Open = 0
Minimal closure = 1
Significant closure = 2
Complete obliteration = 3

Which skull is from an older individual?

4. Look at the illustration (or your lab specimens) to compare the surface of the pubic symphysis of A and B. Which is older? What's the difference between them?

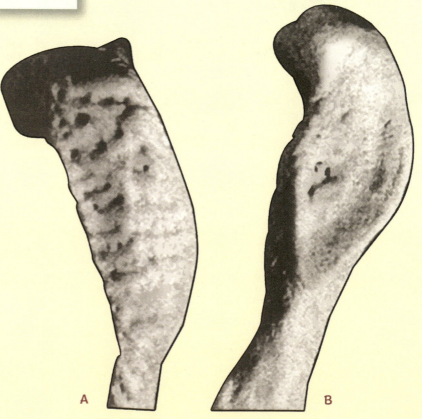

**SELF-TEST
8.3**

NAME _____

SECTION _____   DATE _____

1. What are the two main categories of age-related changes in the skeleton?

   a.

   b.

2. What are two specific techniques we can use to determine age within each of the categories referred to above?

   a.

   b.

3. In the following, each of a through c below represents an individual with bones in various stages of fusion. Using Figure 8.8 on the epiphyseal union of bone ends, figure out the age range for each of the bones, then combine the information to estimate the individual's age. An example is done for you below. Phrase your answer in terms such as "at least ___ years," or "not older than ___ years," or "between ___ and ___ years."

   Example: head of humerus fused to diaphysis   at least 13 years
                     head of femur unfused to diaphysis   not older than 20 years
                                     age of individual   between 13 and 20 years

   a. iliac crest unfused to body of ilium   _____

      head of humerus fused to diaphysis   _____

                      age of individual   _____

   b. iliac crest fused to body of ilium   _____

      acromion process fused to scapula   _____

                      age of individual   _____

c. distal end of radius fused to diaphysis   _____

   distal end of tibia unfused to diaphysis   _____

                     age of individual   _____

Determining Ancestry

Although forensic anthropologists must determine ancestry—also traditionally referred to as **race**—as accurately as possible, this is difficult to do. Populations vary widely, with much overlap among various groups. Still, some extent of past reproductive isolation in groups has resulted in features that are found with much greater frequency in some skeletons than in others. The issue of ancestry/race in biological anthropology will be discussed further in Chapter 15.

Terminology to describe these categories of people from various geographical regions varies. The three most widely used general categories in the United States are African, Asian, and European ancestry. The European category includes East Indians; and Asian and Native American skulls have many similarities because of their shared ancestry. Australian aboriginal peoples possess a number of distinctive skull features, but such skulls are rarely found in the United States.

Some studies have focused on mainly quantitative, or **osteometric**, traits (*e.g., Ayres et al., 1990*), while others deal with qualitative, or **anthroposcopic**, traits (*e.g., Hrdlička, 1920; Hinkes, 1990; Rhine, 1990*). Both types of traits used together provide the greatest accuracy.

Quantitative (Osteometric) Features

Two examples of quanitative traits are cranial shape and nasal shape, which you learned earlier in this lab.

Cranial Index (Ubelaker, 1999; Byers, 2005)

up to 74.9 =	narrow or long-headed (dolicocephalic)	more often African Origin
75.0–79.9 =	average (mesocephalic)	more often European Origin
80.0–84.9 =	round-headed (brachycephalic)	more often Asian Origin
over 85.0 =	very round-headed (hyperbrachycephalic)	

Nasal Index (Bass, 1995; Ubelaker, 1999; Byers, 2005)

53 and up =	wide-nosed (platyrhiny)	more often African Origin
48–52.9 =	medium-nosed (mesorhiny)	more often Asian Origin
up to 47.9 =	narrow-nosed (leptorhiny)	more often European Origin

Qualitative Features (Anthroposcopic Traits)

Table 8.3 lists just a small sample of the many traits that are considered when attempting to determine ancestry. Most of these can be observed in Photos 8.6–8.8, as indicated.

TABLE 8.3: Selected Traits for Determining Ancestry

	AFRICAN ORIGIN	EUROPEAN ORIGIN	ASIAN ORIGIN
Nasal root (superior nasal margin)	low, gently rounded	high, narrow, peaked	low, peaked
Lower border of nasal aperture	"guttered"	sharp sill, forms ridge	flatter, often indistinct
Orbital shape	squared	tear-drop, sloping	rounded
Malar tubercle	absent	usually absent	usually pronounced, "droopy"
Dental arcade shape	broad anteriorly; rectangular	narrow anteriorly; parabolic	broad posteriorly, rounded
Lingual side of incisors	flat	flat	shovel-shaped (see *Atlas*, p. 254)

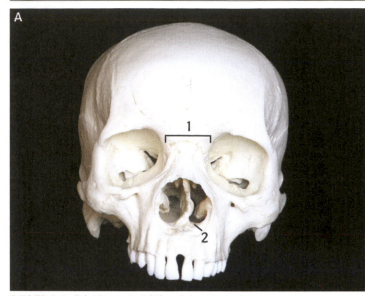

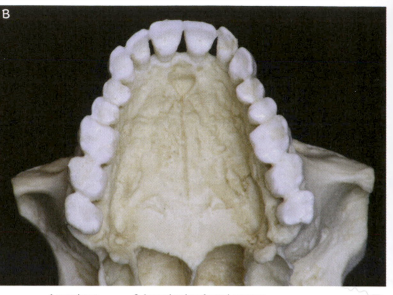

PHOTO 8.6 (**A**) *African skull* (**B**) *and dental arcade*   1. nasal root   2. lower border of nasal aperture

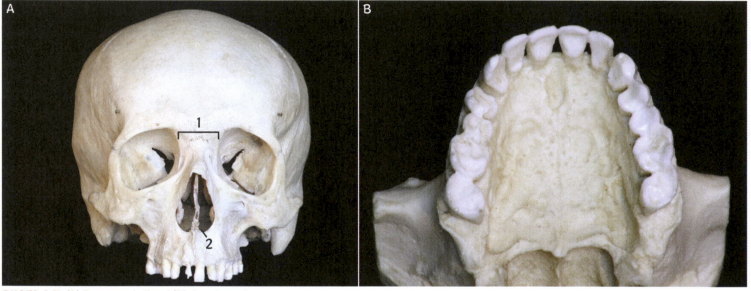

PHOTO 8.7 (**A**) *European skull and* (**B**) *dental arcade*   1. nasal root   2. lower border of nasal aperture

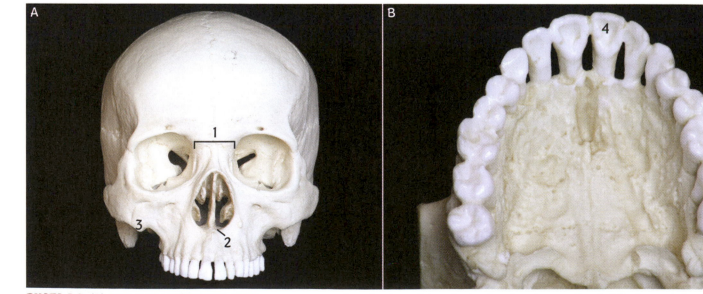

PHOTO 8.8 (**A**) *Asian skull and* (**B**) *dental arcade*   1. nasal root   2. lower border of nasal aperture   3. malar tubercle   4. shovel-shaped incisors

How Tall Were They?

Height, or stature, can be reconstructed by measuring various bones. This is possible because of a high degree of predictability in the proportion of our bones (especially limb bones) to our total height, as well as the fact that leg bones (the most accurate to use) make up part of our height during life. An anthropometric tool called an *osteometric board* is used to take measurements on various bones (Figure 8.10). The bone measurements are plugged into a formula to give an estimate of total height, accompanied by some margin of error (Trotter, 1970). Because body proportions can differ depending upon sex and ancestry, different formulae are used for different populations (Krogman and Iscan, 1986). Each population, however, experiences more variation within than it does when compared to others.

Note: Keep in mind that actual height often differs from the last recorded height of an individual because of inaccuracy of self-reported height and to shrinkage occurring with age. When was the last time you were accurately measured?

For additional information and exercises dealing with human biological variation, see One Step Further after Lab Exercise 8.4, and Chapter 15.

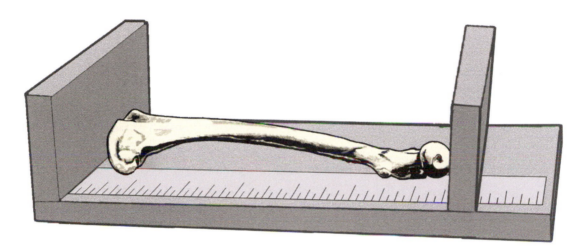

FIGURE 8.10 *Osteometric board with femur being measured*

LAB EXERCISE
8.4

NAME _____

SECTION _____   DATE _____

1. Measure three skulls from your lab to determine the cranial index (your instructor may have you use measurements taken earlier in this lab or provide you with measurements as a time-saving technique).

$$\text{Cranial index} = \frac{\text{Cranial breadth}}{\text{Cranial length}} \times 100$$

	SKULL 1	SKULL 2	SKULL 3
Cranial breadth			
Cranial length			
Cranial index			

2. Use the sliding calipers to estimate the relative width of the nose on three skulls (don't perform these measurements on a classmate!) by measuring nasal height and nasal breadth. *Again, be careful; the bone is extremely delicate in this area.*

$$\text{Nasal index} = \frac{\text{Nasal breadth}}{\text{Nasal height}} \times 100$$

	SKULL 1	SKULL 2	SKULL 3
Nasal breadth			
Nasal length			
Nasal index			

3. Observe the features, and compare them to the three skulls shown in the photos (or to your lab collection skulls). Enter an *Af* if you think the form of a feature is more likely to be African, *As* for Asian, and *Eu* for European.

	Skull 1	Skull 2	Skull 3
Nasal root (superior nasal margin)			
Lower border of nasal aperture			
Nasal aperture width			
Orbital shape			
Malar tubercle			
Dental arcade shape			
Lingual side of incisors			

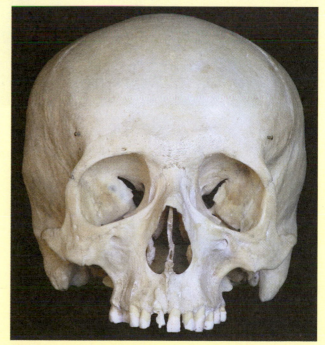

Skull 1

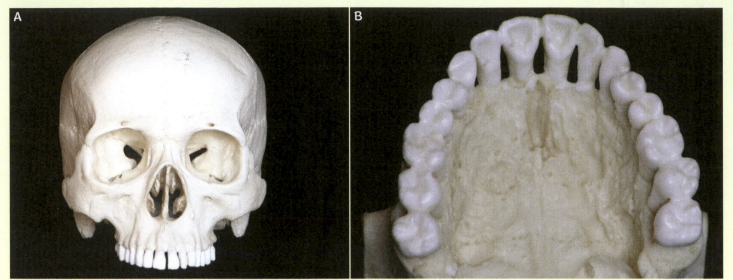

Skull 2   Dental arcade

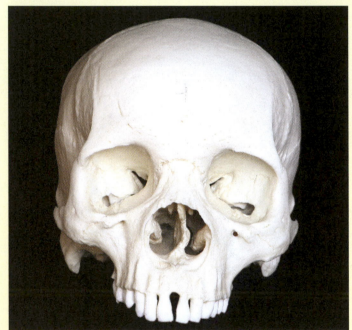

Skull 3

4. If you looked at the same three skulls in your lab collection for questions 1 through 3, were your answers consistent for the quantitative data together with the qualitative data? Keep in mind that your sample size is small, so inconsistencies between results of the various means of assessing ancestry are possible.

5. In the absence of an osteometric board, you can improvise with a tape measure taped to a table. Measure the maximum length of a femur (in cm), and use the following formula (this one happens to be for Asian males) to reconstruct stature. (See Figure 8.10)

femur length: _____

formula (Trotter, 1970):

femur (2.15) + 72.57   [femur length × 2.15 + 72.57]

stature _____ (cm)

_____ (inches: 2.54 cm = 1 inch)

The standard error for this formula is 3.80—meaning that the actual stature may have been 3.8 cm greater or lesser than the estimated stature you calculate after completing your formula.

SELF-TEST 8.4

NAME _____

SECTION _____ DATE _____

1. What are two qualitative methods and two quantitative methods to determine ancestry?

2. Why is determination of ancestry so difficult?

3. If you find a decayed skeleton with only one complete long bone remaining intact and you want to reconstruct the stature of this individual, what steps would you take?

Incidentally, you find your skeleton in Thailand, the bone is a femur, and it measures 52.8 cm long. The diameter of the femoral head falls into the male range.

ONE STEP FURTHER

NAME _____

SECTION _____ DATE _____

Additional Lab Exercise 8.1

ADDITIONAL MATERIALS NEEDED:

- Three upper or lower dentitions with differing degrees of tooth wear (label them A through C; photos provided here in case lab specimens aren't available)

Earlier in this chapter you used dental eruption patterns to estimate the age of some young individuals and were introduced to the concept of dental attrition as an approximate way to gauge age in adults. In this additional exercise you will put this second concept to use by ordering a few sets of dentition according to the wear on their teeth.

In this lab exercise you will observe dental attrition from a *comparative perspective*, gaining some practice in differentiating older and younger dentitions rather than assigning an age to them based on a chart from an ancient population with very different attrition rates. If you have a variety of dentitions in your lab collection, you will arrange them in order of what best represents the youngest to the oldest specimen. Alternatively, you could use dentition photos A through C.

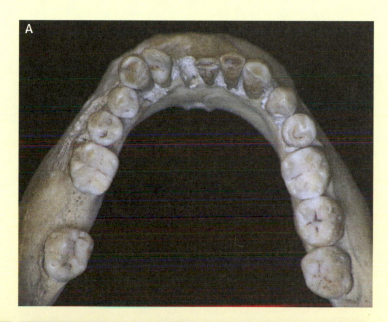

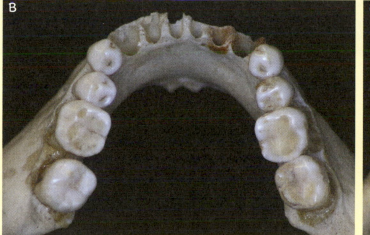

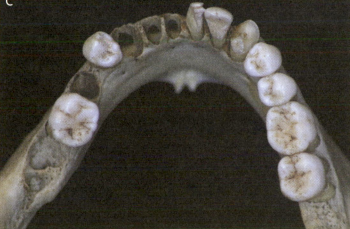

1. Observe the dentitions provided in your lab (or Photos A through C) and fill out the chart below, after reading about the aspects to look for on the molars, listed below. Also, take a look at Figure 7.8, which depicts the tooth layers (enamel, dentin).

   - Are all teeth erupted? (Does the dentition represent an adult individual?)

   - Is there a smooth extension of enamel across the occlusal surface of the tooth, or is the enamel worn in places, exposing the dentin? The dentin exposure will appear as thin ridges, starting with the highest points on the cusps.

   - The teeth will show less wear as you move from front (mesial) to back (distal) along the tooth row, because M1 erupts before M3. Therefore, M1 may exhibit considerable wear while M3 may appear relatively "new."

SPECIMEN	A			B			C		
	M1	M2	M3	M1	M2	M3	M1	M2	M3
Fully erupted?*									
Dentin exposure (none, little, much)									
		A			B			C	
Age ranking (1 youngest, 3 oldest)									

*M3 fails to erupt in some individuals (photos B and C)

2. If you had compared only one of the three molars on all of the dentitions, would your age ranking have been the same?

ONE STEP FURTHER

NAME _____

SECTION _____ DATE _____

Additional Lab Exercise 8.2

ADDITIONAL MATERIALS NEEDED:

- Femur, tibia, and humerus from same individual (measurements provided here if lab specimens aren't available)

Intuitively, it makes sense that a tall person would have a relatively long femur and someone with a long femur would have a relatively long humerus. These traits (variables) are said to **covary**. Covariance can be expressed mathematically, and an equation can describe the relationship between the variables. Based on this relationship, if we know a measurement of one of these variables, we can predict the measurement of the other. You used this principle earlier in this lab when you conducted a height estimation from a femur.

More Stature Estimation

In this section of the lab, you will practice more with stature reconstruction using formulae from various populations, and examine how different parts of the skeleton may differ in their accuracy for predicting stature. Because populations and the two sexes have somewhat different body proportions, we must rely on our expertise in sexing skeletons and determining ancestry to reconstruct stature most accurately.

1. If you have a femur, a tibia, and a humerus from the same individual in your lab collection, you will measure those bones and record the measurements in the first column. Measure the maximum length of the femur and the humerus. The tibia length should be measured from the most superior point of the lateral condyle to the bottom of the medial malleolus.

   If you lack lab specimens, you may use the measurements from a male skeleton, provided below the chart, to fill out the chart.

BONE USED	LENGTH (in cm)	FORMULA (with measurement plugged in)	STATURE ESTIMATE (in cm)	RANGE (use standard error)	ESTIMATE IN FEET & INCHES
Femur					
Tibia					
Humerus					

(An additional row is added in case your instructor asks you to measure another bone or combination of bones.)

Sample measurements (to use if needed in place of lab specimens):

femur:	42.0 cm
tibia:	31.7 cm
humerus:	30.3 cm

2. We will assume for the moment that your skeleton is of European ancestry. Do you know the sex of your skeleton if you are using bones from your lab collection? (If not, assume in this exercise that it is a male.)

   a. Use the appropriate formula from those below and fill in the rest of the chart on the previous page.

Stature Formulae

European male

femur	2.32 (femur length) + 65.53 ± 3.94 (standard error, SE)
tibia	2.42 (tibia length) + 81.93 ± 4.0 (SE)
humerus	2.89 (humerus) + 78.10 ± 4.57 (SE)

European female

femur	2.47 (femur length) + 54.10 ± 3.72 (SE)
tibia	2.90 (tibia length) + 61.53 ± 3.66 (SE)
humerus	3.36 (humerus) + 57.97 ± 4.45 (SE)

Mexican female (to use for Question #4)

femur	2.59 (femur length) + 49.74 ± 3.82 (SE)

(Trotter and Gleser, 1952, 1977; Genovés, 1967; Burns, 2007)

   b. Your reconstructed stature should be given in terms of a range (e.g., 5'4" to 5'7"). To obtain a range for your stature estimate (SE), subtract the standard error (in cm) from your total estimated height (in cm). This gives the lowest margin of the reconstructed height range. Add the SE to obtain the highest margin of the range.

   c. Dividing the lowest and highest possible reconstructed stature estimates by 2.54 will give you height in inches. Convert to feet (and inches) by dividing again, by 12.

3. Are the stature estimates based on the three bones different from one another? Are two of them closer estimates to each other than is the third? If so, why do you suppose that is so? Which do you think is the most accurate? Why?

4. To see how different your stature estimate would be if you would not accurately assess sex and/or ancestry, recalculate the estimate for just the femur, using the formula above for the Mexican female.

   a. Record your calculation and your resulting height (convert to feet and inches) below.

   b. Was the second stature estimate using a formula from a different ancestry close to the first one?

5. Is length of femur an example of a continuous or a discontinuous trait?

ONE STEP FURTHER

NAME _____

SECTION _____ DATE _____

More Anthroposcopy: Skeletal Traits *(only if skulls are available in your lab)*

Take a look at each of the skulls in your lab. Compare them for the presence of any of the traits indicated below. All of these traits fall within the normal range of human variation, but some of them are present at a somewhat higher frequency in certain populations than in others. Although some may be caused by disease agents, most are caused by genetic processes. Your appreciation of the breadth of human skeleton variation should increase as you observe more bones and more features.

Briefly note any of the following that you observe in your skeletal collection. Note the total number of skeletons you looked at, and the number that possess any of the features.

1. Frequently, within the lambdoidal suture, small bones are "trapped" within the suture lines. These typically are referred to as *wormian bones* (one example of which is an *Inca bone*). Do any see any skeletons with these bones? (*Atlas*, p. 233, Photo 7.2, p. 251)

2. On the frontal bone, do any of the skulls have a suture line down the middle? A certain percentage of people have retained the metopic suture throughout life (*Atlas*, p. 253).

3. An osteoma is a benign bony outgrowth, most often found mostly on skull and facial bones (*Atlas* p. 236). They are slow growing and asymptomatic. Are there any skulls in your collection with such bumps on the skull? Any with other signs of disease? If so, describe briefly below.

4. A mandibular torus is common (almost 10% of the U.S. population, for example; more common in some other populations). You may notice a bony growth on the lingual (inner) side of at least one of the mandibles in your lab collection and also may have at least one classmate who notices such a bulge in his/her own mouth! These can be felt and seen easily and often are **bilateral** (on both sides of the mandible). If seen, note it below.

5. Are all the teeth erupted? Do any skulls appear to be from a fully adult individual but missing the third molar? If so, is the tooth (teeth) missing from the maxilla or the mandible? This relatively common condition is known as M3 agenesis (p. 211, Photo B).

Note: A Statistical Forensic Anthropology Program

FORDISC is a computer program created by Ousley and Jantz (2005) to assist forensic anthropologists with skeletal identification by comparison to a reference sample. A large data base was compiled, and **discriminant function analysis** is used to determine which continuous variables discriminate between two or more groups. Once a statistical relationship is determined between particular measurements of individuals and the naturally occurring group in which one belongs, we can use the known variables (*e.g.,* femoral head diameter) to predict the group into which one fits (*e.g.,* male or female).

This can be highly useful for determining the sex and ancestry of skeletal remains, although, because much overlap occurs between the sexes and ancestries, we must use a number of such traits to strengthen our conclusions.

Some features are more useful than others and are weighed more heavily in the analysis. We must remember, however, that analysis of individuals not included in the reference populations of the comparative database may yield questionable results (*e.g.,* Ramsthaler et al., 2007; Walker, 2008).

Other researchers have established databases and conducted discriminant function analyses for various additional populations for sexing the mandible (Franklin *et al.,* 2008) and the pelvis (Steyen, M., Işcan, M.Y., 2008).

Comparative Osteology and Functional Complexes

"Have you ever wondered . . . ?"

- How do scientists know how dinosaurs or other extinct species walked or what they ate?

OBJECTIVES

- Understand the importance of the comparative perspective
- Learn how form–function relationships work
- Become familiar with form–function relationships in terms of specific dental complexes and locomotor complexes
- Learn to interpret main functional types of teeth for each dietary type
- Recognize various forms of the postcranial skeleton to be able to interpret locomotor behavior
- Learn to use intermembral indices to help interpret locomotor categories

MATERIALS NEEDED

- Preferably, skeletal material of various species, at least to represent as much of the following as possible:
  - at least part of posterior tooth rows to show the four main functions of:
    - puncture/crushing (sharp, pointy cusps—bat, tarsier, etc.)
    - shearing (high cusps and connecting ridges—goat, deer, cow)
    - crushing/grinding (low, rounded cusps—human, pig, chimp)
    - tearing (large canines and sharp, high-cusped premolars and/or molars—dog, cat)
- Preferably, long bones (particularly humerus, femur, ulna) and scapulae of various species to represent stable versus mobile, arboreal versus terrestrial tendencies

  (*Note: The above items can be substituted/supplemented with photos in the lab manual.*)
- Foods (or substitutes) listed in Lab Exercise 9.1, so students can experiment with which kind of food gets placed where in the mouth, and use of anterior versus posterior teeth: sunflower seeds (shelled and unshelled), carrots, beef jerky, spinach/lettuce, whole apple
- Scissors (optional for Lab Exercise 9.2, #2; to cut out photos in Appendix D): one pair for each of two to five lab pairs
- Number and letter labels to group the postcranial bones, and set up lab "stations."

(One Step Further will require additional materials; see Additional Lab Exercise 9.1.)

*(**Note:** The instructor may want to print out photos from the online Instructor Manual for lab exercises.)*

The way an animal moves is determined by the shape of its body. Specific bony and muscular features permit, as well as limit, certain motions. An anatomical *feature*, together with the *manner in which it is used*, describes a **form-function** relationship. These parts of the anatomy are referred to as functional complexes. An example is a **pre-hensile** (grasping) **tail**, whose particular bony and muscular features (its **form**) are directly associated with its grasping abilities (its **function**). We can use our knowledge of form–function relationships to make inferences about how extinct animals moved and why certain features may have evolved. Thus, our knowledge of the present allows us to interpret the past.

Evidence from the Teeth and Skull

The first vertebrates had no teeth, nor jaws to house them. These were the **Agnathans** (G *a*: without; *gnath*: jaws). The first vertebrate teeth were thought to have evolved from fish scales. We've come a long way since then. Because we're mammals, we share with other mammals the feature of differentiated, or **heterodont**, teeth. Mammals have incisors, canines, premolars, and molars (see Figure 9.1A). By contrast, the jaws of reptiles and other nonmammalian vertebrates (illustrated by the crocodile in Figure 9.1B), are populated by one basic form of tooth.

The form of teeth reflects their function in the diet of a species over time. The diet influences the evolution of tooth form and even jaw form. Teeth are by far the most commonly found body part in the fossil record. The teeth are covered with enamel, a hard, highly mineralized substance that often allows them to escape rapid decay. Further, teeth are small enough to escape the effects of scavenging, by simply falling to the ground and soon becoming embedded in the sediment and left as a permanent record of an organism's existence.

The teeth hide many "stories"—if you know how to read them. By studying only a few teeth of an individual, we might be able to learn something about these factors:

- *Age*
  - Tooth eruption
  - Attrition (tooth wear)
- *Sex*: The size of teeth and jaws (especially canine tooth size) can differ in males and females.
- *Health*: Dental caries and abscesses reflect dental health and general nutrition.
- *Mating systems*: The evolution of canine dimorphism may be influenced partly by the type of mating system.
- *Behavioral patterns*: The use of specific body parts causes characteristic wear patterns.
- *Evolutionary relationships*: Comparative anatomy can indicate an organism's place in the biological classification system.
- *Diet*: Tooth morphology is an indication of diet.

In this and subsequent labs we will focus on the last two items on this list. Learning about teeth can establish the *evolutionary relationships* of modern forms based on similarities to extinct ones; and by identifying form–function relationships in modern species, we can make inferences about *diets* of extinct species. We'll review a bit of dental anatomy.

- What are the four *types of teeth*, from the front to the back of the tooth row?

- Review the anatomical directions for teeth. Draw a *dental arcade*, label anatomical directions: mesial, distal, lingual, buccal, occlusal surface (see Figure 7.7, *Atlas* p. 22, and br. ed. p. 22).

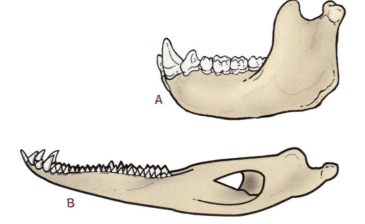

FIGURE 9.1 *Heterodont (A) and homodont (B) dentition*

- Review the *dental formula* concept. Our dental formula, which we share with Old World monkeys and apes (as members of the Infraorder Catarrhini) is $\frac{2}{2} \frac{1}{1} \frac{2}{2} \frac{3}{3}$.

- Review *dental terminology*, using humans as an example. I1 and I2 are the central and lateral incisor, and C1 is the canine. P3 and P4 are the third and fourth premolars (P1 and P2 were lost over evolutionary time). M1, M2, and M3 are the first through third molars.
  - top versus bottom: I^1, $I^2 - I_1$, I_2
  - left versus right: LM_1 (left lower first molar)
  - deciduous versus permanent: d, then lower case tooth (dm: deciduous molar)
  - Rdi^2 (right upper deciduous second/lateral incisor)

On the molars a great deal of attention is directed to the form of the **occlusal surface** (where the upper and lower teeth oppose each other). All bumps, grooves, valleys, and other defining features have names. The primary features on the molars are the bumps, or cusps (*Atlas* p. 35, Figure 3.9).

The evolution of cusp size, form, and position on the tooth can be tracked through time. Primates are *generalized* in that we retain that same basic pattern of distinctive cusps, unlike cows or deer, whose molars have undergone considerable change in adapting to a grazing or browsing diet, and whose cusps are no longer distinguishable from one another.

Tooth Function

Teeth are considered accessory organs to the digestive system, because they assist in beginning the digestive process. Functions of the **anterior dentition** (incisors and canines) differ from those of the **posterior dentition** (premolars and molars). The anterior dentition is responsible for **ingestion**, the taking in of food. The posterior dentition has the task of physically processing food, called **mechanical digestion**. The form of the posterior dentition (also called cheek teeth) more directly reflects dietary adaptations than does the anterior dentition.

For many mammalian species, the anterior dentition has social functions in addition to dietary ones. In some primates, the incisor form has evolved for a grooming function, and large canines presumably were selected because of the advantage they provide in threat displays and fighting—also apparent in some nonprimates such as the walrus.

The posterior dentition breaks down food mechanically in one of four main ways, depending upon cusp form, as illustrated in the photos:

1. *Puncture-crushing/piercing*: Small, sharp, pointy cusps break up hard insect exoskeletons (Photo 9.1).

2. *Shearing:* High cusps and the crests that link them cut through leafy vegetation (Photo 9.2).

3. *Crushing, grinding:* Low, rounded cusps occlude with low basins to masticate a variety of foods; sometimes useful for hard or slippery foods such as nuts and fruits (Photo 9.3).

4. *Tearing:* Large, pointy cusps with long, sharp edges cut foods into smaller bits without excessive preparation before swallowing; used particularly for meat-eating (Photo 9.4).

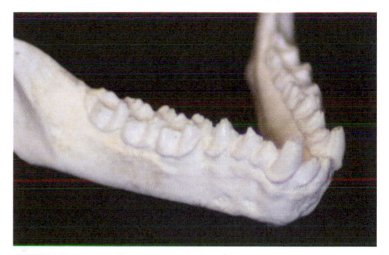

PHOTO 9.1 *Dentition for puncture-crushing/piercing*

PHOTO 9.2 *Dentition for shearing*

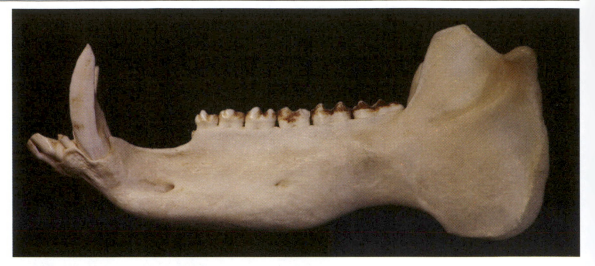

PHOTO 9.3 *Dentition for crushing and grinding*

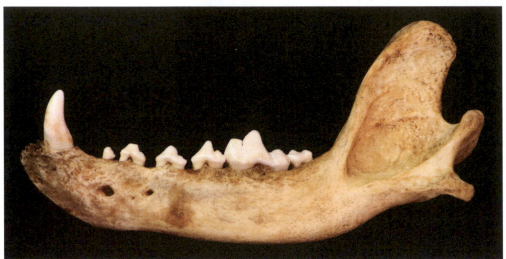

PHOTO 9.4 *Dentition for tearing*

Tooth Form

Molars can be classified in various ways, and the number of terms that refer to types and parts of the teeth is overwhelming. We will mention only several of the main forms. One of the first subcategories to consider is whether the molar teeth of a species are *high-crowned* or *low-crowned*.

High-Crowned Teeth If a tooth sticks up far above the gumline, it is high-crowned, or *hypsodont* (G *hypso*: high; *dont*: tooth). These teeth are present in herbivores such as deer, cows, and horses. In some species (particularly rodents), teeth continue to grow as they are worn down by abrasive foods, and enamel ridges make grinding more efficient.

Two types of hypsodont molars are *lophodont* (G *loph*: crest) and *selenodont* (G *selen*: moon) (Photo 9.5). Lophodont teeth have elongated ridges (lophs) that connect the cusps. Selenodont teeth (such as that in deer and cows) have cusps that have been elongated in

an anterior–posterior direction to increase cutting surfaces. Old World monkeys possess *bilophodont* (two-crested) molars, in which two crests connect the pairs of cusps in a medio-lateral direction (Photo 9.6).

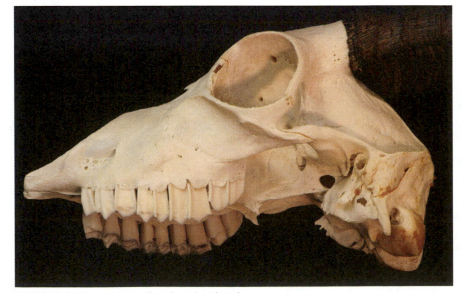

PHOTO 9.5 *Hypsodont teeth: selenodont (goat)*

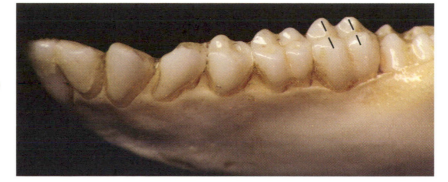

PHOTO 9.6 *Bilophodont molars (vervet monkey)*

Low-Crowned Teeth If a molar tooth is relatively low-crowned, it is described as *brachydont* (G *brachy*: short). One important type of brachydont tooth is exhibited by many species of mammal that eat a variety of foods (hard, soft, and everything in between). They may have square-shaped molars (quadrate), with low, rounded cusps. These teeth, termed *bunodont* (G *bun*: hill, mound), are found in humans (and many other primates), bears, and pigs (Photo 9.7).

Some members of the Order Carnivora (dogs and cats, but not bears) have a last upper premolar and first lower molar that is large and blade-like. These are the *carnassial* (L *carn*: flesh) teeth, used for slicing and chopping (Photo 9.8).

Skull Form

Keep in mind that the bony development of the skull depends on the size and shape of chewing muscles and the magnitude and direction of force generated in the skull while chewing.

- If you touch the side of your head in the region of your temple and clench and unclench your teeth, you'll feel the action of the temporalis muscle.

- The next time you have the opportunity to pet a large dog, feel the crown of its head (the top, toward the back). You may feel a bony bump. That is a sagittal crest, the site of attachment for the temporalis muscle.

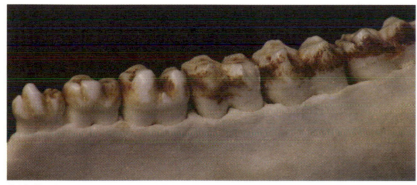

PHOTO 9.7 *Bunodont molars (peccary)*

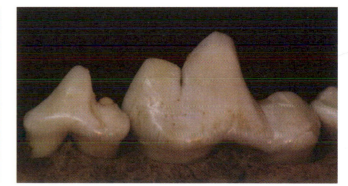

PHOTO 9.8 *Carnassial teeth (dog).*

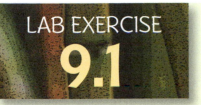

LAB EXERCISE
9.1

NAME _____

SECTION _____   DATE _____

1. Review the main four molar tooth functions and the tooth types. Then take a look at the dentitions of various mammalian species in your lab, or from a combination of your specimens and these photos. For each, list the type of mechanical function (puncture–crushing, shearing, etc.) undertaken by the molars, as well as its presumed diet. Use the chart on the following page.

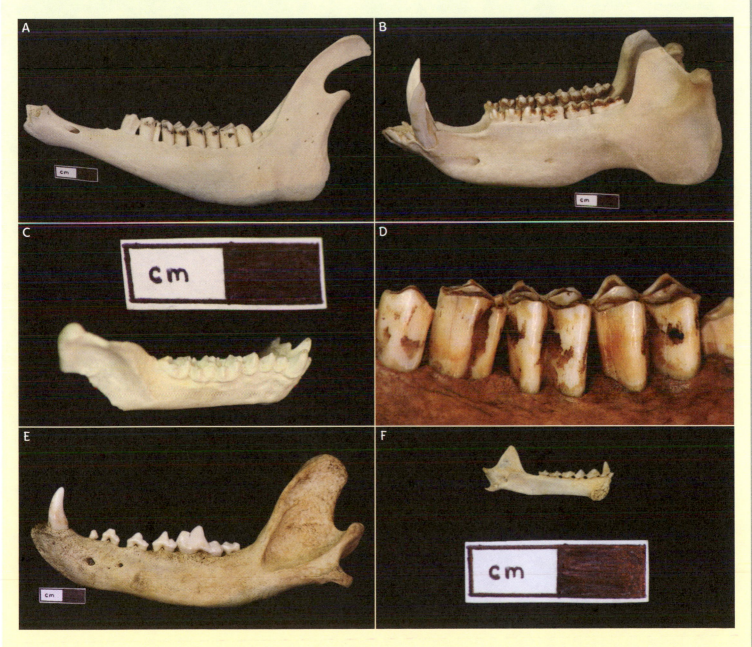

SPECIMEN	MECHANICAL FUNCTION	PRESUMED DIET	SPECIES (OPTIONAL)
A			
B			
C			
D			
E			
F			

2. Experiment to see which foods require processing with which teeth. Try each food type, and fill out the table regarding tooth use and form.

	SUNFLOWER SEEDS	CARROTS	BEEF JERKY	SPINACH OR LETTUCE	WHOLE APPLE	*SUNFLOWER SEED IN SHELL
Use of anterior dentition? (yes/no)						
Use of posterior dentition? (yes/no)						
Best kind of posterior teeth to break down food						

*This approximates the dentition needed to effectively break down the exoskeleton of a large insect, such as a cockroach or a beetle.

Evidence from the Postcranial Skeleton

Functional complexes occur throughout the body wherever form–function relationships have developed over time. For example, by looking at the bony human shoulder joint (e.g., the humeral head, how it articulates with the glenoid fossa of the scapula), we can see the potential range of motion. By applying laws of biomechanics, we know that the size and location of muscle attachment sites on bone indicate the size and orientation of muscles, and we can extrapolate the degree of speed or strength generated at that point.

We study postcranial remains for much the same reason that we study dental remains. Once we are familiar with form–function relationships in modern species, we can make inferences about fossils, including our extinct relatives. Just as teeth and diet are directly related, so are postcranial morphology (form) and **positional behavior—posture** and **locomotion**. Within each individual's body, the range of motion at every joint is limited by the morphology of the bone ends contributing to the joint, and the surrounding ligaments and muscle attachments. Because individual variation is found within species, some individuals have a morphology that is better suited than others to perform a specific motion. The most efficient forms for certain movements are selected by natural selection over time.

Thus, positional behavior is influenced by morphology, as well as by body size and use of substrates. Different forms of features will be selected for in **arboreal** species than in **terrestrial** species, because the challenges of arboreality and terrestriality are different.

The vast majority of primates are **quadrupeds** —using all four limbs in locomotion. Although many primates are arboreal, some species are terrestrially adapted—spending most of their time on the ground. Two main differences between arboreal and terrestrial quadrupedal primates are in *joint form* and *body segment ratios*.

The joints in **arboreal quadrupeds** are mobile, with fewer bony restrictions and more rounded joint surfaces than terrestrial species. **Terrestrial quadrupeds** are likely to have more stable joints, with their range of motion limited by the surrounding bony restrictions. For example, parts of a terrestrial baboon's femur are more similar to a deer's femur than that of a spider monkey. This is an example of convergent evolution, in which a similar form evolves as a result of similar environmental pressures to fulfill a similar function.

In arboreal quadrupeds, the **center of gravity** tends to be lower, closer to the **base of support**. Arboreal species typically have shorter limbs relative to their trunk, which lowers their body (and

center of gravity) and brings it closer to the substrate (see Figure 9.2). Because terrestrial animals do not have to worry about falling far, they tend to have longer limbs relative to their trunk, which enhances speed.

The forelimbs and hindlimbs of quadrupeds are approximately equal in length. This is more true for terrestrial quadrupeds than for arboreal ones, whose legs (hindlimbs) often are longer, enabling them to leap farther. The relative length of forelimbs and hindlimbs reflects their use. Primates with longer arms have a *forelimb-dominated* mode of locomotion, and longer legs indicate *hindlimb-dominated* locomotion (see Figure 9.3). Other main primate locomotor categories are brachiation arm-swinging, arboreal leaping, and bipedalism. We will deal with these more later in this chapter.

In this part of the lab, you will compare various bones to determine functional differences between species. You will be paying particular attention to the articular surface area of a joint. See Table 9.1 for features to look for on some selected bones.

FIGURE 9.2 (A) Arboreal and (B) terrestrial primates

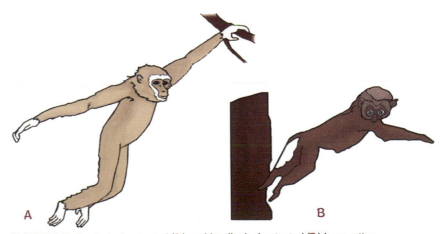

FIGURE 9.3 Forelimb-dominated (A) and hindlimb-dominated (B) locomotion

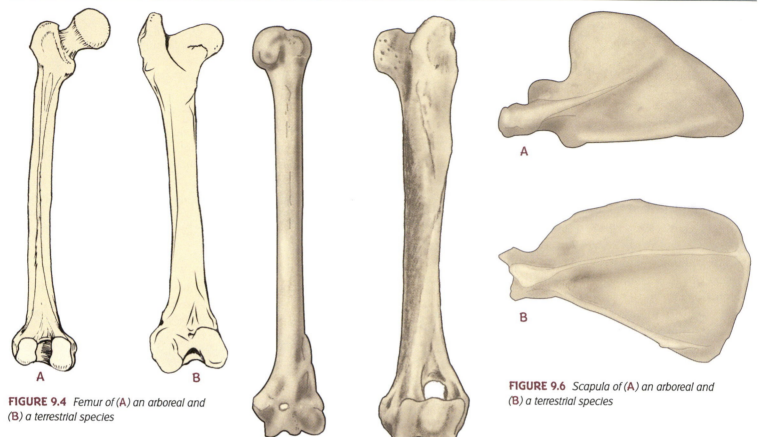

FIGURE 9.4 Femur of (A) an arboreal and (B) a terrestrial species

FIGURE 9.5 Humerus of (A) an arboreal and (B) a terrestrial species

FIGURE 9.6 Scapula of (A) an arboreal and (B) a terrestrial species

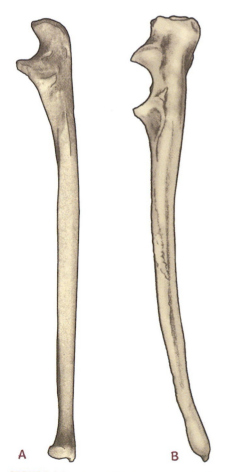

FIGURE 9.7 Ulna of (A) an arboreal and (B) a terrestrial species

TABLE 9.1: Functional Features of Selected Bones

	ARBOREAL (MORE MOBILITY)	TERRESTRIAL (MORE STABILITY)
Femur (Fig. 9.4)		
Femoral head	Rounded, globular	Less rounded, articular surface extends onto femoral neck
Greater trochanter	Low-set	Extends higher than femoral head
Humerus (Fig. 9.5)		
Humeral head	Rounded, globular	Less rounded, more ovoid
Tuberosities	Smaller, lower-set	Larger, bulkier
Scapula (Fig. 9.6)		
Size and shape	Shorter, broader	Longer, narrower
Placement	More dorsal placement	More lateral placement (functionally lengthens forelimb, increases stride length)
Ulna (Fig. 9.7)		
Olecranon process	Reduced (allows for full elbow extension)	Large (prevents full extension; doesn't fit inside olecranon fossa)

LAB EXERCISE
9.2

NAME _____

SECTION _____ DATE _____

In this exercise you will identify four types of bone (homologous bones) from a few different species and make inferences about the locomotion of each depending upon the morphology of the bone ends. Use the photos in Appendix D in addition to bones from your lab collection. Your instructor may provide some human bones for comparison, and assistance in identifying which bone is of what type.

1. Using ourselves as an example, we first will learn about some general features of locomotion. For this brief exercise, stand up.

   a. Where is your base of support?

   b. How can you make the base of support wider?

   c. How is your base of support different from that of a gorilla?

   d. Based on our limb-length ratios, our locomotion is _____- dominated.
   (hindlimb or forelimb)

2. From Appendix D, group the same types of bones together by cutting out the photos and physically putting them together. If available, use your real bone specimens. Which bones did you group together (photos are labeled A through L)?

Specimen	Bone
__ __ __	_____
__ __ __	_____
__ __ __	_____
__ __ __	_____

3. Now make some inferences about function for some of these bones. By examining the joint surface and surrounding area, determine how mobile or stable a joint is and possibly make inferences about movements that could have taken place at that joint.

SPECIMEN	EMPHASIS ON MOBILITY OR STABILITY?	LIKELY TO BE TERRESTRIALLY OR ARBOREALLY ADAPTED?	COMMENTS
A			
B	N/A		
C			
D			
E			
F	N/A		
I			
L			

SELF-TEST 9.1

NAME _____

SECTION _____ DATE _____

1. What type of molars do you have, according to the functional categories discussed in this lab?

2. What is your dental formula?

3. How do anterior and posterior dentition differ functionally?

4. What are the four main functional types of posterior dentitions in mammals?

   a.

   b.

   c.

   d.

5. Why should we study form–function relationships in living species?

6. Which has a relatively larger base of support, a penguin or a mouse?

7. What is a functional complex?

8. What are the two categories of positional behavior?

    a.

    b.

9. What are some primary differences in articular surface area between arboreally and terrestrially adapted mammal species?

10. What are some primary differences in limb segment ratios between arboreally and terrestrially adapted primates?

NAME _____

SECTION _____ DATE _____

Additional Lab Exercise 9.1

ADDITIONAL MATERIALS NEEDED:

- Osteometric board or tape measure (taped to a table)
- Humerus, radius, femur, and tibia from one individual (human)
- Limb bones of four nonhuman primate species—humerus, radius, femur, and tibia—each from same individual; label each species with letters A to D
- If nonhuman primate specimens are unavailable, use illustrations in lab manual to substitute

As mentioned previously, the study of joint form and body segment ratios is used to examine locomotion. Earlier in this chapter we noted the difference between hindlimb-dominated and forelimb-dominated locomotion. You'll now quantify this ratio of forelimbs to hindlimbs using the **intermembral index**. This index differs depending on the type of locomotion a species exhibits.

The formula for intermembral index is
$$\frac{\text{humerus} + \text{radius length}}{\text{femur} + \text{tibia length}} \times 100$$

The intermembral (IM) index indicates the following relationships:

- Approximately 100   forelimbs and hindlimbs of equal height
- Lower than 100   longer hindlimbs than forelimbs
- Greater than 100   longer forelimbs than hindlimbs

Other indices provide additional important information and help to avoid lumping disparate species into the same locomotor group. These include the **brachial index** and the **crural index**, which reflect the relative length of the upper vs. lower arm and upper vs. lower leg, respectively. The formulae for the brachial index and crural index are:

Brachial index

$$\frac{\text{Radius length}}{\text{Humerus length}} \times 100$$

Crural index

$$\frac{\text{Tibia length}}{\text{Femur length}} \times 100$$

Table 9.2 indicates some general associations between limb length and locomotion. This is a *general* guide, so keep in mind that all information should be taken together, including the information studied about joint surfaces and bone shape earlier in the chapter.

1. Using an osteometric board or a tape measure taped to the table, measure the *maximum length* of the humerus and the radius. For the tibia, measure from the *most superior point of the lateral condyle to the bottom of the medial malleolus*. Measure the *bicondylar length* of the femur (from the bottom of the condyles to a point even with the top of the femoral head).

    If you do not have measurable nonhuman primate specimens, use the illustrations labeled A through E, and measure the appropriate bones with a ruler or a sliding caliper. Your raw measurements obviously will be different from those taken on real bones, but the information you are seeking are *indices (relative lengths)*.

TABLE 9.2: Locomotor Categories and Associated Limb Proportions

GENERAL LOCOMOTOR CATEGORIES	RELATIVE LIMB PROPORTIONS	EXAMPLES
Arboreal quadrupedalism	Somewhat longer hindlimbs, to significantly longer hindlimbs than forelimbs	Squirrel monkey, langur
Terrestrial quadrupedalism	Limbs of approximately equal length	Baboon, vervet
Brachiation	Forelimbs much longer than hindlimbs	Gibbon
Arboreal leaper (including vertical clinger/leaper)	Hindlimbs much longer than forelimbs Forearm longer than upper arm	Tarsier, sifaka, galago (bushbaby)
Bipedalism	Hindlimbs much longer than forelimbs Upper arm longer than forearm	Human

Fill in the measurements in the chart below, then calculate the three indices using the formulae from page 231.

	A	B	C	D	E (Human)
Humerus (cm)					
Radius (cm)					
Brachial index					
Femur (cm)					
Tibia (cm)					
Crural index					
Intermembral index					

2. Compare your indices to the description of primate locomotor categories in Table 9.2. Into what categories do specimens A through E (pages 233 and 234) best fit? (E will be obvious.)

A _____   D _____

B _____   E _____

C _____

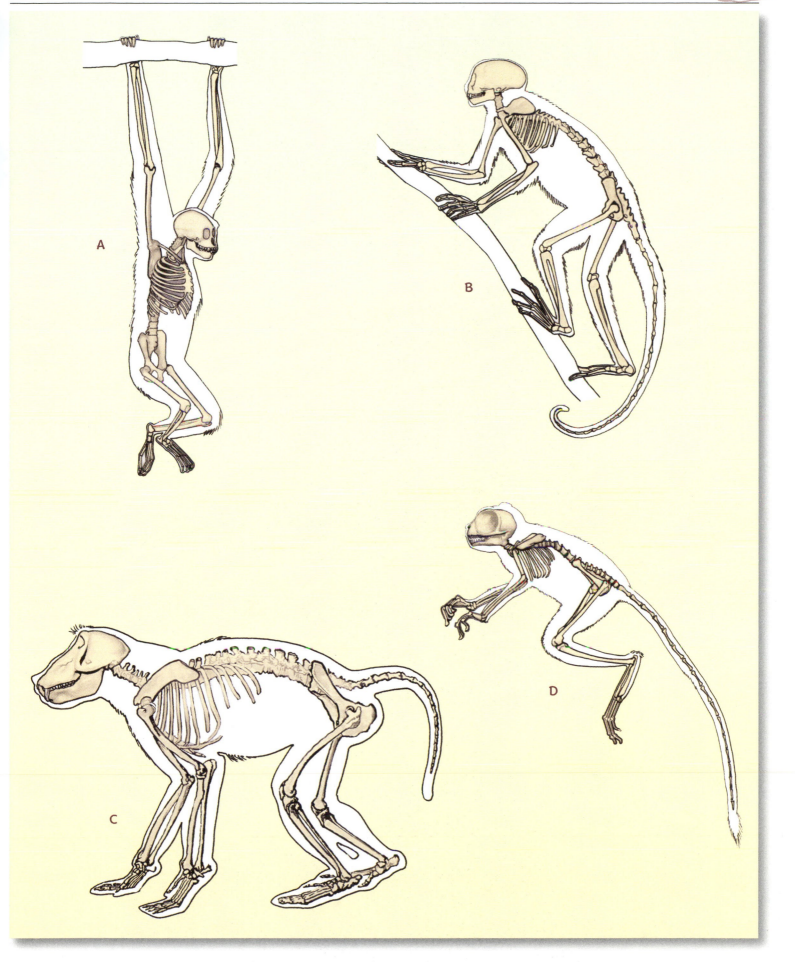

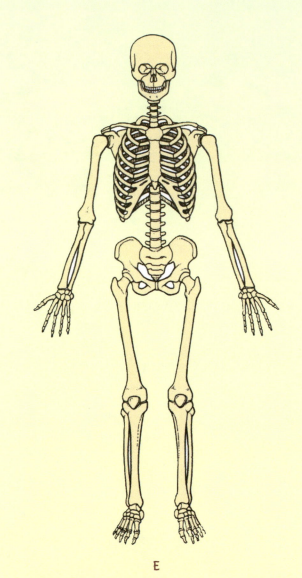

E

Biological Classification and the Living Primates

"Have you ever wondered . . . ?"

- What is the difference between a monkey and an ape?

OBJECTIVES

- Become familiar with the basis for biological classification
- Understand the concept of homology and its use in classifying living organisms
- Know the characteristics of the primate order
- Distinguish characteristics of the major groups and subgroups of primates
- Learn to identify primates vs. nonprimates based on skeletal features
- Provide an introduction to main schools of thought in systematics, some principles of cladistics, and how to interpret a cladogram

MATERIALS NEEDED

- Preferably, as many as possible of the following skulls:
  - dog or cat
  - lemur
  - other strepsirhine
  - tarsier
  - two or three New World monkeys
  - one or two Old World monkeys
  - one or two apes

(*Note: The above items can be substituted/supplemented with photos in lab manual.*)

- Number and letter labels to group the postcranial bones and set up lab "stations"

If we go back far enough in time, we will see that all living organisms have a shared ancestry. That the complex nature of our genetic blueprint is shared among all species is a strong line of evidence for this connection. The Kingdom Animalia encompasses an enormously diverse range of living creatures, from fleas, to lizards, to humans. Groups with a more recent common ancestry share more features with one another than do groups that share a common ancestor in the distant past. This chapter demonstrates how we can classify organisms into groups on the basis of similar characteristics that arose from a shared ancestry.

Establishing Evolutionary Relationships

Our shared ancestry with the flea can be traced far back in time, before humans, bears, or even mammals or vertebrates existed. Our shared ancestor is found early in the Paleozoic Era, which began about 600 million years ago. Many types of invertebrates existed at that time, but this was long before the first vertebrate appeared.

Over time, vertebrates evolved and diversified into various groups. One of the groups evolved into a creature with live-bearing young, fur, relatively large brain, teeth specialized for different functions, and a constant internal body temperature. These mammals originated within the Mesozoic Era, more than 200 million years ago. Mammals diversified, giving rise to the groups that included the taxonomic Order Carnivora, of which bears are a member, and the Order Primates, the order in which humans are a member.

Thus, the more distant shared ancestry of the human and the flea resulted in few shared features, but the more recent common ancestry of the bear and the human resulted in more shared features, which also are shared with many other mammalian species. The features that groups share as a result of common ancestry are called **homologous features**, or **homologies**. Figure 10.1 illustrates some of the species within the Kingdom Animalia, with a homologous feature (the humerus) illustrated in those species who possess this arm bone.

The group called the vertebrates contains a bony internal skeleton. It forms the **Subphylum Vertebrata**. Because similar characteristics are used to group (classify) organisms, we have to know how the characteristics that form the basis for our classifications arose in the first place. Similarities between groups of organisms can arise in two primary ways: analogies and homologies.

Analogies

The fish and the dolphin in Figure 10.1 are superficially similar in body form, reflecting adaptations to similar conditions rather than descent from a common ancestor possessing that body form. This is an example of an **analogy**, in which a feature evolves independently in different groups as a result of similar evolutionary pressures resulting in similar adaptations. Dolphins evolved from land mammals but converged upon a fish body form as a result of their gradually adapting to an aquatic environment. **Convergent evolution** caused analogous features to appear in fish and dolphins, which share a distant ancestry.

The bird's wing and the bat's wing provide another good example of an analogous characteristic that arose independently in the two groups. Other examples of analogies are the body form of a rabbit and that of a bandicoot (an Australian marsupial), and aquatic adaptations of seals and sea lions, each of which evolved separately from land-adapted mammals.

Homologies

Alternatively, the features of the two groups may be similar because their common ancestor had the feature and both descendant groups inherited it. As mentioned, a feature deriving from a common ancestor is termed a **homology**. For example, dogs and bears both have a humerus because they share a common ancestor (some early carnivore) that had a humerus. Cats and crocodiles both have femurs because they share a common ancestor (some early reptile of the Mesozoic Era) that had a femur. Another example of homology is the lack of a tail in humans and in apes. *Homologous features are useful for classification, because they reflect evolutionary relationships.*

Primitive Features Versus Derived Features

Two other concepts that are important in understanding evolutionary relationships are **primitive features** and **derived features**. A vertebral column is a primitive feature for vertebrates; the common ancestor of vertebrates had a vertebral column. Within the vertebrate group are the mammals. The features shared by and unique to mammals among the vertebrates are derived features, distinct and changed from those of the common ancestor. For example, only primates have opposable thumbs, so this is a derived feature shared only by other primates, not with all mammals.

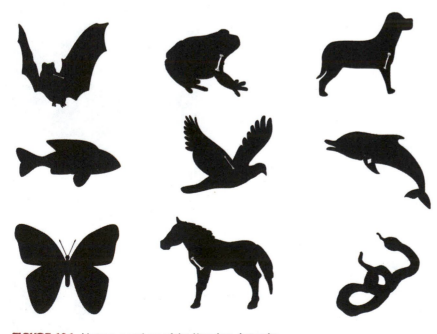

FIGURE 10.1 *Various members of the Kingdom Animalia*

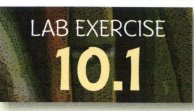

LAB EXERCISE 10.1

NAME _____

SECTION _____ DATE _____

Of the array of varied creatures within the Kingdom Animalia, some fly, some crawl, some leap, and some swim. This exercise asks you to place a number of them into taxonomic groups and decide which groups are related most closely to which other groups.

1. Start with a small sample to work with first, consisting of: fish, horse, frog, dolphin, butterfly, pigeon, dog, bat, and snake. You could dissect them to see the underlying structures, or refer to Figure 10.1 for the illustrations of various animals in the Kingdom Animalia, with part of the bony forelimb visible in some for comparison.

2. What separation would you make first? Which has an ancestry that is the most distant from the others?

   _____. Once that creature is separated from the others, all eight of the other species stand together in a group. What is an important feature common to all eight species?

3. Of those eight remaining animals, figure out which ones are mammals. Which of the following characteristics would help you decide. Why?

   fur   vertebral column

   limbs   mammary glands

   opposable thumbs   homeothermy (warm-blooded)

4. Is the humerus bone of the bird and bat an example of analogy or homology? (Check with your instructor on this one!)

Biological Classification

Classifications are information-retrieval systems that order objects into groups on the basis of similarities. These hierarchical systems consist of sets with subsets, each lower set sharing an increasing number of characteristics. Biological classification specifically orders living organisms into groups and subgroups based on their evolutionary relationships.

John Ray (British), **Casper Bauhin** (Swiss), and **Carl Linnaeus** (Swedish) each devised a biological classification system independently. Although Ray and Bauhin lived and worked in an earlier time than Linnaeus did, the latter's work alone is what is remembered. The system of **binomial nomenclature** uses two names—the **genus** and the **species**. For example, in *Australopithecus africanus*, *Australopithecus* is the genus and *africanus*, the most basic unit, is the species.

The **binomen** is a combination of names for genus and species that is unique and universal. Latin, which is no longer the primary language of any country, enables scientists worldwide to communicate without favoring one language over another. Although common names differ among countries, scientific names are the same everywhere. For example, dog is *perro* in Argentina and Mexico, *chien* in Quebec and France, but scientists all over the world use the term *Canis familiaris.*

The biological classification hierarchy for the orangutan looks like this:

Kingdom	Animalia
Phylum	Chordata
Subphylum	Vertebrata
Class	Mammalia (mammals—not birds, reptiles)
Order	Primates (prosimians, monkeys, apes)
Family	Pongidae (ape family)
Genus	*Pongo*
Species	*Pongo pygmaeus*

Alternative Classification Schemes

The science of naming organisms is called **taxonomy**. A **taxon** (*pl:* **taxa**) is a taxonomic group. At higher levels of classification, members of a taxon share fewer characteristics and a common ancestor farther back in time. At lower levels, members of a taxon share increasing numbers of characteristics and a more recent common ancestor. Groups of species are classified on the basis of their evolutionary relationships. Alternative ways of classifying organisms are based on two facets of such relationships:

1. Recency of divergence—how recently two groups shared a common ancestor

2. To what extent the groups diverged—how much each group has changed in the time since they shared a common ancestor

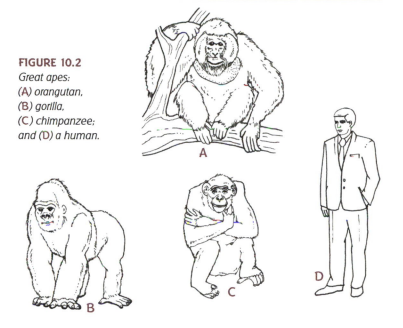

FIGURE 10.2
Great apes:
(A) *orangutan,*
(B) *gorilla,*
(C) *chimpanzee;*
and (D) *a human.*

Figure 10.2 presents illustrations of three apes and a human. Through biochemical and fossil evidence, we know that orangutans diverged from the evolutionary line leading to African apes (chimpanzees and gorillas) and humans more than 15 million years ago, while humans diverged from the African apes 7 or 8 million years ago. Therefore, African apes and humans share a more recent common ancestor with one another and are related to each other more closely than any of the three are to the orangutan. Humans, however, have diverged much more since the time of the common ancestor. We differ more from the common ancestor in appearance and (presumably!) in behavior than any of the other great apes.

The more traditional classification, based upon the school of thought called **evolutionary taxonomy,** would place humans apart from all of the great apes because of our greater degree of change since our split from the common ancestor. The newer (now more common) school of thought is **cladistics,** which emphasizes the actual timeframe of evolutionary divergence. The One Step Further feature at the end of the chapter provides more information on this topic, together with an additional lab exercise and questions to answer.

The Order Primates

The primates constitute an order of mammals. Examples of other orders within the Class Mammalia are

- Rodentia (rodents)
- Chiroptera (bats)
- Artiodactyla and Perissodactyla (the two hoofed mammal orders).

The Order **Primates** is thought to have originated from insectivore-like (shrew/hedgehog order) stock approximately

65 million years ago. The evolution of primates is discussed further in Chapter 12.

Homologous skeletal features can be used to classify the primates in terms of their place in the Class Mammalia, and their subgroupings within the primate order. Although we now can also use a number of genetics techniques for classification, in this lab we will cover skeletal features that are useful for grouping the primates. At right is a list of primate characteristics, or evolutionary trends of the order. Figure 10.3 illustrates some of these features that serve to distinguish *most* primates from *most* other mammalian orders. Although some other groups possess some of these features, primates have all or most of these as a *suite* of characteristics.

Distribution, Habitat, Diet

Extant (living) primates are distributed throughout much of the tropics and subtropics, although their numbers are drastically declining, mostly a result of habitat encroachment. They are found in tropical Africa, India, and Southeast Asia, as well as South and Central America (and a few even in North America, in Mexico)—see Figure 10.4. The primate inhabitants of Madagascar, besides the relatively recent addition of humans, are a diverse group that includes all lemur-like forms.

Primates inhabit a variety of habitats, from wet rainforest to quite dry savanna. As an order, primates are highly adaptable and sometimes coexist successfully with humans. Most primates eat a basically vegetarian diet, but they may specialize in certain classes of foods. These dietary types are:

- *folivory* (leaf-eating)
- *frugivory* (fruit-eating)
- *gramnivory* (seed-eating)
- *gummivory* (gum-eating)

Some are primarily *insectivorous*. Many are *omnivorous* and eat a variety of plant and animal matter. As you saw in Chapter 9, dietary adaptations are reflected in the dentition.

Characteristics of Primates

*1. Unique ear region
 — petrosal bulla (*Atlas*, p. 9, Figure 1.15)
*2. Retention of unspecialized limb skeleton
 — retention of five fingers and five toes and retention of clavicle; this is unlike hoofed mammals, for example, which have lost most of their digits and have no clavicle
*3. Nails (rather than claws) on digits; tactile pads
*4. Grasping hind feet with opposable first toes; grasping hands; some with opposable thumb
*5. Increased emphasis on vision:
 — forward-facing eyes, allowing for better depth perception
 — expanded occipital and temporal lobes (visual centers)
 — color vision (in most primates)
*6. Complete ring of bone around orbit: postorbital bar
*7. Enlarged brain relative to body size; complex, more elaborate neocortex
*8. Less emphasis on olfaction:
 — shortened snout
 — small olfactory bulbs
*9. Fewer teeth; primitive cusp pattern preserved
10. Longer fetal nourishment, intrauterine development, prolonged stages of lifespan
11. Longer period of infant dependency and parental care
12. Most are gregarious (live in social groups) with well-developed communication systems

*Features that are especially important because they also can be observed in the fossil record.

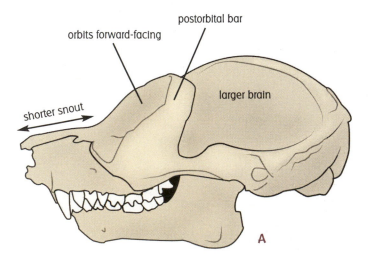

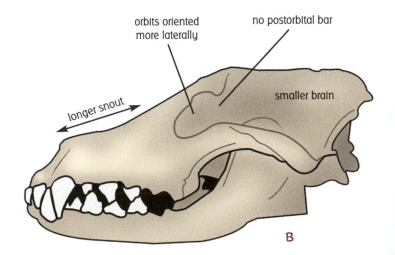

FIGURE 10.3 *Some comparative features of (A) primate and (B) nonprimate*

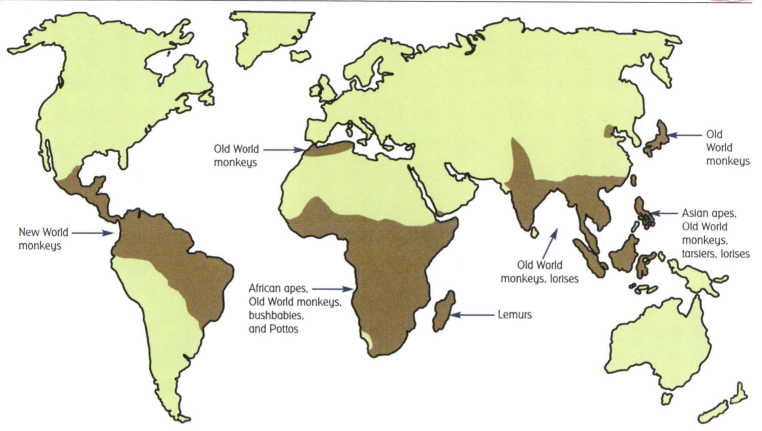

FIGURE 10.4 *Primate distribution*

LAB EXERCISE
10.2

NAME _____

SECTION _____ DATE _____

In examining a number of mammal skeletons—for example, bear, lion, opossum, wolf, raccoon, pig, and elephant, in addition to several primate species—what characteristics would you use to decide whether a skeleton is a primate?

1. Circle the characteristics you would use.

fur   opposable thumbs

forward-facing eyes   relatively small olfactory bulbs

relatively large brain   mammary glands

2. For the characteristics you did not circle, why didn't you think they would be useful to differentiate primates from nonprimates?

3. Fill out the chart below, using the photos on the next page or skulls in your lab collection.

	DOG	MONKEY
Postorbital bar?		
Cranium size relative to body size (or face)		
Emphasis on olfaction (based on snout size)		
Type of teeth (from Chapter 9)		
*Opposable first toes or thumbs?		
*Nails or claws?		
*Not observable in the photo, but this is basic information		

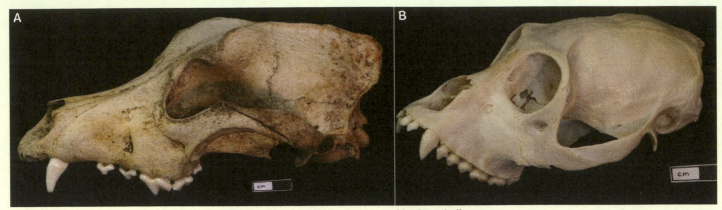

Dog skull   Monkey skull

4. Look at the photos below or your lab specimens and *note the form* of the listed features in the chart below. You will use your answers later to place the specimens into suborders (Strepsirhini and Haplorhini).

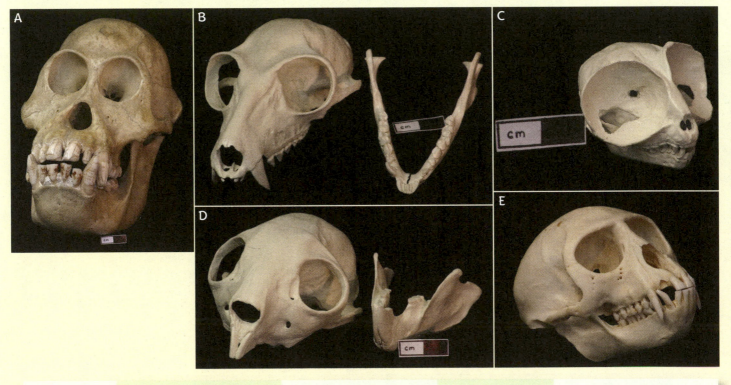

SPECIMEN	FUSED MANDIBULAR SYMPHYSIS? (IS THE MANDIBLE ONE BONE OR TWO?)*	CRANIUM SIZE (BRAINCASE) RELATIVE TO FACE	FULLY ENCLOSED ORBIT?	TOOTHCOMB? (LOWER INCISORS JUT FORWARD)
A				
B				
C				
D				
E				

*If a suture line is visible, mandibular symphysis is unfused.

Primate Classification

Suborders The primates can be divided into two suborders—the **Strepsirhini** and the **Haplorhini**—named for the form of their nose. Strepsirhini refers to the "turned nose" (comma-shaped nostrils), as contrasted with Haplorhini, the "simple nose." Each of these two suborders is made up of richly varied primates that can be subclassified into various infraorders, superfamilies, families, and so forth.

- Strepsirhines exhibit a number of primitive characteristics that are shared by most mammals, but they are united by two important **derived features** (unique to the group): a toothcomb (*Atlas* p. 37) and a grooming claw. The best-known example of a strepsirhine is a lemur.

- The haplorhines are more obviously "human-like" and include monkeys of both the New World (the Americas) and the Old World (Africa and Asia), the apes (chimpanzees, gorillas, orangutans and gibbons), and humans.

Figure 10.5 shows selected differences between these suborders.

Traditional Classification The traditional classification of the primates split the primates into two suborders— **Prosimii** (G *pro* – before; *simia* – ape) and **Anthropoidea** (G *anthrop* – man; *oid* - like)—instead of Strepsirhini and Haplorhini. The primate members of the two groups in both the traditional and the newer classification are virtually the same, with the exception of the tarsier (discussed next).

FIGURE 10.5 *Selected characteristics of the primate suborders*

*derived features for strepsirhines

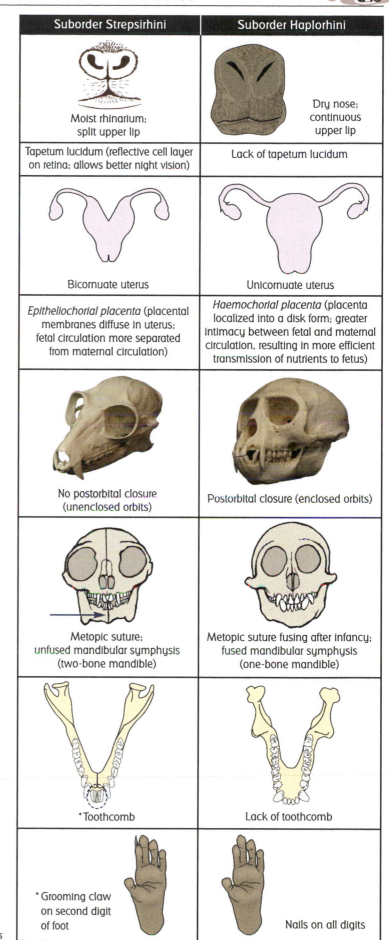

Suborder Strepsirhini	Suborder Haplorhini
Moist rhinarium; split upper lip	Dry nose; continuous upper lip
Tapetum lucidum (reflective cell layer on retina; allows better night vision)	Lack of tapetum lucidum
Bicornuate uterus	Unicornuate uterus
Epitheliochorial placenta (placental membranes diffuse in uterus; fetal circulation more separated from maternal circulation)	*Haemochorial placenta* (placenta localized into a disk form; greater intimacy between fetal and maternal circulation, resulting in more efficient transmission of nutrients to fetus)
No postorbital closure (unenclosed orbits)	Postorbital closure (enclosed orbits)
Metopic suture; unfused mandibular symphysis (two-bone mandible)	Metopic suture fusing after infancy; fused mandibular symphysis (one-bone mandible)
*Toothcomb	Lack of toothcomb
*Grooming claw on second digit of foot	Nails on all digits

Infraorder Levels Although strepsirhines and haplorhines each include infraorders and lower-level taxa, we will focus on the haplorhines only, as they are related more closely to us. Figure 10.6 is a partial classification of the primate order. The Haplorhini has three infraorders:

1. **Tarsiiformes** (tarsiers)
2. **Platyrrhini** (G *plat*: broad; *rhin*: nose)
3. **Catarrhini** (G *cat*: downward; *rhin*: nose)

Tarsiers (see Photo 10.1) are distinct from the other haplorhines and were traditionally classified with the strepsirhines in the old suborder Prosimii. The platyrrhines (New World monkeys) and catarrhines (Old World monkeys, apes, and humans) are more similar to each other. Important differences are found in the ear region (Photo 10.2); (note the bony ear tube, the ectotympanic tube, on the catarrhine) and the nose (Figure 10.7).

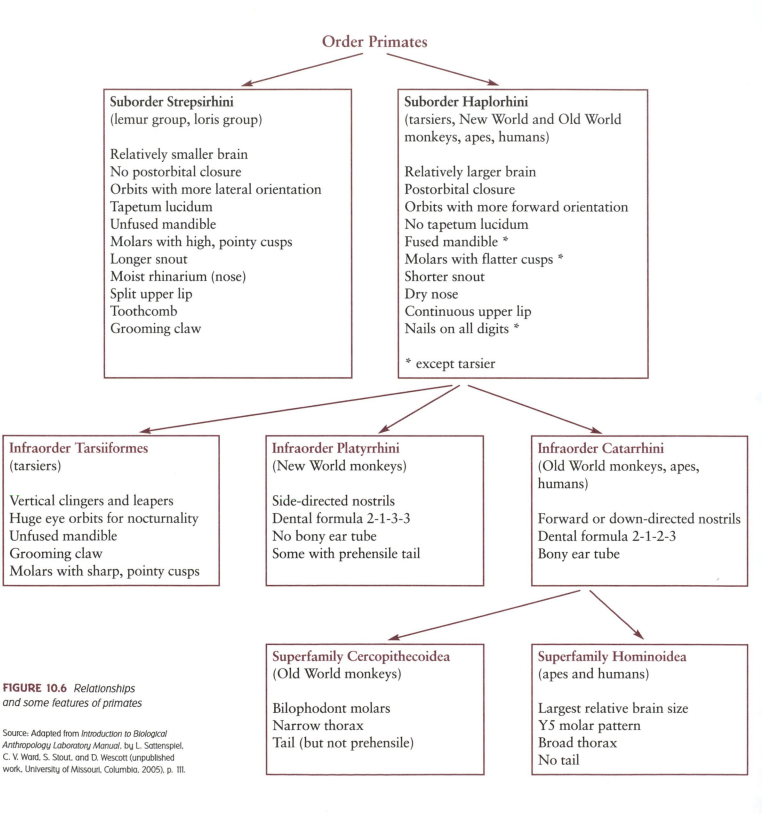

FIGURE 10.6 *Relationships and some features of primates*

Source: Adapted from *Introduction to Biological Anthropology Laboratory Manual*, by L. Sattenspiel, C. V. Ward, S. Stout, and D. Wescott (unpublished work, University of Missouri, Columbia, 2005), p. 111.

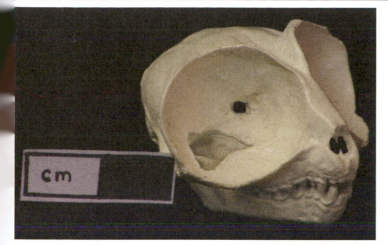

PHOTO 10.1 *Tarsier skull*

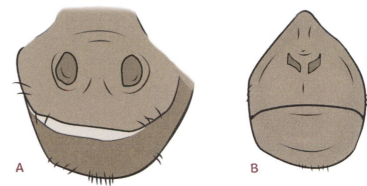

FIGURE 10.7 *Nose shape and nostril orientation in platyrrhines (A) and catarrhines (B)*

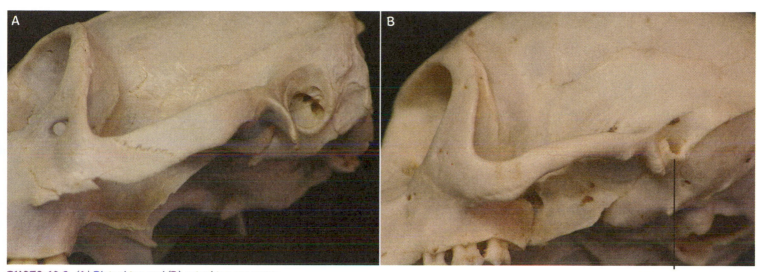

PHOTO 10.2 *(A) Platyrrhine and (B) catarrhine ear region*

bony ear tube

Superfamily Level As we move down to lower levels in the biological classification system, members of the taxa share more features. We will continue to focus on the haplorhines, keeping in mind that the strepsirhines also have their own taxonomic subgroupings.

Within the Platyrrhini there is only one superfamily of New World monkeys, the **Ceboidea**. We will not classify the lower levels within the Ceboidea. Examples of New World monkeys include spider monkeys, capuchins, squirrel monkeys, marmosets, and tamarins.

Within the Catarrhini there are two superfamilies: the **Cercopithe-coidea** (Old World monkeys) and the **Hominoidea** (ape and human group). Some differences between the two superfamilies are given in Figure 10.6 and are observable in Figure 10.8. (see also *Atlas*

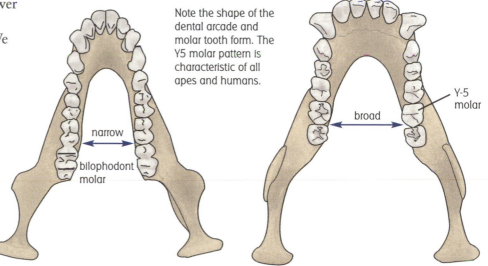

Note the shape of the dental arcade and molar tooth form. The Y5 molar pattern is characteristic of all apes and humans.

narrow

bilophodont molar

broad

Y-5 molar

FIGURE 10.8 *Examples of differences between (A) a cercopithecoid and (B) a hominoid*

p. 59, Photo 3.50D for bilophodont molar and p. 67, Photo 3.65, for Y-5 molar pattern.)

LAB EXERCISE
10.3

NAME _____

SECTION _____   DATE _____

1. Using Figure 10.5 as guide, decide which of the specimens in photos A–E on page 244 (not the photos on this page) are strepsirhines and which are haplorhines. List them below.

Strepsirhines:

Haplorhines:

2. Fill out the chart with reference to the photos A–E, shown below:

SPECIMEN	SIZE OF ORBITS RELATIVE TO BRAIN SIZE (SMALL OR LARGE)	FUSED MANDIBULAR SYMPHYSIS?	FULLY ENCLOSED ORBITS?	DENTAL FORMULA (IF OBSERVABLE)	BONY EAR TUBE? (IF OBSERVABLE)
A					
B					
C					
D					
E					

3. Which of the specimens on p. 249 are haplorhines? _____

   Which are strepsirhines? _____

4. Is one of the specimens on p. 249 a tarsier? _____ If so, which one? _____

5. From p. 249, which are platyrrhines _____, and which are catarrhines?

   _____

6. Using Photos A through C below, answer the following questions for each. Be careful to use characteristics that are *distinguishing for that group* at that *specific level in the taxonomic hierarchy*! For example, if deciding whether an animal is a platyrrhine or a catarrhine, be sure to name features that distinguish members of Platyrrhini from Catarrhini. Figures 10.5 and 10.6 can serve as a guide.

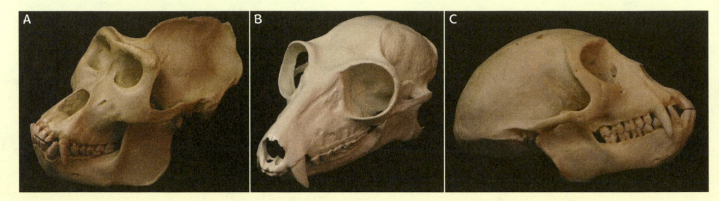

Photo A

  1. Is this a primate? _____ Why or why not?

  2. Is this a strepsirhine or a haplorhine? _____ How do you know?

  3. If a haplorhine, is it a tarsier, a platyrrhine or a catarrhine? _____ How do you know?

Photo B

1. Is this a primate? _____ Why or why not?

2. Is this a strepsirhine or a haplorhine? _____ How do you know?

3. If a haplorhine, is it a tarsier, a platyrrhine or a catarrhine? _____ How do you know?

Photo C

1. Is this a primate? _____ Why or why not?

2. Is this a strepsirhine or a haplorhine? _____ How do you know?

3. If a haplorhine, is it a tarsier, platyrrhine or catarrhine? _____ How do you know?

SELF-TEST 10.1

NAME _____

SECTION _____   DATE _____

1. Would you say the following represent examples of a homology or an analogy? Why?

   a. bird humerus and bat humerus

   b. vertebral column of a fish and vertebral column of a cat

   c. butterfly wing and bird wing

2. What is an important difference between evolutionary taxonomists and cladists in the way the living organisms are classified?

3. Which charactersistics are the most useful to use for classification, primitive or derived?

4. Define binomen.

   Give an example:

5. Match the following characteristics with the correct taxon. Only one of them has more than one correct response.

   _____ 1. no tail   A. Catarrhini

   _____ 2. laterally directed nostrils   B. Hominoidea

   _____ 3. bony ear tube   C. Platyrrhini

   _____ 4. some have prehensile tails   D. Strepsirhini

   _____ 5. two-part mandible   E. Cercopithecoidea

6. Name two strepsirhine characteristics that differentiate them from haplorhines.

   a.

   b.

7. Name two catarrhine characteristics that differentiate them from platyrrhines.

   a.

   b.

8. Name two haplorhine characteristics (that differentiate them from strepsirhines).

   a.

   b.

9. Name two platyrrhine characteristics (that differentiate them from catarrhines).

   a.

   b.

10. Name two differences between hominoids and cercopithecoids.

   a.

   b.

ONE STEP FURTHER

NAME _____

SECTION _____ DATE _____

Additional Lab Exercise 10.1

If taxonomy is the science of naming organisms, **systematics** is the theoretical and philosophical framework for the system of naming that is used. The schools of thought mentioned previously—*evolutionary taxonomy* and *cladistics*—are part of the systematics framework. The manner in which a researcher classifies living organisms depends partly on how one looks at the evolutionary process, and the accuracy with which he/she believes that a biological classification should reflect evolutionary history.

A more traditional way of depicting evolutionary history is a sort of tree, with branches representing various evolutionary lines. Such an evolutionary (or phylogenetic) tree imparts a great deal of information, including: ancestor–descendant relationships, how long ago evolutionary branching occurred, and for how long each species existed. Evolutionary taxonomists use **evolutionary trees**.

Cladistics is concerned with evolutionary relationships and highlights *branching patterns* that demonstrate the taxa that shared an ancestry more recently versus longer ago. Relationships are represented graphically by a **cladogram** (p. 254), which does not include a time factor and does not specify ancestor–descendant relationships. A cladogram is constructed using the following basic steps:

1. Select the taxonomic group to undergo analysis
2. Identify **characters**—any feature of an organism that forms the basis for comparison; for example, tail
3. Identify **character states**—all possible forms of each character; for example, tails may be present or absent, prehensile (grasping) or non-prehensile
4. Determine whether each character state is the primitive form or the derived form of the character (*e.g.*, a tail in primates is the primitive form, while apes/humans have the derived form—lack of a tail); this usually is accomplished by comparison to a taxonomic group outside of, but closely related to, the group under analysis
5. Group taxa according to shared character states that are derived (not primitive)

Cladistics has its own, extensive set of associated terminology. A few terms have been presented, and below are two more that relate specifically to interpreting a cladogram. See the cladogram on the next page and identify each:

- **Clade:** each of the five lines shown here represents an evolutionary lineage, or clade (G *clad*: branch)
- **Node:** branching point for each clade (*e.g.*, **A**); a hypothetical ancestral form that possesses a particular set of features. Features present at **A** (on the next page) are shared by all taxa above that level; thus, taxa **V** and **VI** will share these features.

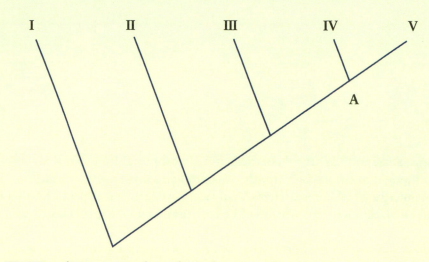

I, II, III, IV, and V represent hypothetical taxonomic groups.

The following questions refer to the next cladogram that focuses on the primates. In this case, the Order Insectivora is the **outgroup** (the taxonomic group outside of, but related to, the group under analysis).

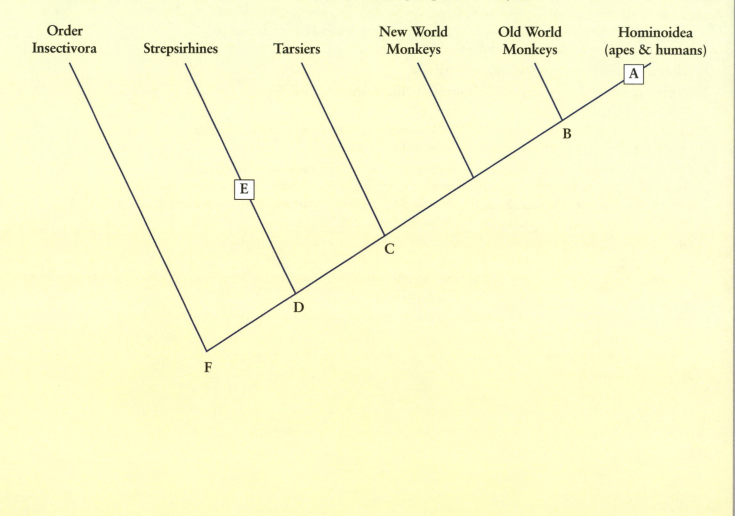

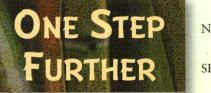

ONE STEP FURTHER

NAME _____

SECTION _____ DATE _____

Additional Lab Exercise **10.1** (cont.)

With your lab partner, observe the cladogram at the bottom of p. 254 and identify the nodes and the clades. From the list of primate features given below, fill in blanks 1 through 6. Some blanks should have more than one feature listed.

toothcomb
2123 dental formula
post-orbital closure
forward-facing eyes
dry nose and continuous upper lip
post-orbital bar
Y5 molar pattern
opposable big toe
grooming claw
lack of tapetum lucidum
moist rhinarium and split upper lip

1. Point A (on the Hominoid clade)   _____

2. Node B   _____

3. Node C   _____

4. Point E (on the Strepsirhine clade) _____

5. Node D   _____

6. Node F   _____

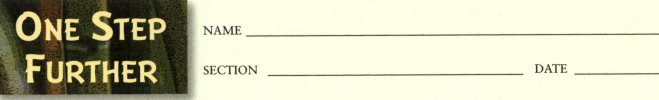

NAME _____

SECTION _____ DATE _____

Additional Self-Test Questions

Based on the bulleted characteristics, classify each primate below.

1. This primate has:

   • dry nose
   • one-part mandible
   • 2 1 3 3 dental formula

   What is it?

   suborder _____

   infraorder _____

2. This primate has:

   • no tapetum lucidum (reflective cell layer in eye for night vision)
   • 2123 dental formula
   • no tail

   What is it?

   suborder _____

   infraorder _____

   superfamily _____

3. In the traditional version of primate classification, tarsiers were included with the:

   a. monkeys   c. prosimians
   b. anthropoids   d. tree shrews

4. Features that have undergone much change since the last common ancestor, or are recently adapted features, are

   a. primitive
   b. homologous
   c. derived
   d. analogous

5. List five features that differentiate primates from other mammalian groups.

   a.   d.

   b.   e.

   c.

6. Cladistics or Evolutionary taxonomy? (put a **C** or **ET** in the blank)

   Which school of systematics emphasizes:

   _____ a. amount of change (evolution) of groups since the shared common ancestor

   _____ b. recency of divergence from the common ancestor; branching patterns

7. Hominoid or Cercopithecoid? (put an **H** or a **C** in the blank)

   _____ a. narrow thorax

   _____ b. Y-5 molar pattern

   _____ c. tail

   _____ d. bilophodont molars

   _____ e. broad palate

   _____ f. larger relative brain size

Bonus:

What are two characteristics that are primitive for mammals but derived for vertebrates?

Fill in the blanks below.

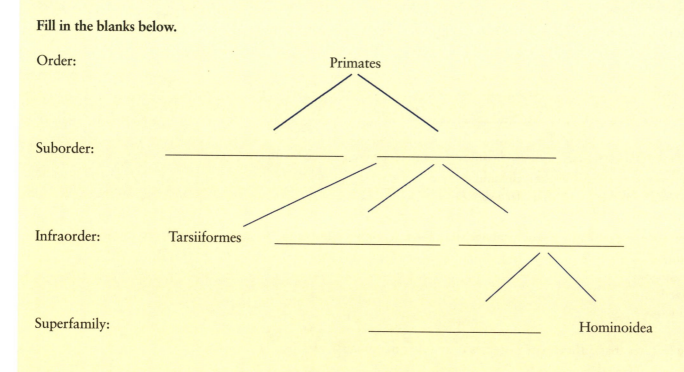

Order: Primates

Suborder: _____   _____

Infraorder: Tarsiiformes   _____   _____

Superfamily: _____   Hominoidea

Observing the Behavior of Living Primates

Now that you are familiar with the main primate groups, you will apply that knowledge to study them in a systematic way. If it is feasible to visit a zoo or other captive animal facility for this lab, you probably will gain a different perspective on nonhuman primates than you held previously.

The study of animal behavior involves quantifying phenomena that are observed, and collecting data in the most unbiased and objective manner possible. Not only are captive primates intrinsically interesting, but data collected on them also may be useful in dealing with zoo management issues such as gauging the effects of a new enclosure or new cagemates.

In this lab, you will learn some specific techniques to observe primates as well as other animals. In lieu of an accessible zoo or other facility with at least two primate species, a video may be substituted. (See One Step Further, p. 277).

Captive Primates

Captive primates exhibit a somewhat different range of behaviors than they would in their natural habitat. They are provided food regularly, and their diet is different from what their wild counterparts would be eating; they move about on different substrates than they would in nature; and they are not free to migrate from one group to another. Thus, their ability to express choice in mates is more limited than it would be in the wild. Still, behaviors specific to each species distinguish them from all others, whether in the wild or in a captive setting. From captive primates, observers can obtain a good sense of the behavioral characteristics of various species.

Preparation

Success in conducting this research depends on following instructions closely. Careful organization allows you to easily assemble your report and will make for your instructor's more feasible evaluation of your work. Before you begin observing and collecting data, read over the entire lab to be sure the instructions are clear.

You will need the following items at the zoo:

- classification sheet with physical characteristics of primates from Figure 10.6 in Chapter 10
- blank paper (graph paper or lined paper)
- clipboard or notebook
- watch (preferably digital)

Optional:

- three extra copies of Lab Exercise 11.1
- ruler (particularly if you don't have graph paper)
- binoculars or opera glasses (primates may be housed a distance away—for example, on an island)
- camera or videocamera
- tape recorder

Please follow all instructions posted at the zoo and don't feed or interact with the animals. You will be attempting to obtain the most natural behavior you can retrieve in this setting. Always treat the animals with respect.

You will differentiate the various types of primates at the zoo and record some basic information on their physical and behavioral features, as well as facts on ecology and distribution from the zoo signs (supplemented by information from other sources as needed). You will use basic observational techniques to collect data.

LAB EXERCISE
11.1

NAME _____

SECTION _____ DATE _____

List up to eight primate species at the zoo for which you may record information. This lab can be feasibly conducted even if only two or three primate species are present.

Common Name   **Scientific Name**

1. _____   _____

2. _____   _____

3. _____   _____

4. _____   _____

5. _____   _____

6. _____   _____

7. _____   _____

8. _____   _____

Classification of Primates, Characteristics, Geographical Distribution

For at least four species of *primate* at the zoo (this number may be modified at the instructor's discretion), fill out items A through D. For A, B, and C, additional information may be necessary to look up in a text or on the Internet. Be sure to cite any sources used. Figure 10.6 in Chapter 10 will be useful here.

A. Common name and scientific name of primate

Below, write the common name and the scientific name. The proper way to write a scientific name is to either *italicize* (if using the computer) or <u>underline</u> *both the genus and species* names (and subspecies if it has one), capitalizing only the first letter of the genus name (for example, *Saguinus oedipus*).

_____   _____

B. Classification

1. To which suborder does the primate belong (Strepsirhini or Haplorhini)?

_____

How can you tell which suborder, *by looking at the individuals before you*? (What features are observable to *you* that indicate its classification?)

2. To what infraorder does the species belong? _____

3. To which superfamily does the species belong? _____

C. Habitats, geographical distribution

1. In what kind of habitat is the primate found? (e.g., savanna, rainforest)

2. Where is the primate found geographically? (continent, region)

D. Observed features and behaviors

1. What is the primate's body size? (Compare it to commonly seen animals, or approximate body weight, if known.)

2. Look at its hands. Is there anything unusual about the fingers or thumb? How similar or different do they appear compared to our hands? (*Hint*: Look at fingernails and opposability of thumb.)

3. Does this primate have a tail? If so, is it prehensile (grasping)? What does the tail do, even if nonprehensile? How long is the tail in relation to its body length?

4. What is its primary mode of locomotion (how does it move around)?

5. How many individuals are in the exhibit, and how old do they appear to be? How many males and how many females?

6. Is this a sexually dimorphic species? (In **sexual dimorphism**, males and females may have different body sizes.)

7. Describe the primate's pelage (coat).

8. Are the primates feeding? If so, what are they eating?

9. Observe the animals in the exhibit for about 5 minutes, and describe some behaviors you see.

Primate Behavioral Observations

Now you will learn some common animal observational techniques. You will choose one species of primate at the zoo and apply three different data collection techniques to that species: **ad libitum sampling**, **instantaneous sampling**, and **scan sampling**. An important objective is to learn to distinguish which sampling methods are best for which species and/or situations.

If possible, choose species that are visible in their exhibit so you can collect data successfully. In the ad libitum, or "diary" approach, record all behaviors for all animals (Altmann, 1974; Martin and Bateson, 1993).

Ad Libitum Sampling

On the "*Ad Libitum* Sampling" sheet, record your chosen primate species.

You will spend *one-half hour* collecting data on the study species, keeping a detailed running list of *all behaviors*

performed by all animals, including references to the time. For example:

> From 11:32 to 11:35, the female groomed her own leg.
>
> At 11:35, she got up, quadrupedally walked over to the male, and sat down one foot away from him."

Detail is important. If your animals are inactive, even more specificity is needed. For example, instead of "The male sat for 10 minutes, and the female stood nearby," you might write something like:

> Beginning at 3:27, the male sat still on his haunches on the ground, looking forward; licked lips; rolled eyes.
>
> At 3:29 he closed his eyes and rested for 2 minutes, at times twitching his left little finger. At the same time, the female was standing quadrupedally, watching me.

LAB EXERCISE
11.2

NAME _____

SECTION _____ DATE _____

Ad Libitum Sampling

Species: _____ Date: _____

Conditions: _____ Starting time: _____

Focal Animal Instantaneous Sampling

The focal animal instantaneous sampling method is really a combination of two different techniques that are useful for the collection (and later analysis) of data on a number of variables at once.

1. In **instantaneous sampling** (Altmann, 1974; Martin and Bateson, 1993), data are recorded at *predetermined intervals* (*e.g.,* every 30 seconds, or every 2 minutes).

2. **Focal animal sampling** allows the observer to concentrate and collect data more accurately on the behavior of *one individual at a time* (Altmann, 1974; Martin and Bateson, 1993).

This lab has two options, depending upon time constraints and your instructor's directions.

    Option 1:   Create your own data sheet, or

    Option 2:   Use the data sheet "Focal Animal Instantaneous Sampling" in Lab Exercise 11.3

Normally you would spend some time observing your animals to obtain an idea of their general behavior. Because you have just watched them and recorded their behavior, this step isn't necessary.

Option 1: Ethogram and Data Sheet Preparation

An ethogram (also called a behavioral taxonomy; see Lehner, 1987) is a catalog of the behaviors in the behavioral repertoire of a species.

1. After spending at least 20 additional minutes observing the animals, *list all* of the *behaviors* you see.

2. Immediately afterward, while this is still fresh in your mind, *define* each behavior descriptively. For example:

> quadrupedal stand: position in which all four limbs are approximately perpendicular to the torso. This behavior can be on any substrate as long as the body is approximately parallel to the ground.

Each behavior should be *mutually exclusive*. This means that each behavior should be defined so it is distinguishable from all other behaviors, because you will be recording only one behavior at a time. For example, if an animal is sitting *and* grooming, you must decide whether to record "sitting" and "grooming" or separately devise a category that takes into account both sitting and grooming. You must be clear in your definitions, followed by consistency in your data collection.

3. Categorize the various types of behaviors, such as

> *locomotor behaviors* (run, walk, leap),

> *social behaviors* (groom, wrestle, hug),

> and so on.

4. Compose your data checksheet. See the sample data sheet for Focal Animal Instantaneous Sampling, along with the codes. Using the categories from your ethogram, make a similar data sheet and codes. Include only the behaviors that you actually observed. Again, take care to make your behavioral categories mutually exclusive.

Option 2: Use of Prepared Data Sheet

Focal Animal Instantaneous Sampling Use the Focal Animal Instantaneous Sampling sheet in Lab Exercise 11.3 and continue below. You may modify the data sheet to include behaviors you noted during your preliminary observations.

1. For the focal animal instantaneous sampling method, collect data for at least one-half hour, using either the data checksheet provided or one you devised. Collect data at 2-minute intervals. This is your *time interval*. Before you begin, you may refer to the example on p. 270.

2. Choose your focal animal. Data collection is more interesting and instructive if you choose an animal that is exhibiting some behavior other than sleeping.

3. If you have a watch that can be set to beep at 2-minute intervals, set it now. Fill in the information at the top of the data sheet, note the starting time, then wait for the 2-minute interval.

4. Exactly 2 minutes *after* the starting time, jot down on the data sheet what your focal animal is doing, along with the code for the observed behavior. This will have been your first *sample point*. Continue for at least another 28 minutes.

Keep in mind that in this method you will *not* be listing *all* behaviors during the entire sample interval, only that occurring at the instant of the sample point. Thus, only *one* behavior is listed at every sample. (This is one reason for making categories mutually exclusive.) If a behavior you observe is not listed, add it to the data sheet and to the codes.

Scan Sampling

In scan sampling (Altmann, 1974; Martin and Bateson, 1993), the general activity for all animals in the exhibit is recorded simultaneously, at predetermined intervals. This method is used to record either general categories of behavior or to focus attention on only one or two specific types of behavior to the exclusion of all others.

As in focal animal instantaneous sampling, you'll be taking data only *at the sample point* between the sampling intervals. Use 2-minute samples for this technique as well. An example is provided on p. 272.

NAME _____

SECTION _____ DATE _____

Focal Animal Instantaneous Sampling

(use 2-minute intervals and the accompanying codes on the next page)

Species: _____ Date: _____

Conditions: _____ Focal animal description:

Description: _____

Starting time: _____

Time	Context (general activity)	Position	Social Behavior	Substrate	Food Type (if feeding)	Comments

Codes for Focal Animal Instantaneous Sampling

Context: F   Feed: includes foraging (searching for food), ingesting (getting food into mouth), and chewing
 R   Rest: in a stationary posture for at least 10 seconds after time interval begins
 T   Travel: moving from one area of the exhibit to another
 S   Social: interacting with another individual of its species

Positions:

Si	Sit
St – b	Stand bipedally
St – q	Quadrupedally
Li	Lie
Clg	Cling
Qw	Quadrupedal walk
R	Run
Le	Leap
Clb	Climb
O	Other (then specify)

Social behaviors:

P	Sit in close proximity (w/in 1 meter)
H	Hug
Gr	Groom (other)
Pl	Play (specify how)
T	Threaten
C	Chase
M	Mounting
O	Other

Substrate:

Br	Branch
Sh	Shelf
G	Ground
F	Fence
O	Other

Focal Animal Instantaneous Sampling
(use 2-minute intervals and the accompanying codes)

Species: **Lemur catta**   Date: **9/23/09**

Conditions: **sunny, warm**   Focal animal description:
adult female

Starting time: **2:12**

Time	Context (general activity)	Position	Social Behavior	Substrate	Food Type (if feeding)	Comments
2:12	f	Si	P	Br	apple	
2:14	f	Si		Br	potato	
2:16	R	Li	P	Sh		Had threatened a female
2:18						

LAB EXERCISE
11.4

NAME _____

SECTION _____ DATE _____

Scan Sampling Data Checksheet

(use 2-minute intervals)

At each sample point, note down the number of individuals in the group that are feeding, those that are resting, traveling, or engaging in social behavior.

Species: _____   Date: _____

Conditions: _____   Starting time: _____

Time	# Feeding	# Resting	# Traveling	# Social	Total
Total					

Example: Scan Sampling Data Checksheet

(2-minute intervals)

At each sample point, note down the number of individuals in the group that are feeding, those that are resting, traveling, or engaging in social behavior.

Species: **Macaca mulatta**   Date: **9/23/09**

Conditions: **cloudy, cool, construction noise**   Starting time: **2:32 p.m.**

Time	# Feeding	# Resting	# Traveling	# Social	Total
2:32	/ / /		/ / / /		7
2:34		/ / / / /	/ /		7
2:36	/ / /	/ /		/ /	7
2:38		/ / / / /		/ /	7
Total	6	12	6	4	28

LAB EXERCISE
11.4 (CONT.)

NAME _____

SECTION _____ DATE _____

Completing the Lab

Use your observations and completed forms to complete the lab.

1. Based on the *ad libitum* observations, make a statement about the amount of time your primates spent in various activities.

2. Do the same for the *focal animal instantaneous sampling* method. With the total number of observations as your sample size, figure the percentages of time spent (or, rather, samples observed) for each different behavior. You may write this out in a simple list as shown here, or you may make a table for the results if you wish. For example:

   feeding   22%

   sitting   10%

   grooming   16%

   etc.

3. Figure out totals for the *scan sampling* technique.

These techniques can be modified to best answer your research questions and allow you to acquire the most accurate data. The data sheets included here are offered for your use or as models for your own. Whatever technique is used, researchers must state their methodology clearly so other researchers can usefully compare the results to their own data.

SELF-TEST
11.1

NAME _____

SECTION _____ DATE _____

1. On a separate paper, write approximately a page comparing the three methods of data collection you used. For each method, list advantages and disadvantages, considering the following:

What might be a situation that calls for *ad libitum* data collection?

For focal animal sampling?

For scan sampling?

Might one method work better for some species than others, or for some behaviors rather than others? Why?

Which seems more objective, and which more subjective?

2. What are some cues that were useful to you in distinguishing among different individuals of the same species in the zoo?

3. What are some reasons for studying primates in captivity?

ONE STEP FURTHER

NAME _____

SECTION _____ DATE _____

Additional Lab Exercise 11.1

ADDITIONAL MATERIALS NEEDED:

- Alternative exercise on primate behavior using videos instead of animals at a captive facility

Instructions to Instructor:

- Suggested video for Lab Exercise 11.1: "Life in the Trees" (BBC, part of Life on Earth series with David Attenborough), or other video exhibiting a variety of primates in their natural habitats. (Another suggestion is "Prime Time Primates," PBS Home Video, Scientific American Frontiers).
- For the remaining Lab Exercises (11.2–11.4), a video (or videos) that focus on one species could be used, with the sound (if narrated) off or very low. Any video that contains sustained activity of primates should be fine, such as:
  - ◆ "Five Species" or others of the Documentary Educational Resources from The Primate Series by Anne Zeller
  - ◆ "Bleeding Heart Baboons," Parthenon Entertainment
  - ◆ "Great Apes," PBS Home Video
  - ◆ "The New Chimpanzees," National Geographic Special

Instructions to Student:

1. Read the first two pages of the chapter to familiarize yourself with this exercise, realizing that only some of the material will apply to an alternative study.

2. **Lab Exercise 11.1** can be conducted using a video that shows several species of primates.

3. Read the section on "Primate Behavioral Observations" (on p. 263) regarding the next portion of the assignment.

For the remainder of the assignment, your instructor will decide whether you will observe the same segment of a video several times (to compare three different data collection techniques) or use different videos about various primates to record data using the three techniques.

4. **Lab Exercise 11.2: *Ad Libitum* Sampling.** Watch the video segment, first filling in the blanks noting the species, date, time, etc., at the top of the data sheet. Follow the instructions you read in "Primate Behavioral Observations" on page 263, and record all behaviors of all individuals as the video plays.

5. **Lab Exercise 11.3: Focal Animal Sampling**

   a. Read the instructions for Focal Animal Instantaneous Sampling (on p. 267). You will follow the directions for Option 2 and use the data sheet provided. (You may skip the discussion entitled "Option 1: Ethogram and Data Sheet Preparation.")

   b. Familiarize yourself with the data sheet in Lab Exercise 11.3 entitled "Focal Animal Instantaneous Sampling" and the code sheet on the following page. A sample filled-out data sheet is found on the same page as the code sheet. Review the instructions with your instructor.

c.   Your instructor should play the first few minutes of the video for you so you can choose a focal animal upon which to collect data (ignoring all others in the video), and so you can get an idea of how the data sheet will work.

   d.   Watch the video (for one-half hour) and collect data, using the data sheet provided.

6. **Lab Exercise 11.4: Scan Sampling**

   a.   Look at the "Scan Sampling Data Checksheet" in Lab Exercise 11.4, and carefully review the scan sampling directions on page 267. A sample filled-out data sheet is provided.

   b.   Watch the video (for approximately one-half hour), and collect data using the "Scan Sampling Data Sheet.

   c.   Complete the remainder of Lab Exercise 11.4, followed by Self-Test 11.1.

Early Primates from the Paleocene Through the Miocene

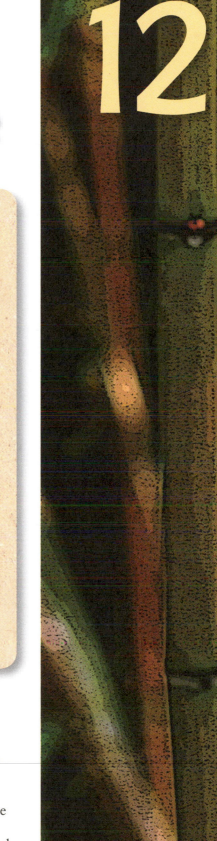

12

"Have you ever wondered . . . ?"

- The first primates were from Africa, right?
- If modern primates evolved from early primates, from whom did the early primates evolve?

OBJECTIVES

- Learn the major groups of extinct primate species, especially those leading to later primates, including humans
- Recognize extinct species by identifying fossil casts, learn similarities to and differences from modern species
- Learn the distribution of extinct primates in time and space
- Learn the principles of relative and absolute dating methods

MATERIALS NEEDED

- Preferably, as many as possible of the following skulls/casts:
  - *Agyptopithecus*
  - *Proconsul*
  - *Dryopithecus*
  - *Sivapithecus*
  - Lemur
  - Tarsier
  - A New World monkey
  - An Old World monkey
  - A chimpanzee
  - An orangutan
  - A gorilla

  (**Note:** *The above items can be substituted/supplemented with photos in lab manual and* A Photographic Atlas for Physical Anthropology.)
- Number and letter labels to group the postcranial bones and set up lab "stations"

By studying the earliest primates, we can put human evolutionary history into the context of all of primate evolution. In this lab we will identify a sampling of the main groups of fossil primates and learn some of their distinguishing features.

We study earth's history from the fossil record. Defined broadly, **fossils** are evidence of past life forms. They can take the form of an imprint or cast, or actually have gone through the process of **fossilization** (see Figure 12.1). When an animal dies and is buried, minerals from the sediment in which it lies replaces the organic material in bone, particle by particle. This is a slow process, and the time it takes depends upon the sediment and its mineral content, as well as the ambient temperature at which the process occurs.

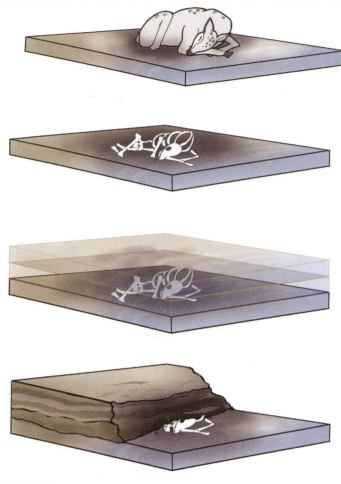

FIGURE 12.1 *Fossilization process*

Geological Time Scale

A **geological time scale** is shown in Table 12.1. This table covers only the time range of the **Phanerozoic Eon**. Previous to the Phanerozoic Eon was the **Precambrian Eon**, which lasted from the time of earth's formation through 542 million years ago (mya). In this chapter the focus is primarily on the **Cenozoic Era**, because this is the portion of time during which the primates evolved.

The geological time scale is a hierarchical system of classifying time (similar to biological classification), with larger blocks of time divided into smaller blocks (eons divided into eras, eras into periods, and periods into epochs). Scientists have divided these blocks of time in accordance with the rise and fall of major groups of organisms.

Information and exercises regarding techniques for dating fossils are covered in One Step Further, at the end of the chapter.

Plate Tectonics

The earth's plates that underlie the continents are in motion—known as **plate tectonics**, or **continental drift.** The position of the continents influences the geographical distribution patterns of all living things, including the primates. The **paleoclimate** has changed considerably through time, and this has influenced the type of habitats and, thus, survivability of the flora and fauna within it. Over the entire Cenozoic Era, the primary trend has been one of cooling and drying, but with many fluctuations.

TABLE 12.1: Geological Time Scale within the Phanerozoic Eon

ERA	PERIOD	EPOCH
Cenozoic Era (66 mya to the present)	Quaternary (1.8 mya to the present) Tertiary (66–1.8 mya)	Holocene (10,000 years ago to the present) Pleistocene (1.8 mya – 10,000 ya) Pliocene (5.3 – 1.8 mya) Miocene (23 – 5.3 mya) Oligocene (34 – 23 mya) Eocene (56 – 34 mya) Paleocene (66 – 56 mya)
Mesozoic Era (251 – 66 mya)	Cretaceous (146 – 66 mya) Jurassic (205 – 146 mya) Triassic (251 – 205 mya)	
Paleozoic Era (542 – 251 mya)	Permian (299 – 251 mya) Carboniferous (359 – 299 mya) Devonian (416 – 359 mya) Silurian (444 – 416 mya) Ordovician (488 – 444 mya) Cambrian (542 – 488 mya)	mya = million years ago ya = years ago

Primate Beginnings in the Paleocene Epoch (66 mya to 56 mya)

The earliest known primates were from a seemingly unlikely place: North America! Keep in mind that the earth looked quite different 66 million years ago, back in the **Paleocene** epoch (66 mya to 56 mya). North America, Europe, and Asia were joined in one huge landmass, called **Laurasia**. In the southern hemisphere, another landmass, **Gondwanaland**, was in the process of splitting apart into what would be Africa, South America, Antarctica, and Australia. India was an island continent and hadn't "docked" at Asia, so the Himalayas didn't yet exist.

Much of the globe was warm and humid, with little difference between the northern and southern latitudes. From Minnesota to Argentina, tropical rainforests dominated. England had alligator-filled swamps, and the Ozarks were a vast, low, forested plain with slow streams and swamps.

Primates were an early branch of the mammalian tree, very near the trunk. Soon after early mammals began to diverge into distinct groups, primates and primate-like creatures already were present, by 63 million years ago. An extinct taxonomic group called the **Plesiadapiformes** (G *plesi*: near, recent; L *adapi*: rabbit) consists of early mammals with certain primate-like characteristics.

Some researchers consider Plesiadapiformes to be primates because of their petrosal bulla, more rounded molar cusps, and arboreal features of the postcranial skeleton (Szalay and Delson, 1979; Szalay, 1981). Others (e.g., Rasmussen, 2002) disagree and would place this group in a different but closely related mammalian order. This interpretation, in turn, was challenged by scientists who again support the idea of Plesiadapiformes as primates (Bloch and Silcox, 2006). Whatever they were, they existed in North America and Europe, with a few in China.

Although the fossil evidence doesn't allow us to confidently answer questions about the origin of Plesiadapiformes and their specific relationships with modern primates, we do know that they were a diverse group of about 75 species, ranging from the size of a small mouse to that of a medium house cat. Some groups had more primate-like features than others. Two examples from this group are the genera ***Purgatorius*** (early Paleocene of North America) and ***Plesiadapis*** (Paleocene to early Eocene, widespread in North America and Europe) (Figure. 12.2; *Atlas* p. 260; br. ed. p. 32). A more complete list of fossil primate genera can be found in Appendix E. Selected plesiadapiform features are listed in Table 12.2 and compared with primate characteristics. A number of the primate features you are familiar with can be observed as well in fossils.

Some of the Plesiadapiformes lasted through much of the following epoch, the Eocene, then became extinct. Their extinction may have been brought about by competition

FIGURE 12.2 *Plesiadapis*

TABLE 12.2: Plesiadapiforms Compared to Primates

PLESIADAPIFORM FEATURES	PRIMATE FEATURES
Small brain size	Large relative brain size
No postorbital bar	Postorbital bar
Laterally-facing eye orbits	Forward-facing eye orbits
Prognathic (forward-protuding) face	Shortened snout
Possible petrosal bulla	Petrosal bulla
Large, ever-growing incisors	Canine usually largest tooth
Lack of opposable big toe	Opposable big toe
Claws on digits	Nails on digits

with rodents, which were fast becoming the most numerous mammalian species (Van Valen and Sloan, 1965).

The "True" Primates of the Eocene Epoch (56 to 34 mya)

During the **Eocene** epoch the earth did not undergo drastic changes, but the main tectonic event of importance for primate distribution was the increasing separation of North America from Europe as the Laurasian landmass broke apart. By the end of the epoch, the two were parts of separate landmasses. Around this time, a severe drop in temperature also influenced the ecology and distribution of many species.

Primates of the Eocene epoch were present in North America, Europe, Asia, and Africa. In the Eocene epoch, Europe had more than 200 primate species—comparable to the total number of primate species alive today. The two best-known and best-represented groups that inhabited North America and Europe were the taxonomic superfamilies

Adapoidea (Adapoids) and **Omomyoidea** (Omomyoids). All of the primate features with which you now are familiar also were present in these early primates.

Adapoids: Ancestors of Strepsirhines

One of the main Eocene groups includes the probable ancestors of the strepsirhines. These adapoids, having more than 80 different species, ranged in size from a large rat to a large housecat. There is widespread agreement that members of this group gave rise to the strepsirhines (including, among others, the lemurs and lorises of today). Among the best known of these primates are the genera **Cantius** (North America and Europe), **Notharctus** (North America), and **Adapis** (Europe) (see Figure 12.3; *Atlas* pp. 264–265; br. ed. pp. 36–37). A few representatives also are found in Africa and Asia.

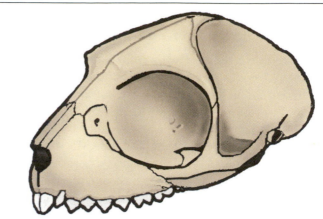

FIGURE 12.4 *Necrolemur*

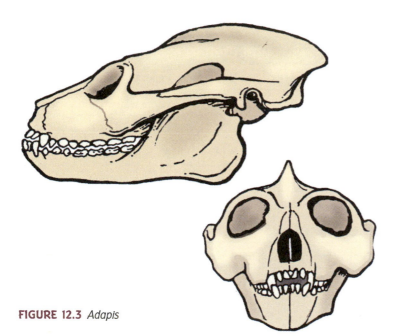

FIGURE 12.3 *Adapis*

Omomyoids: Possible Ancestors of Haplorhines

Similar in appearance to the modern tarsier, the omomyoids are even more numerous than the adapoids, with more than 90 species. Like the adapoids, the omoyoids are best known from North America and Europe, but some representatives were present in Asia and possibly in Africa. The ancestral haplorhine may have arisen from the Omomyoidea.

Omomyoids typically were smaller in body size, on average, than adapoids. Some of the better-known omomyoids are **Necrolemur** (Europe), **Tetonius** (North America), and **Rooneyia** (North America) (see Figure 12.4; *Atlas* pp. 263, 267, 270; br. ed. pp. 35, 39, 42).

Other Eocene Primates from Africa, Asia, and Europe

Although all of the known fossils from North America and Europe from the Eocene epoch fit relatively neatly into either the Omomyoidea or the Adapoidea, such is not the case for Eocene fossil primates from Asia and Africa. Representatives of the omomyoids and adapoids are found in Asia and Africa, but some fossils are quite distinct from them. An excellent example from Asia is **Eosimias** (Figure 12.5), a tiny late Eocene primate from China that appears to exhibit features of the **anthropoids** (the group includes monkeys, apes, and humans) before their divergence into platyrrhines and catarrhines (Gebo et al., 2000).

Other Eocene Asian primates that also may represent early anthropoids are **Amphipithecus** and **Pondaungia** (Fleagle, 1999). In Africa, the very late Eocene **Catopithecus** (*Atlas* p. 271; br. ed. p. 43) is clearly an anthropoid and even possesses catarrhine features (Simons and Rasmussen, 1996), It is one of the members of a fossil primate family from a site in Egypt (described next).

The newest Eocene fossil primate is an exciting and important addition to the primate order: **Darwinius masillae** (Franzen et al., 2009). This small juvenile female (estimated to arrive at 650–900 g if she had reached adulthood) was

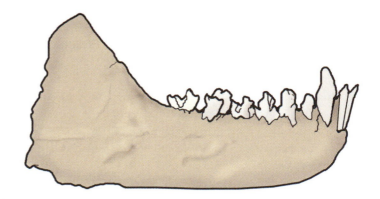

FIGURE 12.5 *Eosimias*

ound at a fossil site in Germany and has features of an early aplorhine. The interpretation is undisputed because "Ida," s she is known, is the most complete fossil primate ever ound. She even came complete with a digestive tract conaining the remains of her last meal!

The Oligocene Primates (34 to 23 mya)

As a result of the extreme drop in temperature at the end of the Eocene epoch, what had been appropriate primate habitat in the northern hemisphere became inhospitable to the tropically adapted primates. This virtually eliminated them from the region. Primates in North America and Europe either became extinct or migrated southward, most suffering the former fate. Thus, the **Oligocene** epoch has very few fossil primates worldwide. The primary exception consists of the rich fossil deposits in the Egyptian **Fayum Depression**, a region that was a lush gallery (riverine) forest during the Oligocene epoch. Time-wise, the lower Fayum deposits are near the boundary between the Eocene and the Oligocene (about 23 mya), extending up through the earliest part of the Miocene (Fleagle, 1999).

The continents were active, causing a great deal of tectonic and volcanic activity. Africa and Europe crowded around an existing inland sea, enclosing it into what we now call the Mediterranean Sea. India had begun its collision course with Asia, starting the uplift we now know as the Himalayas. Australia and South America separated from Antarctica so that all became island continents.

During the Oligocene, two fossil primate families were present at the site:

1. **Parapithecidae:** *Apidium* is a primary example of this family. This anthropoid, from about 36 million ago, has some similarities to New World monkeys, which you will see when you compare the figure with a platyrrhine specimen (see Figure 12.6; *Atlas* p. 272; br. ed. p. 44). Thus, some researchers think a creature with features similar to *Apidium* may be an ancestor of the platyrrhines and catarrhines. *Apidium* was about the size of a squirrel monkey (or a large squirrel).

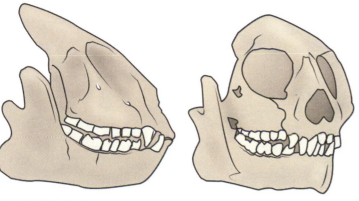

FIGURE 12.6 *Apidium*

2. **Propliopithecidae:** *Aegyptopithecus,* the best-known representative of this family, dates from about 33 mya (Photo 12.1; *Atlas* p. 272–273; br. ed. pp. 44–45). This howler monkey-sized primate is most likely an early catarrhine and may have given rise to both the cercopithecoid (Old World monkey) and hominoid (ape/human group) lines. *Aegyptopithecus* is a good candidate for ancestry for the both of these groups of Old World anthropoids because it is generalized enough to have given rise to both groups rather than exhibiting specific features of either one.

Aegyptopithecus teeth are comparable to those of hominoids and are the first in the fossil record to exhibit the **Y5 molar cusp pattern** (*Atlas* p. 67, Figure. 3.65). The tooth pattern of the Old World monkey (bilophodonty) appears after the hominoid molar pattern.

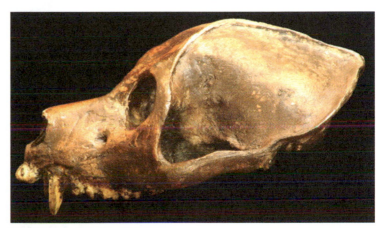

PHOTO 12.1 *Aegyptopithecus*

Miocene Hominoids (23 to 53 mya)

In the **Miocene** epoch, the previous cooling trend reversed temporarily and the world experienced warmer temperatures for a time. Geological processes were hard at work forming the earth's surface much as we know it today. For example, the tectonic activity that brought India into place along the Asian continent continued and the Himalayas rose dramatically.

A variety of catarrhine primates of the superfamily Hominoidea existed in Africa, Asia, and Europe during the Miocene. These apes, most of which were small-bodied compared to their modern relatives, are termed the **Miocene hominoids.** They were primarily arboreal, with ape-like heads and a body with a mixture of ape-like and monkey-like features. As in the modern hominoids, they had no tail. In contrast to the relatively few apes now (only four or five genera), the Miocene epoch yielded about 30 genera!

African Forms

The earliest of these genera was **Proconsul** (Photo 12.2), first discovered in Kenya in 1948. Its relationship to modern apes was assumed quickly, and it was named in reference to its presumed ancestry of chimpanzees. A famous pipe-smoking chimpanzee named Consul (Photo 12.3) had resided at the Belle Vue Zoo in England, so the fossil form was named as its progenitor. Four species of *Proconsul* existed between 22 and 14 million years ago in East Africa, ranging from cocker spaniel-sized to chimp-sized. In addition to *Proconsul*, about 18 genera of ape existed in Africa during the Miocene.

During the early part of the Miocene epoch, Africa was an island continent. The previous isolation of Antarctica from South America and Australia brought about a change in ocean currents such that the warm tropical waters and cold polar waters mixed less. This had the effect of lowering the circum-polar temperatures and leading to a buildup of the Antarctic ice cap. Although the Miocene was generally warmer than the Oligocene, the cold polar temperatures caused much seawater to be trapped in ice, which lowered the sea levels. This had an important consequence for primate distribution: it opened up a land bridge from Africa to Europe 17 to 18 million years ago. After this connection between the continents, we begin to see Miocene hominoids in Europe and Asia, presumably descendants of the African forms.

Asian Forms

The Asian hominoid **Sivapithecus** (Photo 12.4; *Atlas* pp. 277–280; br. ed. pp. 49–52), from India and Pakistan, appeared about 15 million years ago. You will be comparing it to living apes to determine its possible relationships.

Another important and fascinating Asian hominoid, related to *Sivapithecus*, was **Gigantopithecus**, one species of which appeared in India and Pakistan in the late Miocene (about 9 mya). Another, larger, species of *Gigantopithecus* persisted until less than a million years ago in China and Vietnam, and even coexisted with *Homo erectus*. Although known only from its jaws and teeth, this clearly was the largest primate that ever lived, with a larger dentition than even the gorilla (see Figure 12.7). Representatives of about five other genera existed during the Miocene of Asia.

European Forms

About eight genera of European ape existed between 13 and 8 million years ago. The most famous of these is **Dryopithecus** (see Figure 12.8; *Atlas* p. 276; br. ed. p. 48), which was the size of a large monkey (or a small golden retriever). About nine additional genera of Miocene ape lived in Europe,

PHOTO 12.2 *Proconsul*

PHOTO 12.3 *Consul, the performing chimpanzee*

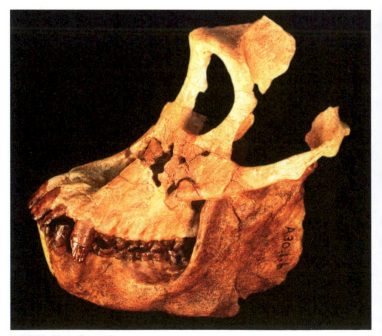

PHOTO 12.4 *Sivapithecus*

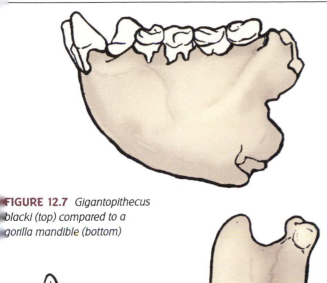

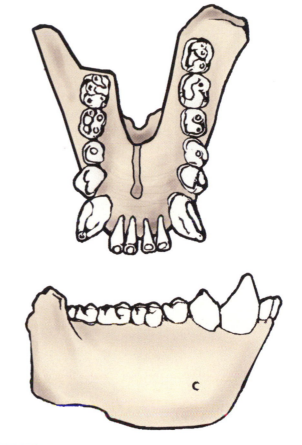

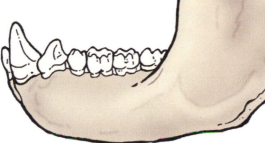

FIGURE 12.7 *Gigantopithecus blacki (top) compared to a gorilla mandible (bottom)*

FIGURE 12.8 *Dryopithecus mandible*

including the newly discovered **Pierolapithecus catalaunicus**. Discoverers of *Pierolapithecus* interpreted it to be a member of the group that gave rise to all of the great apes and humans (Moya-Sola et al., 2004). Alternatively, an early representative of the group may have given rise to the African ape/human line (Begun and Ward, 2005). Another European fossil ape is **Ouranopithecus macedoniensis**, which existed in Greece late in the Miocene, about 9 to 10 million years ago (*Atlas* p. 281; br. ed. p. 53). *Ouranopithecus* has been proposed as a possible ancestor of African apes and humans (de Bonis et al., 1990; Begun, 2003; Koufos and de Bonis, 2004).

LAB EXERCISE
12.1

NAME _____

SECTION _____ DATE _____

1. Compare the illustration of a Plesiadapiform primate (*Plesiadapis*, below) (*Atlas* p. 260; br. ed. p. 32) with the skull (or the photo below) of a strepsirhine (*Atlas* p. 102; br. ed. p. 8).

   a. Fill out the chart below. Refer to Table 12.2 for body parts that are not shown in the accompanying illustration or photo.

SKULL FEATURES	PLESIADAPIFORM	STREPSIRHINE
Postorbital bar		
Position of orbits: lateral or forward-facing?		
Relative size of braincase (compared to face)		
Prognathism: length of snout relative to cranium		
Form of incisors and incisor size relative to canines and molars		
POSTCRANIAL FEATURES		
Nails versus claws*		
Opposable big toe?*		

*not observable from photos, but information is in this chapter

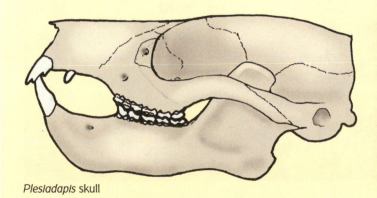

Plesiadapis skull

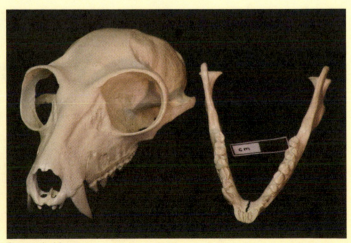

Ring-tailed lemur

b. Why do some researchers consider plesiadapiformes to be members of the primate order?

c. Which of the plesiadapiform features are decidedly unlike those of primates?

2. a. Compare the fossil and living forms listed below, using a combination of specimens and accompanying illustrations and photos on this page and the next. (*Adapis: Atlas* p. 265, br. ed. p. 37; Ring-tailed lemur: *Atlas* pp. 102; *Necrolemur: Atlas* p. 267, br. ed. p. 39; Tarsier: *Atlas* pp. 112–113; *Eosimias*). If you can't determine a specific feature, put a "not obs" (not observable) in the blank. Figures 10.5 and 10.6 may also provide useful information.

SKULL FEATURE	ADAPIS (ADAPOID)	LEMUR* (LEMUR)	NECROLEMUR (OMOMYOID)	TARSIER (TARSIUS)	EOSIMIAS
Postorbital bar?					
Postorbital closure?					
Position of orbits					
Relative size of braincase					
Snout length relative to cranium					
Fused mandibular symphysis?					
Size of anterior versus posterior dentition					

*Other strepsirhine skulls may be substituted for the lemur.

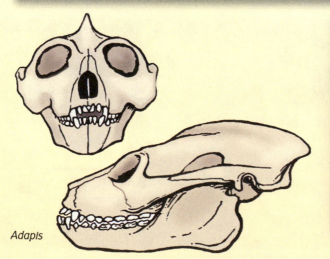

Adapis

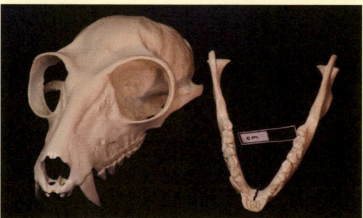

Ring-tailed lemur

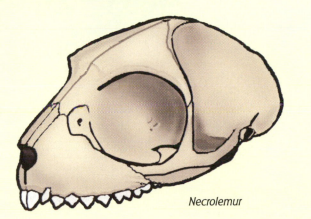

Necrolemur

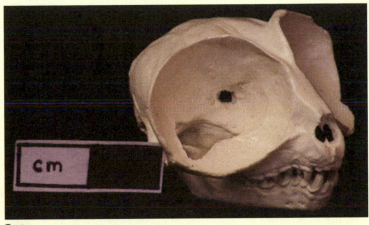

Tarsier

Eosimias

b. Using lab specimens or the accompanying photos, look at the relative size of orbits of the tarsier versus those of a monkey and a lemur (see photo from question #1). What can we tell about the activity patterns (diurnal versus nocturnal) from fossilized remains?

c. Adapoids are thought to be ancestral to what modern forms?

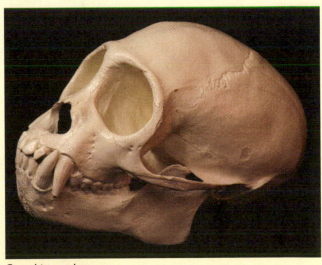

Capuchin monkey

d. Omomyoids may be ancestral to what modern forms?

3. Compare the skulls of the Fayum primates *Apidium* and *Aegyptopithecus* to a New World monkey, an Old World monkey, and an African ape.

   a. Fill out the chart below using specimens or the accompanying photos and illustrations (use capuchin photo on p. 289) (*Apidium*: Atlas p. 272, br. ed. p. 44; *Aegyptopithecus*: Atlas p. 272–273, br. ed. p. 44–45; chimpanzee: Atlas pp. 140–142). Again, not all features will be visible from the photos alone. Figures 10.5, 10.6, and 10.8, as well as Photo 10.2, may provide useful information.

SKULL FEATURES	*APIDIUM*	CAPUCHIN MONKEY (OR OTHER NEW WORLD MONKEY)	*AEGYPTOPITHECUS*	VERVET (OR OTHER OLD WORLD MONKEY)	CHIMPANZEE (OR GORILLA)
Postorbital closure?					
Dental formula					
Length of snout					
Molar form* (bilophodont versus Y5 pattern)	NA	NA			
Form of ear region (bony tube?)					

*If actual specimen is available

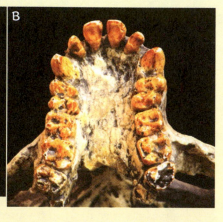

Aegyptopithecus (**A**) skull and (**B**) dental arcade

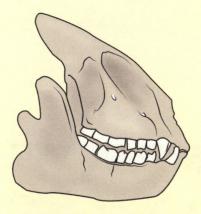

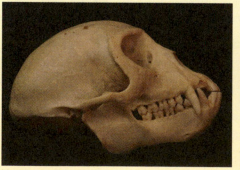

Vervet monkey

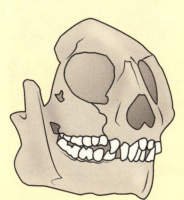

Apidium

Chimpanzee

LAB EXERCISE
12.1 (CONT.)

NAME _____

SECTION _____ DATE _____

b. In which features is *Apidium* similar to a capuchin?

c. In which features is *Aegyptopithecus* similar to an Old World monkey?

  To the chimpanzee (or gorilla)?

4. Examine skulls, accompanying photos, and/or figures to make the following comparisons (*Proconsul*; *Dryopithecus*: *Atlas* p. 276, br. ed. p. 48; Chimpanzee: *Atlas* p. 140–142; see chimpanzee and vervet photos on the next page). Keep in mind that for some specimens or species, a feature may be unobservable here (particularly if a postcranial feature).

	PROCONSUL	DRYOPITHECUS	CHIMPANZEE**	VERVET (OR OTHER OLD WORLD MONKEY)**
Shape of dental arcade				*
Relative brain size (compared to face)		*		
Molar form (bilophodont versus Y5 pattern)				
Tail?*				

*Not observable from photos
**Another Old World monkey skull may be substituted for a vervet, and a gorilla may be substituted for a chimpanzee.

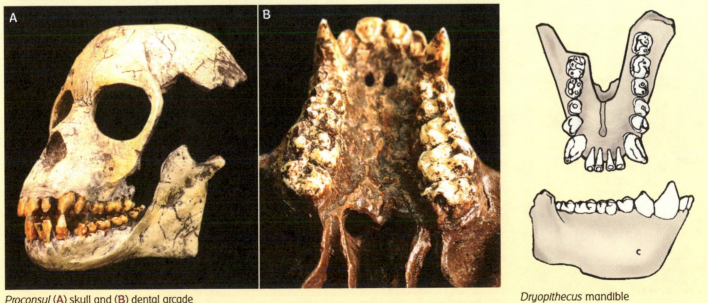

Proconsul (A) skull and (B) dental arcade

Dryopithecus mandible

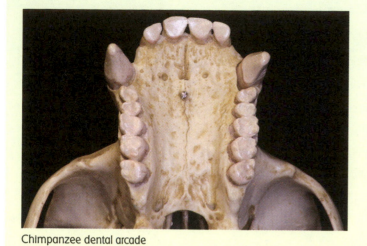

Chimpanzee dental arcade

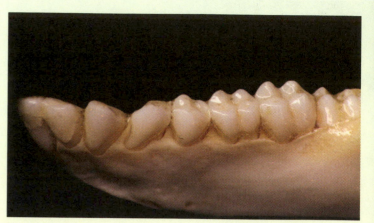

Vervet dentition

5. a. Compare *Sivapithecus* (below) to the photos of an orangutan and an African ape on the following page (*Sivapithecus*: *Atlas* pp. 277–280, br. ed. p. 49–52; Orangutan: *Atlas* pp. 136–139; Chimpanzee: *Atlas* pp. 140–142), and fill out the chart.

	SIVAPITHECUS	ORANGUTAN	GORILLA (OR CHIMPANZEE)
Interorbital distance (greater versus smaller?)			
Shape of orbits			
Size and shape of zygomatic arch			
Relative size of central versus lateral incisors			
Size of supraorbital ridge			
Shape of subnasal region (alveolar prognathism?)			

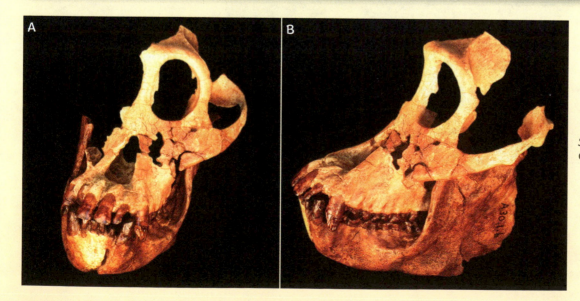

Sivapithecus (A) anterior and (B) lateral view

NAME _____

SECTION _____   DATE _____

Orangutan (**A**) anterior and (**B**) lateral view

Gorilla (**C**) anterior and (**D**) lateral view

b. *Sivapithecus* is most similar to which of the modern apes? In what features?

SELF-TEST
12.1

NAME _____

SECTION _____ DATE _____

1. What are five primate features that would be apparent from fossils?

2. For the Oligocene primates:

    a. *Apidium* and *Parapithecus* have the dental formula of 2-1-3-3. What kinds of living primate have this dental formula?

    b. *Aegyptopithecus* has a dental formula of 2-1-2-3. What kinds of living primate have this dental formula?

    c. All of the Oligocene primates have no bony ear tube (ectotympanic tube). To what primate haplorhine group is this similar?

3. a. Of the features you have observed, name one that *Aegyptopithecus* shares with other anthropoids.

    b. With other catarrhines? Name one.

    c. With hominoids? Name one.

4. If you find a fossil sample made up of numerous adult individuals of the same species, some having a larger body size and larger canines, what might this indicate?

5. Which occurred earlier in time, *Proconsul* or *Dryopithecus*?

   Where was each found?

   Why is the timing of their existence significant in terms of the possible evolutionary relationship between the two?

6. Compare the *Gigantopithecus* specimen to a gorilla mandible. How is it similar?

   How is it different?

NAME _____

SECTION _____ DATE _____

Additional Lab Exercise 12.1

How Old Was This Fossil? Dating Techniques

When we talk about geological time, sedimentation, and fossilization, we must have a temporal frame of reference for the past. That frame of reference can be either an actual point in time or a comparison with another sedimentary layer or fossil. These describe two main categories of dating techniques: **absolute dating** and **relative dating**. It is beyond the scope of this lab manual to discuss individual methods, but the following exercises reinforce the general principles of absolute (radiometric, chronometric) methods and relative (comparative) methods.

Relative Dating: Stratigraphy

The diagram below represents an "outcrop," a rocky exposure such as those seen on the sides of cliffs or along road cuts made to create freeways. In outcrops we often can see layers, called **strata** (singular = **stratum**), also called **beds**. Each stratum is the result of some previous natural geological event or process, such as a flood or erosion. Over time, the accumulation of these processes causes layers of sediment to pile up and form sedimentary sequences. According to the well-established Principle of Superposition, the older strata are deeper in the earth and the younger ones closer to the surface. Not shown in the diagram here (or dealt with here) are the many complex geological events that can occur to interfere with neat, clear layers. These include folding events, faulting, erosion, intrusions by other sediment types, and so on.

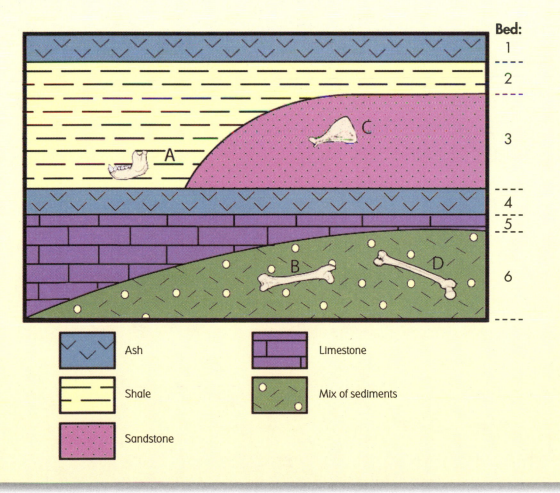

When fossils have been deposited in sedimentary rocks, the *relative ages* of the fossils can be determined through comparison of the strata in which they are contained. Thus, relative dating will answer questions about "what's older" or "what's younger" rather than "when did it live?"

Following the diagram on p. 297 is a key for interpreting the fossil beds, as well as some other useful information. Examine the diagram, the key, and the hints below, then answer the questions that follow.

A Few Hints

- Ash is sediment resulting from volcanic activity.
- A mix of silt, pebbles, and other unsorted sediments are the result of flooding.
- Sandy sediment (including resulting sandstone) often reflects an extended dry period.
- From absolute dating techniques, we know that Bed 2 is about 3 million years old.
- Bed 4 is about 4.5 million years old.
- Shales are usually deposited in slow-moving water such as in former lakes, lagoons, river deltas, and floodplains.

---

1. List the fossils in order from the *most recent to the oldest*.

2. Which bed (note the number) contains Fossil C?

3. A volcano 100 miles from this fossil locality has erupted several times, each time spewing ash for hundreds of miles. Which stratum or strata formed during times of volcanic activity?

4. Which fossil likely represented a species that lived in or near a lake?

5. Which fossil (or fossils) was (were) deposited around the time of flooding?

6. What do you know about the age of Fossil A?

7. Which strata probably formed during arid (dry) periods of time?

Stratigraphy (or biostratigraphy, if life forms are compared among strata) is only one of the many relative dating techniques. Others include paleomagnetism, fluorine dating, and faunal correlation.

ONE STEP FURTHER

NAME _____

SECTION _____ DATE _____

Absolute Dating: Radiometry

Only after the discovery of radioactivity, around A.D. 1900, were we successful in obtaining absolute dates for geologic events. As a result of techniques that depend upon radioactivity, we know that the Earth formed about 4.6 billion years ago, and that dinosaurs became extinct 66 million years ago.

To use absolute dating on rock, it must contain radioactive isotopes. Radioactive isotopes (parent atoms) decay into more stable "daughter" atoms and, in the process, release energy (radiation). Because the decay occurs at a **constant rate**, it can be used to measure time elapsed. The relative amount of parent and daughter atoms can be used to determine the age of the rock, within a certain margin of error. The decay rate is measured in terms of **half-life**, the time it takes for ½ of the parent atoms to decay to form the daughter atoms.

One radiometric technique is called Potassium-Argon dating. Potassium 40 (K^{40}) decays to Argon 40 (Ar^{40}) at a half-life of 1.3 billion years. At the time of the rock's formation (time zero), there is only K^{40} and no Ar^{40}. After 1.3 billion years, half of the original K^{40} atoms have been transformed into Ar^{40} atoms.

1. A rock specimen contains 30 mmol (millimoles) of K^{40} and 30 mmol of Ar^{40}. How old is the rock?

2. Would a specimen containing 30 mmol of K^{40} and only 5 mmol of Ar^{40} be younger or older than the rock in the previous question?

3. Approximately how old is a rock specimen that has 15 mmol of K^{40} and 45 mmol of Ar^{40}?
    a. 2.6 billion years old
    b. 650,000,000 years old
    c. 1.3 billion years old
    d. Cannot answer from the information given

    The simple diagrams below show four rock specimens (A through D), with letters representing the atoms embedded in the structure of minerals forming the rock. The parent atoms of this hypothetical radioactive isotope have a half-life of 5 million years.
    The key is:

    P   Parent atoms

    D   Daughter atoms

    X   atoms other than P and D

```
PXXXXXXXXXPXXXXXXXXXPXXXXXPXXPXX
XXXXXXXPPXXXXXXXXXXXPXXXXXXPXPXXX
XXPXXXXXXPXXXPPXXXXXPXXXXXXXPXXXX
XXXXXPXXXXXPXXXXPXXXXXXXXXPXXXXXX
XXPXXXXPXXXXXXPXXXPXXXXPXXXXXPXXX
PXXXXPXXXXXPXXXPXXXXXXXPXXXXXPXXXP
XPPXXXXXXXXXPXXXXXPXXXXPXXXXXPXXXX
XXXXXXPXXXXXXPXXXXPXXXPXXXXXPXXXX
```

                                                    Specimen A

```
DXXXXXXXXXXPXXXXXXXXDXXXX
XXXXXXXPDXXXXXXXXXXPXXXXDX
XXPXXXXXXDXXPDXXPXXXXXXXD          Specimen B
XXXXXPXXXXXXXXXXXXXXXPXXXXX
XXDXXXXPXXXXXXDXXXXPXXDXX
PXXXXDXXXXXPXXXXXXXXXXDXX
XPDXXXXXPXXXXXXXXXDXXXPXXX
XXXXXXDXXXXXXXXXDXXXXXPXX
XXXXXDXXPXXPXXXXXXXXXXDXX
```

```
DXXXXXXXXXXDXXXXXXXXDXXXX
XXXXXXXDDXXXXXXXXXXDXXXXXX
XXDXXXXXXDXXDDXXDXXXXXXXX          Specimen C
XXXXXDXXXXXDXXXXXXXXXXXX
XXDXXXXDXXXXXXDXXXXDXXXXX
DXXXXDXXXXXDXXXXXDXXXXXXX
XXXXXXXXXXXXXXXDXXXXXXXX
```

```
XXXDXXXXXXXDXXXXXXDXXXX
XXXXXXXPDXXXXXXXXXXXXXXX
XXDXXXXXXDXXPDXXDXXXXXX          Specimen D
XXXXXDXXXXXDXXXXXXXXXDXX
XXDXXXXXDXXXXDXXXDXXXXX
DXXXXDXXXXXDXXXXXXPXXDX
XDDXXXXXDXXXXXXXXXDXXXDX
XXXXXXDXXXXDXXXPXXXXXXX
```

4. Fill in the blanks to arrange the rock specimens from oldest to youngest.

_____ _____ _____ _____

    Oldest   Youngest

5. Approximately how old is Specimen A?

6. How old is Specimen B?

7. The age of Specimen C is:
   a. 10 million years old
   b. 5 million years old
   c. older than 20 million years

8. Does the size of the rock specimen affect the results? Why or why not?

Keep in mind that these techniques have sources of error. In particular, an accurate radiometric date can be obtained only if the mineral remained a closed system during the entire period since its formation. One simple safeguard is to use only fresh, unweathered material rather than chemically altered samples. Some other commonly used radiometric techniques are Carbon-14 and Uranium 238. Among additional techniques of absolute dating, some use organic material instead of rock.

Source: Mélida Gutierrez, unpublished geology laboratory exercise.

ONE STEP FURTHER

NAME _____

SECTION _____ DATE _____

Additional Self-Test Questions

1. What was the primary climatic change during the Cenozoic Era?

2. Where were the earliest known primates found?

3. What are a few features of Eocene primates from North America?

4. Where were the earliest anthropoid primates found, and from what epoch?

5. What two groups of primates were found in the Fayum deposits of Egypt from the Oligocene?

6. What are the seven epochs of the Cenozoic Era, in order from the most recent to the oldest?

7. List four features of Plesiadapiformes (the earliest possible primates).

8. Fill in the blanks below for each fossil primate regarding the continent upon which it was found and the approximate age according to epoch.

Fossil primate:	Where was it found?	In which epoch of the Cenozoic Era?
Gigantopithecus	_____	_____
Proconsul	_____	_____
Plesiadapiformes	_____	_____
Aegyptopithecus	_____	_____

Who's in Our Family?

13

"Have you ever wondered . . . ?"

- What didn't the apes keep evolving?
- I've heard of the famous fossil Lucy, but who *was* she?
- Who's in our (taxonomic) family?

OBJECTIVES

- Understand the mechanics of bipedalism
- Learn to interpret locomotor behavior from skeletal features of apes, modern humans, and extinct hominids
- Recognize the importance of using living groups as a comparative base for interpreting fossils
- Learn skeletal differences between humans and apes for interpreting human fossils
- Identify early members of the human family through fossil casts; know similarities to and differences from modern species
- Understand the distribution of extinct members of our family in time and space
- Address difficulties of establishing evolutionary relationships among members of the human line and our closest living relatives

MATERIALS NEEDED

- Preferably, as many as possible of the following skulls/casts:
  - Modern human skull
  - Hand bones of human and an ape
  - Skull of chimpanzee (or other ape)
  - Fetal skull
  - Young ape skull
  - Human pelvic bone(s)
  - Ape pelvic bone(s)
  - Human femur
  - Femur of chimp (or other ape)
  - Human foot
  - Australopith pelvic bone(s)
  - *A. afarensis* skull cast
  - *A. africanus* skull cast
  - Robust australopith skull cast
  - Taung child fossil cast

  (**Note:** *Above items can be substituted/supplemented with photos in lab manual and* A Photographic Atlas for Physical Anthropology.)

- Number and letter labels to group the postcranial bones and set up lab "stations"

(One Step Further will require additional materials; see Additional Lab Exercises 13.1 and 13.2.)

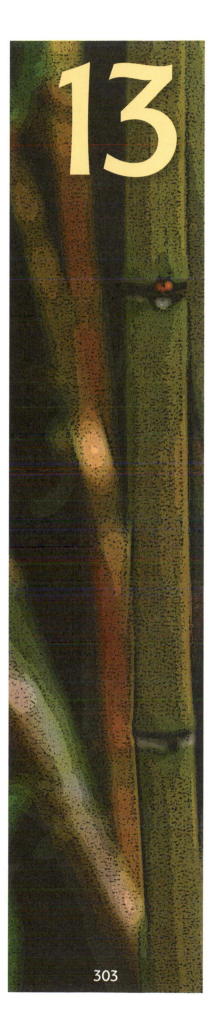

Between 6 and 8 million years ago a population of ape-like primates roamed eastern Africa, moving about using all four limbs, sometimes on the ground, sometimes in trees. This group of creatures then split into various populations, eventually evolving into the African apes (chimpanzee and gorilla) on the one hand and the human line on the other. According to our interpretation of the fossil record, our extinct ancestors exhibited, after the ape/human split, anatomical correlates of **bipedalism**.

The Comparative Basis

To assess fossils and place them in a taxonomic scheme, we must have some comparative basis. To interpret human evolutionary history, we must be familiar with human loco-motor adaptations, as well as those of our closest living relatives, the African apes. We would expect an extinct common ancestor of humans and the African apes to have shared homologous features with both living groups, but evidence certainly supports the idea that living African apes are more similar anatomically to that common ancestor than are modern humans (see Figure 13.1). Apes didn't "stop evolving," but many more obvious changes accumulated on the human branch of the evolutionary tree. Thus, although it is easy to differentiate modern humans from modern African apes on the basis of anatomical characteristics, it gets more difficult to compare early members of the human family with apes or our ape-like ancestors. The earliest human ancestors were quite ape-like.

In this chapter we compare the anatomy of African apes and humans in the cranial and postcranial skeleton, with special reference to the anatomical adaptations for humans to bipedal locomotion.

FIGURE 13.1 *Human divergence from the apes*

Bipedalism: the Hallmark of Humanity

Although there are many four-legged runners, climbers, and others, humans are the only ones to walk upright on two legs habitually. Our mode of locomotion has advantages and disadvantages, but presumably the advantages outweighed the disadvantages and provided important survival value. We display many unique features of muscle and bone related to bipedalism, and while modern African apes are *capable* of walking bipedally, they do not exhibit the anatomical adaptations for doing so. African apes are known as **knuckle-walkers**, a type of quadruped.

Human bipedalism is unique in its **striding gait**. Although most of us walk every day, we rarely think about the "mechanics" as we are doing so. In bipedalism the walking cycle has two phases:

1. In the **stance phase**, the foot is in contact with the substrate and supports the weight. This phase has three parts: the heel strike, the flat foot (or midstance), and the toe-off (leaving the ground for the next step) (Figure 13.2).

2. In the **swing phase**, the foot comes off the substrate and is being repositioned for the next stance phase (Figure 13.3). Here, the leg comes forward and around toward the center (called *adduction*). In humans, some of the gluteal muscles are positioned on the side; these act as stabilizers for the contralateral side so we don't fall over to the side when one foot is off the ground. Our legs come in at the knees so the center of gravity doesn't have to be shifted laterally back and forth much while walking.

Compared to most other animals, humans are "unbalanced" in locomotion. Think about it: We are balancing all of our weight on just one leg about half the time we are

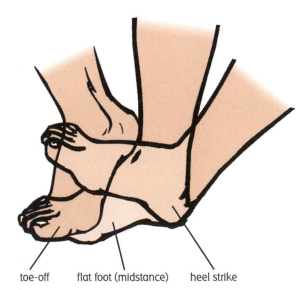

FIGURE 13.2 *Foot in stance phase*

toe-off   flat foot (midstance)   heel strike

FIGURE 13.3 *Foot in
swing phase*

walking! This causes balance problems that are dealt with
by our having redistributed (during our evolutionary past)
the orientation and function of various muscles and their
associated skeletal supporting structures.

Three main aspects of our locomotion are

1. *propulsion* (push-off),
2. *stabilization* (so we don't fall over trying to balance on
   one leg), and
3. *adduction* (swinging our leg around to the center with
   each step).

Certain muscle groups allow each of these actions, and
we will see the differences in the hip and leg bones in humans
versus apes resulting from this difference in muscle function.

NAME _____

SECTION _____ DATE _____

Go through the following exercise with your lab partner.

1. Stand up. In slow motion, lift one leg, take a step forward, and place your foot on the ground in the same way you do when you walk. Continuing slowly, take another step. In what area of your body do you feel your muscles tense when you lift your leg to first take that step? (Where are the muscles located?)

2. Just before you put your foot down on the heel and transfer the weight to your forward foot, what is your other leg doing? (What area in your other leg feels tense?)

3. Take several steps at a normal pace. Notice how your leg swings around naturally to the center before you put your leg down, enabling you to walk a straight line. Where do you think the muscle group that causes this is found?

   As mentioned, humans have balance problems that our quadrupedal relatives do not, because of our mode of locomotion.

4. Remain standing, and pretend that you are about to cross a log lying across a deep gorge between two cliffs. How would you position yourself to best avoid a fall? What if you expect someone to try to push you over? How will your body position change?

   In the quadrupedal locomotion of a chimpanzee, the legs don't adduct naturally toward the center as ours do and instead move along two parallel (parasagittal) planes. When a chimp walks upright, its center of gravity shifts with each step so that its upper body shifts as well.

5. Walk like an upright chimp. Don't adduct your legs as you walk. Keep them parallel to each other. Describe what your upper body does naturally as a result. Does it shift from side to side?

6. Males and females have slightly different centers of gravity caused by a difference in body proportion. Squat on the ground and have someone place a marker (such as a dry erase marker) on its end 8 to 10 inches out in front of you, between your feet. Put your hands behind your back. Lean down and attempt to knock over the marker with your nose.

Who is more successful at knocking over the marker?

What does this say about the location of the center of gravity in males and females?

Ape-Human Anatomical Comparisons

We assume that gorillas and chimpanzees are more similar than are humans to the common ancestor of African apes and humans, but what was the ancestral locomotor pattern? Although some researchers support the idea of knuckle-walking as the ancestral condition, additional fossil evidence will answer the question more satisfactorily.

Adaptations to Bipedalism

The many differences between the postcranial skeleton of a human and an ape result from many generations of selection for the most efficient locomotion for each (Figure 13.4). Our important first step will be to learn about a few of the many such differences so we can make inferences about the features of our fossil relatives. The features we point out here will be familiar to you from Chapter 7.

Vertebral Column

The characteristic curves you observed in the human vertebral column (Figure 7.10 and *Atlas* p. 184, Figure 5.74B) are absent in the apes. The difference in size between cervical and lumbar vertebrae is more marked in humans because the difference in the amount of weight born by the cervical vertebrae (the head) differs from the lumbar vertebrae (the entire upper body). Apes have a less marked difference because all four limbs share in weight-bearing. Therefore, the lumbar vertebrae don't have to be as large.

The ape ilia (singular = ilium) are more posterior, so they are closer to each other and the intervening sacrum is thus narrower. In the human, because the ilia are out to the sides, the bones are farther apart, spanned by the wider sacrum.

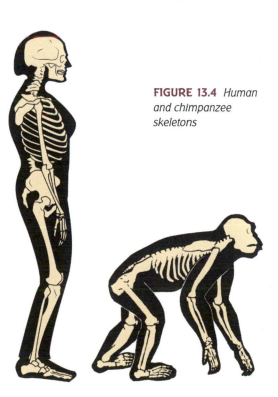

FIGURE 13.4 *Human and chimpanzee skeletons*

Pelvis

On the ape pelvis the ilium is long and skinny (*Atlas* p. 184, Figure 5.72) and the gluteal muscles function as powerful hip extensors. In humans the gluteal muscles act as stabilizers for the hip, so there has been selection for shifting these muscles toward the sides as their function changed. The bony support, the ilium, now has a lateral orientation (Figure 13.5 and *Atlas* p. 184, Figure 5.73 A and B).

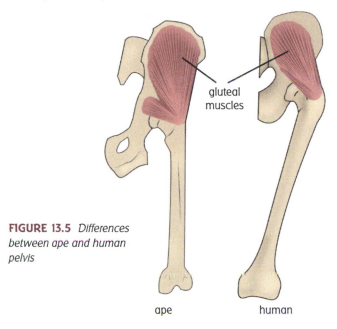

gluteal muscles

FIGURE 13.5 *Differences between ape and human pelvis*

ape   human

A major muscle of propulsion in humans is the *rectus femoris* of the quadriceps muscle group. The rectus femoris is not significant in apes, but the origin of this muscle on the human pelvis causes a large projection, the *anterior inferior iliac spine* (Figure 13.6). This feature is very small on an ape innominate. The muscle actually crosses two joints, its action producing movement at both the hip and the knee. It inserts on the *anterior tibial tuberosity*, which also is large in humans and small in apes. If you stand up, lift your leg (flex leg at hip), then straighten your knee (extend leg at knee), you will experience the rectus femoris in action.

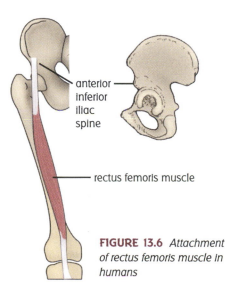

anterior inferior iliac spine

rectus femoris muscle

FIGURE 13.6 *Attachment of rectus femoris muscle in humans*

Femur

The pulling of the leg around toward the center as you step forward is caused by the adductor muscle group, muscles of which run from your posterior pelvis to the linea aspera on your posterior femur (Figure 13.7). The muscle is relatively weak in apes, so the linea aspera is small compared to the marked one observed on a human femur.

If you look in a mirror, or at your classmates when they're in a standing position (anatomical position), you'll see that the legs come in toward the center, from hip to knee. This is a result of the articulations at the hip and the knee, caused by the shape of the joint surfaces. The femur thus creates an angle with the tibia upon which it rests, called the *bicondylar angle* (also called the carrying angle; Figure 13.8).

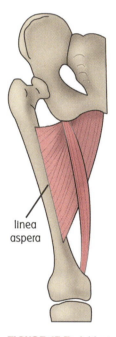

FIGURE 13.7 *Adductor muscles inserting onto a human posterior femur at linea aspera*

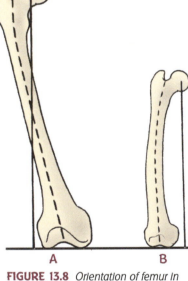

FIGURE 13.8 *Orientation of femur in (A) humans and (B) apes*

Feet

Human feet are well designed for terrestrial distance walking, with toes all in a line, the most medial of which is greatly developed to absorb forces and assist in propulsion, and ligaments bind our foot bones into arches to serve as shock absorbers. Our heel strike, in which all of our body weight is transmitted through the calcaneus, has selected for a large such bone in humans (Figure 13.9 and *Atlas* p. 194, Figure 5.100B) compared to an ape calcaneus.

Apes retain an arboreally adapted grasping big toe, not so different in size from the other toes, and a longitudinal arch is not necessary. Ape toes are longer, and metatarsals and phalanges are more curved than ours, in another arboreal adaptation.

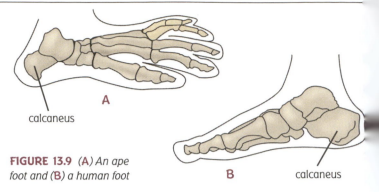

FIGURE 13.9 *(A) An ape foot and (B) a human foot*

Hands

Similar to the differences between human and ape foot bones, our metatarsals and phalanges are straighter and those of apes are more curved. The terminal phalanx of the thumb provides an expanded area for muscle attachment in humans (Photo 13.1A). This is not the case in apes, in which the thumb tip is thinner and lacks the extensive muscle attachment sites (Photo 13.1B).

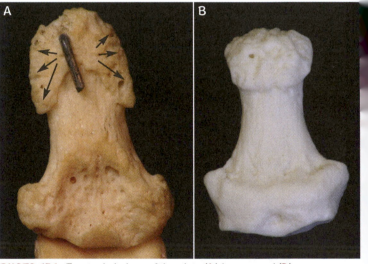

PHOTO 13.1 *Terminal phalanx of thumb in (A) human and (B) ape*

Cranial and Dental Differences Between Humans and Apes

While adaptations to bipedalism were some of the earliest apparent changes from the common ancestor of humans and African apes, dental and cranial features changed as well and are visible in fossils of early hominids. The key, again, is to use our comparative base of living apes and humans to see differences in skulls and dentition. Basic knowledge of ape and human cranial and dental differences and similarities is essential to interpret the fossil record, which is made up largely of jaws and teeth. The numerous distinguishing features of ape versus human skulls and teeth are far too numerous to detail here, but we'll highlight some of the major ones.

Cranium

The position of the foramen magnum is the only cranial feature indicating body posture, because it is the entry point for the spinal cord. The foramen magnum is more anterior in humans (Photo 13.2A; *Atlas* p. 87, Figure 4.16), and more posterior in apes (Photo 13.2B; *Atlas* p. 142, Figure 4.164).

The much greater cranial capacity of humans influences cranial shape such that our skull is higher, with the maximum breadth high on the parietals (Photo 13.3). Humans exhibit virtually no postorbital constriction compared to the apes (Photo 13.4), because the human brain fills the space behind the orbits.

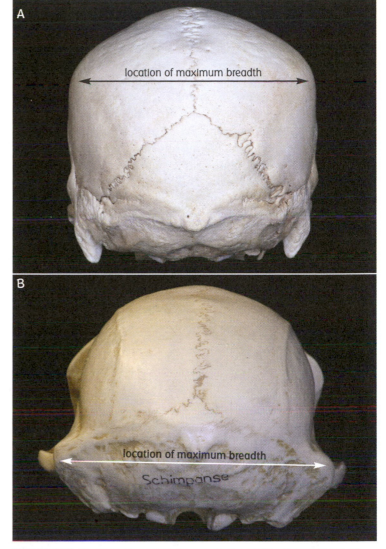

PHOTO 13.3 *Posterior view of (A) human skull and (B) chimpanzee skull*

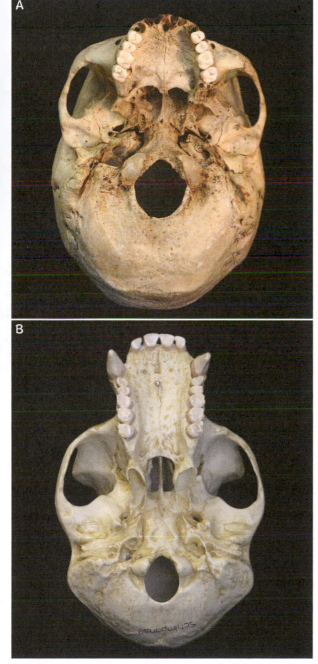

PHOTO 13.2 *Ventral view of (A) human skull and (B) chimpanzee skull*

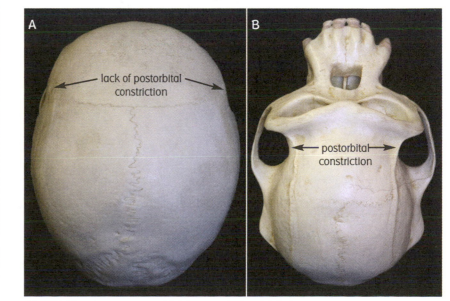

PHOTO 13.4 *Superior view of (A) human skull and (B) chimpanzee skull*

Face and Jaws

Humans are **orthognathic**. Our face is quite vertical, in contrast to the **prognathic** appearance of the apes, with their forward-jutting jaw (Photo 13.5). Our dental arcade is **parabolic,** or rounded (*see* Photo 13.2A; *Atlas* p. 87, Figure 4.16) as opposed to the rectangular shape observable in the ape tooth rows (Photo 13.2B). The human mandible is gracile, and chewing forces are buttressed by the bony anterior projection of the chin. The apes' mandible is robust, and chewing forces are buttressed on the internal aspect of the mandible, with a **simian shelf** (Photo 13.6).

Also related to chewing force is the development of a sagittal crest in gorillas (p. 293, Photos C and D; *Atlas* p. 146) and some male chimpanzees, and the flaring of the zygomatic arches. Both of these features are related to extensive development of the temporalis muscle.

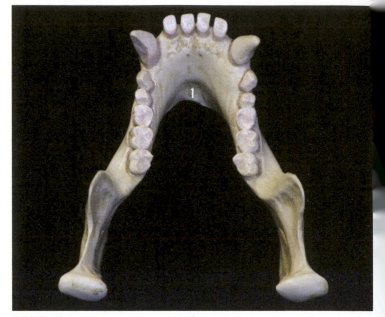

PHOTO 13.6 *Chimpanzee mandible demonstrating simian shelf*
1. simian shelf

Teeth

The large canines of apes are part of a functional complex called a **canine shearing complex,** or **honing triad** (Photo 13.7). In addition to large canines are spaces (each is a **diastema**) in which each canine fits in the upper and lower tooth rows, and a lower premolar just posterior to the bottom space that is sharpened as it sharpens the upper canine. This tooth is called the **sectorial P_3.** While it is the first premolar in the tooth row, P_1 and P_2 have been lost through evolutionary time; the remaining premolars in catarrhines are P_3 and P_4 (*Atlas* p. 67, Figures 3.65, 3.66; p. 71, Figure. 3.72). The size relationship of molars differs in apes and humans such that in apes, molar size increases somewhat toward the back (M3>M2>M1). In humans, molar size decreases toward the back (M1>M2>M3).

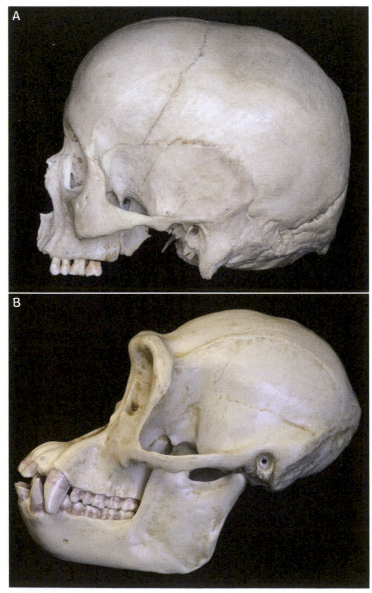

PHOTO 13.5 *Lateral view of (A) human and (B) chimpanzee skull*

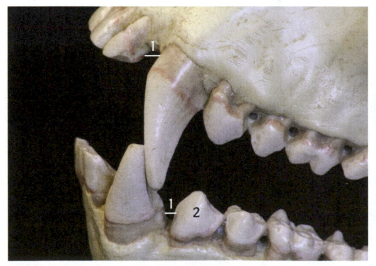

PHOTO 13.7 *Gorilla mandible demonstrating canine shearing complex*
1. diastema   2. sectorial P_3

LAB EXERCISE

13.2

NAME _____

SECTION _____ DATE _____

1. Observing the skulls of young individuals of different species is useful. How do the human fetal skull (A) and the chimp infant skull (B) shown here look more or less similar to one another than do adults of the two species? (Photo 13.5; *Atlas* p. 96, Figure 4.38; p. 143, Figure 4.166)

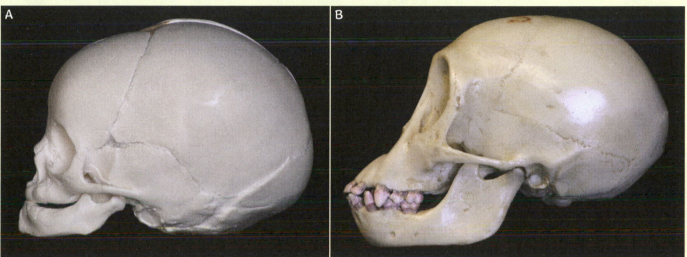

(A) Human fetal skull and (B) chimpanzee infant skull

2. Examine Figures 13.5, 13.6, 13.8, and 13.9, and the photos on the next page (or your lab specimens). Describe your observed differences between ape and human with regard to differences related to bipedalism (*Atlas* p. 184, Figure 5.72; p.192).

	CHIMPANZEE	HUMAN
Pelvis Ilium shape, length		
Orientation of iliac blades (posterior versus lateral)		
Size of anterior inferior iliac spine		
Femur Bicondylar angle?		
Orientation of femoral head, height of greater trochanter		
Size of linea aspera		
Foot Position of big toe		
Size of calcaneus		
Relative thickness of big toe to other toes		

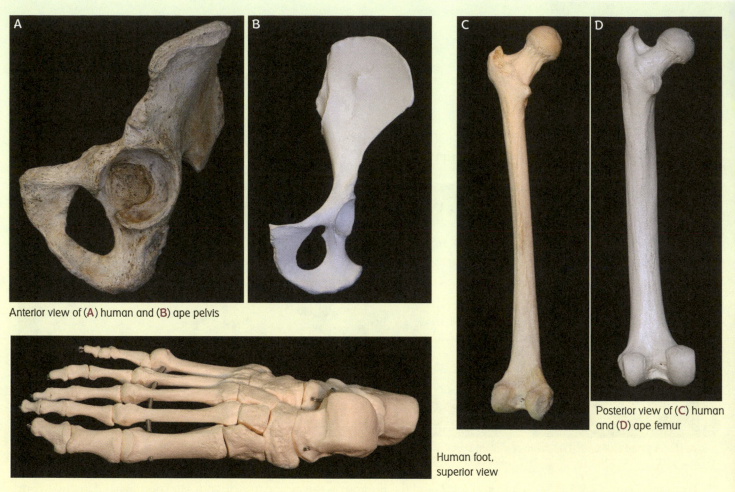

Anterior view of (A) human and (B) ape pelvis

Posterior view of (C) human and (D) ape femur

Human foot, superior view

3. Compare the cranial and dental features of an ape and a human, and fill out the chart, using lab specimens, photos 13.2 through 13.7, or the text.

	CHIMPANZEE	HUMAN
Position of foramen magnum		
Shape of dental arcade		
Relative size of molars: M1, M2, M3		
Location of maximum skull breadth (viewed from back)		
Degree of postorbital constriction		
Cranial capacity (cranium size relative to facial skull)		
Degree of prognathism		
Canine shearing complex: Canine size Diastema Shape of P₃		
Chin versus simian shelf		

Early Members of the Human Line

The human fossil record now contains a dazzling array of fossilized bone, stone tools, and other evidence from our evolutionary history. The last several years alone have yielded unprecedented numbers of fossils, far exceeding our expectations. As the record has become more complete, however, it is ever more difficult to "connect the dots" and link the various hominid forms to one another through time.

What to Call Them?

Discussion of human evolution is complicated by lack of agreement among paleontologists about how to refer to the various species that have existed along the human line after the human/African ape split. Thus far, all such species found exhibit bipedal adaptations.

All of these species used to be called hominids, or members of the family Hominidae, to be distinguished from the great ape family Pongidae (chimps, gorillas, and orangutans). Now, most agree, all of the great apes should not be placed together in the same family, because the African apes (chimps, gorillas) are more closely related to us than to the Asian apes, the orangutans. Many researchers now include *humans and human ancestors/relatives, as well as the African apes* in the family Hominidae. Humans and their ancestors then are classified separately into their own subfamily, Homininae.

In attempting to make sense of the past, researchers' interpretations of the fossil record vary widely as they use their knowledge to classify and categorize in ways with which everyone does not necessarily agree. Textbooks present material in different ways, each author offering a slightly different view. This is the nature of science. The goal here is to introduce many of the known fossil forms and their morphology rather to delve into the various classification schemes that have been interpreted from the fossil evidence.

To avoid much of the confusion in terminology of taxonomic names, I refer to all of our bipedal relatives after our split from the African apes as *members of the human line*.

This group is composed of about 18 species, far too many to learn individually. For reference, a relatively complete list of these fossil species, along with their geographical location and time range, is found in Appendix F. We feasibly can subdivide the member of the human line into three informal subgroups in order to introduce them.

The two subgroups that occurred earlier in time are more similar to one another, and occurred only in Africa. They have in common a relatively small brain and ape-like head, perched on a rather human-like body. These two subgroups are:

- the earliest members of the human line
- the australopiths

Later in time, the third group appeared, finally spreading into regions outside of Africa. More easily distinguished from the other two, the third group is:

- the genus of humans, *Homo*.

Now we will briefly review the range of forms in each of the two earlier subgroups, then move on to lab exercises that focus on some of the better known representatives of these groups. The following chapter, Chapter 14, is devoted to the varied members of the genus *Homo*.

Earliest Members of the Human Line

One of the most recent finds is that of *Sahelanthropus tchadensis* (*Atlas* p. 282; br. ed. p. 54), found in Chad, Central Africa (Brunet, et. al., 2002) (Photo 13.8). Some researchers have interpreted this early (7–6 mya) fossil to represent the earliest split from the ape line. Two species found in East Africa are *Ororrin tugenensis* (approximately 6 mya) and *Ardipithecus ramidus* (5.8–4.4 mya). Although all exhibit bipedal adaptations, each has various primitive features, causing some controversy amongs researchers regarding their status in the human line.

PHOTO 13.8 *Sahelanthropus tchadensis*

The Australopiths

Still quite ape-like in some cranial features, the australopiths all undoubtedly are bipedal and include the likely candidate for the ancestor of *Homo*. They are mentioned here in order of their first appearance in the fossil record.

The earliest member of the genus *Australopithecus* is *A. anamensis* (4.2–3.9 mya), whose still primitive features make it a likely potential link between the earliest members of the human line and the later *Australopithecus* species. The various *A. anamensis* specimens have been found over three decades in East Africa.

Following quickly on the heels of this species was "Lucy." The most famous and most complete australopith specimen, Lucy was found in Ethiopia in 1974 by Donald Johanson. At the time, she was the earliest known biped, and a new species was named for her—*Australopithecus afarensis*. Additional surveying since that time has yielded dozens of individuals of this species, which existed between about 3.9 and 2.9 million years ago (Photo 13.9; *Atlas* pp. 286–287; br. ed. pp. 58–59). Because *A. afarensis* fossils are so well represented for much of the skeleton, the skeletal adaptations of this species (especially those for bipedalism) serve as a comparative basis for a number of lab exercises in this chapter.

PHOTO 13.9 *Australopithecus afarensis*

A controversial but potentially significant discovery in 2001 was *Kenyanthropus platyops* (from about 3.5 mya), a fossil form that is in many ways similar to *A. afarensis*, but with a flatter face (Photo 13.10). Not everyone recognizes *Kenyanthropus* as a valid species, but if it is, it may be near the ancestry of the genus *Homo*. Another potential *Homo* ancestor is *A. africanus*, from South Africa (Photo 13.11; *Atlas* p. 289; br. ed. p. 61), often referred to as a **gracile australopith** (as distinct from the robust group, below). This was the earliest australopith to be discovered, when the fossil of a young individual (the "Taung child") was brought to Raymond Dart in 1924.

Numerous adult individuals of this species have been found since then in South Africa, dating between about 3

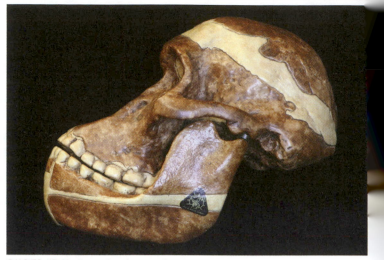

PHOTO 13.11 *Australopithecus africanus*

and 2 million years ago. Overlapping in time with *A. africanus* was the relatively recent find, *A. garhi* (meaning "surprise" in the language of the local Afar region), so named because of the surprise with which its discoverer, Tim White, greeted its uncovering. It is the only species, other than members of the genus *Homo*, to be found associated with stone tools!

The three remaining australopith species are all **robust australopiths**, sharing a number of cranial and dental adaptations related to feeding on hard objects that require much chewing force. The earliest species was *A. aethiopicus* (Photo 13.12; *Atlas* p. 288; br. ed. p. 60), which lived in East Africa. *Australopithecus robustus* (found in South Africa) and *A. boisei* (found in East Africa) overlapped in time, with *A. boisei* existing until more recently, up to about 1.2 million years ago. Some researchers place these species in their own genus, *Paranthropus*. It is agreed that all have become extinct without leaving any descendants.

By studying the morphology (form) of the australopith fossil specimens and comparing them to apes and to humans in the following lab exercises, you will better understand their placement on the human line.

PHOTO 13.10 *Kenyanthropus platyops*

PHOTO 13.12 *Australopithecus (Paranthropus) aethiopicus*

LAB EXERCISE 13.3

NAME _____

SECTION _____ DATE _____

1. Observe lab specimens and the photos in this and the previous lab exercise. Compare postcranial bones of *Australopithecus afarensis* (Lucy) to those of a chimpanzee and a human (*Atlas* p. 287, Figures 8.66, 8.67; br. ed. p. 59, Figures. 3.66, 3.77), and fill out the chart below. Answer from a comparative perspective. For example, for orientation of iliac blades, you might say, "more laterally placed" (for *A. afarensis* compared to a chimpanzee) and "slightly more posteriorly placed" (for *A. afarensis* compared to a human). See next page for *A. afarensis* proximal femur.

	A. AFARENSIS COMPARED TO A CHIMPANZEE	*A. AFARENSIS* COMPARED TO A HUMAN
Pelvis Ilium shape, length		
Orientation of iliac blades		
Size of anterior inferior iliac spine		
Femur Bicondylar angle?		
Orientation of femoral head, height of greater trochanter		
Size of linea aspera		

*In the absence of *A. afarensis* lab specimens and/or the *Atlas*, few features will be visible.

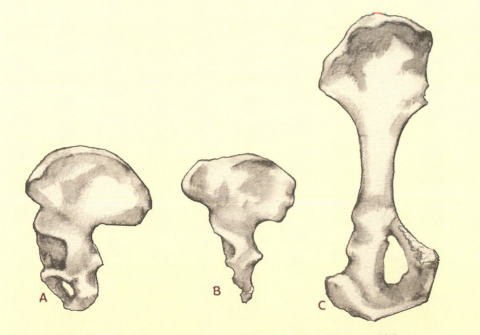

Comparison of innominate bone of (A) a human, (B) an australopithecine, and (C) an ape

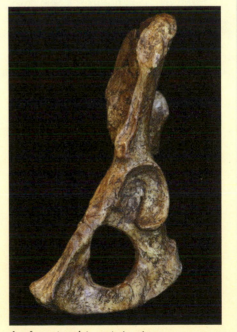

A. afarensis pelvis, anterior view

Proximal femur of *A. afarensis*, posterior view

2. In the chart, describe the cranial and dental features of *A. afarensis* compared to a chimp and to a human, using the lab specimens and photos 13.2 through 13.5, and on the following page (*see also Atlas* pp. 286–287; br. ed. pp. 58–59).

	A. AFARENSIS COMPARED TO A CHIMPANZEE	*A. AFARENSIS* COMPARED TO A HUMAN
Position of foramen magnum		
Shape of dental arcade		
Relative size of molars: M1, M2, M3		
Location of maximum skull breadth (viewed from back)		
Degree of postorbital constriction		
Cranial capacity (cranium size relative to facial skull)		
Degree of prognathism		
Canine shearing complex: Canine size Diastema Shape of P_3		
Chin versus receding mandibular symphysis		

LAB EXERCISE
13.3 (CONT.)

NAME _____

SECTION _____ DATE _____

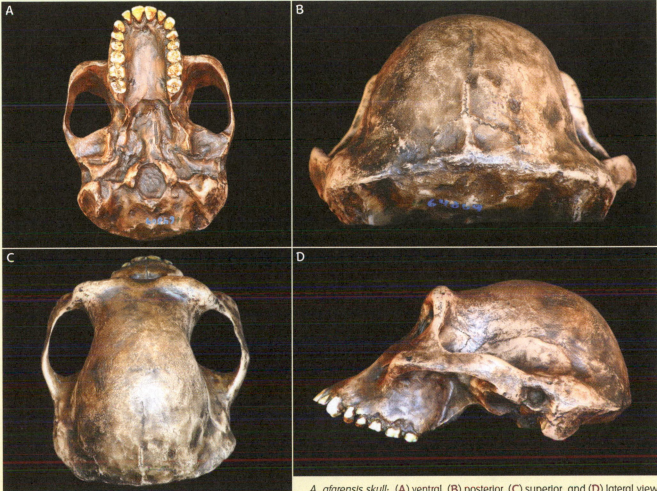

A. afarensis skull: (**A**) ventral, (**B**) posterior, (**C**) superior, and (**D**) lateral views

3. For the following exercise on cranial and dental features, observe *A. africanus* and a robust australopith from the photos here (*Atlas* pp. 288–293; br. ed. pp. 60–65) and compare them to the specimens or photos of *A. afarensis*, a chimp, and a human. Fill out the chart on page 321.

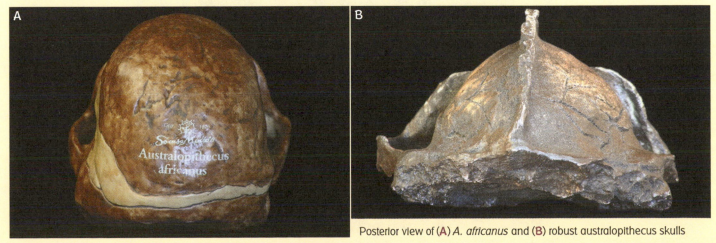

Posterior view of (**A**) *A. africanus* and (**B**) robust australopithecus skulls

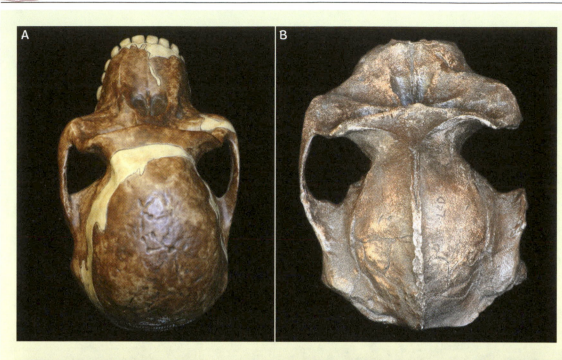

Superior view of (A) *A. africanus* and (B) robust australopith skulls

Lateral view of (A) *A. africanus* and (B) robust australopith skulls

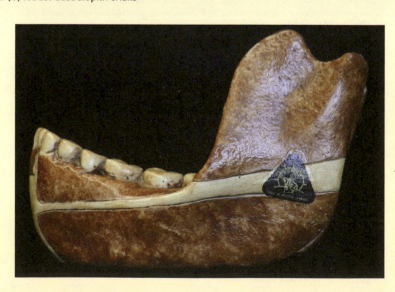

A. africanus mandible

LAB EXERCISE
13.3 (CONT.)

NAME _____

SECTION _____ DATE _____

	CHIMP	A. AFARENSIS	A. AFRICANUS	ROBUST AUSTRALOPITH	HUMAN
Location of maximum skull breadth					
Degree of postorbital constriction					
Degree of zygomatic flare					
Cranium size relative to facial skull					
Degree of prognathism					
Facial profile shape					
Sagittal crest? (ridge on top of skull)					
Shape of occipital and nuchal region					
Canine shearing complex: Canine size Diastema Shape of P_3					
Chin versus retreating mandibular symphysis					

4. Regarding the robust australopiths, what do you think the molar tooth form and size, degree of zygomatic flare, and presence of sagittal crest are related to?

5. The relative size of the anterior and posterior dentition changes through time. Tooth proportions can be measured to track that change. Measure the width (side to side) of one of the central upper incisors, and the width of an upper second molar (lingual side to buccal side) from the same side. Then calculate an index to obtain a ratio of incisor-to-molar width.

$$\frac{\text{Incisor width}}{\text{Molar width}} \times 100$$

	INCISOR WIDTH	M² WIDTH	INDEX
Chimpanzee			
A. afarensis			
A. africanus			
Robustus australopith			
Modern human			

6. Which specimen is most similar to which other specimen?

   Do you observe any trends in changes of tooth proportion over time?

7. Compare the photo of the Taung child (*Atlas* p. 288, Figure 8.69; br. ed. p. 60, Figure. 3.69), *Australopithecus africanus*, with the modern fetal human skull and that of the baby chimp in Lab Exercise 13.2. Why do you think the discoverer of the Taung child, Raymond Dart, insisted that the Taung skull was on the human, not the ape, line? What features may have led him to this conclusion?

Taung child skull, mandible, and endocast

SELF-TEST
13.1

NAME _____

SECTION _____ DATE _____

1. What are at least three skeletal differences between apes and humans that relate to locomotion?

   a.

   b.

   c.

2. What are at least three cranial or dental differences between apes and humans?

   a.

   b.

   c.

3. What are the two phases of the walking cycle? Briefly describe each.

   a.

   b.

4. What is a primary shared adaptation among all species on the human line?

5. What are the three main groups of species on the human line?

   a.

   b.

   c.

6. What are two features that differ between the robust australopiths and the other early (pre-*Homo)* members of the human line? Describe the feature for each group.

7. a. Overall, does the skull of an *A. afarensis* look more ape-like or more human-like?

    b. What features mostly contribute to this overall appearance?

8. Why is *A. afarensis* known to be on the human, rather than ape, line?

9. a. Does the australopith pelvis look more ape-like or more human-like?

    b. What features mostly contribute to this overall appearance?

ONE STEP FURTHER

NAME _____

SECTION _____ DATE _____

Additional Lab Exercise **13.1**

ADDITIONAL MATERIALS NEEDED:

- Spreading calipers
- Graduated cylinders or large measuring cups with mL marks (a 2-cup measuring cup holds 500 mL, which would be too small for a modern human skull, but it could be filled more than once)
- Small, hard-packing seeds (such as flax seeds) or balls (such as lead shot)
- If desired, some extra bowls to dump seed/shot into while measuring

Cranial Capacity

Brain size will be discussed further in Chapter 14, but it is introduced here as an important feature that changes over time in human evolution. Brain size is inferred from **cranial capacity**, which is basically how much brain a skull can hold. Cranial capacity is measured and reported in cubic centimeters (cc). In this exercise you will learn to *estimate cranial capacity based on cranial measurements*, as well as to measure the *actual volume of skulls*. Keep in mind that differences in cranial capacity *within a species* are not related to intelligence but, instead, are simply an expression of biological variation among individuals.

Because the formulae you will use are specifically for humans, you will not collect cranial measurement data for the ape, but you will compare the actual volume technique using the formula for cranial capacity for humans. You also can compare your results to Chapter 14's brain size/body weight chart with actual cranial capacity estimates from the published literature.

1. Fill out the chart below by first taking the measurements, then calculating the formulae. If necessary, refer back to Chapter 8 (p. 182) for the skull landmarks (Photo 8.1 A through C) and techniques for cranial measurement (Figures 8.1 and 8.2). Also see the figure for the cranial height measurement. Measure two human skulls of known sex (preferably one male and one female).

	HUMAN 1	HUMAN 2
Cranial length		
Cranial breadth		
Cranial height		
Cranial capacity (see formula below)		

Measuring cranial height

Lee-Pearson cranial capacity formulae: (from Lee and Pearson, 1901)
For males: 0.365 (cranial length × cranial breadth × cranial height) + 359.34
For females: 0.375 (cranial length × cranial breadth × cranial height) + 296.40

2. For each skull, measure the cranial volume as follows: Turn over the skull so the inferior aspect is up, and pour the seed/shot into the foramen magnum up to the rim. Then pour the seed back out into the graduated cylinder or measuring cup. (The cranial capacity may be larger than a single graduated cylinder or a measuring cup can hold, so be prepared to use a third container for dumping the seeds/shot after measuring if you have to fill the measuring vessel again.) Record the volume in the chart below. Each milliliter (mL) equals 1 cubic centimeter, so the conversion is easy.

	HUMAN 1	HUMAN 2	APE
Cranial volume			

3. How comparable were your results of the estimated (via formula) and the actual cranial capacities?

ONE STEP FURTHER

NAME _____

SECTION _____ DATE _____

Additional Lab Exercise 13.2

ADDITIONAL MATERIALS NEEDED:

- Three kinds of foods with various degrees of toughness, such as:
  - strawberries (or other soft food that requires little chewing)
  - Cheerios or other crunchy cereal
  - carrot pieces (or other hard food)

Jaw Muscles

In Chapter 9 you learned some functional anatomy of the dentition: how different parts of the tooth row are used for different types of food and how different forms of dentition reflect dietary patterns. Jaw musculature was introduced briefly. We'll learn more about that in this exercise and how it can influence cranial architecture.

The two main muscles involved in chewing are the temporalis and the masseter muscles. Note the difference in size and muscle orientation between the human, the gorilla, and the australopith (see figure below). As the temporalis grows, it inserts higher and higher on the temporal bone, and in some species additional insertion area is needed. Continued muscle growth produces electrical impulses that stimulate bone growth, resulting in the sagittal crest.

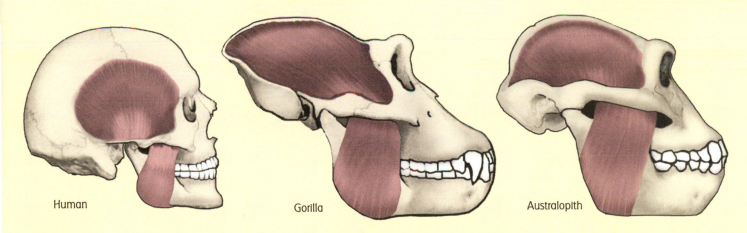

Human   Gorilla   Australopith

In this exercise you will compare the way your jaw muscles feel when you chew different types of foods, and gain an appreciation for the way in which food types may provide selective pressure for the evolution of various forms of jaw musculature.

As you chew each of the types of food (soft, medium, hard), feel your chewing muscles. The temporalis is felt on the sides of the head above the temples, and the masseter on the lateral sides of the mandible in the region between the molars and the gonial angle.

1. Describe how much you can feel the contractions of the two muscles for the three different foods.

2. Which teeth do you use the most while chewing?

3. Which of hominids do you assume would have eaten the toughest foods, based on the ratio of anterior (incisors and canines) and posterior (molars and premolars) tooth size?

4. Look once again at the figure on page 327 of the jaw muscles in the human, the gorilla, and a robust australopith. Why is the temporalis so extensive in the latter two?

5. Briefly describe the association between molar size and jaw muscle size, with particular reference to the robust australopiths.

ONE STEP FURTHER

NAME _____

SECTION _____ DATE _____

Additional Self-Test Questions

1. Did the robust australopithecines leave any descendants? If so, what species?

2. Where are gracile australopithecines found?

3. Which member of the human line shows the earliest adaptations to bipedalsim?

4. What feature on the skull relates to bipedalism?

5. Are the following features associated with apes (A) or humans (H)?

    _____ 1. rounded dental arcade

    _____ 2. femur with bicondylar angle

    _____ 3. non-opposable big toe

    _____ 4. ilium of pelvis oriented to the sides

    _____ 5. foramen magnum more posterior

6. Based on your readings and your lab exercises, describe a few changes over time between the earliest members of the human line through the end of the time period of australopiths.

The Genus *Homo*

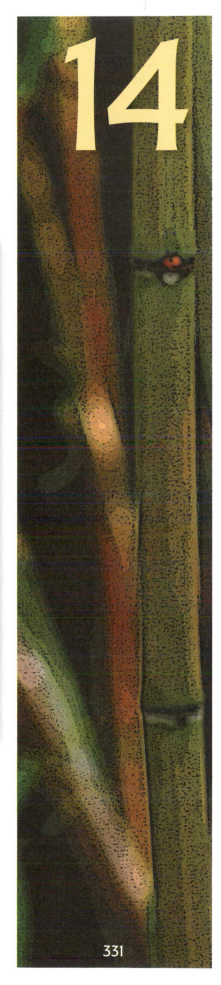

14

"Have you ever wondered . . . ?"

- Did we evolve from Neanderthals?
- Did they ever find the "Missing Link?"

OBJECTIVES

- Recognize extinct members of genus *Homo* by identifying fossil casts
- Become familiar with features that are similar to and different from other extinct and modern species when compared to various *Homo* species
- Learn the distribution of extinct members of the genus *Homo* in time and space
- Understand that interpretation of the human fossil record is complex and debatable, and that not all paleontologists agree on the classification schemes proposed

MATERIALS NEEDED

- Preferably, as many as possible of the following skulls/casts:
  - Modern human skull
  - Early *Homo* skull cast (*Homo habilis* or *H. rudolfensis*)
  - Chimpanzee skull (or other ape)
  - *Homo ergaster* or *Homo erectus* skull cast
  - "Archaic" *Homo sapiens* skull cast
  - Neanderthal skull cast
  - Early anatomically modern human skull cast

  (Note: The above items can be substituted or supplemented with photos in lab manual and A Photographic Atlas for Physical Anthropology.*)*

- Number and letter labels to group the bones and set up lab "stations"

The roots of the genus *Homo* go back approximately 2.4 million years to eastern Africa. *Homo* has changed greatly over time, with several recognized species in the genus (between five and ten, depending upon the author), and the numbers keep growing as the fossil record is uncovered further. Again, a list of most fossil human species is found in Appendix F. This chapter is divided into two main sections, the first dealing with earlier *Homo* and the second with later members of the genus.

Early *Homo*

The earliest known member of our genus was found by Mary and Louis Leakey. Formally named by Louis Leakey, Philip Tobias, and John Napier, its scientific name was suggested by Raymond Dart, the South African paleontologist who discovered the Taung child fossil, among many others. **Homo habilis** roughly translates from the Latin as "handy man," named as such because of its presumed association with stone tools. Though it was similar to *Australopithecus africanus* in many ways, its brain was significantly larger and its face and dentition smaller.

Numerous additional specimens of early *Homo* were found later in East and South Africa from about 2.4 to 1.4 million years ago, and also attributed to *Homo habilis* (Photo 14.1A). Some researchers, however, interpreted the wide range of variation in these fossils as evidence for two species, which differ from each other in cranial and post-cranial features. Thus, some of the *Homo habilis* specimens were placed in a new species: **Homo rudolfensis** (Photo 14.1B; *Atlas* p. 295; br. ed. p. 67), although not all accept it as a valid species. For our purposes here, we can consider the features of these two similar forms together, as listed below. (Some features that distinguish between the two forms are listed in Appendix G).

Features of *Homo habilis/rudolfensis* as compared to *A. africanus* are:

1. Cranium size and shape:
   - Higher cranium
   - Larger cranial capacity: average of 650 cc (25%–40% larger than australopiths); largest was ~775 cc
   - Less postorbital constriction
   - More rounded cranium
   - Face smaller relative to cranium

2. Diet and chewing:
   - More vertical face (less prognathic, more orthognathic)
   - Smaller, thinner mandible

- Mandible more parabolic and less V-shaped
- Shortened length of posterior tooth row
- Teeth more human-shaped: premolars and molars smaller, incisors larger

The relatively simple stone tools associated with early *Homo* are called **Olduwan** (Fig. 14.1), after the site in Tanzania (Olduvai Gorge) where they were first discovered. Technological advances accompanied the anatomical changes throughout the evolution of humans. Keep in mind that only one of the early *Homo* species (to be more specific, one population within a species) evolved into later forms. Many think that *Homo rudolfensis* has the features that likely were exhibited by a human ancestor.

Homo erectus/Homo ergaster

In the late 1800s, a Dutch doctor, Eugene Dubois, went to the Dutch East Indies to find "the Missing Link." After a great deal of searching, he found a skullcap and a femur on the Indonesian island of Java. Assuming that he'd found the "ape-man" he was looking for, he named a new species for his find—*Pithecanthropus erectus*, later renamed **Homo erectus**. But the assumption that a single fossil represented the missing link was mistaken. Like any family tree, the human evolutionary past is represented by many branches, so the idea of a single half-human half-ape form is a myth. After Dubois' find, additional fossils with similar features were found in Asia and in Africa.

Similar to the case for *Homo habilis*, the variation of fossils attributed to *Homo erectus*, as well as its time range and geographical distribution, raise doubts that all such fossils belong to one wide-ranging species. Many researchers agree that they represent two species—*Homo erectus* and

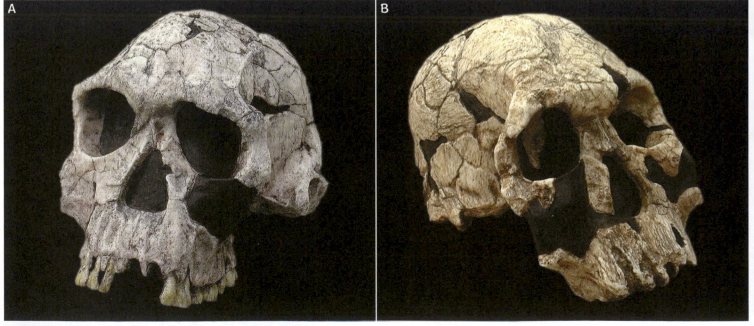

PHOTO 14.1 *Early Homo: Homo habilis (**A**) and H. rudolfensis (**B**)*

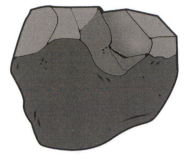
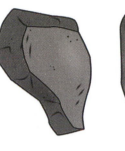
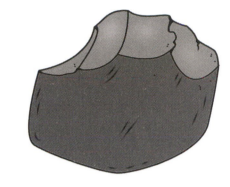

IGURE 14.1 *Examples of Olduwan tools*

Homo ergaster (G *erg*: work)(Photo 14.2; *Atlas* p. 296–297, ~03; br. ed. pp. 68–69, 75).

Homo erectus is the Asian species, and many researchers ~hink it represents an evolutionary dead-end. *Homo ergaster* ~s found in Africa and may represent the ancestor of later ~umans. ***Homo erectus/ergaster*** closely followed early pop- ~lations of *Homo habilis* in time and existed over a long ~eriod, from about 1.8 million years ago to as recently as ~50,000 years ago in the Far East. The most recent African ~orms are dated at about 500,000 years ago. These two ~pecies have numerous similarities. Features of both, com- ~ared to the earlier *Homo habilis/H. rudolphensis*, include:

- thicker bone
- long, low skull
- cranial capacity of 850–1100 cc
- sagittal keel (thickening along top of skull)
- large supraorbital torus (larger than *H. habilis*)
- shorter face

- less postorbital constriction
- receding forehead
- sharp nuchal torus, set high on occipital, V-shaped
- maximum breadth near base of skull
- projecting nasal region
- vertical or receding mandibular symphysis (no chin)
- taller at adulthood
- less sexual dimorphism
- basically modern postcrania; more muscled and robust than modern humans

Why was *Homo erectus/ergaster* so important? Presum- ably, *Homo ergaster* respresented the first of the human line to leave Africa. In addition, they were the first known to control fire. Their stone tools, called the **Acheulean** type, were better developed than Olduwan tools. A typical Acheulean tool is a large, bifaced, and often tear-drop-shaped tool, the **hand axe** (Photo 14.3). Hand axes are found in

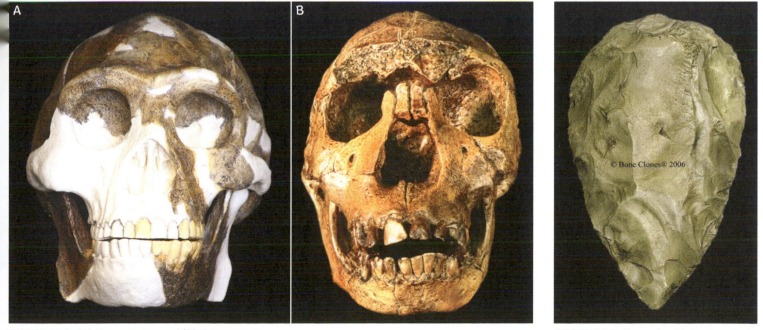

PHOTO 14.2 (A) *Homo erectus* and (B) *Homo ergaster*

PHOTO 14.3 *Example of Acheulean tool*

Africa and in Europe but not in eastern Asia. Experiments show that they probably were used on meat, bone, wood, and hides. These ubiquitous hand axes have been referred to as the "Swiss Army knife of the Lower Paleolithic."

Dmanisi: An Early Enigma

In the former Soviet Union, in what is now the Republic of Georgia, an unexpected find was uncovered in 1991—fossils dated at about 1.7 million years ago, an apparent early *Homo erectus/ergaster* migrant from Africa. Remains of more individuals were found in 1999. The features show similarities to *H. erectus/ergaster*, but it is smaller and more primitive, with a much smaller brain size (Photo 14.4). Some researchers consider this to be *H. erectus/ergaster*, a few assign it to its own species (*Homo georgicus*), and some don't yet attempt to assign it a name.

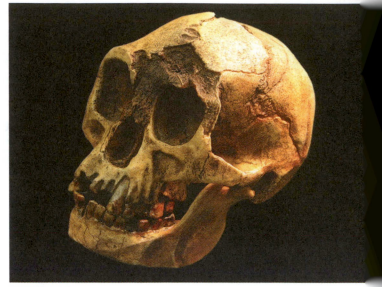

PHOTO 14.5 *Homo floresiensis*

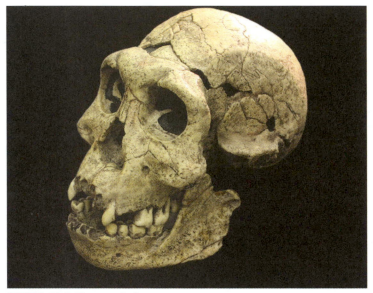

PHOTO 14.4 *Dmanisi skull*

Homo floresiensis: A Later Enigma

You likely have heard of the Hobbit—not the main character in the Tolkien novel, but his namesake, the fossil remains of a diminutive form of human in Indonesia that was announced to surprise and controversy in 2004 (Brown et al., 2004) (Photo 14.5). The situation did seem more like fantasy than science, from the fossil discoveries of as many as 12 small (3½ foot tall) people in a huge cave in a verdant forest, to their association with giant rats, komodo dragons, and pygmy elephants.

The cave site, Ling Bua, on the island of Flores, has yielded a number of mysterious questions:

1. Why were these people so small, with such small brains? (380 cc!) Do they represent descendants of *Homo erectus* that became smaller in their island isolation over time?

2. Do the remains represent a new species, **Homo floresiensis**, as some insist? Or did they suffer from microcephaly

or from Laron syndrome, both of which result in a smaller brain size and other physical manifestations (Martin et al., 2006; Hershkovitz et al., 2007)?

3. Why are their stone tools so sophisticated if they were made by such small-brained humans?

4. Why did they exist so recently in time? Dating of the remains shows that the species (if it actually was a species) existed at that site from about 94,000 years ago to only 13,000 years ago!

The debate continues, although the idea of a new species now seems more acceptable. The phenomenon "island dwarfing," which is controversial but likely for a number of other species, may have applied to these humans as it probably did to the pygmy elephants with which they were found. Island populations may exhibit tremendous differences in size from mainland forms because of a combination of genetic drift and natural selection—in this case, lack of selection for large body size if predator risk is low. This human form, despite its existence in relatively recent times, is presented in this section with its likely relatives, *Homo erectus/ergaster*. However, a recent study of the feet from the original specimen has contributed new information crucial to the species' interpretation.

While the extreme relative length of the foot has been previously noted, the new analysis revealed a mix of primitive and derived foot features for this clearly bipedal early human (Jungers et al., 2009). The authors suggest the possibility that a species even more primitive than *Homo erectus/ergaster* may have given rise to *Homo floresiensis*.

The following exercise allows for comparisons among some of these earlier members of our genus and their stone tools.

LAB EXERCISE
14.1

NAME _____

SECTION _____ DATE _____

1. Take a look at Olduwan tools (refer to Figure 14.1).

   a. What would make you think they are tools and not just rocks?

   b. In what specific ways do these tools differ from Acheulean tools? It may be helpful to draw them as part of your answer.

2. Compare the earlier members of the genus *Homo* with a predecessor as well as a modern human to highlight changes occurring over time. Use the photos on the next two pages and from Lab Exercise 13.3 (also see *Atlas* pp. 289, 290, 295–298, 303; br. ed. p. 61, 62, 67–70, 75) or fossil casts. Many of your descriptions may be in relative terms (larger, smaller, etc.).

	A. AFRICANUS	*H. HABILIS* OR *H. RUDOLFENSIS*	*H. ERECTUS* OR *H. ERGASTER*	MODERN HUMAN
Shape of dental arcade				
Size of front teeth relative to back				
Relative size of molars: M1, M2, M3				
Sagittal keel?				
Location of maximum skull breadth				
Degree of postorbital constriction				
Cranial shape (height versus length)				
Cranium size relative to facial skull				
Supraorbital ridge size				
Degree of prognathism				
Shape of occipital and nuchal region (nuchal torus?)				
Mandibular symphysis form (receding, vertical, chin)				

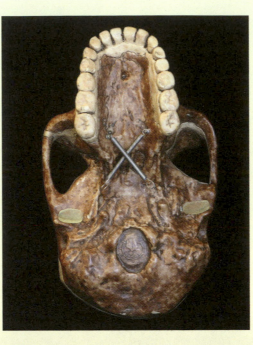

Australpithecus africanus,
ventral view

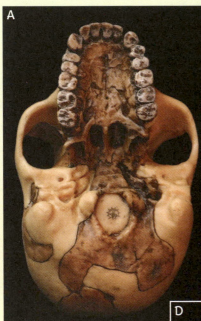

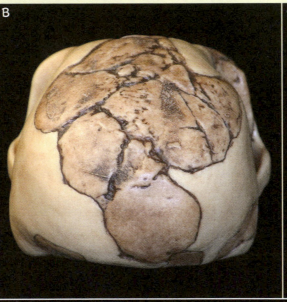

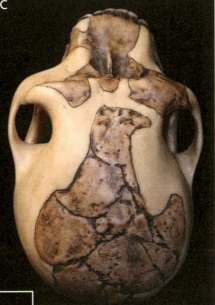

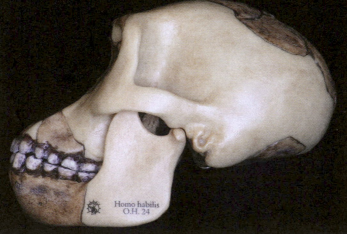

Homo habilis: **(A)** ventral,
(B) posterior, **(C)** superior,
and **(D)** lateral views

LAB EXERCISE
14.1 (CONT.)

NAME _____

SECTION _____ DATE _____

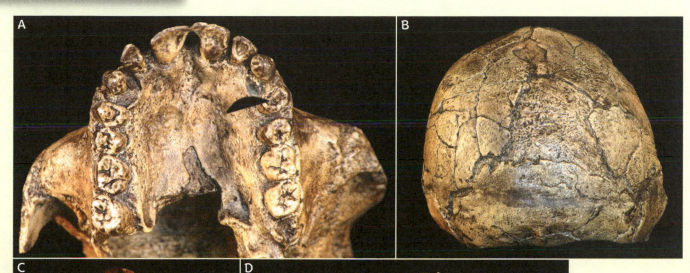

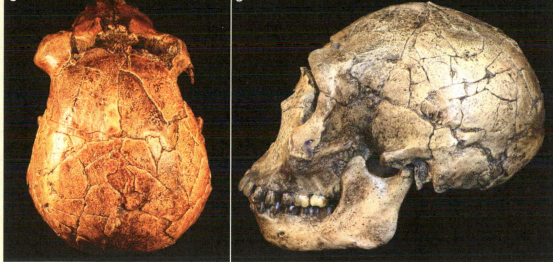

Homo ergaster: (**A**) ventral,
(**B**) posterior, (**C**) superior,
and (**D**) lateral views

Modern human dental arcade
(see also Photos 13.2 and 13.5A)

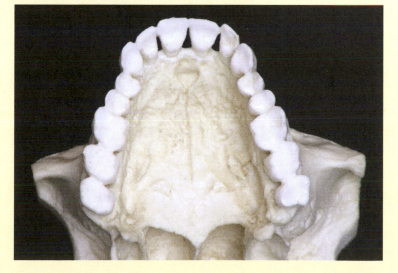

3. You've observed several cranial features. Which ones are directly related to (or appear to be a result of) increased cranial capacity?

4. Although bigger brains are known to be related to higher intelligence in a general sense, within a species, individuals with a larger head size aren't smarter than their smaller-headed companions. Brain size has a great deal of intra-specific (within species) variation. When comparing various species, a significant aspect to study is *relative brain size*—brain size compared to body size.

   To determine the significance of this correlation, we can gauge the ratio of brain size to body size. The chart below provides you with data on average cranial capacity (cc) and average body weight for several species. It is up to you to calculate the ratio by dividing the cranial capacity by body weight. Obviously, a species with a value of .05 has a smaller relative brain size than one with a 0.12 value.

$$\frac{\text{cranial capacity (in cubic cm)}}{\text{body weight (in kg)}} = \text{brain/body size ratio}$$

Fill out the chart for the species listed.

SPECIES	CRANIAL CAPACITY (CC)	AVERAGE APPROXIMATE BODY WEIGHT (KG)	BRAIN/BODY SIZE RATIO
Chimpanzee	395[1]	54[3]	
Gorilla	506[1]	120[3]	
A. afarensis	438	37[5]	
A. africanus	440	35[5]	
Robust australopiths	515[2]	39[2]	
H. habilis	631	42[5]	
H. erectus	985[2]	56[4]	
H. sapiens	1325[1]	63[4]	

Adapted from *Introduction to Biological Anthropology Laboratory Manual*, by L. Sattenspiel, C. V. Ward, S. Stout, and D. Wescott (unpublished work, University of Missouri, Columbia, 2001), p. 130.

Data obtained:

[1] *Introduction to Physical Anthropology*, 8th ed., by R. Jurmain, H. Nelson, L. Kilgore, and W. Trevathan (Belmont, CA: Wadsworth/Thomson Learning, 2003).

[2] *Biological Anthropology*, by M. A. Park (New York: McGraw-Hill, 2005).

[3] *Primate Adaptation and Evolution*, 2nd ed. by J. G. F. Fleagle (New York: Academic Press, 1999).

[4] *Biological Anthropology* by C. Stanford, J. S. Allen, and S. C. Anton (Upper Saddle River, NJ: Pearson Prentice Hall).

[5] "Body size and proportions in early hominids," H. McHenry, in *American Journal of Physical Anthropology*, 87:407–431.

5. Is this what you would expect? From what you have found among the species listed above, at what point (or points) in human evolution did the most significant increase in relative brain size occur?

Later *Homo*: "Archaic" *Homo sapiens*

Evidence points to indications that humans lived and died approximately 780,000 years ago in what is now Spain. Several fossils from two sites have provided paleontologists with another issue over which to disagree. The fossils appear to be distinct from *Homo erectus/ergaster* in that they are more modern. The fossils' discoverers gave them a new scientific name—*Homo antecessor*—and proposed that they may represent the ancestral group from which evolved both Neanderthals and modern humans (Bermudéz de Castro et al., 1997). Few researchers consider the taxon valid at this time.

By 400,000 years ago, humans with a mix of *Homo erectus* and **Homo sapiens** features were present in Africa, Asia, and Europe. This loosely defined group often has been referred to as **"archaic" Homo sapiens**, or **transitional forms** (Photo 14.6; *Atlas* p. 307–312; br. ed. p. 79–84), and frequently not attributed to any particular species. Humans living during this time vary from each other and appear to lack a suite of features that would distinguish them as one species.

Recently, some researchers have been assigning scientific names to them, but there is continued lack of agreement about what names to use and which fossils should be ascribed to which species. Many, however, now assign these early human fossils, found between about 400,000 and 150,000 years ago, to the species **Homo heidelbergensis**, named after the German city near the site where they were first discovered.

Relative to *Homo erectus/ergaster*, some features exhibited by the "Archaic" *Homo sapiens* were:

- larger cranial capacity
- decreased postorbital constriction
- higher skull, shorter skull (front to back)
- occipital more rounded (less angular)
- forehead more rounded
- smaller teeth and jaws

Compared to modern humans, some features are:
- heavier face
- larger teeth
- lower, longer skulls
- large supraorbital ridge, varied, often not continuous across frontal bone, but arched over each eye

These newer members of the genus *Homo* were culturally more diverse than *H. erectus/ergaster*, with advances including new and more varied tools, some primitive shelters, and more efficient hunting techniques. Although use of Acheulean tools continued for a time, they began to be interspersed with new tool-making techniques, particularly one undertaken to create **Levalloisian** flake tools. In this technique the core was modified to produce more predictable sizes and shapes of flakes. The hafting of points onto shafts for spears also occurred during this time.

Around the time of the disappearance of these people, approximately 150,000 years ago, two groups of people appeared—the **Neanderthals** and the **anatomically modern humans**.

Special Case of the Neanderthals

The first discovery of a fossil that was recognized as human at the time of its discovery was of a Neanderthal partial skeleton, found near Dusseldorf, Germany in the mid-1800s. First thought to be the bones of a cave bear, a high school science teacher recognized them as human.

Neanderthals existed in the Middle East and Europe from about 130,000 years ago until about 30,000 years ago. The most distinctive specimens are those that first appeared about 75,000 years ago in Europe, during the height of the Pleistocene ice ages. These are referred to as "classic" Neanderthals, and are best exemplified by specimens such as those pictured (Photo 14.7; *Atlas* pp. 314–319; br. ed. pp. 86–89), and by the features listed on page 340. The Neandethals frequently inhabited caves and were efficient game hunters. Their stone tools were more complex and varied than previous tools, using a tool technology referred to as the **Mousterian** industry (Photo 14.8).

The place of the Neanderthals in our evolutionary history —or whether they even *had* a place in our history—continues to be debated. Some researchers see Neanderthals as a defunct side branch and an evolutionary dead-end, representing a separate species, *Homo neandertalensis*. Others are

PHOTO 14.6 *"Archaic" Homo sapiens (Homo heidelbergensis)*

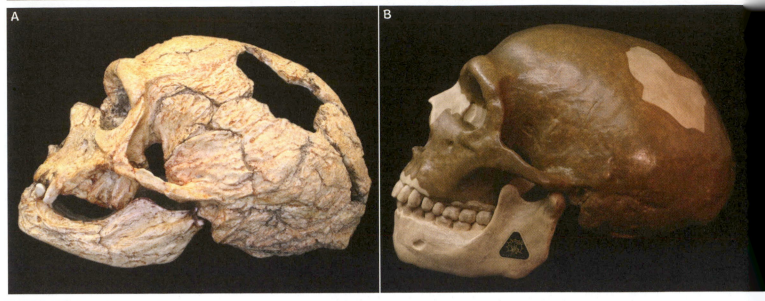

PHOTO 14.7 *Neanderthal specimens*

PHOTO 14.8 *Examples of Mousterian tools*

convinced that some Neanderthal traits are present in modern human populations and that they are a subspecies of *Homo sapiens* (*H. sapiens neandertalensis*). Mitochondrial DNA taken from the humerus of a Neanderthal was interpreted to indicate a split between anatomically modern humans and Neanderthals between 550,000 and 690,000 years ago, too long ago for a shared gene pool (Krings et al., 1997). Additional DNA studies and statistical simulation support that conclusion (Currat and Excoffier, 2004; Pennisi, 2007).

Neanderthal features relative to modern humans are:

- long, low skull
- average cranial capacity 1520 cc
- maximum breadth midway down skull
- occipital bun (large bump on back of skull)
- large supraorbital ridge
- rounded orbits
- midfacial prognathism ("puffy" maxillary region, which houses the maxillary sinuses)
- more rounded ("swept back") zygomatic arches
- broad nasal aperture (opening)
- retromolar space (space behind the lower third molar, in front of the ascending ramus of the mandible)
- vertical mandibular symphysis (no chin)
- massive limbs

Anatomically Modern Humans

Anatomically modern humans, referred to as *Homo sapiens* or *Homo sapiens sapiens* (Photo 14.9; *Atlas* pp. 320–322; br. ed. pp. 92–94) first appeared in Africa about 150,000 years ago and reached Europe by about 35,000 years ago. Dates on their arrival in Asia are less clear, but certainly by 25,000 years ago and possibly by 40,000 years ago. These earliest Africans of our species were from what is now Ethiopia, South Africa, and Tanzania. The very earliest, discovered quite recently, is from Ethiopia, and dates from between 160,000 and 154,000 years ago (White et al., 2003). By about 100,000 years ago, these humans already had migrated to Israel.

The best known of the anatomically modern humans of Europe, was from the French site of **Cro Magnon,** a term that came to be synonymous with the earliest Europeans. These humans used a variety of Upper Paleolithic tools, which comprised the tool technologies referred to as Aurignacian, Gravettian, Solutrean, Magdalenian, and Perigordian. Their new tools included the atlatl (spear thrower),

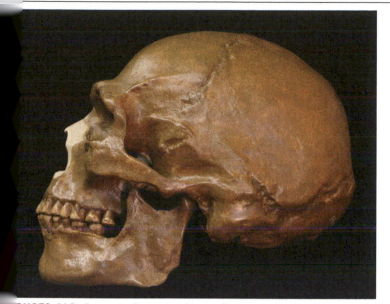

PHOTO 14.9 *Anatomically modern human (Predmöst, Czechoslovakia)*

spears, javelins, harpoons for fishing, clubs, stone missiles, boomerangs, bolas (stones tied together, probably to snare birds), and burins (a wood-working tool). Their tools were made from a wide variety of raw materials, such as bone, antler, and wood. From these materials they made awls, needles, pins, fasteners, and fish hooks.

Features of anatomically modern humans compared to Neanderthals include:

- shorter, higher skull
- 1200–1700 cc (avg. 1325)
- more vertical forehead
- small supraorbital ridge
- maximum breadth high on parietals
- more angular orbits
- more squared-off zygomatic arches
- narrow nasal aperture
- chin (mental protuberance)
- smaller teeth, jaws
- skeleton more slightly built

Obviously, our story does not end here, but from this point on, technological changes have transformed our species to a much greater extent than have anatomical ones. Our differences from one another, though they may be noticeable, are superficial compared to the vast changes we have undertaken over our entire evolutionary history. The final chapter deals with the biological variation present in modern-day human popuations.

LAB EXERCISE
14.2

NAME _____

SECTION _____ DATE _____

1. Compare various human forms, using lab specimens or Photos 14.6, 14.7, and 14.9, and those shown on the next pages (*Atlas* pp. 307–312, 314–319, 320–322; br. ed. p. 79–84, 86–89, 92–94).

	"ARCHAIC" H. SAPIENS	NEANDERTHAL	EARLY ANAT. MODERN HUMAN	MODERN HUMAn
Size of front teeth relative to back				
Dentition/teeth size relative to face size				
Location of maximum skull breadth				
Degree of postorbital constriction				
Cranial shape (height versus length				
Cranium size relative to facial skull				
Supraorbital ridge size				
Degree of prognathism				
Form of midfacial region (prognathic?)				
Shape of occipital and nuchal region (bun or torus?)				
Mandibular symphysis form (receding, vertical, chin)				
Retromolar space?*				

*Not observable from photos

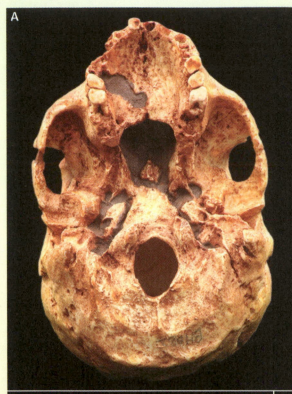

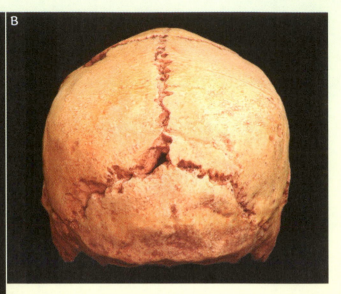

"Archaic" *Homo sapiens (Homo heidelbergensis):* (**A**) ventral, (**B**) posterior, (**C**) superior, and (**D**) lateral views

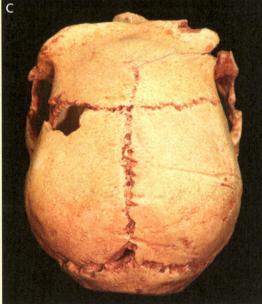

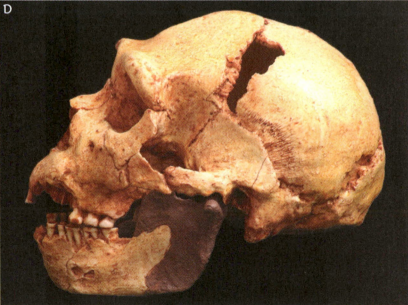

LAB EXERCISE
14.2 (CONT.)

NAME _____

SECTION _____ DATE _____

Neanderthal: **(A)** posterior, **(B)** superior, and **(C)** lateral views

Anatomically modern human: **(A)** posterior, **(B)** superior, and **(C)** lateral views

2. If skulls are available, you will conduct some quantitative comparisons of Neanderthals with modern humans. Measure and calculate indices for the following: a Neanderthal, an early anatomically modern, and a recent human skull. Fill out the chart below as you work.

   a. Calculate the cranial index. (You learned the technique in Chapter 8):

$$\frac{\text{cranial breadth}}{\text{cranial length}} \times 100 = \text{cranial index}$$

   b. Use the sliding calipers to measure the comparative length of the anterior and posterior tooth rows.

     — Measure the width of the *anterior tooth row* from the outside (buccal/labial side) of canines on the right and left sides.

     — Measure the length of the *posterior tooth row* from the mesial surface of the first premolar to the distal surface of the third molar.

     — Calculate an index to represent the ratio of the two parts of the dental arcade.

$$\frac{\text{anterior tooth row}}{\text{posterior tooth row}} \times 100$$

   c. Compare tooth proportions: central incisor width relative to second molar width, using the same technique as that used in Chapter 13.

$$\frac{\text{central incisor width}}{\text{second molar width}} \times 100$$

	NEANDERTHAL	EARLY A.M. HUMAN	MODERN HUMAN
Cranial breadth			
Cranial length			
Cranial index			
Anterior tooth row			
Posterior tooth row			
Index			
Central incisor width			
Second molar width			
Index			

3. Based on your measurements, what can you say about the differences between Neanderthals and modern humans in terms of:

Cranial shape?

Anterior versus posterior teeth?

Tooth proportions?

SELF-TEST 14.1

NAME _____

SECTION _____ DATE _____

1. What are at least four changes in the cranium or dentition that occurred between the earliest members of the human line and early members of the genus *Homo*?

   a.

   b.

   c.

   d.

2. Name (without looking at your chart, if possible) two characteristics of *Homo erectus/ergaster* that are not observed in the other species studied so far.

   a.

   b.

3. What are at least four characteristics that appear to unite all members of the species *Homo sapiens*?

   a.

   b.

   c.

   d.

4. Which of the following "inventions" was first used by which of the species you learned about in Chapter 13 or Chapter 14?

   a. Walking bipedally _____

   b. Burying their dead _____

   c. Use of Acheulean tools _____

   d. Control of fire _____

   e. Use of Olduwan tools _____

   f. Use of Mousterian tools _____

   g. Use of Upper Paleolithic tools _____

   h. Building nuclear reactors _____

5. Name and explain three *trends* that occurred *over the course of human evolution*. These could have to do with skull shape, facial morphology, or tooth and jaw proportions. Describe how each trend showed continual change over time, and include descriptive examples of which fossil forms had which form of each trait you discuss.

   a.

   b.

   c.

6. Is there such a thing as the "Missing Link?" Briefly explain your answer.

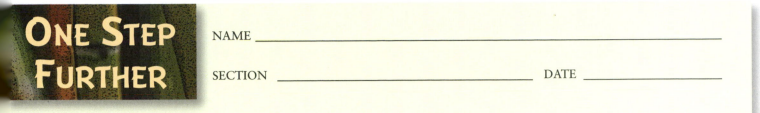

ONE STEP FURTHER

NAME _____

SECTION _____ DATE _____

Additional Lab Exercise 14.1

The views on the relationship between Neanderthals and modern humans are still controversial. Studies of cranial and postcranial remains, as well as genetic data and mathematical simulations of gene flow, contribute evidence to either one side or the other. You'll make your own contribution here by studying some of the differences between the two types of human.

Take a look at the illustrations of a Neanderthal and a modern human skeleton. You already have made a number of comparisons of the cranial anatomy, so focus here on the postcranial anatomy.

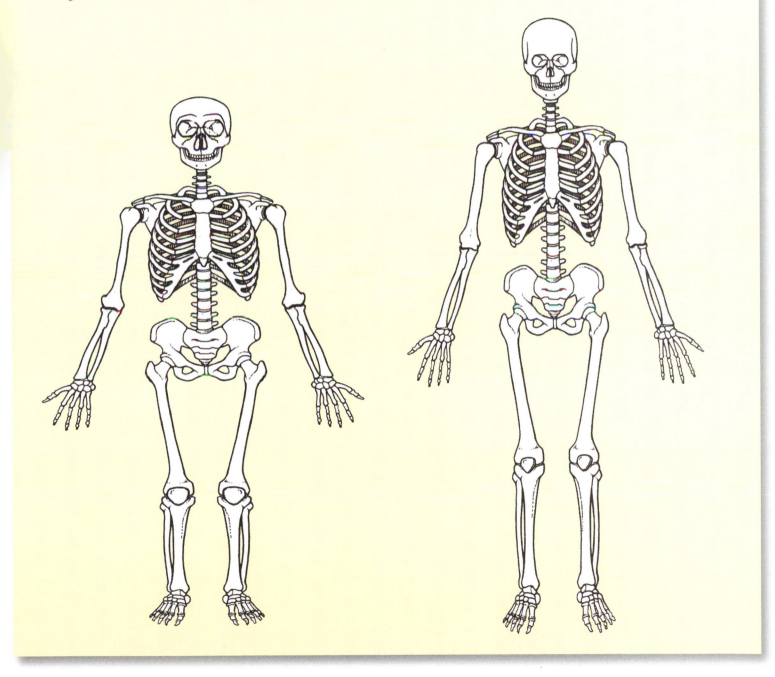

1. Describe the shape of each of the anatomical regions listed, in as much detail as you can, focusing on the differences between the two forms.

	NEANDERTHAL	MODERN HUMAN
Thorax		
Pelvis		
Intermembral index		
Crural index		
General description of skeleton, body shape		

2. Did you get a "feel" for whether the differences would be enough to warrant being placed in different species? Think of the variation you have seen among modern human skeletons. Does the Neanderthal skeleton fall within, or outside of, that range of variation? Use examples from your observations.

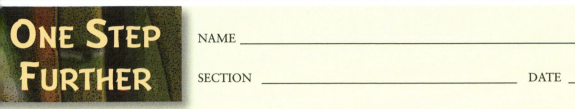

Additional Self-Test Questions

1. What are three features of Neanderthals that differentiate them from modern humans?

2. Why do some researchers think that more than one species is present in the material originally attributed to the species *Homo habilis*?

3. Which is the earliest species on the human line to be found outside of Africa?

4. What are a couple of differences in dentition of *Homo* compared to the australopiths?

5. Where have most of the Neanderthal fossils been found?

6. What was the climate like during the Pleistocene?

Modern Human Biological Variation

"Have you ever wondered . . . ?"

- How many races are there?
- If every individual has different fingerprints, what about identical twins?

OBJECTIVES

- Learn about intergroup and intragroup variations in modern human populations
- Understand the term "race" and the difficulties involved in categorizing humans
- Observe dermatoglyphic patterns as an example of inter-individual variation, using techniques involved in fingerprint identification
- Collect anthropometric data as further evidence for human biological variation
- Observe the continuous nature of anthropometric data through additional practice with basic statistics, particularly measures of central tendency and measures of dispersion

MATERIALS NEEDED

- Ink pad (blue or black)
- Magnifying lenses (at least one per several sets of lab partners)
- Tape measure or stadiometer (for measuring height)
- Sliding calipers (can substitute tape measure or ruler)
- PTC taste papers, if not already used for Chapter 5 (or for those students missing that lab)

By now you have gained a sense of the ways humans may vary from one another. In Chapter 1 you measured some aspect of your fellow classmates. Chapters 2, 3, 4, and 5 dealt with examples of genetic variation. Chapter 6 emphasized the important role of individual variation in natural selection. In Chapters 7 and 8 you learned the basics of skeletal anatomy and differences among skeletons, especially pertaining to sex, age, and ancestry. If your university has various skeletons on hand, you had the opportunity to observe that no two skeletons of the same species are exactly alike, even if they are of the same sex, age, and ancestry.

This chapter focuses on the biological variation among modern humans, in terms of both **intergroup variation** (differences *between* populations) and **intragroup variation** (individual differences occurring *within* populations). The first brief lab section deals with how we attempt to place people into groups, and the associated questions and issues that arise in doing so. In the second, more extensive, lab, you will collect data on a number of

353

traits that vary from individual to individual. Keep in mind that the features in individuals (both those that are observable and those we cannot see) result from a combination of genetics and the environment. Thus:

$$genotype + environment = phenotype$$

Intergroup Variation: Race and Ancestry

Before we discuss the nature of intergroup variation, you w. undertake a lab exercise to observe how human classificatic isn't as clear-cut as it seems.

LAB EXERCISE
15.1

NAME _____

SECTION _____ DATE _____

Work through the following exercise with your lab partner, discussing your answers as you go.

1. Look at the four photos below labeled A through D.

a. If you are asked to classify these four individuals, how would you group them? Any together? Each in separate groups?

b. What was the basis for your classification? Did you have one criterion, or more than one?

c. Did they fit neatly into what you may think of as "races?"

2. Now take a look at the following set of twelve photos, labeled A through L. Using the same criterion (or criteria) you used for question 1, attempt to place these people into categories, or "races."

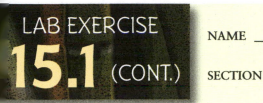

LAB EXERCISE 15.1 (CONT.)

NAME _____

SECTION _____ DATE _____

a. How many categories do you have? Using letters for your categories, list the photos you would put into which groups.

b. Do your categories seem as "neat" as for question number 1?

c. Would you find any additional criteria useful? If you use additional criteria to classify these people, does that change your groupings? Do you have more groups? Fewer?

Race: Biologically Real?

Anthropologists have reached a consensus that **race**, as traditionally used, has no biological basis (American Association of Physical Anthropologists, 1996; American Anthropological Association, 1998). Although human groups do differ, no consistent set of criteria can be used reliably to group all humans into discrete categories that accurately reflect historical patterns of ancestry. The criterion of skin color traditionally groups people of disparate ancestries, which reflects the fact only that around the globe, darker skin is found nearer the equator. This arbitrary grouping characteristic was chosen because it can be easily observed, but it frequently has been associated mistakenly with behavioral characteristics and used as a basis for discrimination.

The nature of human variation reflects gradual changes when moving geographically from one region to another. This gradual change over space, known as a **cline**, results from constant interbreeding among human populations, with more mixing between neighboring groups than distant groups. Human populations have a great deal of overlap—so much so that more genetic variation exists *within* each population than *between* different populations (Rosenberg et al., 2002). Differences among populations relate to the fact that that gene frequency changes occur differently in different groups, as a result of random processes as well as natural selection.

3. What is your ancestry? What geographical regions did your recent ancestors come from? This may relate to your **ethnicity,** the group whose customs you identify with most closely.

Intragroup Variation: Differences Among Individuals

Members of a species vary in an infinite number of ways, caused by both genetic variation and environmental influence. We'll examine some ways in which individuals vary from one another. You will collect data on some of these traits and learn how we refer to the type of variation exhibited and some techniques for analyzing and describing this variation.

Discrete Traits

Many traits have a strong genetic influence, caused by genes on either one or a number of chromosomes. These traits are likely to fall into two or more categories, and we can count their presence or absence. **Discrete traits** were introduced in Chapter 5, and you used simple observation (anthroposcopy) to record them. Such traits are in contrast to the continuous traits (which are measurable) that we touched on in Chapter 1. Discrete traits have a **discontinuous distribution** and can be portrayed graphically with a bar graph, pie chart, or the like.

The first example of inter-individual variation that we will examine lies in our hands—**dermatoglyphics** (Gr. *derma*: skin; *glyphe*: to carve)—fingerprints and palm prints.

Inter-individual Variation: Dermatoglyphics

Dermatoglyphics is the study of the ridges of skin on primates' hands and feet (palms, soles, fingers, toes). These ridges may have evolved along with the grasping fingers of our early primate ancestors, because they offer the benefit of increased friction for climbing. Fingerprints (and other friction ridges) begin their development as dots, which enlarge and fuse to eventually form ridges during our third and fourth month as a fetus (e.g., Allison, 1973) and remain basically unchanged throughout our lives.

Fingerprints provide an excellent expression of inter-individual variation. They are highly heritable (determined by multiple genes on various chromosomes), resulting in very similar, but not identical, fingerprints of identical twins.

We are most familiar with the use of dermatoglyphics in the context of fingerprints used in crime-solving. Because of their high degree of heritability, however, they also are useful in investigating family relationships. Fingerprints and palm prints are studied in biomedicine as well, because particular dermatoglyphic patterns are genetically linked to various inherited conditions. Evidence of regional differences in the frequency of fingerprint patterns from historical periods of relative genetic isolation may allow this information to contribute to population studies.

Fingerprint Patterns

The three primary patterns in fingerprints are **arches, loops**, and **whorls**, each with a variety of common sub-types (Henry, 1934; Figure 15.1). Certain digits tend to retain certain patterns, as you may see during this lab. The two primary types of information we obtain from fingerprints are:

1. pattern type (arches, loops, whorls, etc.), and
2. **ridge counts**, in which we use landmarks within the prints as a basis from which to identify patterns unique to individuals.

The combination of patterns and ridge counts in each individual is unique, and although related individuals may have similar prints, they are not identical. The main types and subtypes of fingerprint classification, devised in the late 1800s, are:

1. arch
   a. simple arch
   b. tented arch

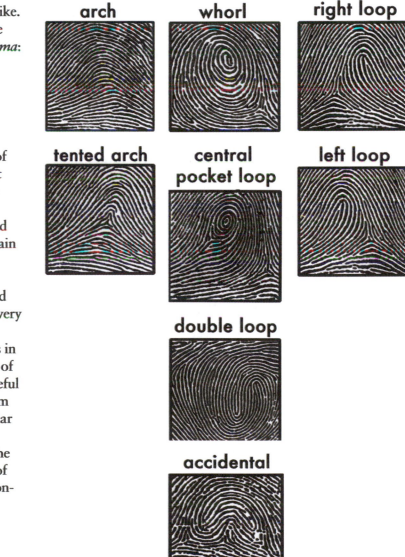

FIGURE 15.1 *Types of fingerprints*

2. loop
   a. right loop
   b. left loop

3. whorl
   a. plain
   b. central pocket loop
   c. double loop
   d. accidental

(Henry, 1934; Cummins and Midlo, 1961)

Before actually collecting your fingerprints in Lab Exercise 15.2, take a preliminary look at all of your fingertips and see if you can identify some of the basic patterns. Your fingerprints may not be represented here, as many patterns are somewhat rare.

Look at the fingerprint on one of your fingers (not your thumb). See if you can find these two features:

1. either the top of a loop or the center of a whorl, and

2. a triangular shape in which lines are bifurcated.

These describe the **core** and the **triradius** (Figure 15.2). The core typically is found at the center of the fingerprint pattern. The triradius is also called the **Delta**, and, like its namesake Greek letter, it is triangle-shaped.

Loops have one triradius, whorls have two, and arches have none. **Ridge counting** entails counting the number of friction ridges from the core to the triradius (Figure 15.2). Because only loops and whorls have a triradias, ridge-counting cannot be conducted for arches.

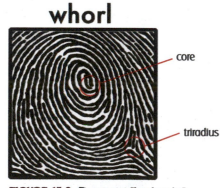

FIGURE 15.2 *Fingerprint "landmarks"*

A Brief Note on Palm Prints

Although we will spend little time here on palm prints, be aware that these also exhibit certain patterns. For example, most people have two primary lines on their palms, one

extending superomedially from the lateral side and the other inferolaterally from the medial side (Photo 15.1). A proportion of the population, however, has a single primary line that crosses from the medial to the lateral side (Photo 15.2). This **palmar crease** (traditionally called a **simian crease** because of its appearance in nonhuman primates) occurs in approximately 3 percent of the "chromosomally normal" population and a large proportion of individuals exhibiting various chromosomal anomalies.

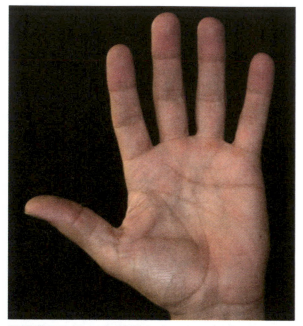

PHOTO 15.1 *Normal palm print*

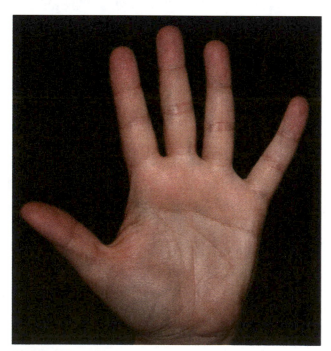

PHOTO 15.2 *Mid-palmar crease*

LAB EXERCISE 15.2

NAME _____

SECTION _____ DATE _____

1. Use the chart below to collect your fingerprint data with your lab partner. Relax your hand and have your lab partner roll each of your fingers carefully from one side to the other on the ink pad, then roll each of them on the chart below in the proper box. Keep in mind that Digit I is the thumb, Digit V is the pinkie finger, etc.

2. Fill in the blanks in the rows below each fingerprint to classify the pattern as best you can, and conduct the ridge count. Remember that ridge-counting can be conducted only for loop and whorl patterns, not arches.

Right Hand

	DIGIT I	DIGIT II	DIGIT III	DIGIT IV	DIGIT V
Pattern					
Ridge Count					

Left Hand

	DIGIT I	DIGIT II	DIGIT III	DIGIT IV	DIGIT V
Pattern					
Ridge Count					

3. Fill in the information below for your left hand and right hand totals.

Totals for left hand:

Ridge count _____

Number of arches _____

Number of loops _____

Number of whorls _____

Totals for right hand:

Ridge count _____

Number of arches _____

Number of loops _____

Number of whorls _____

4. Did the type or ridge counts of your fingers or that of your lab partner show any patterns? (For example, did your index fingers both have higher ridge counts than the other fingers, or was one type of fingerprint more common for thumbs versus pinkies?)

5. Now you'll look for any patterns as a class in terms of differences between the sexes, between left and right hands, etc.

   Use the data from number 3 (page 361) for all of your classmates, to fill in the Totals Data Chart. You will need to collect the data for each male and female in class, for left and right hands. (Depending on time constraints, your instructor may consolidate this information for the entire class.)

6. Using the information from the Totals Data Chart, calculate the averages for each category (male versus female; left hand versus right hand) to fill in the blanks below.

   Male:

   Mean ridge count   _____

   Mean number of arches   _____

   Mean number of loops   _____

   Mean number of whorls   _____

   Female:

   Mean ridge count   _____

   Mean number of arches   _____

   Mean number of loops   _____

   Mean number of whorls   _____

   Class Totals for Right Hand (males and females):

   Mean total ridge count   _____

   Mean number of arches   _____

   Mean number of loops   _____

   Mean number of whorls   _____

   Class Totals for Left Hand (males and females):

   Mean total ridge count   _____

   Mean number of arches   _____

   Mean number of loops   _____

   Mean number of whorls   _____

7. Did you observe any differences between males and females in ridge counts or fingerprint patterns? (Earlier work did claim a difference between males and females, later disputed for ridge counts.)

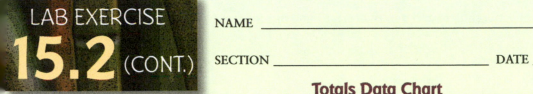

LAB EXERCISE
15.2 (CONT.)

NAME _____

SECTION _____ DATE _____

Totals Data Chart

MALES	RIDGE COUNT			NO. OF ARCHES			NO. OF LOOPS			NO. OF WHORLS		
	LEFT	RIGHT	TOTAL	LEFT	RIGHT	TOTAL	LEFT	RIGHT	TOTAL	LEFT	RIGHT	TOTAL
1												
2												
3												
4												
5												
6												
7												
8												
9												
10												
11												
12												
13												
14												
15												
16												
17												
18												
19												
20												
TOTAL												

FEMALES	RIDGE COUNT			NO. OF ARCHES			NO. OF LOOPS			NO. OF WHORLS		
	LEFT	RIGHT	TOTAL	LEFT	RIGHT	TOTAL	LEFT	RIGHT	TOTAL	LEFT	RIGHT	TOTAL
1												
2												
3												
4												
5												
6												
7												
8												
9												
10												
11												
12												
13												
14												
15												
16												
17												
18												
19												
20												
TOTAL												

8. Did you observe any differences between left hand and right hand fingerprint patterns or ridge counts?

9. Look at your palms and describe the primary lines (or line):

   a. Do they follow a typical pattern, as described on page 360 and shown in Photo 15.1?

   b. If they differ from the typical pattern shown, describe how they differ. Do your palms differ from one another?

   c. Do they differ in any major way from those of your lab partner?

LAB EXERCISE
15.2 (CONT.)

NAME _____

SECTION _____ DATE _____

Continuous Traits

As was introduced in Chapter 1 and again in Chapter 5, traits that exhibit a continuous range of variation are known as **continuous traits**. They frequently have a stronger environmental component and often result from the action of various genes. Because continuous traits can be measured, we depend a great deal on recording measurements to study variations within species. Lab Exercise 15.3 requires little introduction or background. You will work with your lab partner to collect some anthropometric data on each another. You were introduced to this concept in Chapter 8, with measurements of cranial shape.

1. For each of the items below, collect data on yourself and your lab partner, and fill out the accompanying chart. For the leg, arm, and finger, measure only the right side.

   - **Stature** (standing height): With a stadiometer or a tape measure taped to the wall, measure from top of head to heels (in stocking feet).

   - **Sitting-height**: Using a tape measure or a stadiometer; measure the distance between the top of the head and a flat, hard-sitting substrate.

   - **Leg length**: While standing, the person being measured holds one end of the tape measure on the anterior inferior iliac spine, and the lab partner pulls down the tape to the medial malleolus. (Researchers vary the method used for measuring leg length; many people have uneven leg lengths, so if you measure both legs, this may be observed.)

   - **Arm length**: Using a tape measure, start at scapular acromion process and measure to the ulnar styloid process.

   - **Finger length**: Using sliding calipers (the blunt, not the sharp end), measure from the center of the knuckle (articulation of metacarpal and proximal phalanx) to the fingertip.

MEASUREMENT	YOURSELF	YOUR LAB PARTNER
Stature (cm)		
Sitting height (cm)		
Arm length (cm)		
Leg length (cm)		
Finger length of digit II (mm)		
Finger length of digit IV (mm)		

(An additional row is left blank in case your instructor wishes you to collect data on additional traits—*e.g.*, skinfold thickness if you have calipers.)

2. Indices can give an indication of relative proportion. The indices you will calculate are:

	YOURSELF	YOUR LAB PARTNER
Relative leg length $$\frac{\text{Leg length}}{\text{Standing height}} \times 100$$		
Ratio of arm to leg length $$\frac{\text{Arm length}}{\text{Leg length}} \times 100$$		
Ratio of digit II to digit IV $$\frac{\text{Digit II}}{\text{Digit IV}} \times 100$$		

3. Compare your measurements and indices with those of your lab partner, and those of at least five other students. Briefly describe the range of variation in both raw measurements and indices. Were the differences more or less among individuals than you would have expected?

4. Think about the ways in which humans vary in size, shape, or other features. With your lab partner, think of a situation (realistic or hypothetical) in which a form of a feature you observed or measured for modern humans during this lab exercise (either in this chapter or in a previous chapter) might provide an advantage, and thus be selected for by natural selection.

SELF-TEST
15.1

NAME _____

SECTION _____ DATE _____

1. Did your views about race (ancestry) change from before you did this lab? What did you learn about the categorization of human groups?

2. Is there more variation between human groups or within each group? Explain your answer.

3. What are at least two reasons for studying dermatoglyphics?

4. What are the three main types of fingerprint pattern?

5. What are a few differences between discrete traits and continuous traits? Your answer may include reference to the difference in the way they are presented graphically, and/or the influence of genes versus environment on the expression of the two different types of traits.

ONE STEP FURTHER

NAME _____

SECTION _____   DATE _____

Additional Lab Exercise 15.1

1. With your lab partner, choose one anthropomorphic trait that can be documented with a raw measurement, not an index. Ask for the data on this trait from all of your classmates so you will have measurements from the entire class. Record the data separately for males and for females in case your instructor later asks you to compare the data between the sexes with regard to this trait.

2. What are the mean, median, and mode for this trait for the entire class? (Refer back to Chapter 1 if needed.)

3. The standard deviation is a measure of the variability in a set of measurements of a population. More specifically, the standard deviation indicates how much the values in a poplulation differ from the mean of that population. For example, let's say the average height of women in the United States is 5'5" (65") and the standard deviation is 3.5". Thus, most women in the United States are within 3.5" of 5'5" that is, between 5'1.5" and 5'8.5" (between 61.5" and 68.5"). In a population with little variation, values are fairly close to the mean, and the standard deviation is low. In a poplulation with much variation, values are quite different from the mean, and the standard deviation is fairly high.

4. Now you will calculate the standard deviation for your measurement in your population (your class). An example, in blue type, accompanies each step, but for a very small data set!

   a. What is the mean of your sample? (From the previous question—again, this is the mean of your entire class, males and females together).

      If your measurements are: 35, 30, 40, 45, and 50, your mean is 40.

   b. Subtract the mean from each measurement, noting each (you will get some negative numbers here, of course). These numbers represent their difference (deviance) from the mean.

      35 − 40 = −5
      30 − 40 = − 10
      40 − 40 = 0
      45 − 40 = 5
      50 − 40 = 10

c. Square each of the differences (deviations) from the mean.

$$-5^2 = 25$$
$$-10^2 = 100$$
$$0^2 = 0$$
$$-5^2 = 25$$
$$-10^2 = 100$$

d. Take the sum all of the squares.

$$25 + 100 + 0 + 25 + 100 = 250$$

e. Divide your result by the total number of items on the list (in this case, 5). (If you were trying to extrapolate from your sample to the entire population, you would divide by the total number of items on the list minus one.)

$$\frac{250}{5} + 50$$

f. Take the square root of this resulting number. The answer is the standard deviation from the mean. What is the standard deviation for your measurement, for your class?

$$\sqrt{50} - 7.07$$

g. Find classmates who used a different measurement than you did to calculate the standard deviation. Was your class more variable or less variable for that other measurement than for the one you used? What was the standard deviation for the other measurement?

For future reference, the formula for standard deviation is:

$$\sigma = \sqrt{\frac{\Sigma (x_i - \bar{x})^2}{N}}$$

The symbols are defined as:

σ = standard deviation
N = number of items
Σ = sum (of)
x_i = each item
$\bar{X}$ = mean

The Instructor's Manual offers additional exercises using these data for an additional basic statistical test that allows us to compare two groups—for example, the two sexes.

Concluding Comments

The topics covered in this lab manual, as mentioned at the beginning, are tied together by the thread of an underlying evolutionary framework. Evolution works in populations to cause significant changes over time, such as those we have studied in human evolutionary history. All four evolutionary forces: natural selection, mutation, migration, and genetic drift, have contributed to these changes, with both random and nonrandom factors acting to change gene frequencies from generation to generation (as we saw in our toothpick "populations").

You've learned about the genetic basis for evolution: the structure of the genetic material, how genetic material is passed on through the generations and results in physical characteristics (the phenotype), and how genetic variation is produced (mutations) and reshuffled (in gamete production) to create innumerable combinations of genotypes. You've studied the outcome of this genetic variation, particularly in terms of the skeletal variations exhibited within the human species, and how natural selection results in a diverse range of adaptations according to various environmental pressures over time.

Physical anthropology places humans in perspective within our historical and biological world. Our evolutionary past has resulted in who we are today as a species. You looked more closely at the range of variation of some modern human traits and learned that most of the observed variation is among individuals rather than between human groups. The close genetic relationship we share with all the other members of our species is evidence for our relatively recent shared common ancestor.

Cut-Outs
One Step Further
Lab Exercise 3.1

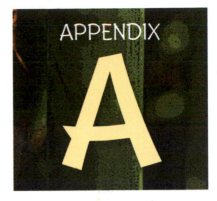

DNA Bases for Original Strands	
PURINES	**PYRIMIDINES**
A	T
A	T
A	T
A	T
A	T
G	C
G	C
G	C
G	C
G	C

There willl be one extra pair of bases

Free DNA Bases for Newly Forming Strands	
PURINES	**PYRIMIDINES**
A	T
A	T
A	T
A	T
A	T
G	C
G	C
G	C
G	C
G	C

There willl be one extra pair of bases

RNA Bases	
PURINES	**PYRIMIDINES**
A	U
A	U
A	U
A	U
A	U
G	C
G	C
G	C
G	C
G	C

There willl be one extra pair of bases

Amino Acids

Ribosome

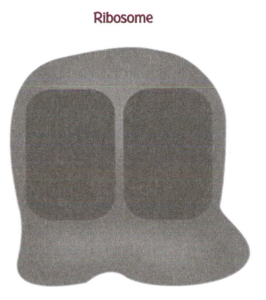

tRNA Molecules

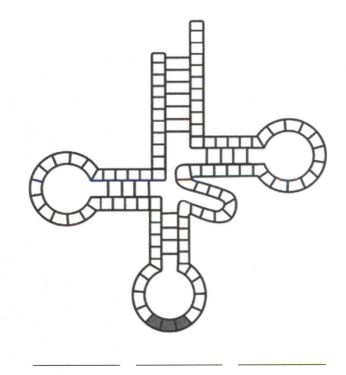

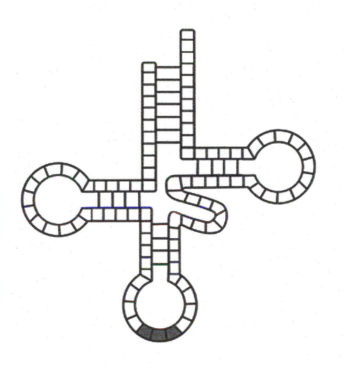

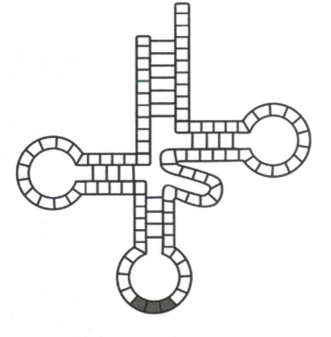

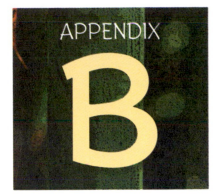
Chromosomes in a Dividing Cell

(for use in Lab Exercise 4.1, number 2)

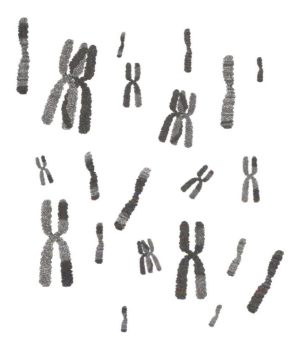

Latin and Greek Roots for Selected Anatomical Terms

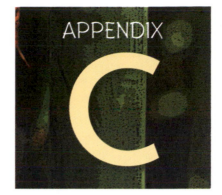

Feature (or Bone)	Root	Language	Meaning
coronal suture	coron	L	crown
cribriform plate	cribr	L	sieve
crista galli	crist	L	crest
foramen, foramina	foram	L	opening
fossa	foss	L	ditch, trench
crista galli	gall	L	rooster
glabella	glab	L	smooth
lambdoidal suture	lambd	G	similar to Greek letter lambda
foramen magnum	magn	L	large
mandible	mand	L	chew
mandible	mandibul	L	jaw
metopic suture	metop	G	forehead
nasal, nasion	nas	L	nose
orbit	orbi	F	circle
parietal	parie	L	wall
sagittal sutur	sagitt	L	arrow
sella turcica	sell	L	saddle
stapes	stape	L	stirrup
tympanum (eardrum)	tympan	G	drum
zygomatic	zyg	G	yoke

(for use in Lab Exercise 9.2, number 2)

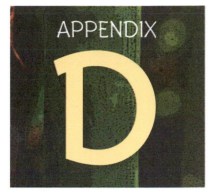

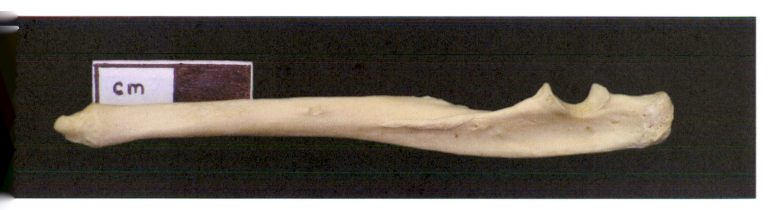

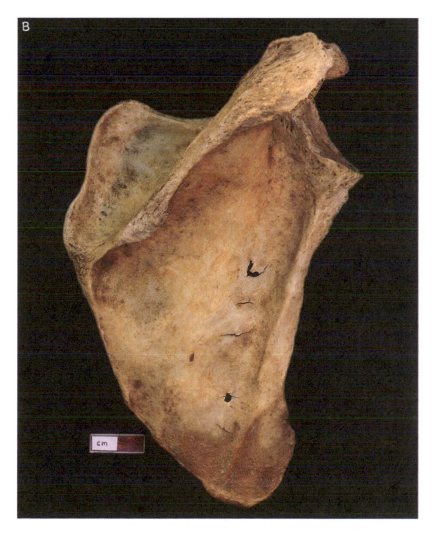

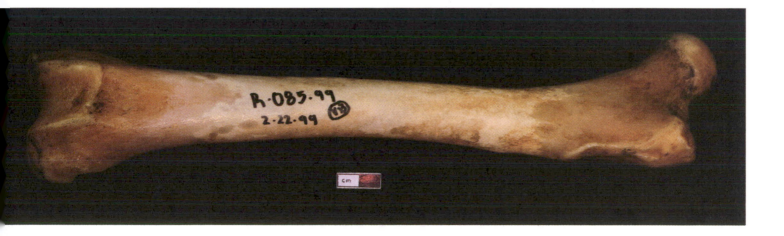

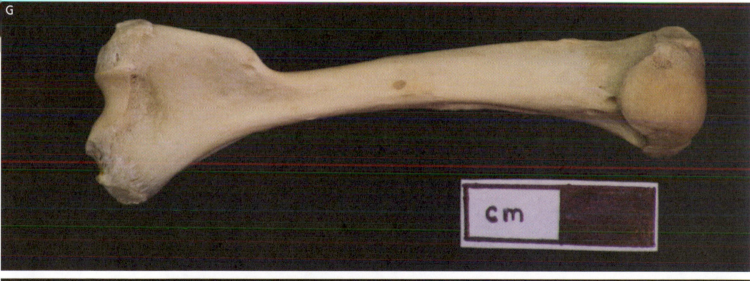

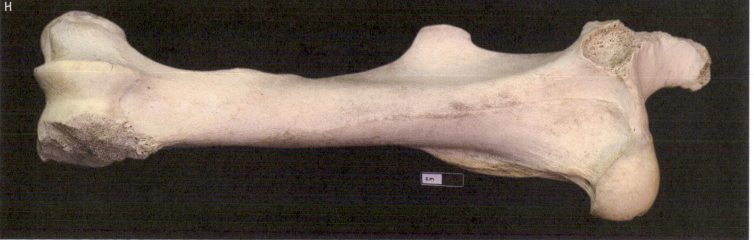

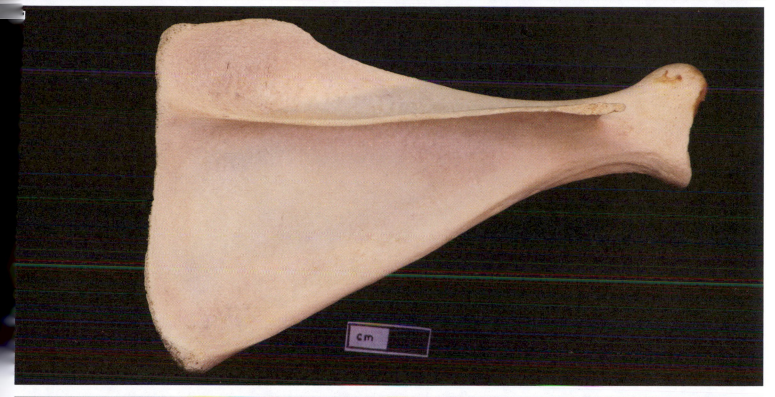

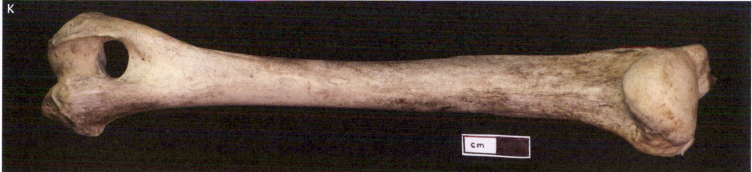

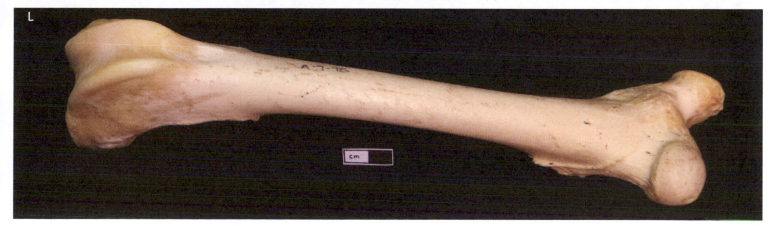

Fossil Primates: Paleocene through Miocene

New World primates not included)

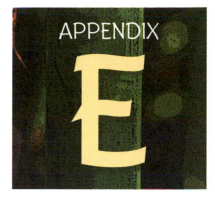

Scientific Name*	Taxonomic Group**	Epoch within Cenozoic Era	Geographical Distribution
Purgatorius	Plesiadapiformes	Early Paleocene	North America
Plesiadapis	Plesiadapiformes	Paleocene, early Eocene	North America, Europe
Cantius	Adapoidea	Eocene	North America, Europe
Notharctus	Adapoidea	Eocene	North America
Adapis	Adapoidea	Eocene	Europe
Necrolemur	Omomyoidea	Eocene	Europe
Tetonius	Omomyoidea	Eocene	North America
Rooneyia	Omomyoidea	Eocene	North America
Eosimias	Possible early anthropoid	Eocene	Asia
Amphipithecus	Anthropoidea	Eocene	Asia
Pondaungia	Anthropoidea	Eocene	Asia
Catopithecus	Anthropoidea	Oligocene	Africa (Egypt)
Apidium	Parapithecidae	Oligocene	Africa (Egypt)
Aegyptopithecus	Propliopithecidae	Oligocene	Africa (Egypt)
Proconsul	Hominoidea	Miocene	Africa
Dryopithecus	Hominoidea	Miocene	Europe
Sivapithecus	Hominoidea	Miocene	Asia
Gigantopithecus	Hominoidea	Miocene through Pleistocene	Asia
Pierolapithecus catalaunicus	Hominoidea	Miocene	Europe
Ouranopithecus macedoniensis	Hominoidea	Miocene	Europe

*(genus only listed if more than one species) **(not necessarily formal grouping)

Fossil Members of the Human Line (Hominids/Hominins)

APPENDIX

F

Species	Time Range	Geographical Distribution
Earliest members of the human line		
Sahelanthropus tchadensis	7–6 mya	Central Africa (Chad)
Ororrin tugenensis	~ 6 mya	East Africa
Ardipithecus spp. (A. ramidus, 4.4 mya)	5.8–4.4 mya	East Africa
Australopiths		
Australopithecus anamensis	4.2–3.9 mya	East Africa
Australopithecus afarensis	3.9–2.9 mya	East Africa
Kenyanthropus platyops *	~ 3.5 mya	East Africa
Australopithecus africanus	3–2 mya	South Africa
Australopithecus gahri *	~ 2.5 mya	East Africa
Australopithecus (Paranthropus) aethiopicus	~ 2.5 mya	East Africa
Australopithecus (Paranthropus) robustus	2–1.5 mya	South Africa
Australopithecus (Paranthropus) boisei	2.4–1.2 mya	East Africa
Genus *Homo*		
Homo habilis / Homo rudolfensis	2.4–1.4 mya	Africa
Homo erectus / Homo ergaster	1.8 mya–50,000 ya	Africa, Asia, possibly Europe
Homo antecessor *	850,000–780,000 ya	Europe
Homo heidelbergensis	~400,000–150,000 ya	Africa, Europe, possibly Asia**
Homo floresiensis *	94,000–13,000 ya	Indonesia (island of Flores)
Homo neandertalensis	130,000–~30,000 ya	Europe and Middle East
Homo sapiens	~160,000 ya to present	Worldwide; earliest members in Africa

Taxonomic designation not accepted by all researchers   **depends upon species designation of particular fossils*

Features of *Homo rudolfensis* and *Homo habilis*

H. rudolfensis (2.4–1.6 mya – E. Africa)	H. habilis (2.0–1.6 mya – E. and S. Africa)
Larger body size; 1.5 m tall	Smaller body size
Larger absolute, but smaller relative cranial capacity	Larger supraorbital ridge
Smaller supraorbital ridge	Facial bones smaller, nose more developed
More robust facial features	More gracile facial features
More orthognathic	More prognathic
Large palate	Smaller palate
More robust mandible	Thinner jaw
Larger posterior teeth (but narrow molars)	Smaller molars
More human-like femur	Postcranium more primitive; relatively long arms

Wood, B. A. 1991. *Koobi Fora Research Project. Vol. 4: The Hominid Cranial Remains.* Oxford, England. Clarendon Press; McKee, J. K., F. E. Poirier, and W. S. McGraw. 2005. *Understanding Human Evolution*, 5th ed. Upper Saddle River, NJ: Pearson Prentice Hall.

References

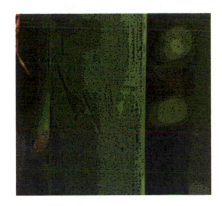

Adams, M. D., et al. 2000. The genome sequence of *Drosophila melanogaster. Science* 287:2185–2195.

Allison, H. C. 1973. *Personal identification.* Boston: Holbrook Press.

Altmann, J. 1974. Observational study of behavior: Sampling methods. *Behaviour* 49:227–267.

American Anthropological Association. 1998. AAA statement on race. *Anthropology Newsletter,* http://www.aaanet.org

American Association of Physical Anthropologists. 1996. Statement on biological aspects of race. *American Journal of Physical Anthropology* 101:569–570.

Ayers, J., R. L. Jantz, and P. H. Moore-Jansen. 1990. Giles & Elliot race discriminant functions revisited: A test using recent forensic cases. In: G. W. Gill and J. S. Rhine (Eds.), *Skeletal Attribution of Race: Methods for Forensic Anthropology.* Albuquerque, NM: Maxwell Museum of Anthropology Papers No. 4, pp. 65–71.

Bartoshuk L. M., V. B. Duffy, and I. J. Miller. 1994. PTC/PROP tasting: anatomy, psychophysics, and sex effects. *Physiol Behav.* 56:1165–1171.

Bartoshuk L. M., V. B. Duffy, L. A. Succhina, J. Prutkin, and K. Fast. 1998. PROP (6-n-propylthiouracil) supertasters and the saltiness of NaCl. *Ann NY Acad Sci.* 855:793–796.

Bass, W. M. 1995. *Human Osteology: A Laboratory and Field Manual*, 4th ed. Columbia: MO: Archaeological Society (Special Publication No. 2).

Begun, D. 2003. Planet of the apes. *Scientific American* 289:74–83.

Begun, D. R., and C. V. Ward. 2005. Comment on "*Pierolapithecus catalaunicus*, a new Middle Miocene great ape from Spain." *Science* 308:203.

Blattner, F. R., G. Plunkett III, C. A. Bloch, N. T. Perna, V. Burland, M. Riley, J. Collado-Vides, J. D. Glasner, C. K. Rode, G. F. Mayhew, J. Gregor, N. W. Davis, H. A. Kirkpatrick, M. A. Goeden, D. J. Rose, B. Mau, and Y. Shao. 1997. The complete genome sequence of *Escherichia coli* K–12. *Science* 277:1453–1462.

Bloch, J. I., and M. T. Silcox. 2006. Cranial anatomy of the Paleocene plesiadapiform *Carpolestes simpsoni* (Mammalia, Primates) using ultra high-resolution X-ray computed tomography, and the relationships of plesiadapiforms to Euprimates. *J. Hum. Evol.* 50:1–35.

Brothwell, D. R. 1981. *Digging Up Bones*, 3rd ed. New York: Cornell University Press.

Brown, P., T. Sutikna, M. J. Morwood, R. P. Soejono, E. Jatmiko, W. Saptomo, and R. Awe Due. 2004. A new small-bodied hominin from the Late Pleistocene of Flores, Indonesia. *Nature* 431:1055–1061.

Brunet, M., F. Guy, D. Pilbeam, H. T. Mackaye, A. Likius, D. Ahounta, A. Beauvailain, C. Blondel, H. Bocherens, J-R. Boisserie, L. De Bonis, Y. Coppens, J. Dejax, C. Denys, P. Duringer, V. Eisenmann, G. Fanone, P. Fronty, and D. Geraads. 2002. A new hominid from the Upper Miocene of Chad, Central Africa. *Nature* 418:145–151.

Buikstra, J. E., and Ubelaker, D. H. 1994. *Standards for Data Collection from Human Skeletal Remains*. Fayetteville: Arkansas Archeological Survey.

Bukovsky A., M. R. Caudle, M. Svetlikova, J. Wimalasena, M. E. Ayala, and R. Dominguez. 2005. *Endocrine* 26:301–316.

Burns, K. R. 2007. *Forensic Anthropology Training Manual*, 2nd ed. Upper Saddle River, NJ: Pearson Prentice Hall.

Byers, S. 2005. *Introduction to Forensic Anthropology : A Textbook*, 2nd ed. Boston: Allyn and Bacon.

Cummins, H., and C. Midlo. 1961. *Finger Prints, Palms and Soles: An Introduction to Dermatoglyphics*. New York: Dover.

Currat, M., and L. Excoffier. 2004. Modern humans did not admix with Neanderthals during their range expansion into Europe. *PLoS Biology* 2:e421. doi:10.1371/journal.pbio.0020421.

de Bonis, L., G. Bouvrain, D. Geraads, and G. Koufos. 1990. New hominid skull material from the late Miocene of Macedonia in northern Greece. *Nature* 345:712–714.

Fleagle, J. G. F. 1999. *Primate Adaptation and Evolution*, 2nd ed. New York: Academic Press.

France, D. L. 1986. Osteometry at muscle origin and insertion in sex determination. *Am. J. Phys. Anthropol.* 76:515–526.

Franklin D., P. P. O'Higgins, C. E. Oxnard, and I. Dadour I. 2008. Discriminant function sexing of the mandible of indigenous South Africans. *Forensic Sci Int.* 179:84.e1–5.

Franzen, J. L., P.D. Gingerich, J. Habersetzer, J. H. Hurum, W. von Koenigswald, and B. H. Smith. 2009. Complete primate skeleton from the Middle Eocene of Messel in Germany: Morphology and paleobiology. *PLoS One* 4:e5723.

Gadsby, P. 2000. Tourist in a taste lab. *Discover* 21:70–75.

Gebo, D. L., M. Dagosto, K. C. Beard, T. Qi, and J. Wang. 2000. The oldest known anthropoid post-cranial fossils and the early evolution of higher primates. *Nature* 404:276–278.

Genoves, S. C. 1967. Proportionality of long bones and their relation to stature among mesoamericans. *Am. J. Phys. Anthropol.* 26:67–78.

Giles, E., and O. Elliot. 1963. Sex determination by discriminant function analysis of crania. *Am J. Phys. Anthropol.* 21:53–68.

Hardy, G. H. 1908. Mendelian proportions in a mixed population. *Science* 28:49–50.

Henry, Sir E. R. 1934. *Classification and Uses of Fingerprints*. Chicago: Chicago Medical Book.

Hershkovitz, I., L. Kornreich, and Z. Laron. 2007. Comparative skeletal features between *Homo floresiensis* and patients with primary growth hormone insensitivity (Laron Syndrome). *Am. J. Phys. Anthropol.* 134:198–208.

Hinkes, M. J. 1990. Shovel-shaped incisors in human identification. *Skeletal Attribution of Race: Methods for Forensic Anthropology*. Albuquerque, NM: Maxwell Museum of Anthropology Papers No. 4, pp. 21–26.

Hrdlička, A. 1920. Shovel-shaped teeth. *Am J. Phys. Anthropol.* 3:429–465.

Johnson J., M. Skaznik-Wikiel, H. J. Lee, Y. Kiikura, J. C. Tilly, and J. L. Tilly. 2006. Setting the record straight on data supporting postnatal oogenesis in female mammals. *Cell Cycle*, Nov. 20; 4(11) (e-pub ahead of print).

Jurmain, R., H. Nelson, L. Kilgore, and W. Trevathan. 2003. *Introduction to Physical Anthropology*, 8th ed. Belmont, CA: Wadsworth/Thompson Learning.

Katz, D., and J. M. Suchey. 1986. Age determination of the male *Os pubis*. *Am. J. Phys. Anthropol.* 69:427–435.

Koufos, G. D., and L. de Bonis L. 2004. The deciduous lower dentition of *Ouranopithecus macedoniensis* (Primates, Hominoidea) from the late Miocene deposits of Macedonia, Greece. *J Hum Evol.* 46:699–718.

Krings, M. A., A. Stone, R. Schmitz, H. Kraintzi, M. Stoneking, and S. Paabo. 1997. Neanderthal DNA sequences and the origin of modern humans. *Cell* 90:19–30.

Krogman W. M., and M. Y. Iscan. 1986. *The Human Skeleton in Forensic Medicine*, 2nd ed. Springfield, IL: Charles C Thomas.

Lee, A., and K. Pearson. 1901. Data for the problem of evolution in man. IV: A first study of the correlation of the human skull. *Philosophical Transaction of the Royal Society of London.* 196: 225–264.

Lehner, P. N. 1987. Design and execution of animal behavior research: an overview. *Journal of Animal Science* 65:1213–1219.

Malthus, T. R. 1826. *An Essay on the Principle of Population as It Affects the Future Improvement of Society,* 6th ed. London: J. Johnson.

Mange, E. J., and A. P. Mange. 1994. *Basic Human Genetics.* Sunderland, MA: Sinauer.

Martin, N. G. 1975. No evidence for a genetic basis of tongue rolling or hand clasping. *J. Hered.* 66:179–180.

Martin, P., and P. Bateson. 1993. *Measuring Behaviour: An Introductory Guide,* 2nd ed. Cambridge, MA: Cambridge University Press,

Martin, R. D., A. M. MacLarnon, J. L. Phillips, L. Dussubieux, P. R. Williams, and W. B. Dobyns. 2006. Comment on "The Brain of LB1, *Homo floresiensis.*" *Science* 312:999.

McHenry, H. 1992. Body size and proportions in early hominids. *Am. J. Phys. Anthropol.* 87:407–431.

McKee, J. K., F. E. Poirier, and W. S. McGraw. 2005. *Understanding Human Evolution,* 5th ed. Upper Saddle River, NJ: Pearson Prentice Hall.

McKern, T. W., and T. D. Stewart. 1957. Skeletal age changes in young American males. *U.S. Army Quartermaster Research and Development Command* (Technical Report EP-45).

Moya-Sola, S., M. Köhler, D. M. Alba, I. Casanovas-Vilar, and J. Galindo. 2004. *Pierolapithecus catalaunicus,* a new Middle Miocene great ape from Spain. *Science* 306:1339–1344.

National Institute of Child Health and Human Development. Turners page: http://turners.nichd.nih.gov/ClinFrIntro.html. Klinefelter's page: http://www.nichd.nih.gov/publications/pubs/klinefelter.htm#xwhat

Ousley, S. D., and R. L. Jantz. 2005. *FORDISC 3.0.* Knoxville: University of Tennessee, Department of Anthropology, Forensic Anthropology Center.

Park, M. A. 2005. *Biological Anthropology.* New York: McGraw-Hill.

Pennisi, E. 2007. No sex please, we're Neanderthals. *Science* 316:967.

Phenice, T. W. 1969. A newly developed visual method for sexing the *Os pubis. Am. J. Phys. Anthropol.* 30:297–302.

Ramsthaler, F., K. Kreutz, and M. A. Verhoff. 2007. Accuracy of metric sex analysis of skeletal remains using Fordisc based on a recent skull collection. *Int J Legal Med.* 121:477–482.

Rasmussen, D. T. 2002. Early catarrhines of the African Eocone and Oligocene. In *The Primate Fossil Record.* W. C. Hartwig, Ed. Cambridge, MA: Cambridge University Press, pp. 203–220.

Rat Genome Sequencing Project Consortium. 2004. Genome sequence of the Brown Norway rat yields insights into mammalian evolution. *Nature* 428: 493–521.

Rhine, S. 1990. Non-metric skull racing. *Skeletal Attribution of Race: Methods for Forensic Anthropology.* Albuquerque, NM: Maxwell Museum of Anthropology Papers No. 4, pp. 9–20.

Rosenberg, N. A., J. K. Pritchard, J. L. Weber, H. M. Cann, K. K. Kidd, L. A. Zhivotovsky, and M. W. Feldman. 2002. Genetic structure of human populations. *Science* 298:2381–2385.

Sattenspiel, L., C. V. Ward, S. Stout, and D. Wescott. *Introduction to Biological Anthropology Laboratory Manual* (unpublished work, University of Missouri, Columbia, 2001, pp. 111 and 130).

Scientific American Frontiers Archives: http://www.pbs.org/safarchive/4_class/45_pguides/pguide_904/4494_peppers.html#act2

Shahbake, M., I. Hutchinson, D. G. Laing, and A. L. Jinks. 2005. Rapid quantitative assessment of fungiform papillae density in the human tongue. *Brain Res.* 1052:196–201.

Simons, E. L., and D. T. Rasmussen. 1996. Skull of *Catopithecus browni,* an early tertiary catarrhine. *Am. J. Phys. Anth.* 100:261–292.

Stanford, C., J. S. Allen, and S. C. Anton. 2006. *Biological Anthropology*. Upper Saddle River, NJ: Pearson Prentice Hall.

Steyen, M., and M. Y. Iscan. 2008. Metric sex determination from the pelvis in modern Greeks. *Forensic Sci Int*. 179:86.e1–6.

Szalay, F. S. 1981. Phylogeny and the problem of adaptive significance: the case of the earliest primates. *Folia Primatol*. 36:157–182.

Szalay, F. S., and E. Delson. 1979. *Evolutionary History of the Primates*. New York: Academic Press.

Todd, T. W. 1920. Age changes in the pubic bone I: The male white pubis. *Am. J. Phys. Anthropol*. 3:285–334.

Todd, T. W. 1921. Age changes in the pubic bone II: The pubis of the male negro–white hybrid; III: The pubis of the white female; IV: The pubis of the female white–negro hybrid. *Am. J. Phys. Anthropol*. 4:1–70.

Trotter, M. 1970. Estimation of stature from intact long limb bones. In: T. D. Stewart (ed.) *Personal Identification in Mass Disasters*. Washington, DC: National Museum of Natural History.

Trotter, M., and G. C. Gleser. 1977. Corrigenda to "Estimation of stature from long limb bones of American Whites and Negroes, Am. J. Phys. Anthrop." (1952). *Am. J. Phys. Anthropol*. 47:355–356.

Trotter, M., and G. C. Gleser. 1952. Estimation of stature from long limb bones of American Whites and Negroes. *Am. J. Phys. Anthropol*. 10:463–514.

Ubelaker, D. H. 1978. *Human Skeletal Remains: Excavation, Analysis, Interpretation*. Chicago: Aldine.

Ubelaker, D. H. 1999. *Human Skeletal Remains: Excavation, Analysis, Interpretation*, 2nd ed. Chicago: Aldine.

Van Valen, L., and R. Sloan. 1965. The earliest primates. *Science* 150:743–745.

Walker, P. L. 2008. Sexing skulls using discriminant function analysis of visually assessed traits. *Am. J. Phys. Anthropol*. 136:39–50.

Watson, J. D., and F. H. C. Crick. 1953. Molecular structure of nucleic acids: a structure for deoxyribose nucleic acid. *Nature* 171:737–738.

Weinberg, W. 1908. Über den nachweis der vererbung beim menshcen. Jahresh. Wuertt. *Ver. vaterl. Natkd*. 64:369–382.

White, T., B. Asfaw, D. DeGusta, H. Gilbert, G. D. Richards, G. Suwa, and F. C. Howell. 2003. Pleistocene *Homo sapiens* from Middle Awash, Ethiopia. *Nature* 423:742–747.

Whitehead, P. F., W. K. Sacco, and S. B. Hochgraf. 2005. *A Photographic Atlas for Physical Anthropology*. Englewood, CO: Morton.

Glossary

ABO blood group A blood type system coded for by alleles at a locus on chromosome 9; three primary alleles (I^A, I^B, I^O) determine blood type (A, B, O, or AB).

absolute dating Techniques of estimating the actual age, in years, of organic or inorganic materials; chronometric dating, radiometric dating.

Acheulean Refers to a tool kit associated with *Homo erectus* in Africa and early "archaic" *Homo sapiens* in Europe; classified as Lower Paleolithic tools.

ad libitum Sampling technique in which all observed behaviors are recorded on all visible animals.

Adapis Member of extinct superfamily Adapoidea from the Eocene of Europe.

Adapoidea Superfamily of Eocene primates, within which lie the likely ancestors of strepsirhines; most occurred in North America and Europe.

adaptation An evolutionary shift in a population in response to environmental change; a feature that acts to increase survival or reproductive success in individuals and is a result of natural selection.

adaptive significance Selective processes resulting in the evolution of a specific feature; reason for the evolution of a specific feature.

adenine One of the four bases in DNA and RNA.

Aegyptopithecus Best-known representative of extinct family Propliopithecidae from the Oligocene of Egypt; an early catarrhine that may have given rise to the Old World monkey and ape/human lines.

agglutination Clumping effect of serum antibodies with antigens of red blood cells of a different blood type.

Agnathans Members of the extinct Class Agnatha; these fish were the earliest vertebrates.

allele Alternative form of a specific gene; different alleles code for different forms of a trait.

amino acids The subunits making up proteins; 20 common types are found in most proteins.

Amphipithecus Eocene primate from Asia; may represent an early anthropoid.

analogy/analogous features Similar features in different taxonomic groups arising independently under similar evolutionary pressures.

anaphase The stage of cell division in which the chromosomes migrate to opposite poles of the cell.

anatomical position In a human, a standing position with the arms down at the sides and the palms of the hands facing forward, thumbs out to the sides.

anatomical terminology Words used to describe directions and position of bodies and body parts.

anatomically modern humans Taxonomic designation *Homo sapiens sapiens*, denoting our own species and subspecies; first appeared in Africa about 150,000 years ago.

anemia A condition in which red blood cells fail to deliver oxygen to the body's tissues.

aneuploidy The condition of having an incorrect number of chromosomes.

anterior A direction term meaning toward the front of the body

anterior dentition Teeth at the front of the dental arcade: incisors and canines.

Anthropoidea One of the two suborders of Order Primates in the traditional classification scheme; consists of monkeys, apes, and humans.

Anthropoids Group that includes monkeys, apes, and humans; traditionally a formal taxonomic suborder of primates.

anthropometry The measurement of humans.

anthroposcopy Qualitative examination of human features.

antibodies Proteins formed by the body's immune system in response to specific invading antigens.

anticodon Triplet of three exposed bases on a tRNA molecule; complementary to mRNA **codon**.

antigens Molecules that provoke an immune response (antibody production).

Apidium Member of extinct family Parapithecidae from the Oligocene of Egypt; exhibit similarities to New World monkeys.

appendicular skeleton Portion of the skeleton that develops later; consists of limb bones and bones of the pelvic and pectoral girdles.

arboreal Means tree-living.

arch Dermatoglyphic term referring to a type of fingerprint, commonly found on the thumb, characterized by a gentle curve.

"archaic" *Homo sapiens* Fossil specimens distributed in Africa, Asia, and Europe from about 800,000 years ago to about 30,000 years ago; known also as **transitional forms** because they exhibit a combination of *Homo erectus* and anatomically modern human features.

Ardipithecus ramidus Early member of the human line from East Africa, dated at approximately 4.4 million years ago.

arms On a chromosome, the portions extending from the centromere.

articular cartilage Layer of cartilage covering the epiphyseal ends of long bones.

artificial selection The process whereby humans select for specific traits in domesticated plants or animals; selective breeding.

attrition (dental attrition) Wear on the **occlusal surface** of teeth.

Australopithecus aethiopicus Oldest member of the robust australopith group; found in East Africa.

Australopithecus afarensis East African hominid species of the primitive australopith group; species includes "Lucy" specimen.

Australopithecus africanus African early hominid species, also referred to as the "gracile" form of australopith.

Australopithecus anamensis Oldest and most primitive member of the australopith group from East Africa, dated at between 4.2 and 3.9 million years ago; represents the earliest evidence for bipedality.

Australopithecus boisei Member of robust australopith group having the most massive teeth and jaws; found in East Africa.

Australopithecus robustus Member of robust australopith group; found in South Africa.

australopiths Group of early hominids from Africa that exhibit many primitive features, composed of approximately 11 species.

autosomal dominant Mode of inheritance in which an allele is expressed whenever it is present.

autosomal recessive Mode of inheritance in which an allele must have been inherited by both parents to be expressed.

autosomal trait Trait coded-for by a gene on a chromosome numbered 1–22.

autosomes All chromosomes except the sex chromosomes.

axial skeleton Portion of the skeleton that develops first; consists of midline structures such as skull, vertebral column, rib cage, sternum, and hyoid.

B

base One of four types of chemical substances bonded to the sugar molecules in DNA and RNA nucleotides; DNA bases are adenine, cytosine, guanine, and thymine, and RNA bases are adenine, cytosine, guanine, and uracil.

base of support Area between the supporting body parts in contact with the substrate.

base pairs Bases occurring in pairs along the DNA molecule, making up the "rungs" of the DNA double helix (adenine bonds with thymine, cytosine with guanine).

bed Stratigraphic layer of sediment pertaining to a given time period.

bell-shaped curve Graphical representation of continuous data whose mean, median, and mode are the same; **normal curve**.

bilateral Pertaining to both sides (of an organism).

bilophodont Refers to molar teeth in which two crests connect the pairs of cusps in a mediolateral direction; typical of Old World monkeys.

binomen Refers to the combination of genus and species as part of the Latin binomial classification scheme used worldwide; scientific name.

binomial nomenclature Classificatory system for organisms devised by Carl Linnaeus featuring the binomen (genus and species).

biological variation Differences among individuals of a species in the form of physical features or genetic makeup.

bipedal/bipedalism Adaptations to habitual upright walking on two legs.

brachial index Ratio that reflects the relative length of the upper arm versus lower arm.

C

cancellous (spongy) bone Bone usually found deep within bone, surrounding the marrow cavity and within the ends of long bones; contains many large spaces filled with mostly red marrow.

canine shearing complex Also called the **honing triad**; a combination of three features found in apes: large canines, **diastema**, and **sectorial P₃**.

Cantius Member of extinct primate superfamily Adapoidea, from the Eocene of North America and Europe.

carrier An individual who possesses a recessive allele for a genetic trait disorder but is unaffected himself or herself.

Catarrhini Infraorder of haplorhine primates that includes Old World monkeys, apes, and humans.

Catopithecus Early catarrhine from the late Eocene of Egypt.

caudal Term meaning closer to the tip of the tail.

eboidea Superfamily of platyrrhine primates; New World monkeys.

cell Basic structural and functional unit of living things.

Cenozoic Era Most recent era of Phanerozoic Eon; time range from 65 million years ago to present.

center of gravity The point at which an object's mass is concentrated.

centriole Organelle composed of microtubules; organizes the cytoskeleton for cell division.

centromere Portion of the chromosome found at junction of arms; consists of tightly coiled DNA.

cephalic Refers to the skull or head.

Cercopithecoidea Superfamily of catarrhines consisting of Old World monkeys.

character Any feature of an organism used to establish evolutionary relationships.

character state Pertains to whether the form of a character is primitive or derived.

chromatid One of the two sides of a chromosome in its doubled state after replication of its DNA.

chromatin Condition of genetic material during interphase portion of cell cycle when cell is not dividing.

chromosomal anomaly Having too many or too few chromosomes (also called **chromosomal aberration**).

chromosomal mutations Mistakes that result in an extra or missing piece of chromosome, entire chromosome, or set of chromosomes.

chromosomes Nuclear bodies made of the genetic material DNA, coiled around various proteins.

circumvallate V-shaped row of **papillae** at the back of the tongue.

clade Evolutionary line representing a group of organisms that share a common ancestor; includes the common ancestor and all its descendants.

cladistics School of thought about taxonomy and classification that emphasizes recency of common ancestry for establishing evolutionary relationships.

cladogram Graphical representation of evolutionary relationships used by cladists.

cline Gradual change in a trait over geographical space.

cloning Process of producing a genetically identical individual (or individuals).

codominant Describes the condition when a heterozygote's two alleles for a given locus are both expressed in the phenotype.

codon Triplet of three bases on an mRNA strand read by ribosomes during protein synthesis; each codon determines a specific amino acid.

compact (dense) bone Bone usually found in more superficial portions of bone, thickest in diaphysis of long bones; provides protection and support and resists stress.

continental drift *See* **plate tectonics.**

continuous traits Phenotypes whose forms are measurable.

continuous variation Result of measuring characteristics of living organisms; typically can be represented by a **normal (bell-shaped) curve.**

convergent evolution Features in distantly related groups that become more similar over time because of selective forces acting in similar ways.

core Point of reference in a fingerprint at or near the center of the pattern area.

coronal (frontal) plane Imaginary plane dividing the body into front and back portions.

covary Correlation of two variables such that they change in the same way in certain conditions.

cranial Refers to the skull or head.

Cro Magnon Fossil site in France of an early anatomically modern human; term referring to early anatomically modern humans in Europe.

crossing over Exchange of portions of maternally and paternally derived chromosomes of a homologous pair; occurs during Prophase I of meiosis.

crural index Ratio that reflects the relative length of the upper versus lower leg.

cytokinesis Process by which a single cell cleaves into two at the end of cell division.

cytoplasm Watery, jelly-like substance within a cell but outside of the nucleus.

cytosine One of the four bases in DNA and RNA.

cytoskeleton Network of microtubules and microfilaments; dispersed in cytoplasm to provide a structural framework for cell division.

D

Darwinius masillae Newly found fossil primate of the superfamily Adapoidea; important for its potential place as a link between the strepsirhine and haplorhine suborders as well as for its completeness (95%).

daughter atoms The isotopes that result from radioactive decay.

deep Refers to position away from body's surface; internal.

degenerative changes Modifications occurring as a result of age, wear, and disease.

deletion Type of mutation in which one (or more) nucleotides is removed from the DNA molecule.

delta Point of reference in a fingerprint; bifurcation near the base of the dermatoglyphic pattern, exhibits triangular form similar to the Greek letter.

dense (compact) bone Bone usually found in more superficial portions of bone, thickest in diaphysis of long bones; provides protection and support; resists stress.

dental formula Number of teeth in an upper and lower quadrant of mammalian jaw.

deoxyribonucleic acid (DNA) A nucleic acid in the form of a long, linear molecule composed of bases, sugar, and phosphate molecules; the genetic material of all organisms.

deoxyribose The specific type of sugar molecule in DNA.

derived features Features that have undergone change from the ancestral form, as differentiated from **primitive features.**

dermatoglyphics The science of the study of dermal ridges of fingers, toes, palms, and soles.

diaphysis Shaft of a long bone; portion between epiphyseal plates.

diastema A space in the tooth row; in the canine shearing complex, the space in the lower tooth row for the upper canine to fit, and vice versa.

differential reproductive success The condition in which individuals within a population reproduce at different rates; a result of natural selection.

differentiation Embryological process dictated by the DNA that results in differential development of stem cells into various cellular types.

diploë Porous portion of flat bones of skull.

diploid Term that describes the number of chromosomes in somatic cells.

discrete traits Phenotypes whose forms fall into one or the other of a number of distinguishable categories.

discriminant function analysis Statistical technique used to determine which variables discriminate between two or more groups.

disomy Normal condition in which the set of chromosomes in a human zygote includes 23 homologous pairs.

disjunction Separation of chromosome pairs or sister **chromatids** during **anaphase** of cell division.

distal Position on the limbs relatively farther from attachment of limb to trunk of body.

Dmanisi Fossil site at which an early possible *Homo erectus* was found, located in Georgia of the former Soviet Union, dated at 1.7 million years ago.

DNA fingerprinting Identification technique in which segments of noncoding DNA from two or more individuals are compared to establish the degree of similarity, and thus of relatedness.

dominant An allele that is always expressed when present.

dorsal Position on body closer to the back; term used more frequently for quadrupeds.

double helix Common manner of referring to the double-stranded, helical (twisted) nature of DNA's structure.

Down syndrome The condition produced by having an extra chromosome 21 (**Trisomy 21**).

Dryopithecus European Miocene ape.

E

early "archaics" Fossil hominid specimens occurring between about 800,000 years ago and 150,000 years ago.

egg cells Gametes present in females, originating in the ovaries; human egg cells have 23 chromsomes.

endoplasmic reticulum (ER) Membranous network of channels in cytoplasm, continuous with nuclear membrane, that forms a pathway for transporting substances within the cell and stores synthesized molecules.

enzyme Class of proteins that speed up chemical reactions in cells.

Eocene Epoch within Cenozoic Era in which the first "true" primates appeared and diversified; time range from 55 to 38 million years ago.

Eosimias Tiny late Eocene primate from China, a likely early representative of anthropoids.

epigenetics New area of genetics that investigates the causes of expression and lack thereof in regions of DNA.

epiphyseal line Remnant of epiphyseal plate.

epiphyseal plate Portion at end of diaphysis where bone growth occurs as cartilaginous cells divide, to be replaced later by bone cells (same portion as metaphysis).

epiphyses Portions at ends of a bone; the last to fuse (ossify); separated from rest of bone by epiphyseal plate during development.

essential amino acids Amino acids not produced by the body and must be taken in as protein. *See also* **amino acids.**

ethnicity The group with which one identifies; often exhibits particular cultural and linguistic traits.

eukaryotes Organisms whose genetic material is enclosed within a nuclear membrane within the cell.

euploidy Having the correct number of chromosomes.

evolution A change in gene frequency within a population over time, caused by one or more of the **evolutionary forces.**

evolutionary forces Four factors that cause gene frequencies to change in a population: natural selection, mutation, migration, and genetic drift.

evolutionary taxonomy School of thought about taxonomy and classification that regards the amount of divergence from a common ancestor as a valid criterion for classification.

evolutionary tree Graphical representation that portrays the relatedness of species; length of branches denotes length of time passed.

cets Smooth areas on bone where articulation occurs.

yum Depression Geological formation in Egypt that yields any known primate fossils from the late Eocene and ligocene epochs.

atures Characteristics of bone related to function and muscle evelopment.

liform Thread-like papillae (structures that house taste buds) ear the back of the tongue; contain nerve endings sensitive to ouch.

tness Degree of reproductive success of an individual relative o other members of the population.

at bones Bones of cranium, shoulder, pelvis, and rib cage.

ocal animal sampling Animal behavior technique that uses observations of one individual at a time.

oliate Ridged papillae (structures that house taste buds) near he back and on the lateral borders of the tongue.

ontanels Spaces between bones on infant skull that allow room for growth; also called "soft spots."

form of a trait The specific appearance of a characteristic, for example, brown hair; **phenotype**.

formative changes Bony modifications occurring during the process of growth and development.

form-function Relationship between the morphology of a feature to the manner in which the feature is used.

fossilization Process by which organic material in hard parts (bone, teeth, shell) is replaced, particle by particle, by minerals in the sediment; premineralization.

founder effect A form of genetic drift in which a small sub-population is reproductively isolated from the main population, "founding" a new population.

frameshift mutation An insertion or deletion mutation that results in a shift in the "reading frame" of all the rest of the codons on an mRNA strand.

frequency Rate of occurrence in a population; expressed as a percent.

frontal (coronal) plane Imaginary plane dividing body into front and back portions.

functional complexes A holistic view of an adaptation: anatomy and associated use of a feature.

fungiform Mushroom-shaped papillae (structures that house taste buds) throughout the tongue.

G

gametes Haploid cells that pass on genetic material to offspring at fertilization; sperm and egg cells.

gene A segment of DNA coding for a specific polypeptide (or protein).

gene flow (migration) Movement of genes from one population's gene pool to another, causing change in gene frequencies of both former and new gene pools.

gene frequency Within a population, the percent of each type of gene that exists for a specific trait.

gene pool All the genes in a population at a specific point in time.

genetic code The specific amino acids determined by each type of codon of mRNA.

genetic drift (random genetic drift) Random fluctuations in gene frequency of a population between generations; particularly in a small population, gene frequencies do not accurately represent those of the parental population.

genotype The allele pair present for a specific locus in an individual.

genotypic ratio Number of homozygous dominant to heterozygous to homozygous genotypes for a particular parental cross.

genus (pl: genera) Taxonomic level above the species and below the subfamily; a group of closely related species.

geological time scale Hierarchical classification of time on earth into eons, eras, periods, and epochs based upon the rise and fall of major groups of organisms.

Gigantopithecus Genus of ape originating in the Miocene but existing until well into the Pleistocene; largest known primate.

Golgi body and vesicles Delivery system of cell, which collects, modifies, packages, and distributes molecules that are synthesized at one location and used at another.

Gondwanaland Landmass in the southern hemisphere that consisted of what would become Africa, South America, Antarctica, and Australia.

gracile australopiths The more slender form of early hominid; primarily *Australopithecus africanus*.

guanine One of the four bases in both DNA and RNA.

H

hair follicle Small, sac-like pocket in the epidermis that houses the base (bulb and root) of each hair.

half-life In the process of radioactive decay, the time it takes for one-half of the atoms of an unstable (radioactive) isotope to decay into an isotopic variant of another element; used for absolute dating.

hand axe Bifaced, teardrop-shaped stone tool; the most common and widely distributed tool in the Acheulean tool kit.

haploid Term that describes the number of chromosomes in gametes; one-half the full chromosomal complement, or one set of chromosomes (1n).

Haplorhini Primate suborder that includes tarsiers, monkeys, apes, and humans.

Hardy-Weinberg formula Mathematical formula used to express the relationship between allele and genotype frequency of a population; $p^2 + 2pq + q^2 = 1$, where p represents the dominant allele, q the recessive allele, and the number 1 the entire population (100%).

Hardy-Weinberg law A mathematical relationship existing between allele frequency and genotype frequency such that the frequencies of particular genotypes can be predicted from allele frequencies; allele and genotype frequencies will remain constant from one generation to the next (in equilibrium) if mating is random and there is no action of the evolutionary forces.

hemizygous The condition of males for an X-linked trait; because males have only one X chromosome, they cannot be homozygous or heterozygous for X-linked traits.

hemoglobin Protein in red blood cells that carries oxygen from the lungs to the body's tissues.

heterodont The situation of having teeth within the jaw differentiated into different types to serve various functions.

heterozygous The condition of having inherited two different alleles at a particular locus.

Hominidae The taxonomic group defined variously as modern humans and our extinct relatives after the split from the African apes, or humans plus our extinct relatives *and* the African apes.

Hominoidea Superfamily of the catarrhine infraorder composed of apes and humans.

Homo Members of the human genus; exhibits derived dental and cranial features relative to the common ancestor of African apes and humans.

Homo erectus Species of early members of genus *Homo* characterized by large brain; the first such species to be found outside Africa; may combine two species, *H. erectus* (from Asia) and *H. ergaster* (from Africa).

Homo ergaster Species designation for fossil specimens that co-existed with and were similar to *H. erectus*.

Homo floresiensis Recently discovered species of diminutive, small-brained human on Indonesian island of Flores, perhaps an offshoot of **Homo erectus**, dated at between 94,000 and 13,000 years ago.

Homo habilis Earliest named members of the genus *Homo*; may consist of members of two species, *H. habilis* and *H. rudolfensis*.

Homo heidelbergensis Species designation accepted by some for a number of "archaic" *Homo sapiens* living between approximately 400,000 and 150,000 years ago; typically refers to European and African forms.

Homo rudolfensis Species designation of some early members of the genus *Homo*; distinguishable from *Homo habilis* by a number of cranial and postcranial features.

Homo sapiens sapiens Taxonomic designation of our own species and subspecies; first appeared in Africa about 150,000 years ago.

homology/homologous feature A characteristic that is similar in various groups of organisms because of their origin from a common ancestor possessing that characteristic.

homologous pairs Chromosomal couples of each type of chromosome (pair number 1, 2, etc.).

Homonoid Member of superfamily **Hominoidea**.

homozygous The condition of having inherited the same two alleles from the parents at a specific locus.

homozygous dominant The condition in which two alleles inherited at a specific locus both code for the dominant form of the trait.

homozygous recessive The condition in which two alleles inherited at a specific locus both code for the recessive form of the trait.

honing triad Also called **canine shearing complex**; combination of three features found in apes: large canines, **diastema**, and **sectorial P$_3$**.

horizontal plane Imaginary plane dividing the body into upper and lower parts.

hydrogen bond Weak linkage between two negatively charged atoms that share a hydrogen atom.

hypothesis A statement proposed to explain some phenomenon; framed to be testable/falsifiable.

I

independent assortment Random distribution of each pair of chromosomes into daughter cells during **meiosis**.

inferior Refers to portion of body closer to bottom of feet.

ingestion Getting the food into the mouth.

insertion (muscle) Site at which muscle tendon attaches to the bone that is movable relative to the other bone; usually located on the more distal bone.

insertion (mutation) Type of mutation in which one (or more) nucleotides is mistakenly added to the DNA molecule.

instantaneous sampling A technique of time sampling in which behavior is sampled periodically at sample points between a set time interval.

intermembral index Relative proportions of forelimbs and hindlimbs expressed as a percentage of forelimb to hindlimb.

interphase Stage of the cell cycle in which cell division is not occurring; cell growth, DNA replication, and organelle replication are in progress.

irregular bones Category of bone that includes vertebrae, facial bones, and some wrist and ankle bones.

aryotype The chromosomal complement of an individual; also, a organized arrangement of an individual's chromosomes.

nyanthropus Early member of human line in East Africa, ccurring at the same time as *A. afarensis*, approximately 3.5 illion years ago.

nuckle-walker Specialized mode of quadrupedal locomotion the African apes, in which the weight of the front of the body borne by the knuckles.

ndmarks Sites on the skull that serve as points for measure-ent and allow for consistent measurements to be taken on arious individuals.

ate "archaics" Fossil hominid specimens occurring between bout 125,000 years ago and about 30,000 years ago; a primary roup was the Neanderthals.

ateral Refers to position on the body farther from median lane.

aurasia Landmass made up of northern continents consisting of North America, Europe, and Asia.

aw A statement of fact meant to describe, in concise terms, an action or set of actions generally accepted to be true and universal.

Levalloisian Describes prepared core technique used by later "archaic" *Homo sapiens* that produced flakes of a predictable size and shape.

locomotion Body position involving displacement of the body's mass; movement.

locus The position of a gene on a chromosome, consistent for genes on chromosomes for all individuals of a species.

long bones Category of bone that includes limb bones, finger and toe bones.

loop Dermatoglyphic term referring to a type of fingerprint, commonly found on the thumb, characterized by a sharp curve.

"Lucy" Well-known specimen of a 40% complete female *Australopithecus afarensis*, found in Ethiopia.

lysosome Sac-like attachment to cell membrane that digests unneeded molecules; formed from vesicles of Golgi body.

M

M3 agenesis Failure of the third molar to erupt.

mean Measure of central tendency of a data set, arrived at by calculating the sum of observations divided by the number of observations.

mechanical digestion First part of the digestive process, carried out by action of the teeth to break down food into smaller pieces for easier breakdown by digestive enzymes.

medial Position on body closer to the median plane.

median Measure of central tendency representing the middle number in a distribution of scores; half the scores are higher than the median, and half lower.

median (midsagittal) plane Imaginary plane dividing the body into equal left and right halves.

medullary (marrow) cavity Space along the inside of the diaphysis containing yellow marrow (in adults), which consists mostly of fat cells and scattered blood cells.

meiosis The type of cell division occurring in the testes of males and ovaries of females whereby a specialized somatic (diploid) cell divides and produces daughter cells that develop into gametes.

Meiosis I The first meiotic division, in which the number of chromosomes is reduced from 46 to 23; homologous chromosomes are separated into different daughter cells.

Meiosis II The second meiotic division, in which the sister chromatids of each chromosome are separated from each other.

Mendelian traits Genetically simple traits determined by alleles at a single gene locus.

messenger RNA (mRNA) Type of RNA strand synthesized by using a DNA gene as a template; carries the "message" of the DNA sequence of a gene from the nucleus to the cytoplasm during protein synthesis.

metaphase Stage of cell division in which the chromosomes line up along the equator of the cell in preparation for separating to opposite poles of the cell.

metaphysis Region in mature bone where diaphysis meets epiphysis; formed the epiphyseal plate before the cartilage was replaced by bone.

mid-palmar crease Palm print that exhibits a single transverse crease; traditionally called **simian crease.**

midsagittal (median) plane Imaginary line dividing the body into equal left and right halves.

migration (gene flow) Movement of individuals between populations, altering gene frequencies of both original and new populations.

Miocene Epoch within the Cenozoic Era in which apes (Miocene hominoids) diversified and spread geographically; time range from 24 to 5 million years ago.

Miocene hominoids Term used to refer to the approximately 30 genera of early apes occurring between 20 and 5 million years ago; primarily arboreal with a mix of ape-like and monkey-like features but no tail.

missense mutation A substitution mutation in which the mistakenly replaced nucleotide causes a different amino acid to be coded for.

mitochondria Oblong organelle where adenosine triphosphate (ATP) production occurs for cellular energy; possesses its own DNA, called mitochondrial DNA.

mitosis The type of cell division whereby a somatic cell divides and produces two identical daughter cells.

mode Measure of central dispersion describing the score occurring most frequently in a data set.

monogenic Describes a trait whose gene expression is controlled by alleles at a single locus.

monosomy Situation in which one of a homologous pair of chromosomes is missing.

Mousterian Designates tool kit associated with Neanderthals; classified as Middle Paleolithic tools.

mRNA Abbreviation for **messenger RNA**.

mutagens Environmental factors that cause mutation to occur.

mutation Inherited change in the DNA sequence; the only evolutionary force to introduce new variation into the gene pool.

N

nasal Refers to the nose.

natural selection A primary factor causing evolutionary change in populations, in which individuals whose inherited traits allow them to better survive and/or reproduce contribute more offspring to the subsequent generation.

Neanderthals Fossils classified variously as either *Homo sapiens neandertalensis* or *Homo neandertalensis*; relatively specialized group of robustly built early humans occurring between 75,000 and 35,000 years ago.

Necrolemur Member of extinct superfamily Omomyoidea from Europe.

node Branching point for each **clade** on a **cladogram.**

nondisjunction Failure of chromosomes to separate before moving to opposite poles of the cell during anaphase; results in wrong number of chromosomes in the daughter cells after cell division is complete.

nonrandom mating Tendency of individuals of a species to breed with certain other individuals, resulting in changes in gene frequency of populations.

nonsense mutation A substitution mutation resulting in formation of a **stop codon** where there previously was none; causes premature halting of translation and a truncated polypeptide length.

normal curve Graphical representation of continuous data whose mean, median, and mode are the same; **bell-shaped curve.**

Notharctus Member of extinct superfamily Adapoidea from the Eocene of North America.

nuclear membrane Double-layered structure composed of phospholipids and protein molecules that controls passage of material into and out of nucleus.

nucleic acid Acidic substance found in all cells: DNA and RNA.

nucleolus Mass of proteins and ribosomal RNA in the nucleus; site of ribosome production.

nucleotide The most basic unit of both DNA and RNA; consists of one phosphate molecule, one sugar molecule, and one base.

nucleus Structure that contains the genetic material (DNA); separated from the rest of the cell by a **nuclear membrane.**

O

occlusal surface Upper and lower opposing portions of teeth that are in contact when the mouth is closed.

Olduwan tools Earliest of the stone tools, the tool kit associated with *Homo habilis*; classified as Lower Paleolithic tools.

Oligocene Epoch within the Cenozoic Era during which ancestors of New World monkeys and hominoids evolved; time range from 38 to 24 million years ago.

Omomyoidea Extinct primate superfamily from the Eocene; most representatives are from Europe and North America.

opsin Proteins in cone cells of retina that enable perception of color; bind to visual pigments in the red-sensitive cones, green-sensitive cones or blue-sensitive cones, making the visual pigment/opsin complex sensitive to light of a specific wavelength.

organ A structure formed by two or more cellular tissues; carries out a specific function in the body.

organ systems A group of organs working together to perform a bodily function or set of functions.

organelles Components of a cell within the cytoplasm.

organism A single living entity.

origin Site from which a muscle arises; usually on the "fixed" bone and more proximal than the insertion.

Ororrin tugenensis Possible early member of the human line if bipedalism proves to be its locomotor mode after further study, dated at approximately 6 million years ago.

orthognathic Describes the vertical orientation of the human face.

orthograde Upright **bipedal** animals (e.g., humans).

ossification The process of becoming bone.

osteometry Subcategory of anthropometry that deals with measurement of the skeleton.

Ouranopithecus macedoniensis Fossil primate from the late Miocene of Greece, dated at 9 to 10 million years ago; proposed as possible ancestor of African apes and humans.

outgroup In a cladistic analysis to determine evolutionary relationships of a group, the next most closely related group to that which is the study's focus.

Paleocene Epoch within the Cenozoic Era in which primates first evolved; time range from 65 to 55 million years ago.

Paleoclimate Earth's climatic conditions of the past; important in interpreting and analyzing extinct species' adaptations and distribution patterns.

papillae Bumps on the tongue that house the receptor cells (taste buds).

parabolic Refers to the U-shaped, or rounded, form of the dental arcade.

Parapithecidae Extinct primate family from the Oligocene of Egypt; members share similarities to New World monkeys.

parent atoms Radioactive atoms that will decay over time at a constant rate into daughter atoms; isotopes of a particular element that will decay into isotopes of another element.

pedigree A diagram that delineates the genetic relationships of family members over two or more generations; used to observe patterns of inheritance.

peptide bonds Chemical connection holding amino acids together.

periosteum Connective tissue covering bone in places where there is no articular cartilage.

Phanerozoic Eon More recent of the two largest blocks of geological time, from which many evident life forms evolved; time range from 542 million years ago to the present.

phenotype Outwardly observable traits and features of an individual; may be physical or behavioral.

phenotypic ratio Number of offspring from a parental cross potentially expressing the dominant form of trait relative to the number expressing the recessive form.

phosphate molecule Component of DNA and RNA that, together with sugar molecules, makes up the "backbone" of the strands.

phylogenetic Refers to the evolutionary history of a taxonomic group.

phylogenetic tree Graphical representation that portrays the relatedness of species; length of branches denotes length of time passed.

Pierolapithecus catalaunicus Recently discovered European ape from the Miocene epoch that may represent an ancestral form either to the African ape/human line or to the great ape and human line.

plasma membrane Double-layered structure surrounding a cell, composed of phospholipids and protein molecules, that controls passage of material into and out of the cell.

plate tectonics Movement of the continental plates making up the earth's surface.

Platyrrhini Infraorder of haplorhine primates composed of the superfamily Ceboidea, or New World monkeys.

Plesiadapiformes Diverse group of early mammals from the Paleocene of North America and Europe; may represent the earliest primates.

Plesiadapis Member of extinct mammalian group Plesiadapiformes from the Paleocene; found in North America and Europe.

point mutation Type of mutation in which one or up to a few bases is/are mistakenly out of place in the DNA.

polygenic A trait whose gene expression is controlled by alleles at more than one locus.

polymorphic Describes the condition in which when a genetically determined trait has more than one form in a population (a gene with more than one allele); a **polymorphism**.

polynucleotide chain String of nucleotides of DNA or RNA; two such chains make up the DNA molecule.

polypeptide (polypeptide chain) String of amino acids linked end to end by peptide bonds .

Pondaungia Eocene primate from Asia; may represent an early anthropoid.

population bottleneck Form of genetic drift in which a drastic reduction in the number of individuals in a population results in great differences between gene frequencies of the original and the newly reduced population

positional behavior Spatial relationship between the body mass of an individual and its environment.

postcranial skeleton Part of the skeleton from the cervical (neck) vertebrae inferiorly.

posterior Refers to position on body more toward the back.

posterior dentition Teeth at the back of the dental arcade: premolars and molars.

posture Body position that does not involve displacement of the body's mass.

Precambrian eon Largest portion of geological time scale, from the earth's formation to the beginning of the Phanerozoic Eon 542 million years ago.

prehensile Ability to grasp.

primary oocyte Type of cell that undergoes meiosis in the female; found in the ovaries.

primary spermatocytes Type of cell that undergoes meiosis in the male; found in the testes.

primates Taxonomic mammalian group at the level of the order; includes prosimians, monkeys, apes, and humans.

primitive features Features that are similar in form to that of an ancestor (by contrast, see **derived**).

primitive australopith Group of the earliest form of hominid, made up of several species that include *A. afarensis*; members possess numerous features of the ape-human ancestor.

principle of independent assortment Mendel's law stating that the presence of particular "characters" (alleles) of one trait will not affect the expression of genes of another trait.

principle of segregation Mendel's law stating that for any given trait, members of a pair of "characters" (alleles) separate (segregate) from each other during the formation of gametes, so that only one copy (one gene) is passed on from each parent.

Proconsul Early and best-known Miocene **hominoid** from Africa.

prognathic Forward protrusion of the lower face.

prokaryotes Organisms that lack a nucleus surrounding the genetic material; members of kingdom Monera.

pronograde Designates animals in which the backbone is parallel to the ground (quadrupedal).

prophase First phase of cell division, after DNA replication, in which chromosomes condense and become visible and the cell prepares to divide.

Propliopithecidae Extinct primate family from the Oligocene of Africa (found in Egypt in the Fayum); early catarrhines.

Prosimii One of the two suborders of Order Primates in the traditional classification scheme; includes tarsiers, lemurs, and lorises.

protein Molecules with a working or structural function in the body; made up of one or more polypeptides (strings of amino acids).

protein synthesis Process by which proteins are assembled from amino acids according to the sequences of bases in a DNA gene.

proximal Means closer to the attachment of limb to trunk of body (nearer the hip or the shoulder).

Punnett square Mathematical tool used to predict probabilities of various offspring depending upon parental genotypes.

Purgatorius Member of extinct mammalian group Plesiadapiformes from the Paleocene; found in North America.

purine Class of nucleic acid bases that include adenine and guanine.

pyramidine Class of nucleic acid bases that include cytosine, thymine, and uracil.

R

race Traditionally, a human population considered distinct based on physical characteristics; current knowledge does not support a biological basis for racial groups but, instead, represents a category created and developed by society.

range Lower and upper limits for a set of measurements.

recessive An allele that is expressed only when inherited by both parents in the homozygous condition.

recombinant DNA technology Fragment of DNA taken from one organism and integrated into the genome of another.

relative dating Technique of estimating the age of a fossil in which age is not expressed in years but, rather, with reference to comparisons with other fossils or a geological event.

replication (DNA replication) The process of duplicating genetic material prior to cell division; ensures that all cells have the full complement of DNA making up the chromosomes.

reproductive cloning The production of an entire organism from a cell of an existing organism.

Rh blood group A blood type system coded for by alleles at a locus on chromosome; two primary alleles determine blood type (Rh+, Rh−); Rh+ individuals produce antigens on the surface of their red blood cells.

Rh incompatibility Immune response of a mother to her developing fetus if the Rh − mother begins to produce antibodies in response to antigens on her Rh + fetus' red blood cells; can result in potentially fatal anemia.

ribonucleic acid (RNA) A nucleic acid in the form of a long, linear molecule composed of four kinds of bases and sugar and phosphate molecules.

ribose Type of sugar molecule found in RNA.

ribosomal RNA (rRNA) Type of RNA that associates with various proteins to form ribosomes, which "read" the mRNA strand during protein synthesis.

ribosomes Small structures composed of proteins and RNA.

ridge count Dermatoglyphic technique for identifying individuals; count taken of number of dermal ridges between **core** and **triradius (Delta)**.

robust australopith Group of early hominids with massive jaws, teeth, and chewing musculature; includes *Australopithecus robusts*, *A. boisei*, and *A. aethiopicus*.

Rooneyia Member of extinct superfamily Omomyoidea from North America.

rugose Rough area on bone at the site of muscle attachment.

S

Sahelanthropus tchadensis Recent fossil discovery from Central Africa (Chad); some interpret this fossil as the earliest known hominid to split from the ape line.

sample Subset of a population subjected to statistical analysis.

scan sampling A method in which behavior for all animals (or a particular set of animals) is recorded simultaneously at predetermined time intervals.

science Activity that seeks to explain (natural) phenomena; employs the steps of the **scientific method**.

scientific method Rigorous procedure that is used to identify the most probable explanation for natural phenomena.

ctorial P₃ Lower premolar tooth just posterior to the astema, sharpened as the upper canine hones against it.

gregation analysis The process of testing various genetic potheses to determine which of several modes of inheritance responsible for producing specific patterns in a familial line.

lective advantage Greater propensity of individuals with e form best adapted to a specific environment to reproduce, assing on that trait in higher frequency to the next generation.

lective pressure Environmental factors that influence reproductive success of individuals.

esamoid bone Typically small bone forming within joints; an xample is the patella, the largest sesamoid.

ex chromosomes Chromosomes responsible, via their gene products, for determining the sex of an individual; X and Y hromosomes.

ex-linked trait A trait coded-for by a gene on a sex chromosome.

exual dimorphism Differences in size or other characteristics (besides primary or secondary sexual characteristics) in males and females of the same species.

short bones Category of bone that includes the blocky, often cube-shaped bones of wrist and ankle, and sesamoid bones.

silent mutation Substitution mutation whereby a nucleotide is mistakenly replaced by another, but the same amino acid is coded for.

simian crease Traditional term for a palm print that exhibits a single transverse crease; also called **mid-palmar crease**.

simian shelf A thickened area on the internal aspect of the mandible, serves as a buttress for chewing forces.

simple traits Also termed **Mendelian traits**; determined by alleles at a single gene locus.

single base substitution mutation Mistaken replacement of one nucleotide for another, different nucleotide.

sister chromatids Two identical chromatids attached at the centromere.

Sivapithecus Miocene **hominoid** from Asia; extinct relative of orangutan.

somatic cells Cells making up the structural composition of the body; all cells other than gametes; possess the diploid chromosome number.

species A group of individuals that can potentially interbreed and produce fertile offspring (biological definition of species).

sperm cells Gametes present in males, originating in the testes.

spongy (cancellous) bone Type of bone containing many large spaces; concentrated primarily within the ends of long bones; filled with mostly red marrow.

stance phase Phase of **bipedalism** in which the foot is in contact with the substrate and the weight is supported by the foot.

standard deviation In statistics, measure of the variability of a population for a set of measurements.

stop codon (terminating triplet) The sequence of bases making up three types of codons (UGA, UAA, and UAG) that determine the termination of protein synthesis.

strata Stratigraphic layer of sediment.

Strepsirhini Primate suborder that includes the lemur and loris groups.

striding gait Unique gait characteristic of human **bipedal** locomotion.

Subphylum Vertebrata Group of organisms within the Phylum Chordata that share numerous features, the most important of which is a vertebral column and spinal cord.

sugar molecule Component of DNA and RNA that, together with phosphate molecules, makes up the "backbone" of the strands.

superficial Designates a position near the body's surface.

superior Refers to portion of the body located closer to the top of the head.

sutures Margins of skull bones as they abut each other.

swing phase Phase of **bipedalism** in which the foot comes off the substrate and is being repositioned for the next stance phase; leg comes forward and around toward the center (adducts).

systematics Theoretical and philosophical framework behind the manner in which scientists classify organisms.

T

Tarsiiformes Infraorder of haplorhines consisting of tarsiers.

taxon (pl: taxa) A group of organisms belonging to a particular group at a particular level within the biological classification scheme.

telophase Final phase of cell division, in which the nuclear membrane begins forming around chromosomes at each pole of original cell.

terminating triplet *See* **stop codon**

terrestrial Ground-living.

Tetonius Member of extinct superfamily Omomyoidea from North America.

tetrad A pair of homologous chromosomes in their doubled state, during the **crossing over** that occurs early in meiosis.

theory A statement of relationships that rests upon some firm basis; based on confirmed/corroborated hypotheses.

therapeutic cloning Production of human embryos with the goal of harvesting stem cells for medical purposes.

thymine One of the four bases in DNA; not found in RNA; chemically similar to **uracil**.

tissue Group of identical cells forming organs.

trait A feature or characteristic determined either by the inherited properties of an organism or by a combination of inherited and environmental factors.

transcription The first step of protein synthesis in which mRNA is synthesized, using a DNA segment (a gene) as a template; occurs in the nucleus.

transfer RNA (tRNA) Type of RNA whose function is to transport amino acids to their appropriate place along the mRNA strand during protein synthesis.

transitional forms *See* "archaic" *Homo sapiens*

translation The second step of protein synthesis in which mRNA codons are "read" by ribosomes, and "translated" into an amino acid sequence; occurs in the cytoplasm.

transverse plane Imaginary plane dividing body into upper and lower parts.

triradius Point of reference in a fingerprint; bifurcation near the base of the dermatoglyphic pattern; also called the Delta due to its exhibiting a triangular form similar to the Greek letter.

trisomy Situation in which an extra chromosome is present.

Trisomy 21 An extra chromosome 21, which causes **Down syndrome**.

U

universal donors Individuals with type O blood because their blood can be donated to type A and type B individuals without provoking an immune response.

universal recipients Individuals with Type AB blood who can receive all blood types because their blood serum has neither anti-A nor anti-B antibodies with which to attack antigens of blood cells of a different type.

Upper Paleolithic tools Describes a group of several tool kits associated with early anatomically modern humans in Europe.

uracil One of the four bases in RNA; not found in DNA; chemically similar to **thymine**.

V

ventral Designates position on body closer to the belly; term used more frequently for quadrupeds.

W

whorl Dermatoglyphic term referring to a type of fingerprint with a circular pattern.

X

X chromosome Female sex chromosome.

X-linked dominant Trait coded-for by dominant allele on X chromosome; expressed whenever present.

X-linked recessive Trait coded-for by recessive allele on X chromosome; always expressed in males; must be in homozygous condition for expression in females.

X-linked Trait coded for by alleles on the X chromosome.

Y

Y chromosome Male sex chromosome, relating mostly to male sexual development.

Y5 molar cusp pattern Characteristic Y-shape formed by valleys between molar cusps in apes and humans.

Z

zygote Fertilized egg formed by union of male and female gametes.

Photo Credits

American 3B

Copyright 3B Scientific, Hamburg, Germany. www.a3Bs.com.
Used with permission.

Casts Used for Photography

Fetal Skull

Based on Model LT-A25

Articulated Skeleton

Based on Model LT-A10

Bone Clones

© Bone Clones, Inc. Used with permission.

Casts Used for Photography

Asian male skull

African male skull

Comparative maxilla set

Mandrill skull

***Aegyptopithecus zeuxis* skull**

***Proconsul* skull**

***Sivapithecus* skull**

Gorilla hand unassembled

Lucy pelvis & femur

***Australopithecus afarensis* skull**

***Australopithecus aethiopicus* skull**

***Homo erectus* – Peking Man**

***Homo ergaster* skull**

Dmansi *Homo erectus* skull

Photo taken by Tracy Luedke

***Homo floresiensis* skull**

Photo taken by Tracy Luedke

***Sahelanthropus tchadensis* skull**

Photo taken by Tracy Luedke

***Kenyanthropus platyops* skull**

Photo taken by Tracy Luedke

Photos from Bone Clones Website

***Homo heidelbergensis* skull**

***Homo neandertalensis* skull**

Human European male skull

Modern human adult female pelvis

Modern human Asian female skull
Page 192 . . . . Skull 3

10-year-old human child skull
Page 199 . . . . Dentition A

5-year-old human child skull
Page 199 . . . . Dentition B

Taung child skull (*Australopithecus africanus*)
Page 320

***Homo habilis* skull**
Page 330 . . . . Photo 14.1A

***Homo rudolfensis* skull**
Page 330 . . . . Photo 14.1B

***Acheulean* tool (fossil hominid bi-facial hand-axe)**
Page 331 . . . . Photo 14.3

***Mousterian* tools**
Page 338 . . . . Photo 14.8

Chetham's Library

© Chetham's Library, Manchester, United Kingdom. Used with permission.

Consul, the performing chimpanzee
Page 282 . . . . Photo 12.3

Cleveland Museum of Natural History

© The Cleveland Museum of Natural History.

Casts Used for Photography

Male Tarsier
Page 219 . . . . Photo 9.1
Page 223 C
Page 242 C
Page 245 . . . . Photo 10.1
Page 247 C
Page 287 . . . . upper right

Male ring-tailed lemur
Page 242 . . . . B (lower)
Page 248 . . . . B
Page 285
Page 286

Male aye-aye
Page 242 . . . . D

Male capuchin
Page 247 . . . . B
Page 287 . . . . bottom

Chimpanzee femur
Page 312 . . . . D

Chimpanzee pelvis
Page 312 . . . . B

Good-Light Company

Permission granted from Good-Light Company, www.good-lite.com to reproduce a photo of the Pseudo-Isochromatic 24 Plate Color Vision by Dr. Terrance Waggoner.

Color Blind Tests
Page 101

Somso

® SOMSO Modelle. Used with permission.

Casts Used for Photography

Neanderthal reconstruction
Page 338 . . . . Photo 14.7B
Page 343 . . . . A–C (left side)

S 3—Reconstruction of a Skull of *Homo Sapiens Neanderthalensis*, copyright by SOMOSO® Modelle, Germany, 2009

***Homo sapiens sapiens*—Predmöst**
Page 338 . . . . Photo 14.9
Page 343 . . . . A-C (right side)

S 4—Reconstruction of a Skull of a fossil *Homo sapiens sapiens*, copyright SOMSO ® Modelle, Germany, 2009

***Australopithecus africanus*—Sterkfontein**
Page 314 . . . . Photo 13.11
Page 317 . . . . A (lower left)
Page 318 . . . . A (top), A (middle), bottom
Page 334 . . . . A (top)

ZoS 53—Reconstruction of *Australopithecus africanus*, copyright by SOMSO ® Modelle, Germany, 2009

***Homo habilis* skull**
Page 334 . . . . A-D

S 3/1—Reconstruction of a skull of *Homo habilis*, copyright by SOMSO ® Modelle, Germany 2009

Male gorilla skull
Page 248 . . . . A
Page 291 . . . . C, D
Page 310 . . . . Photo 13.7

ZoS 50—Skull of gorilla, male, copyright by SOMSO ® Modelle, Germany 2009

Male chimpanzee skull
Page 288 . . . . lower right
Page 290 . . . . upper left
Page 309 . . . . Photos 13.2B, 13.3B, 13.4B
Page 310 . . . . Photos 13.5B, 13.6

ZoS 53/2 Skull of a chimpanzee, male, copyright by SOMSO ® Modelle, Germany, 2009

Young chimpanzee skull
Page 311 . . . . B

ZoS 53/1—Skull of young chimpanzee, copyright by SOMSO ® Modelle, Germany 2009

Disarticulated plastic human skeleton
Page 143 . . . . Photo 7.10
Page 152 . . . . Photos 7.13, 7.14
Page 154 . . . . Photo 7.18
Page 157 . . . . C, D
Page 171 . . . . Photo 7.33
Page 172 . . . . Photo 7.34
Page 312 . . . . bottom

QS 40/1 and QS 40/2—Unmounted human (half) skeleton, copyright by SOMSO ® Modelle, Germany, 2009

ndex